The
Cosmic
Dance

The
Cosmic
Dance

Science Discovers
the Mysterious Harmony
of the Universe

Giuseppe Del Re

TEMPLETON FOUNDATION PRESS
Philadelphia & London

Templeton Foundation Press
Five Radnor Corporate Center, Suite 120
100 Matsonford Road
Radnor, Pennsylvania 19087

© 2000 by Templeton Foundation Press

When the name of the translator into English of a quotation is not explicitly given, the translation is the author's.

Library of Congress Cataloging-in-Publication Data
Del Re, Giuseppe, 1932-
    The cosmic dance : science discovers the mysterious harmony of the
universe / Giuseppe Del Re ; foreword by Thomas Torrance.
        p. cm.
    Includes bibliographical references and index.
    ISBN 1-890151-25-4 (hardcover : alk. paper)
    1. Science – Philosophy. I. Title.
Q175.D574 1999
501 – dc21   99-38482
                                                                               CIP

Printed in the United States of America

00   01   02   03   04   10   9   8   7   6   5   4   3   2   1

Das All ist ein Harmonisches Eins, jede Kreatur ist nur ein Ton, eine Schattierung einer grossen Harmonie, die man auch im Ganzen und Grossen studieren muss, sonst ist jedes einzelne ein toter Buchstabe.

[The universe is a harmonious whole, each creature is but a note, a shade of a great harmony, which man must study in its entirety and greatness, lest each detail should remain a dead letter.]

— JOHANN WOLFGANG VON GOETHE (1749–1832)

Contents

Foreword

This is a very remarkable book, concerned with a holistic scientific understanding of the universe and its meaning, written by an eminent scientist who is also a very special human being. Giuseppe Del Re was born in Naples, Italy, in 1932, the son of Raffaello Del Re, a scholar in classical literature and philosophy, who was well known for his philological and critical work in Hellenistic philosophy. Giuseppe himself was first a student in classical languages (Latin and Greek) before becoming a professor of theoretical chemistry at the University of Naples. The main achievements in his primary research field, quantum chemistry, are marked by the "Del Re method" for the determination of atom charges in molecules (1958), and by the introduction of "maximum localization hybrids" in the molecular orbital method. Both procedures are still widely used. In his fundamental epistemology he propounds a basic unitary outlook upon reality seeking to overcome the dualistic frame of mind, long endemic in European thought and affecting science and philosophy alike. This is very evident in his examination of the chemical origin of life and his impressive development of "complexity," with special reference to organization as a characteristic of living beings, resolution of the mind-body relation, and the emergence of meaning. At the same time he has devoted special attention to the philosophy of chemistry and its status as an independent discipline.

Professor Del Re has published over 180 scientific papers, and is best known for his work on the electronic states of molecules. He was one of the leading second-generation specialists in quantum chemistry, and is widely recognized for his particular interest in theoretical and epistemological issues in the present post-mechanist era. This is reflected, for example, in his contribution to a work on the brain-mind problem, in which he collaborated with Sir John Eccles, and which he edited for the Pontifical Academy of Sciences. He is a member of the International Academy of the Philosophy of Science (Brussels), and the European Academy for Environmental Questions (Tübingen), and is a founding member of the International Center for Transdisciplinary Research and Studies (Paris). He is a member of the advisory board of three international journals of philosophy, *Hyle* (Karlsruhe), *La Nuova Critica* (Rome) and *Filosofia oggi* (Genoa). He has been a professor in Canada, Germany, France, Peru, Hungary, and most recently at the École Normale Supérieure in Paris.

The early chapters of this book deal with the scientific and philosophical issues now recognized as central for understanding the world: information, which makes a thing what it is; complexity, the newest general concern of science and technology; the order and intelligibility of nature; organization, the dynamical order characteristic of life, determinism, finalism and chance, and the processes associated with them; beauty and variety; meaning and communication; life and its history. Professor Del Re operates with a hierarchical or multi-layered concept of nature in accordance with which the whole reality of a material entity is characterized by a number of levels. This approach shows that science poses questions which point outside what it can investigate — questions which cannot be ignored if we are to make rational and responsible decisions. The great John Archibald Wheeler, a fellow member with Del Re of the International Academy of the Philosophy of Science, has spoken of the third era in physics as "meaning physics." In this brilliant work, Giuseppe Del Re shows that this applies to much more than physics and chemistry, and yet what he calls a science for sciences. That is a science which points beyond science itself to a universal spiritual outlook embracing science, scientifically compatible with its most rigorous research and open-ended results.

This is a work of great relevance to the meaning of science and its openness to spiritual reality. With his musical metaphor Del Re explores the comprehensive outlook upon the world, which appears to be most compatible with the rise of molecular biology, systems theory, and the new cosmology. This approach is not altogether new, for already in the fourth century Athanasius had employed musical terms such as harmony and symphony, to express something of the kind of order, symmetry, and concord which he discerned in the created cosmos. But today Del Re applies that musical analogy or "image" to the scientific view of the universe to which rigorous science now gives rise after the immense developments in our understanding of the physical world. Thus, Del Re uses the "Great Dance Image" to give meaningful expression to the dynamical order of the universe as a coherent, evolving pattern in which all things participate as if in a dance or a ballet, combining general harmony and coherence with evolution, randomness, irreversibility. The intelligible universe is in fact a dynamic open-structured coherent whole made of complex systems connected by a fine network of causal and non-causal relations, and characterized by semantic reference beyond themselves, which is finally to be appreciated as a hierarchy of meaning.

Here Del Re operates with the realization that the whole reality of a material entity comprises a number of levels, which science seeks to describe in terms of "elementary objects" differing in complexity and size, from that which treats a thing as composed of interacting elementary particles to that which treats it as a collection of a few parts. It is this holistic approach (in line with that of Clerk Maxwell in his "Treatise on Electricity and Magnetism"), argues Del Re, that overcomes the limitations of physicalism and mechanism and opens the way to understanding why life can result from a collection of physico-chemical processes. It also shows that in its very rigor science itself poses questions which point outside what it can investigate and which humanity cannot ignore if it is to make rational and responsible choices. This double emphasis upon the non-dualistic, unitary, and open understanding of the universe, and what Del Re thinks of as the "apophatic" or open-structured character of science, together have the effect of demolishing Stephen Weinberg's contention that the more the universe appears to be comprehensible, the more it seems to be pointless (!), and of fulfilling John Wheeler's prophecy about the new era of "meaning physics." "Meaning," Del Re argues, "can and should be treated as something objective, as a fact of reality," which belongs to the purview of science. This book is not concerned with an examination of the details of science, but with the picture of the universe as a coherent whole to which science leads us. Hence in the later chapters Del Re shifts attention to man as a free agent, consideration of whom is fully consistent with science. Only man can use his reason to make rational judgments, engage in objective operations, choose between different courses of action, and reach a unifying spiritual grasp of reality. This calls attention to the relation between science and man's built-in belief in a dimension of reality inaccessible to the senses.

If the Great Dance image suggested by science hints at a coherent, not-necessarily material reality, what, asks Del Re, is "the glue" that ensures coherence between the stars, man, and the spiritual level inaccessible to the analytical methods of science? For a satisfactory answer he turns to information theory and communication, which can be conceived as taking place, although in various forms and degrees of sophistication, among all things animate and inanimate. Communication can be intentional and the attribution of meaning extends to symbols regarded as gates to the spiritual dimension of reality.

Professor Del Re's exploration of the epistemic character of scientific activity, and its built-in semantic thrust toward the spiritual dimension, leads him to the question of "the soul." The "complexity" viewpoint suggests that the soul of a living being is the organized activity which makes its development and persistence possible as a specific being, despite incessant exchange of matter and energy within a changing environment. The properties of the soul include self-consciousness, a major stumbling-block for cognitive science, artificial intelligence, and neuro-science. This is another point where science seems to point to realms which it seems incapable of grasping with its analytic methods.

What then of a "scientific" *Weltanschauung* or a view of the intelligible world, built on the model of science? Del Re argues that a way of interpreting the world to guide man's actions demands a personal commitment and a personal path of justification: it is a spiritual enterprise. Then, with reference to the notion of in-built belief, and to statements of Poincaré and Polanyi about belief and faith, Del Re points out that the principles for our understanding of the world are adopted as an act of faith — even when they are strictly scientific ones. It turns out that what is special to the nature of the starting principle, which man needs for his psychological stability, is that validity results not only from information about the physical world, but from the history of mankind and the inner experience of each person. In this sense the principle that a spiritual dimension of reality exists and the universe is the world of a Creator — the Choreographer of the Great Dance — appears to be the only reasonable choice. What must be kept in mind, however, Del Re insists, is that there are two sorts of truth: logical correctness and faithfulness to reality. "A science refusing a *Weltanschauung* open on the spiritual dimension of reality is not science; it is a delusion liable to make man die from thirst on the bank of a water stream." This holistic account of "a science for sciences" will be welcome to many people today, for it offers a scientific conception of the universe which is distinctly congenial with the Christian faith.

— Thomas F. Torrance

Preface

This book is intended to take you on a voyage through the main ideas and discoveries of contemporary science, from physics to biology; a voyage aimed at finding out how the wonders the scientists have discovered can contribute to a wholesome personal outlook on life and the universe.

The times are over when our voyage would have been a royal visit to the empire which human ingenuity has conquered for our welfare and pleasure; it will be a humble and patient search for the meaning of the greatest concepts of science in the context of poetry, history, and philosophy. We shall be guided in our exploration by an ancient, recently revived idea: that all there is participates as it were in a great harmonious Dance.

In his foreword, Professor Torrance has expressed a high opinion of this book. I do hope he is right; what is sure is that I have tried my best to write a book that can be a source of new ideas and intellectual perspectives for any reader, whether familiar with science or not. I want to warn you, however, that reading it will not always be an easy task. You will be confronted with a wide range of topics, from lasers to alchemy, from deterministic chaos to Chinese wisdom. As a result, certain points are probably less clear than others, certain pieces of information are taken for granted that are not really well known, and there are many digressions and some repetitions. The quotations intended to document the many connections of science with other fields of intellectual endeavor may be too many. Many citations are from outside the English-speaking world, owing not only to my belonging to the culture of continental Europe, but to the intention of showing how many people, in different times, places and languages, have expressed ideas bearing on our quest. These features may at times try your patience. But I do not apologize: the report of an exploration cannot be mere entertainment; as I have said, its main usefulness lies in providing material for further reflection.

Acknowledgments

I owe the considerations presented in this book to a number of scholars and scientists who, directly or indirectly, encouraged me, a theoretical physicist and later a theoretical chemist, to devote part of my time to the world-view that has emerged from the new science. The philosophers of science who encouraged me to expand my interests were particularly Valerio Tonini, Evandro Agazzi, and the Nobel laureate John Eccles. They made possible my membership in the International Academy for the Philosophy of Science of Brussels. In the context of that institution I had the opportunity to meet John A. Wheeler and Thomas F. Torrance. To the latter I owe very much, for I found in him not only a friend, but a thinker whose understanding of the implications of recent science for a world-view worthy of man I could share completely.

Despite all the esteem and encouragement of so many persons, however, I wonder if I should ever have gone so far as to write this book had I not had the encouragement and support of the John Templeton Foundation. They made for me the writing of this book a commitment, and thus helped me to overcome those moments of crisis which are inevitable when a man is at the same time engaged in teaching and research duties. I should like to thank in particular Sir John Templeton, whose ideas on the relation between science and theology have been a source of inspiration for me. I thank Dr. Robert Herrmann, of the Templeton Foundation, for his patient and constant attention to the process of preparation of the text; I should be glad if he would count me as one of his friends. I also wish to express my appreciation to Mrs. Virginia McWeeny Del Re and Professor Roy McWeeny for reading the manuscript and offering critical remarks and suggestions. Last not least, I thank Maria Teresa, my wife, for her invaluable encouragement, advice and assistance.

The
Cosmic
Dance

Chapter 1

The Great Dance Image

A new foundation for man's irrepressible desire to situate himself in the immensity of the Whole is emerging from science. The Great Dance image, a new cosmological metaphor, which recovers the age-old idea of the Harmony of the World, should probably re-place the old "clockwork image." What does it imply? Why can it help man to come to terms with such new ideas as evolution, randomness, irreversibility, emergence of information, indeed with the new conception of the universe as a complex system made of complex systems?

A New Image of the World – Is a *Weltanschauung* of Any Use?– Of Astronomy and Astrology – The Return of Coherence – Birds, Stars, and the Goddess Earth – The Music and the Dance – Rhythm and Timbre in the Music of the Pulsars

The universe is a harmonious whole, each creature is but a note, a shade of a great harmony, which man must study in its entirety and greatness, lest each detail should remain a dead letter.

— JOHANN WOLFGANG VON GOETHE[1]

A New Image of the World

Our ideas about the nature of the physical world have been dramatically affected by the latest advances of science. A central place is being taken by new notions, particularly biological evolution, emergence of order, deterministic chaos, the genetic code. As a result, a new conception of the world is taking shape, and promises to be extremely interesting, for it points to a direction opposing the ubiquitous specialization of our age; indeed, it suggests the possibility of fitting together such diverse notions as the medieval music of the spheres, Einsteinian space-time, and intrinsic irreversibility of natural processes.[2]

In trying to outline the main features of the new conception, one has to use a number of analogies and comparisons. To grasp the general design and operation of such an enormous and complicated object as the whole cosmos, in fact, the human mind needs an analogy with something based on its own direct experience, what one might call a "cosmological metaphor."

The cosmological metaphor, which has dominated science since the time of Galileo and Newton down to our time despite increasing difficulties, has been called "the clockwork image." According to that metaphor, the universe used to be considered, as Robert Boyle (1627–1692) put it,

like a rare clock... where all things are so skillfully contrived that the engine being once set moving all things proceed according to the artificer's design.[3]

1. *Das All ist ein Harmonisches Eins, jede Kreatur ist nur ein Ton, eine Schattierung einer grossen Harmonie, die man auch im Ganzen und Großen studieren muß, sonst ist jedes einzelne ein toter Buchstabe.* We thank Ms. Dorothee Hock, of the "Casa di Goethe," Rome, for informing us that this passage can be found in a letter written by Goethe to C. L. Knebel on November 17, 1784. The letter can be found in *Goethe's Werke:* Herausgegeben in Auftrage der Großherzogin Sophie von Sachsen: IV Abtheilung: Goethes Briefe: 6. Band: Weimar: 1. Juli 1782–31. December 1784.
2. I. Prigogine and I. Stengers, *La nouvelle alliance* (Paris: Gallimard, 1979); I. Prigogine and I. Stengers, *Entre le temps et l'éternité* (Paris: Flammarion, 1992).
3. R. Boyle, quoted by Donald MacKay on the cover of *The Clockwork Image* (London: Inter-Varsity Press, 1974). No reference is given in MacKay's book, but cf. R. Boyle, *De*

The clockwork image summarized what philosophers have called the "mechanistic-deterministic" view of the world. Today, science has had to accept chance and organization as key concepts for understanding and predicting facts, and another cosmological metaphor appears more consistent with what we know about the material universe. It is the image of the Great Dance. This image was introduced at the dawn of civilization by poets and writers, and is dear to astrologers and Tarot experts because it is related to the Platonic and medieval tradition; but it is only now piercing through the barrier of the most advanced and abstruse scientific research. Perhaps its most significant appearance in recent scientific literature has been its use by the mathematical physicist John Archibald Wheeler, founder of that frontier field of theoretical physics called geometrodynamics. Refusing the notion of universal order expressed by the word *cosmos* (which he calls *universe*), Wheeler wrote:

> World: a multiplicity of existences? Yes. Universe? No. The minuet? How harmonious, how fascinating, how beautiful. Yet all the while we watch we know that there is no such thing as a minuet, no adherence with perfect precision to a pattern, only individuals of different shapes and sizes pursuing different plans of motion with different accuracies.[4]

At least another physicist, Fridtjof Capra, has mentioned explicitly the Cosmic Dance, having in mind Eastern religions, in particular the Dance of Shiva.[5]

A most important point, however, is that other illuminating statements about the Dance image can be found outside scientific literature. In his classic book about the Tarot cards, the initiate Oswald Wirth said of the most powerful of the "Greater Trumps" — XXI, the World:

> When we are better instructed, we shall see Reality in a less crude way. The World is a perpetual whirling dance where nothing is at rest: everything turns incessantly, because motion is that which generates things. This concept goes back to prehistoric ages.... The Tarots are inspired by this idea, which is tens of thousands of years old, when they show us the goddess of life running inside a leaf wreath like a squirrel turning its wheel.[6]

---

hypothesis mechanicae excellentia et fundamentis considerationes quaedam, amico proposi-tae — Some considerations proposed to a friend about the excellence and the foundations of the mechanical hypothesis (London: Herringman, 1674).

4. J. A. Wheeler, "World as System Self-Synthetized by Quantum Networking," *IBM Journal of Research and Development* 32 (1988): 4–15.

5. F. Capra, *The Tao of Physics* (New York: Wildwood House, 1975).

6. O. Wirth, *Les Tarots des Imagiers du Moyen Age* (Paris: Claude Tchou, 1966). Not surprisingly (see our chapter ten), the Western tradition about the Dance goes back at least to Hellenistic times, particularly the great Plotinus (ca. 204–270 A.D.). Cf. Francisco

T. S. Eliot (1888–1965), perhaps the greatest poet of the twentieth century, expressed the same idea in his "Four Quartets." At variance with what the physicist Wheeler seems to suggest in his minuet image, Eliot believes that there must be in the Dance of the World some principle of order and some rules, some *invariants*, just as there are invariants in physical theory. This is what he hints at when he writes:

At the still point of the turning world. Neither flesh nor fleshless;
Neither from nor towards; at the still point, there the dance is,
But neither arrest nor movement. And do not call it fixity,
Where past and future are gathered. Neither movement from nor
      towards,
Neither ascent nor decline. Except for the point, the still point,
There would be no dance, and there is only the dance.[7]

A more explicit presentation of the Great Dance was offered by Charles W. Williams (1886–1945), a profoundly Christian Oxford scholar greatly admired by T. S. Eliot:

Imagine that everything which exists takes part in the movement of a great dance — everything, the electrons, all growing and decaying things, all that seems alive and all that doesn't seem alive, men and beasts, trees and stones, everything that changes, and there is nothing anywhere that does not change. That change — that's what we know of the immortal dance; the law in the nature of things — that's the measure of the dance, why one thing changes swiftly and another slowly, why there is seeming accident and incalculable alteration, why men hate and love and grow hungry, and cities that have stood for a century fall in a week, why the smallest wheel and the mightiest world revolve, why blood flows and the heart beats and the brain moves, why your body is poised on your ankle and the Himalayas are rooted in the earth — quick or slow, measurable or immeasurable, there is nothing at all anywhere but the dance.... If you ache, the dance strains you; if you are healthy, the dance carries you. Medicine is the dance: law, religion, music, and poetry — all these are ways of telling ourselves the smallest motion that we've known for an instant before it utterly disappears in the unrepeatable process of *that*.[8]

This passage might be understood as an acknowledgment of the validity of astrological arguments, but in fact it hints at the scientific implications

García Bazán, *Plotino y la gnosis* (Buenos Aires: Fundación para la Educación, la Ciencia y la Cultura, 1981), 234f.

7. T. S. Eliot, *Four Quartets*, "Burnt Norton," II, lines 64–69 in *The Complete Poems and Plays 1909–1950* (New York: Harcourt Brace Jovanovich, 1971), 119.

8. C. W. Williams, *The Greater Trumps* (1932; reprint, Grand Rapids, Michigan: W. B. Eerdmans, 1976), 94–95.

of the Dance of the World. Indeed, Williams's insistence on the Dance image is especially apt to help our minds explore the place and significance of science in our conception of the world, and hence in our intellectual, esthetic, and ethical choices. What makes it so? Why did it appeal to such a hard-core physicist as John Wheeler, who probably did not know and perhaps would not like the writings of Charles Williams? Why should it be accepted by people of our time who, though conscious of such new problems as man's relation to his environment, are not inclined to yield to esotericism and magic, but still believe in science as a path to truth?

To answer these questions one has to consider at greater depth what the cosmos has become for man since the dawn of scientific inquiry, bringing at the same time to the surface other implications of the Great Dance image. Although there have been other studies with an aim similar to ours, more reflection is needed to grasp the significance, for science as well as for man in general, of the *Weltanschauung* — the way of looking at the world — summarized by the Great Dance image. We shall pay special attention to the new outlook on the "harmony of the world" included in this image.

Is a *Weltanschauung* of Any Use?

There are signs that our age, an age when only solutions to practical problems are considered important, may be approaching an end: not a glorious end, perhaps, but an end. A new approach to mankind's persistent problems has yet to be found, but one thing is certain: the men and women of today are tired of being forced always to think in terms of practical means and material welfare. They have witnessed the failure not only of materialistic ideologies, but also of attempts to reduce the problems of "undeveloped" countries to a shortage of material goods. At a time when religion has disappeared from large sections of their society, the overfed people of the West are realizing that after all there is a difference between human beings and cattle. Although at times we might envy the contented life of cows, spending their time in rich meadows protected from any danger, the fact is that we are not cows. We are more like sheep without a shepherd: a metaphor which today, as it did two thousand years ago, means not that we are just like any other animal but that — despite our high living standards — we feel lost. That is to say, we cannot make sense of our lives and of the universe in which we are immersed.

Even when we cannot or dare not say so in so many words, we miss the answers to the eternal questions — "What is man? Where does he come from? Where is he going? Who lives up there on the golden stars?"[9] —

9. This is the form given to these eternal questions by the German poet Heinrich Heine (1797–1856) in the poem "Fragen" (Questions), which we shall have occasion to mention

which many a modern intellectual considers idle; and for us video-games, drugs, ergonomics, horoscopes, or pseudo-religious sects are just as good as science and religion, despite abundant evidence of the unlimited measure of unhappiness and suffering caused by believing in everything and in nothing at the same time. We are sheep without a shepherd, because we no longer have any basic principles on which to construct satisfactory answers to questions related to the meaning of life.

Western society has experienced this "existential dilemma" for several centuries. Now and again, the role of shepherd was taken by certain intellectuals who thought that human unhappiness could be removed by merely suppressing its manifestations. They believed that they could cure people of their existential doubts by convincing them that their instinctive beliefs in truth, justice, and beauty are pathological "epiphenomena," and that their unhappiness stemmed from "taboos" forbidding them to enjoy freely the material pleasures of life. These intellectuals were quite popular between 1950 and 1970, when actual or potential progress in medical sciences made people less afraid of the health consequences of violating certain "taboos"; but there are grounds for wondering whether their own children were not among the first victims of their overly simplistic view. Be that as it may, a shepherd of men — and, like it or not, all educated people play the role of shepherd at least with their own families and acquaintances — should consider every other person, without exception, as a human being, not as a piece of machinery obliged to function according to someone else's ideology.

What have these considerations to do with a cosmological metaphor? An answer can be found in the writings of the great scientists of the seventeenth century. That was the time of Galileo Galilei, René Descartes, and Blaise Pascal,[10] when the image of the world that placed man and the earth at its physical center was being replaced by the Copernican heliocentric description of the solar system, a time when the clockwork image made its first appearance. Much has been written about Galileo and his personal vicissitudes; much less has been said of the existential crisis brought about by the Copernican revolution among the learned and the less learned. John Donne's (1573–1631) lines about this are rightly famous:

And new philosophy calls all in doubt,
The element of fire is quite put out; The Sun is lost, and th'
Earth . . .
'Tis all in pieces, all coherence gone.[11]

---

again. The poem can be found in H. Heine, *Buch der Lieder* (1827) (Munich: Kindler, 1964).
10. Who died in 1662, 1650, 1662, respectively.
11. J. Donne, *Anatomy of the World* (1612), lines 205-207, 213. From J. Donne, *Liriche sacre e profane: Sacred and Profane Poems*, critical English edition and Italian translation by G. Melchiori (Milan: Mondadori, 1983).

The response that is most significant for our age of science was perhaps that of Blaise Pascal, a great scientist with a most modern mind, who even designed the first mechanical calculator. One of his "thoughts" shows the extent to which even those who were creating the new science felt that something of the greatest import had been lost with the collapse of the previous picture of the universe:

> On considering the blindness and misery of man, on looking at the Universe made dumb, and at man without a light, left to himself, and as it were lost in this corner of the Universe, without knowing who placed him there, what he came to do, what he will become on dying, incapable of any knowledge, I become full of fright, as would happen to a man abandoned asleep on a deserted and terrible island, waking up without knowing where he is, and with no means to escape. And thus I wonder how it is possible that we are not overcome by despair because of such a miserable state.[12]

Let us summarize. Many influential minds of today maintain that *Homo sapiens* is not a very special animal, but just like whales, gulls, and worms, he is one of the possible solutions evolution has found for the "survival of the fittest"; and he should follow his "natural drives." The American philosopher John Dewey (1859–1952) expressed the belief that "the brain is primarily an organ of a certain kind of behavior, not of knowing the world."[13] Even granting that view, we are still faced with the fact that, just as each animal species differs from the others in certain special characteristics, also the human species has many distinctive characteristics, not the least of which is a built-in longing for truth, justice, and beauty. Human beings keep looking for those three values everywhere and, what is more, they instinctively see them as facets of the same general notion: a mysterious harmony and coherence among all things and processes, from the lights in the firmament to the everyday choices of ordinary life.

Whatever the explanation may be, the fact is that our psychological health requires that we should be able to believe in the existence of a general pattern to which all things in the universe conform, and that this pattern is characterized by laws and rules, scientific and moral. In other words, to avoid losing our sense of identity, we need a solid concept of the world as a basic practical reference: a *Weltanschauung*.

Of course, for the vast majority of people, including the highly educated, this built-in need cannot be satisfied by abstract philosophical speculation. In fact, we insist on using a German word, uncommon in the everyday English-speaking world, because the term "world-view" by

12. B. Pascal, *Pensées* (New York: E. P. Dutton, 1958), 393.
13. J. Dewey, *Creative Intelligence* (New York: H. Holt & Co., 1917), 36.

which it is often replaced might suggest an explicit, fully conscious theory of the world. Now, a poor laborer in Kinshasa or Lima certainly has a *Weltanschauung*, but it would be too much to expect of him a world-view (cf. chapter thirteen). Therefore, a reference image making it possible to get at least a feeling for the general nature of those rules is required by our psychology. That is, for most of us a working *Weltanschauung* must rest — as was already the case with the Ptolemaic system of the world — on a description of the universe condensed in a familiar image, that is, a "cosmological metaphor."[14]

Of Astronomy and Astrology

What the Dance image points to is, first of all, the existence of a general common pattern of change to which all objects, systems, and organisms conform. Wirth rightly says that this is a very ancient view. In fact, since the dawn of humanity, the sun was recognized as the heavenly object that determined day and night, and was somehow associated with the seasons and with the length of the year. The moon's periodic vanishing matched important cycles on earth: fishermen must have realized quite early that the tides followed the same rhythm as the moon, and women must have done the same about their own bodies. On closer inspection things appeared to be even more complicated, for the sun's yearly course took place against a background of stars, most of which seemed to be fixed with respect to one another, but would change their orientation depending on the season, so that day by day the sun's highest point corresponded to a different place in an almost rigid but rotating pattern of stars. Certain "stars" (the planets Mars, Jupiter, and Venus) even moved with respect to all the others in extremely complicated ways.

The ancient civilizations, living in places where the sky was clear most of the time, realized that all those regularities in the motions of the stars in the sky clearly matched the pattern of the changing seasons, and hence the most important events in a shepherd's or a farmer's life; consequently, they transferred to the stars that animism which more primitive peoples had applied to earthly objects, mainly living beings such as trees and animals. But, more importantly, the idea of the Dance must have already been there, for it was inherent in a life close to nature:

In that open field
If you do not come too close, if you do not come too close,
On a summer midnight, you can hear the music

14. The concept of metaphor and its significance, with many references to the clockwork image, is discussed by H. Blumenfeld, *Paradigmen zu einer Metaphorologie* (Paradigms for a science of metaphors), vol. VI of the series *Archive für Begriffgeschichte* (Bonn: H. Bouvier and Co., 1960).

Of the weak pipe and the little drum
And see them dancing around the bonfire
The association of man and woman
In daunsinge, signifying matrimonie
— A dignified and commodious sacrament.
Two and two, necessarye conjunction,
Holding each other by the hand or the arm
Which betokeneth concorde. Round and round the fire
Leaping through the flames, or joined in circles,
Rustically solemn or in rustic laughter
Lifting heavy feet in clumsy shoes,
Earth feet, loam feet, lifted in country mirth
Mirth of those long since under earth
Nourishing the corn.

                              Keeping time,
Keeping the rhythm in their dancing
As in their living in the living seasons
The time of the seasons and the constellations
The time of milking and the time of harvest
The time of the coupling of man and woman
And that of beasts. Feet rising and falling.
Eating and drinking. Dung and death.[15]

The Babylonians and then the Greeks, who had the extraordinary gift of seeking understanding for no purpose other than understanding, turned the feeling that earthly and heavenly events followed some common pattern into a sort of scientific hypothesis, almost a theory. According to them, those lights in the night sky, each inhabited by a soul, evolved in complete coherence with the flow of events in the whole world they knew. The god or guardian spirit inhabiting a star had a life, thought processes, emotions, which became at least partly manifest through the star's apparent motions, and were closely parallel with the changes of earthly things. T. S. Eliot makes the same point in his modern poetical fashion:

Garlic and sapphires in the mud
Clot the bedded axle-tree.
The trilling wire in the blood
Sings below inveterate scars
Appeasing long forgotten wars.
The dance along the artery
The circulation of the lymph

15. T. S. Eliot, *Four Quartets*, "East Coker," I, lines 24–47.

Are figured in the drift of stars
Ascend to summer in the tree
We move along the moving tree
In light upon the figured leaf
And hear upon the sodden floor
Below, the boarhound and the boar
Pursue their pattern as before
But reconciled among the stars.[16]

We should beware in this connection of our modern habit of thinking in terms of efficient causes or driving forces: although the stars were later attributed a sort of active influence on events taking place on earth, the genuine meaning of what was called "influence" was probably closer to the Greek ἀνάνκη (ananke), a *necessity* not imposed by preceding or subsequent events or causes or decisions, but by the inherent spatiotemporal unity of the universe. This is why astrology had such a great appeal for the Stoics, those philosophers of the Roman Empire who believed that a true man should remain impassive in the face of any event, accepting the will of the gods without asking for anything in exchange.

Rather than "influence," a better term would be "sympathy," whose Greek ancestor, συμπάθεια (sympatheia), meant "undergoing together." For example, if you said that the conjunction of Jupiter and Mars foreboded war, you really meant that, at the time when that conjunction was realized, the overall state of the universe also included a material and psychological situation on earth corresponding to the premises of war. To put it in modern language, prediction of imminent war was based on the idea that events taking place in our region of space match regularities in other parts of the universe, and the underlying general assumption was that the pattern of change of the universe in time and space fits a single, though immensely complicated, design.

We meet here what modern physicists might call a *collective state* of the universe, evolving with a certain rhythm and along a certain melodic line; this does not imply that the single events making up that state are *caused* by other events in the same sense as when one says that the motion of a wheel is caused by the engine through a system of gears. We are not dealing with a chain of causes, but with *coherence*.

The viewpoint that assigned the first place to coherence (and beauty) in man's endeavor to grasp the pattern of the world outside him moved out of sight in the seventeenth century, as a consequence of the enthusiasm for the newly discovered approach of Galileo, to be replaced by mechanism, summarized in the clockwork image. It was a view that considered the universe merely a collection of directly interacting systems.

16. T. S. Eliot, *Four Quartets*, "Burnt Norton," II, lines 49–63.

The internal properties of those systems were at least ideally independent of the environment, and their behavior was completely determined at each moment of time by previous conditions.

Until recently, modern science stuck to that view, which was formalized as a principle by Ernst Mach (1838–1916), an eminent Austrian mathematical physicist who is also known in philosophy of science as inspirer of the Vienna circle — a group of thinkers who followed the idea that science is essentially a logical construction of our minds. According to Mach's principle, the presence of distant bodies does not affect events or processes in any given part of space, because the forces they exert cancel out.[17] Another principle constantly used in cosmology is the *cosmological principle*. It states that the laws of physics are the same everywhere in the universe. This principle is not in opposition to the idea of a general coherence of the events in the whole universe, but Mach's principle is. Mach's principle, however, concerns the laws of physics applicable in a comparatively small region of space, not the effects of *information* arriving from distant bodies. That, as has been realized only in the last few decades, is quite another matter. We will discuss it at length, because communication — that is to say, information transfer — is what gives such great significance to the Great Dance image. For a rough idea of the line of thought to be followed, consider the physical and psychological consequences that could be brought about on earth by the appearance of a supernova in the sky, even if the change in energy reaching earth from the sky were absolutely negligible.

The Return of Coherence

Until about 1950, two points of view governed science. One was physicalism, an extreme version of reductionistic mechanism, according to which all that is perceived by our senses is nothing but atoms and quanta (or even nothing but elementary particles and fundamental fields). The other was vitalism, whose supporters claimed that it is impossible to explain life without thinking of a special force or field or fluid permeating a living organism, somehow organizing the parts of that organism and imparting to them that special quality that we call "being alive."

Physicalism failed to explain life, a failure that was taken by many as a proof of vitalism. In fact, that failure merely proved that reduction to simpler parts or principles, however necessary, is not sufficient to build the edifice of science. The adoption of reductionistic mechanism coincided with the birth of modern science, and for a long time it prevailed. Scientists believed that a description of a complex object in terms

17. J. Rosen: "Chance and Order in Science *via* the Extended Mach Principle," *Epistemologia* (Genoa) 7 (1984): 309–312.

of its parts would tell everything about that object, even though that belief actually rested on reference to very simple physical systems, such as the solar system. Thus, physics became the model of genuine science, despite the fact that at the same time chemistry was toiling toward the discovery of the structure of molecules, opening the way to our present understanding of the nature of life and to the rise of modern biology.

The discovery of molecular structure was the first great advance toward the realization that in most cases the whole is not just the sum of the parts. Yet a psychological barrier prevented most physicists from accepting that novel view; even the eminent British physicist Sir James Jeans (1877–1946), in a short history of science, failed to mention the discoverers of the structure of molecules. The most popular philosophers of science of our time have all been inspired by the idea that physics sets the standards for deciding whether some theory is or is not "scientific."

Major conceptual advances in science now require that we recover a view of the universe in which every single thing or event is in fact related to everything else. The main concepts involved were already known to scientists and thinkers before the triumph of mechanism, but their import in scientific explanations of observed phenomena has been realized only in the last few decades. Two scientists are probably the most representative of this change: the American mathematician Norbert Wiener, founder of cybernetics, and the Belgian physical chemist Ilya Prigogine, discoverer of the importance of steady-state systems. Wiener, whose work was extended to become a general theory of living and nonliving systems by Ludwig von Bertalanffy, showed that already in engineering science effects were known which could make a system behave as an active whole. Prigogine, whom we have already cited, has most clearly seen that the recovery of the ancient view is required precisely by the state of science after the discovery of the great principles of thermodynamics, relativity, and quantum mechanics. He summarizes them by three general concepts: coherence, emergence of information, and irreversibility. In turn, these concepts rest on at least five more specific concepts: information, order, interaction, organization, and feedback.

Prigogine's eight concepts apply to the whole universe as well as to objects in it. When they are not single material points, those objects may be called *systems*, as physics has done for centuries, but the novelty is that emphasis is now placed not on the parts (or particles) constituting each system, but on its behavior as a whole. Using a typical procedure of modern science — reference to a limiting case — we could say that in the new approach, which is called holistic from the Greek word ὅλος (holos, "whole"), every collection of interacting parts is referred to the limiting case where the interactions are so strong that the individual parts merge together and can no longer be recognized as such. In the traditional approach of physics, rightly called reductionistic, the same collection would be referred to the limiting case of noninteracting parts. The reality to be studied is the same; but, although the physicist's approach has unquestionable advantages, such as showing the inconsistency of such notions as a vital fluid, the other suggests conceptual tools of analysis which apply specifically to a unity of many parts, and are needed precisely because the whole is more than the sum of its parts.

 ˙ Those who have followed the evolution of science in recent years find it difficult to accept the fact that the discovery of atomic structure did not lead the great physicists of the earlier part of the twentieth century to see the limits of reductionism; for even such a simple object as an atom has properties that are not just a superposition of the properties of its constituent particles, the electrons and the nucleus. The more complex a system, the more the reductionistic "explanation" lags behind a complete explanation of the behavior of the whole. A reductionistic approach is grossly unsatisfactory when the complexity is that of a living cell.

The change in mental attitude we are speaking of came very late, with the work of such scientists as Wiener, Bertalanffy, and Prigogine, and with the revival of biology between 1940 and 1960. That change took place in the human sciences as well. In fact, the sense given to the word "system" in recent scientific thought is that adopted by the anthropologist Claude Lévi-Strauss, the founder of structuralism: "A system is any ensemble of elements such that none of those elements can be modified without causing a modification of all the others."[18] If "modification of an element" is understood as a change in the way the element works, not necessarily involving a change in its shape or structure, this sense of the word "system" is quite general, and applies to some extent even to the solar system. If, however, the unity results from the cooperation of parts that have adjusted their properties, indeed their internal states, to those of the others, then one is dealing with that special class of systems which includes living beings. A few concrete examples hopefully will clarify the peculiar nature of the systems of this class, which we shall call "systems in the strong sense" whenever it is important to emphasize the difference from systems such as the solar system.

Consider a pair of scissors. They are essentially two knives joined in a certain way, but with them you can easily cut a sheet of paper held in your hand, an operation extremely difficult with a single knife. The scissors have no inherent unity, that is to say, they are merely an assemblage of two parts whose properties do not depend on whether or not they are together; yet they have a property that the parts do not have, namely cutting paper or even tissues held in one's hand. Therefore, al-

18. C. Lévi-Strauss, quoted by F. Wahl, *Qu'est-ce que le structuralisme? 5 Philosophie* (Paris: Seuil, 1973).

though they are not a system in the strong sense, scissors show one of the characteristics of such a system.

Our solar system is not a system in the strong sense, either, but it goes some distance toward being one. Its major features are consistent with the assumption that each planet moves around the sun as if it were alone. Nevertheless, removal of one planet would affect the motions of the others. Even if it did not affect those motions, its removal could be the indirect cause of local catastrophes. For example, the courses of meteorites would be changed; some might hit other planets, possibly causing disasters.

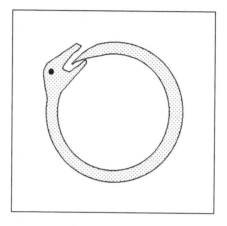

Another step on the way toward systems in the strong sense is illustrated by molecules. Consider, for example, the famous benzene molecule, whose structure recalls the depiction of an Ouroboros (see figure), the mythological serpent holding its tail in its mouth. The molecule is a hexagonal ring of six carbon atoms, each carrying a hydrogen atom held by a bond extending outward from the ring. Suppose you replace one of those hydrogen atoms by something else, such as a chlorine atom or nitro group, by a suitable chemical reaction. Then, as the products of many reactions of the new molecule will show, the properties of the other carbon atoms are affected, some becoming more reactive, others less. Yet such physical characteristics as the atom-atom distances are practically unaffected. Therefore, a molecule does not really possess the kind of unity that makes a collection of parts a system in the strong sense; its unitary behavior is nonetheless strong enough to justify regarding it as the simplest example of a unitary system. We shall come back to this point in the next chapter.

Now consider a solid-state amplifier. If you get hold of the instructions for repair, you will notice that the producer gives the voltages that you must find at a number of places when the amplifier is working correctly. This means two things. First, the device works correctly only when connected to an appropriate voltage and current supply. Second, each component works correctly only if the others work correctly. Thus, the parts of the amplifier are interdependent, and the device works as a whole, even though (as happens with the organs of a living being) it is possible within certain limits to find which particular component is responsible for a malfunction and to replace it. In certain amplifiers, the interdependence of the components is such that if certain of them are short-circuited, the whole device is damaged beyond repair, just as happens to a living organism when it dies.

Finally, consider a cell, the smallest object that can properly be called living, whether belonging to a biological tissue or constituting an independent living being, for instance an amoeba. Although a number of different regions can be distinguished in it, from the standpoint of molecular biology the actual parts of the cell are molecules (ordinary ones and macromolecules) participating in complicated chemical reactions. Those molecules form chains extending over the whole cell, and preside over the metabolism, growth, and reproduction of the cell. The huge number of molecular transformations taking place at each instant form a continuously changing pattern in which no single step can be considered independent of the others. That is to say, a living cell has an extremely high degree of unity resulting from a network of mutually dependent processes. Suitable poisons can alter particular processes, but any such alteration affects the whole cell. In many cases the cell responds by changing its whole organization so as to neutralize the poison; in some cases the alteration is so important that it results in the cell's death. A cell's death is a phenomenon similar to the burnout of an electronic device as in the above example, but the reality it destroys is immensely richer and more complex than that of any artificial device. The difference is not just a matter of scale and number of components.

What emerges from the combined action of the huge number of molecules constituting a living cell is the ability to cope with an enormous variety of changes in the cell's environment, to grow and to organize external raw material into copies of the cell, and to perform various extremely complicated functions. To grasp the nature of those functions, just think of a neuron, one of the cells in the human brain that (as far as present science can tell) make it possible for a person to think. Clearly, there is a *qualitative* difference between the most complex electronic device and a living cell. That qualitative difference is the essential point in the notion of a system in the strong sense: when a large number of parts participate in a tightly organized activity novelties appear that cannot be regarded as the magnification of properties found with a smaller number of components and a lesser degree of organization.

It is important to keep in mind that what is said here is not intended to show that reductionistic explanations are wrong; they are just incomplete. If one said that a man is a being made of two legs, two arms, a brain, and what have you, connected together in such and such a way, one would indeed state a fact, but would omit the most important pieces of information, for example that a man is a being capable of love and (alas!) of the most terrible atrocities. The gap between a fragmentary sort of description based on a system's parts and the reality emerging from the cooperation of those parts to form a whole is what we are exploring here, guided by the image of the Dance. Our exploration is thus largely an exploration of that vast region of half-known realities that today is called "complexity."

Ours will be a journey through the universe in search of those common features that make it a complex system consisting of complex systems. The universe disclosed to us by science appears to be the most beautiful and glorious material thing imaginable, endowed with an internal mysterious order reminiscent of fractals, an eerie by-product of the mathematics of complexity. To begin our journey, let us first of all look briefly at a few concrete examples showing how a holistic view applies to the cosmos of today's science.

Birds, Stars, and the Goddess Earth

Evolution is an almost trivial example of coherence in time and space. Whatever the mechanism for the appearance of a new species may be, there is no doubt that its survival and expansion depend completely on the extent to which it is "tuned" to the environment in which it has to live. In turn, if it survives even for a comparatively short time, it will affect the evolution and the possible appearance of other species. All of this happens as in a complex dance, where a new group of dancers joins the dance in perfect measure at the appropriate place to interpret a new voice in the suite, and at the same time the other dancers make room for them in a harmonious way just by following their own line of melody, while some retire because their part is over and the voice which they interpreted is now silent.

This analogy suggests that, when we say that at a given moment the conditions are ripe for the appearance of a new species, and at the same time we claim that "chance" will decide if and when and what sort of species will appear, we are making two contradictory statements. In order to tell that the conditions are ripe, we must have a clear idea of the expected new species; and we are so to speak fixing its time and place of appearance, so that we leave no room to chance. The contradiction could be removed if we implied that, if we were composing the music of the Dance ourselves, we would start at that time a new melodic line. In fact we are neither the composer nor the choreographer, so we can speak only of a possibility. That is to say, the term "chance" only means that the situation as we know it at a given time and place is compatible with the appearance of a new species, but does not automatically bring it about; what is unknown is the "decision" by whoever or whatever plays the role of the composer, precisely as happens for a voice in a fugue.

To see what is meant by the notion of long-range coherence not falling within a deterministic scheme, consider the case of the migration of the blackcaps, reported by Adolf Portmann. There are hints that the earth's magnetic field provides the reference for the orientation of migrating birds. However, suitable experiments suggest that the migrating birds, at least, of the family *Sylviidae* depend on the positions of the constellations for their orientation. According to Adolf Portmann,

> We know nothing of the consciousness of the little blackcap, and it would be vain to speculate on the "impressions" that the various images of the sky might produce in it. The interiority of the bird appears to us as a whole, but of this whole we can only say that a complicated system of relations with the stars in the sky is preconstituted in it; that the interiority of the bird has been predisposed since its origin to an experimentally verifiable connection with the vision of the night sky, whose constellations, the figures in it, are the determining factors.[19]

This is a beautiful example of a relationship which the Darwinists would explain by assuming a mechanistic chain of mutations and selection, but cannot be accounted for by that explanation alone; for a mechanistic explanation only concerns the historical origin of the behavior we are considering, which actually points to the fact that there is in the universe a fine network of noncausal relations; these relations reach so deeply into the tiniest details that a small bird may depend for its survival on patterns drawn in the sky of its tiny planet by immense globes of nuclear fire tens or hundreds of light years away. If you do not accept Portmann's view about the little blackcaps, just think that the men who crossed the oceans in centuries past relied for orientation on the remote suns shining in the sky.

In reviewing a book (by E. Davourst) on the search for extraterrestrial intelligences, Frank Tipler mentioned a number of points pertaining to a more general aspect of the Great Dance. Two in particular are worth recalling: the argument by B. Carter (1964), based on the weak anthropic principle — according to which the constants entering the fundamental laws of physics could not have values different from the observed ones, if the fact is granted that man exists — suggesting that extraterrestrial

19. A. Portmann, *Aufbruch der Lebensforschung* (Frankfurt a.M.: Suhrkamp, 1965); see also J. L. Gould, "Constant Compass Calibration," *Nature* 375 (1995): 184.

intelligences must be exceedingly rare, if they exist at all; and the attempt by M. Shaposhnikov to predict the mass of an elementary particle using Carter's argument. Tipler wrote:

> This prediction failed, but it is a fascinating thought that there may be a connection between the mass [of an elementary particle] and the rarity of intelligent life in the Universe.[20]

It may be difficult to find an immediate counterpart to correlations of this sort in the Great Dance image, but they are clear suggestions that even physics, the queen of science but the most reductionistic of all disciplines, is being forced to think in terms of a pattern of correlations among the most diverse facts in the universe. The example of the astronavigating blackcap tells us of the role of information exchange in ensuring such coherence; the anthropic principle and its corollaries suggest the existence of a unitary design. Both hint at the existence of the actual Dance and the existence of a great symphony or suite, giving rhythm and shape to the whole material reality in space and time.

One last example is the "Gaia hypothesis," which has aroused so many contrasting reactions. The idea behind that hypothesis, due to James Lovelock, is that the biosphere of earth is a complex system where feedback channels exist that allow it to compensate for internal as well as external perturbations tending to change the status quo; that is to say, the biosphere as a whole exhibits a sort of homeostasis — a capacity to respond to disturbances so as to preserve a particular internal state — akin to the homeostasis characteristic of living organisms.[21]

Lovelock's reference to *Gaia*, the Greek name for the goddess earth, has caused misunderstandings, because it seems to suggest that the earth is a living organism just as is a whale or a mosquito. Similarity, however, does not mean identity. The following points should be kept in mind:

(a) The feedback channels operating in the biosphere are not necessarily as numerous and efficient as in a living organism;

(b) The biosphere is susceptible of several steady states, each possibly reached by what on the human scale is a catastrophic transition caused by a very large perturbation (such as the fall of the meteorite which, according to recent findings, may have caused the extinction of the dinosaurs);

(c) The biosphere probably has a very limited degree of independence; indeed it must "dance in measure" with the rest of the earth and with the universe at large.

20. F. J. Tipler, "Alien Life," *Nature* 354 (1991): 334–335.
21. J. E. Lovelock, "Hands Up for the Gaia Hypothesis," *Nature* 344 (1990) 100–102; cf. *Nature* 207 (1965): 568–570.

Point (b) is especially important. It means that, although ordinary disturbances (say, a sudden increase in the carbon dioxide concentration in a certain part of the globe) may be neutralized by other processes (such as the rapid growth of a denser vegetation), even slightly stronger or self-amplifying disturbances (such as ozone-destroying reactions) can force the biosphere to shift to another steady state — perhaps to one incompatible with the survival of mankind. In a similar situation, a living organism might heal and revert to its normal state, the only state compatible with its environment — but the biosphere *is* the environment, and many states are possible without destroying it: was there not a time, according to paleogeology, when there was no oxygen in the earth's atmosphere, and yet an immense variety of living forms thrived?

With these clarifications, the Gaia hypothesis is not just respectable; it is a beautiful example of what is suggested by the Great Dance image. For example, in the Dance there is feedback, as individual dancers and groups of dancers not only follow the music but continuously adjust their movements to those of the others; but that feedback is strong or weak depending on the circumstances, in particular on the "density" of dancers and the rhythm of the music. Indeed, most of the time the music (and even the choreography) allows a certain freedom to the dancers. This is the feature of the Dance metaphor that throws light on the place random fluctuations and the free actions of human beings may have in a coherent context — such as the earth's biosphere or the whole universe.

The Music and the Dance

Metaphors can have profound significance because, as images or figures, they allow the mind to grasp or discover unsuspected ideal and material relationships between objects. As the Danish historian of science Olaf Pedersen has pointed out, just because they are images

> ...they are always open to more than one interpretation. But far from being a defect this essential openness is the reason why a number of those metaphors have had a very long life and have been able to survive great changes both in science and in the social background against which they first appeared.[22]

Even the clockwork image, although no longer acceptable as a metaphor for the nature of processes in the universe, emphasizes the diachronic, temporal dimension of the world. In this sense it is still valid today. It tells us that, whenever we consider the significance of a clock in our life, we should keep in mind that the clock is part of the universe, and

22. O. Pedersen, *The Book of Nature* (Vatican City: Vatican Observatory Foundation, 1992).

somehow has properties similar to those of the universe as a whole. In light of progress in scientific knowledge, the properties in question can no longer be thought of as those of an inexorable mechanism; yet it remains true that time is embodied in a succession of different states. The novelty in this connection is only that the clock we have to think of when applying the clockwork image to the universe is not like a mechanical clock regulating human activity, but like an electronic clock regulating the internal time of a computer (that is, the rate at which the computer's operating system passes from one state to another in executing instructions). Indeed, the curious and unexpected "computer image" can also be used to describe certain global aspects of the universe, such as the creation and exchange of information.

Reference to a computer clock has special significance in connection with the Great Dance because no dance can be conceived of without a measure. That measure is determined, as it were, by the invisible metronome of the music, which the dance embodies. The metaphor of the Great Dance implies the metaphor of the *Concentus Magnus*, the Great Symphony. That is why it is partly a return to the ancient notion of *Harmonia Mundi* and the Music of the Spheres, developed, however, in the richer and more mature way that has emerged now that science is emerging from the nightmare of scientism.

At first sight, it is somewhat surprising that music should possess a structure and complexity closely matching those discovered in the space of stars and galaxies, in the world of living organisms, in the microcosm of atoms and molecules. The surprise comes from the very paradoxical nature of music: on the one hand, its means of expression is bound in a very precise way to the earth, to the presence of air, and to the conformation of our ears; on the other hand, it seems to be the highest form of art representing nothing but itself and the emotions and feelings of the composer.

Technically speaking, the language and the means of expression of music are one and the same thing, and are limited to earth. That is not true of beauty perceived by our eyes, whether natural or artificial. Although we shall never hear with our ears the actual music of the stars, an echo of their beauty does reach our eyes on a clear winter sky or in a telescope image. Nor will music ever speak explicitly, as poetry does, of the beauty of a sunset or of the glory of God. Poetry is at least partly independent of the means of expression; think of the almost universal appreciation for the *Divine Comedy* of Dante Alighieri and for Homer's *Iliad* even through their translations into many languages. Yet an orchestra, or even a single instrument, can translate into sounds both the pure, immaterial world of mathematics (as in some of Bach's masterpieces) and the immense richness and beauty of the universe (as in Beethoven's Ninth Symphony). This contrast, a cause for wonder and meditation, explains why the temptation to establish a correspondence between music and the most sublime things has been a constant of great civilizations.

The general feeling about music can be reconciled with what science knows about the nature of sound by a number of considerations. First of all, music has a mathematical side, which is of course independent of sounds: the musical intervals as well as the associations of different notes obey rules that can be expressed mathematically; that is true even if they depend on the habits and training of our hearing. The shapes of the curves graphically representing a musical phrase are elegant and completely different from those of noises. Also, the rules of voice movements must be respected (with exceptions reserved to the greatest composers) in order to ensure the greatest independence as well as the greatest coherence of the various parts, along both the melodic line and the harmonic plane. Those elements represent but the "diachronic" and "synchronic" dimensions of a musical message, the former extending in time, the latter extending in the space of the musical frequencies.

The relationship between these dimensions and events taking place in space-time appears immediately, as in a ballet. Groups of dancers will move according to one voice, others according to another: at each moment of time the position of each group of dancers represents a note of an accord, its velocity and direction the melody in which it is engaged. In short, music seems to transform into sounds the regularities of processes in the universe; music expresses a deeply rooted though hidden communion with the infinite variety of all that is and becomes.

Thinking of a ballet and the music it embodies brings out other elements of the image of the Cosmic Dance. As new voices appear, new dancers appear on the stage, and the complexity and beauty become richer and richer; some voices may slowly or suddenly melt into others, to vanish altogether or perhaps to generate a variety of new voices. With respect to the clockwork image, the most peculiar feature is the freedom enjoyed by the dancers: their positions and even their times of appearance are not rigidly fixed. Rather, following the music, the dancers interpret it while taking its history into account, so that even repeated musical passages would not be interpreted in the same way.

Rhythm and Timbre in the Music of the Pulsars

Rather surprisingly, in 1967, centuries after the Music of the Stars had been relegated to the attic of obsolete fantastic notions, the discovery of pulsating stars, or pulsars, brought back to the stage features of processes in the universe that are akin to music. Pulsars send radio-wave signals at extremely regular intervals, between 1/30th of a second and 4 seconds. Their pulses, when received through a suitably tuned radio receiver, appear like bursts of very low frequencies (a few tens of cycles per second) lasting about 3 percent of the total time between pulses. Since the tempos of music have measures between 0.5 and 5 seconds, this means that in the case of a pulsar with a period of about one second, the removal of its very high frequency component will yield beats the length of a musical quaver (an eighth note) or semiquaver, separated by long silences. The pulses have tails, however, which will be heard over a loudspeaker for a much longer time. Because the duration of the pulse corresponds to an oscillation of about 130 Hz, the sound will be a bass beat. Although the rhythm is absolutely regular, minor random changes in the pulsar pulses cause their timbre to change slightly from pulse to pulse. Thus, what is heard when the signal reaching earth from certain pulsars is fed into a sufficiently powerful and appropriately tuned receiver is the beating of a drum. According to Roland Pease, the French composer Gérard Grisey

> ...likens the sound of a pulsar to African drums and says he was inspired by the varying tone colour of the pulses and the regularity of the rhythm.[23]

The idea that pulsars could be treated as musicians must have occurred to many an astronomer as soon as their musical properties were discovered. David Blair noted the first "performance" of pulsar music, which took place in Western Australia in 1988 on the occasion of the fifth Marcel Grossman Conference on General Relativity and Gravitation:

> Perth's Tunc Ensemble, which included saxophone, flute and didgeridoo, played to the live signal of PSR1749-28. [That particular pulsar] was chosen for its drumlike period, its very strong signal and its occasional pulse nulling which gives an interesting syncopated rhythm.[24]

From Blair's report, the Australian performance was evidently on the side of rather light music. In contrast, Gérard Grisey, the French composer mentioned above, wrote very serious music with his work *"Le Noir de l'Etoile."* That composition included the notes of two pulsars, the fast PSR0819 in the Vela nebula (30 pulses per second, heard as a deep bass continuously varying in tone) and the slow, lofty PSR0329-54. The work was presented twice in France and a third time in November 1992 at the Huddersfield Contemporary Music Festival. I do not know how it was set up in those cases; but I like very much to imagine a performance of Grisey's work in an ambiance dear to another modern composer, Xenakis, namely the ancient hall in the ruins of the Abbaye de Cluny on the Boulevard St. Michel in Paris. There you listen to music sitting

23. R. Pease, "Pulsars to Star in Forthcoming UK Festival," *Nature* 360 (1992): 96.
24. D. Blair, "The Music of the Stars," *Nature* 360 (1992): 390.

on the floor, surrounded by bare stone walls. At a certain moment, the lights go out, and a dim bluish luminosity fills the hall. All the instruments are silent. An occasional suppressed coughing is the only sign that other people are present. Then you seem to hear a very weak hollow sound. It grows to the deep bass of a drumbeat and slowly dies off. After a silence that seems infinite, but is actually only a second or so, comes another beat, as deep as the other, but with just a touch of warmth in it; and then again. The drumlike beating goes on, changing the timbre and intensity of its beats but keeping the same steady rhythm. It is as if you were hearing the heartbeats of an enormous animal at sleep.

But now you have overcome the first feeling of awe, and your consciousness goes back to the realization that you are hearing a star pulsating in the depths of space, thousands of light years away and thousands of years in the past. For a moment, music has made you, in the hall of Cluny, one with the life of the universe, with that immense network of messages that spans millions of light years from star to star, from being to being, more mysterious and remote than the network of chemical reactions comprising the life of the strangest living being on earth.

What is the real meaning of such an experience? A person with no sense of poetry may tell you contemptuously that it was all illusion, because it has been a trick of radio-telescopes combined with your belief in scientific theories. Does such a person have any notion at all of what "meaningfulness" is? On another occasion, ask that person what he (or she) thinks a human being is. He (or she) will try to elude the question by pointing out that Sir Karl Popper, the popular epistemologist, has banned out of science all "what is" questions ("What is a star?" "What is life?" "What is man?"). If pushed, that same person may tell you that a human being is merely a biological entity whose only purpose is survival of the individual and of the species — a goal realized in practice by making money and pursuing pleasure. Do not try to convince such a person that things stand otherwise. You will only make a fool of yourself. Your interlocutor will ask how your philosophy can be of use to cure hunger, diseases, and other visible ills of humanity. That response is probably the result of not realizing that there are invisible ills, such as loneliness, despair, disloyalty, and contempt of the rights of other people; such ills can be cured only by helping individuals become conscious of what it means to be a human being. Without a cure of those existential ills, no improvement in material conditions will suffice — as is evident from the conditions of our society. Now, a philosopher's main task is to try to make sense of the reality in which we are immersed by trying to sort out what really exists and what is mere appearance, why existing things change or cease to exist, and what is our place in the universe. Only afterwards are philosophical conclusions used to construct guidelines for action.

The philosopher's role is thus similar to that of the poets, who, as Martin Heidegger (1889–1976) pointed out,[25] have the task of reminding us of the gods — that is, of such things as beauty, wisdom, and heroism. In an age that has rejected all romance and belief, the poets hear the music of the Dance,

> … music heard so deeply
> That it is not heard at all, but you are the music
> While the music lasts. These are only hints and guesses
> Hints followed by guesses; and the rest
> Is prayer, observance, discipline, thought and action, … [26]

and remind us of the paths we should follow in order for our actions to be worthy of human beings. The philosophers should help us to think correctly; they should not be founders of ideologies nor worshippers of their own egos.

All this means that we may accept at face value what we felt when listening to the pulsars. Science and technology have done their part in making it possible for us to hear music from the stars and know that it came from the stars. The cosmic drums are not being beaten, like African tom-toms, to communicate messages between human beings. Yet their music can be meaningful to us. Our feelings have faithfully translated a message that cannot and need not be put into words. The depths of space have a life of their own, a life that, despite its alienness, has at least rhythms in common with ours, and will let us know we are a tiny part of it, if only we take the right approach.

So, you see, in the hall of Cluny we really heard the music of the stars; or, to put it better, we heard one instrument of the whole orchestra, an instrument playing with the tempo and notes our body's ears can detect. Most of the Great Dance Symphony, if we find the time to think, we will hear with the ear of our inner senses — our intelligence and our imagination — at work when we are doing science, philosophy, and poetry.

25. M. Heidegger, *Holzwege*, 5th ed. (Frankfurt a.M.: Klostermann, 1972).
26. T. S. Eliot, *Four Quartets*, "Dry Salvages," lines 209–213.

Chapter 2

Information, Order, and Life

The image of the Dance hints at a coherent, evolving pattern in which all objects in the universe participate. Why do apparently chaotic systems, such as certain African markets, actually work very well? Starting from this question, we shall first explore information, then complexity, the newest problem facing science as a whole, order, which makes nature intelligible, and organization, the kind of order typical of life.

The Souk and the Quelle – Information – Complexity – Unity – Emerging Information – Order – Organization and Life – The Laser and the Market

But the moment my voice, though I sang low and soft, stirred the air of the hall, the dancers started, the quick interweaving crowd shook, lost its form, divided, each figure sprang to its pedestal, and stood, a self-evolving life no more, but a rigid, life-like, marble shape, with the whole form composed into the expression of a single state or act.
— GEORGE MacDONALD (1824–1905)[1]

The Souk and the Quelle

There are pictures which emerge vividly from time to time at the surface of consciousness, and yet we cannot remember how and when they came to us. Such is for me the double image of the Souk of Marrakesh, the famous market of that African city, at the northwestern border of Sahara, and of the Quelle department store, a four-story building in Fürth, near Nuremberg, in Germany.

As to the market of Marrakesh — its image was put in my mind by somebody somewhere in the past. But I know other markets of the same kind, and have seen a photograph, taken in the years before World War II, of the great square of Marrakesh, with a long low porch and a few other buildings at its center, where the Souk is located. Thus, the picture I have in mind should not be far from reality. I see an incredibly dense crowd of men dressed in long robes loudly exchanging greetings and news, discussing prices, carrying handicrafts and food with no evident purpose or destination. Stray dogs wander everywhere, mixing with the goats and donkeys following their masters; occasionally a rat flashes from one hiding place to another. Despite the blazing sun and the contrast of the colors of the buildings and the ground with the black shadows of people and animals, the market conveys a feeling of confusion and unhealthiness. The noise reaches everywhere, and the foul smell of animals, rotting vegetables, sweating men, burning coal, and fried food enwraps everything. If you find the courage to dive into the crowd, you will be called immediately by a fat merchant sitting behind a small stall or on a carpet full of the most incredible mixture of goods, from brilliantine for making your hair a sticky lustrous mass with a cheap perfume smell to little radios of dubious quality. If you agree to play the game, then you start a general conversation about the goods on display, you cautiously

1. G. MacDonald, *Phantastes* (1858; reprint, Grand Rapids, Michigan: W. B. Eerdmans, 1981), 112.

come to the price of what you might buy, you offer one tenth of what the merchant proposes, and finally, after a slowly converging procedure, you pay and leave, convinced that you have been cheated — which is probably false.

The Quelle store I know very well, and you certainly know it or similar ones. It is a clean place, resplendent with polished glass and metal. All the goods are neatly arranged in their cases, the sales women are gracefully made up, and the customers are quiet and well-mannered, exchanging low-voiced greetings only if by chance they meet a friend, and immediately making room for you if you have to pass. On the escalators, in obedience to the rules, people line up on the right, to allow those who are in a hurry to pass on the left. No animals are present — even the customers' dogs must be left outside. A faint pleasant perfume and relaxing music fill the air. Signs indicate where each type of goods is to be found, and the prices are clearly written, including possible discounts, so that even with the cashier the exchange of words is limited to *bitte*, the amount to be paid, and *danke*.

Why am I dwelling on these descriptions? Certainly not to prove that our consumers' civilization is better than any other. We are all human beings; maybe we are fortunate in having received from the past certain values and knowledge that have made our material life easier and healthier, but apart from that, our response to certain ways of selling and buying is merely a matter of habit. The question we should extract from the two pictures is this: Are we right in our feeling that the Souk of Marrakesh is a place of confusion and inefficiency, and that the Quelle store is just the opposite? Or, with reference to the Great Dance: Is the pattern of the Dance present in the chaos of that African market place, and if so, how? Those who are critical of the present stage of our civilization might also ask: Is the Dance at work in the polished machine that is the Quelle store?

The answers to the two subquestions into which the main question has been split are both affirmative: order, organization, and coherence in space and time reign in the Souk of Marrakesh as in the Quelle store of Fürth. If we really wish to convince ourselves that it is so, however, a deeper immersion into the world of complexity than we have experienced so far is necessary. Indeed, our journey must start by exploring that sea where the notions to which we have already given names — system, complexity, information, emergence of information, order, organization, coherence — swim like the colorful fishes of a tropical sea-bottom. Of course, what we are going to consider is basic to any reflection bearing on systems made of many parts; the market examples simply give a vivid picture of the complexity of the systems of living and nonliving beings that make up the Great Dance.

Information

After food and clothes, the most widely consumed commodity in human societies is information, which is conveyed by words, signs, symbols, and pictures. Its name evokes marketplaces, books, newspapers, radios, and television. Yet, only recently has information been recovered as a scientific notion of the same import as energy and matter. With the recognition of its central role in scientific thought, a profound change has taken place in science.

To those who are not familiar with the history of philosophy, it comes as a surprise to learn that the highly sophisticated scientific concept of information is an ancient one, only dismissed four centuries ago by the rise of modern science. Under the name of "form" it had been a central notion in science from the time of Aristotle (384–322 B.C.), the teacher of Alexander the Great of Macedonia, almost twenty centuries before the foundation of modern science in the time of Galileo (1564–1642). The notion of form was abandoned, as far as I can tell, because, when Galileo appeared on the stage, it was being used in all sorts of quibbles intended to explain things from first principles, without considering facts. There is a story of a scientist of the Aristotelian school who, during the terrible pestilence that raged in Milan about 1630, succeeded in proving that the plague could not exist, of course before succumbing to it.[2]

Nor was the notion of information needed again for centuries because new discoveries concerning the rules that govern the behavior of pieces of matter, regardless of their internal shape and structure, kept developing and seemed sufficient to explain everything. To most scientists, the unquestionable success of the underlying mechanistic point of view meant that it needed no improvement as a way to scientific truth. In the nineteenth century, James Clerk Maxwell (1831–1879), the discoverer of electromagnetic waves, to make his discovery acceptable had to show that a mechanical model essentially consisting in a system of gears would act in the same way as the electromagnetic field. Among those scientists who believed that anything but a mechanical explanation would, in fact, be mystical there was none less than the great physicist Lord Kelvin of Largs, to whom we owe, for one thing, the definitive establishment of the concept of energy in mechanics and thermodynamics.[3]

There is perhaps also another reason for the long eclipse of information as a key concept of scientific thought. Since information is just what makes a particular thing different from everything else, it is a property of all that exists; therefore, unless science is forced to acknowledge its exis-

---

2. A. Manzoni, *I promessi sposi* (Milan: Ferrario, 1840); English translation: *The Betrothed*, by A. Colquhoun [London: Dent, Everyman's Library, 1950]).

3. T. F. Torrance, *Transformation and Convergence in the Frame of Knowledge* (Belfast: Christian Journals Ltd., 1984).

tence because of special problems (e.g., genetics), science does not need it. Thus, it is perfectly understandable that the scientists who came after Galileo should have ignored until recently the status of information as a fundamental concept distinct from matter and energy. They had begun rebuilding science with new methods and new procedures starting with the study of the motions of the planets; they had to tread a whole new path from celestial mechanics to biology before they could rediscover, in the last few decades, the vast outlook of Aristotle, who, as a biologist, had started directly from the consideration of living beings and tried to apply the resulting concepts to the whole of reality.

The point so belatedly acknowledged is that matter is something absolutely unqualified until it is shaped. It is like clay. It can take any shape; indeed, one cannot experience its existence except as an object that has a shape, even though when one says "clay exists" one prescinds from shapes. The same is true of matter, but in a far more radical way. We speak of matter as having an independent reality, but in fact, matter is just the *principle* by which things become sensible; what we really see, touch, taste, hear, and smell are lumps of matter characterized by the material of which they are made, the shape they possess, the operations they perform, and so on. What brings matter over from being just the capacity to become anything to becoming "this particular thing" was called by Aristotle "form" and is now called "information."

It should be clear at this point that information in the scientific sense is not the same as communication; it is, so to say, the end result of communication. Take again an example from pottery. The potter has an idea. He or she takes a lump of clay and shapes it according to that idea, making, perhaps, a beautiful amphora. The potter has thus communicated a message to the lump of clay and the lump of clay now contains the information received. Similarly, an engineer prepares the blueprints of a new machine; the mechanics make it from the appropriate materials; the result is an object which operates in a certain way as a whole. Not only does the machine contain the information that distinguishes pieces of different metals from formless, unqualified matter, but the information that was contained in the blueprints has been communicated to those pieces of partly informed matter by the mechanics who have built the machine.

These ideas also apply to energy, simply because energy is either a property of a material object or a special manifestation of matter, as stated by Einstein's equation $E = mc^2$. In practice, we may think of the elementary particles making up the physical world as infinitesimal lumps of matter or energy endowed with information. These objects may form physical systems: electrons form atoms, stars form clusters, and so on. Each system is a new object, which contains the same matter, a different energy (because of the interaction between its parts), and, most important, more information.

The example of the potter shows that information can be understood as the imprinting of a message on matter, as the embodiment of that message; it is what gives a thing its individuality. Let us say this again. The craftsman who makes a vase gives a piece of clay a shape, a form: that action amounts to the transfer of "information," for it is equivalent to writing a message, to transmitting to matter an idea in the potter's mind. The information thus given to the vase remains in it, possibly for thousands of years; therefore, it must be seen as that resident property of the vase that makes it a vase and not something else: it is the what-it-is of the vase. This was the main point of Aristotle's study of this topic more than two thousand years ago;[4] it was also the central notion in a famous 1973 paper by the Nobel laureate Manfred Eigen, who proposed a scheme for the development of life from inorganic matter under the title: *"Wie entsteht Information?"* — how does information come about?[5] Eigen's question can be summarized as follows. We know that the information characterizing a living being is extremely rich and complicated. Now, ordinarily, this information is transmitted from parents to offspring; but, before the appearance of life, it was nowhere to be found: how could it appear? If it emerged spontaneously from nonliving matter, how could that happen against incredibly heavy odds?[6]

It is perhaps positive that the ancient notion of form should have been recovered by science under the name of information (sometimes improperly called "structure"), rather than simply handed down by tradition, for we now see it against the much richer background of modern scientific knowledge. Before a complete merging of ancient "form" and modern "information," however, there is still some way to go. For one thing, too hasty an identification of the two might be misleading. A case in point is when the "quality" of information, that is, its semantic value, is confused with the "information content," introduced by Claude E. Shannon at the dawn of information theory (around 1945) as a measure of the fidelity to the source message of a text received through a communication line.[7] Let C_i denote the information lost in the message received with respect to the message sent; then it can be evaluated through the formula $C_i = -\Sigma_n p_n \log p_n$, where the summation runs over the probabilities $p_1, p_2, \ldots p_N$ (defined as relative frequencies) of the various symbol sequences compatible with the form in which the message under consideration has been received. Let us examine all this in more detail.

Consider the incomplete message "pr.y f.r me." It may correspond to

4. Aristotle, *Metaphysics*, edited and translated by J. Warrington (London: Dent, 1956).

5. M. Eigen, "Wie entsteht Information?" *Berichte der Bunsengesellschaft* 80 (1976): 1059ff.

6. We shall dwell on Eigen's solution and its significance in chapter six.

7. C. E. Shannon and W. Weaver, *The Mathematical Theory of Complexity* (Chicago: University of Illinois Press, 1949).

27 · 27 different complete messages, if the dots are assumed to be low-case letters of the English alphabet. If the message cannot contain but English words, then the possible complete messages compatible with the sequence received are just eight: "pray for me," "prey for me," "pray fur me," "prey fur me," "pray far me," "prey far me," "pray fir me," "prey fir me." Now, the probabilities appearing in Shannon's expression are data derived from available evidence, e.g., from repeated transmission of the same message. We shall say that a letter has a probability of 75 percent if it has appeared at the location of the first dot in three transmissions out of four. Let us now suppose that in a certain case the probability (thus calculated) that the first unknown letter is an "a" is precisely 75 percent, and the probabilities that the second letter is an "o," an "i," an "a," and a "u" are 25 percent, 35 percent, 22 percent, 18 percent, respectively; then the probabilities of the eight messages as expressed in percentages are 18.75, 6.25, 13.50, 4.50, 16.50, 5.50, 26.25, 8.75. Applying the above formula to the message, we obtain for the pertinent information loss $C_i = 1.9177$. This quantity would be zero if all the letters were known; if only the first letter were unknown, with the probabilities given above, it would be 0.5623.

What do these results mean? To get an answer, let us assign an absolute information content to a received message by including the length of the message in the computation. Consider, in the case of our example, all the triplets of words one can make out of a dictionary of 45,000 words. Their number is $N = 15186.4$ billion. The absolute information content of a specific three-word message, if entirely unambiguous, may then be taken as the natural logarithm of that number, i.e., $C_0 = 30.3514$. Therefore, the absolute information content of the message received in the above example is $C_0 - C_i$, namely 28.4337 if two letters are uncertain, and 29.7891 if just one letter is uncertain.

After this example, it is perhaps easier to see that the "semantic" content of the message — that is to say, what the information *means* to a human being — has little to do with the number measuring the information content, unless a reinterpretation of the whole theory is undertaken.[8] Such a reinterpretation is tempting, of course. One might suggest, for example, that a person is much more likely to have sent a message such as "pray for me" than "prey for me" or "pray fir me" because only the first one makes sense; so, why not include meaningfulness in the evaluation of probabilities? This sounds reasonable, but it is not. First, one would be assuming that the sender is a religious person and we know that in the so-called civilized countries people are much more likely to worship sex and money than a God to whom a prayer can be addressed. Second,

8. R. Carnap and Y. BarHillel, *An Outline of a Theory of Semantic Information* (Boston: MIT Research Laboratory of Electronics, Technical Report 247, 1952).

the message might be a coded one. Coding, in fact, is very frequent in certain activities. For example, "prey" might stand for "prices," "fir" for "down," "me" for "buy," in which case the message could be from a stockbroker to his agent. One can find other reasons why yet another form of the complete message is more probable. In sum, since neither the sender nor the recipient, nor the circumstances which have prompted the sending of the message are known, probabilities associated with meaning cannot be estimated.

Even less is the information content related to beauty; Shannon's quantity is by no means intended to distinguish between a line of Shakespeare's *Hamlet* and a nonsense line made with the same number of words or letters. In other words, the standard information content of a message is a notion constructed to provide an objective measure of the degree of certainty about the correspondence between the signals transmitted and received, and is invaluable, but only in that role.

The same is true of information seen as the "essence" of an object or being in its original sense, i.e., that resident set of properties which makes it what it is and nothing else. Called τὸ τί ἦν, *to ti en* ("the what-it-is"), by Aristotle, and *quiddity* in the Middle Ages, it can be associated with information by treating it as the message needed to describe all that identifies that object or being. In this case the message is certainly unambiguous, so that its information content is just C_0. But it should be evident, for example, that an ancient Greek vase and the pottery on sale in certain Spanish sea resorts may require descriptions of the same length, and thus have the same information content, despite the difference in quality and the fact that the former embodies an idea of the artist who made it, while the latter is a product of what our society calls "the abolition of taboos."

We shall have more to say about these questions in the chapter on communication and symbols. Let us now come to a notion closely related to information and in general to that richer form of order which science is recognizing in the universe after the collapse of geocentrism and mechanism.

Complexity

We often speak, inside and outside science, of complex objects. We say that a space probe is a very complex machine, the solution of certain equations is a complex procedure, biology is a very complex science, and so on. We think we understand very well the word "complex," but if asked to say in words what it means we shall find it not so easy. Perhaps, it only means "difficult and complicated," or it can mean "consisting of many interdependent parts." Neither definition is really satisfactory. One could hope that science can provide a satisfactory definition. Unfortunately, that is not the case, for complexity is not something like energy, for which a precise "operational" definition can be given. In fact, one of the pioneers in this field, the French sociologist Edgar Morin, wrote:

La complexité, pour moi, c'est le défi, ce n'est pas la réponse.

Complexity, for me, is the challenge, not the answer.[9]

Nevertheless, science wants clear-cut concepts, and several proposals for a rigorous definition of complexity have been made. Among them, the most reasonable one is probably provided by information theory. A whole spectrum of systems of different complexity can be formed — at least in principle — with given numbers and sorts of building blocks (elementary particles, atoms, molecules, cells, etc.), ranging from systems with parts that are practically independent (interstellar gas, a piece of matter in the plasma state, the cells in a culture where they are very far from each other, etc.) to systems behaving as wholes even under adverse conditions (homeostatic control systems, living beings). In this spectrum, a system will be called complex if at least a measure of interdependence of the parts is indispensable for the system to be what it is, for it brings about properties of the whole that are not sums of the properties of its same parts.

Chemistry provides an example simple enough to serve as a reference. The properties of a molecule are determined not only by the nature of the atoms forming it, but by its structure (which chemists represent with a formula). There are many instances of substances whose molecules contain the same species and numbers of atoms and yet have completely different properties, because their atoms are arranged in different structures. For example, the molecules of methyl ether, a light anesthetic gas, are formed by two carbon atoms, one oxygen atom, and six hydrogen atoms just as are those of ethyl alcohol, the well-known liquid that is a friend to man provided he does not drink too much of it. Six carbon atoms and six hydrogen atoms can form, according to the rules of chemistry, 217 more or less stable molecules, and hence 217 different substances, including the colorless, pungent, inflammable liquid called benzene.

In general, different systems can be formed with the same parts, and they will have different degrees of "complexity." It is possible to devise a quantitative measure of these degrees. Imagine that the parts of the system are completely independent, then divide them into groups of identical parts, and consider that the shortest message (a "string" written in a standard language, say as a binary number). This message is a complete description of the basic set of parts, which has no complexity but

---

9. E. Morin, *Introduction à la pensée complexe* (Paris: ESF, 1990), 134.

that, if any, of the individual parts; it will be satisfactory if it contains a complete description of one part for each group and the number of parts in that group. Suppose the corresponding string has length l_0. Then consider the length l of the string representing (in the same language) the shortest complete description of the actual system. Then the ratio l/l_0 measures the complexity of the system with respect to a simple cluster of its parts (i.e., its *relative* degree of complexity), because the larger the number of properties that do not correspond to properties of the parts, the larger that ratio.

This definition is not beyond criticism, and could be improved. However, it is sufficient for a discussion of the nature of complexity. For one thing, it allows us to realize that the atoms of a molecule do not contain, with respect to their electrons and nuclei, as much additional information as a molecule: this is why a molecule is a system more complex than an atom. The same consideration applies to more familiar objects: we may not be capable of describing completely an entity such as a dog, but there seems to be little doubt — especially after the advent of psychobiology — that, in terms of the difference between what it is as such and the collection of its organs and tissues, a dog is less complex than a human being. A whole ecosystem — think of Gaia, whom we discussed in the preceding chapter — will be more complex than a human being if its unity is such that all the activities of each living being, including human beings, are essential to that unity; but if you consider such activities as art and science outside the scope and control of ecological equilibrium, then the question is open.

A curious but instructive question arises: if an immaterial entity exists, should it be considered complex or simple? The answer is that it is simple, indeed elementary, if what we call "the parts" in our informational definition are thought of as material objects or as objects separated in space; for being immaterial, that entity is not extended in space. In fact, the indivisibility resulting from absence of extension in space may be the reason why the Belgian poet Maurice Maeterlinck (1862–1949) wondered if a distinction between matter and spirit actually applied in the case of particles such as the electron.[10] Yet, from the informational point of view, the very absence of parts means that the complexity of such an immaterial being is necessarily either undefinable or infinite (l_0 is zero). Pursuing to the limit our exercise about complexity, let us now ask: Since this would hold for any immaterial being, what about God? The supreme spiritual Being, one and indivisible by nature, could be thought of as equivalent to an infinite number of immaterial parts, from which an infinite number

10. M. Maeterlinck, *Devant Dieu* (1937), quoted in R. Bodart, *Maurice Maeterlinck* (Paris: Seghers, 1962), 158–160.

of new properties arise. Thus, God is infinite times infinitely complex in the informational sense, though elementary!

This apparent paradox of our theology fiction has a serious side: it proves that it is contradictory for us to pretend to apply our distinctions, except by analogy, to a being whose reality cannot but be above anything we can grasp with our minds. Of course, we citizens of Western civilization at the beginning of the twenty-first century are not always willing to accept the notion that our world of time, space, and matter should not be all there is to know; indeed, we often have trouble accepting the notion that there should be a whole world which we cannot understand precisely because it cannot be assigned a spatiotemporal, scientific reference. We shall have more to say about this in chapter nine, in connection with parapsychology, magic, and other archetypal, nonrational approaches to reality.

Unity

How a unitary behavior can arise (or, as people nowadays would say, "emerge") in a collection of "elementary" objects is the central problem posed by the existence of complexity. The biological bias and the ignorance of chemistry of Aristotelian science had led it to consider the parts of a truly unitary system (say, an organism in activity) as virtual; modern science, founded on mechanics, tends to ignore the possibility that the whole may contain more information than its parts. With the rise of contemporary biology and the end of vitalism the need to reconcile these two extremes has become urgent. The coexistence of a unitary system and of the distinct objects susceptible of a separate study that are its parts is a new field of inquiry.

The approach to sensible reality that reigned almost unquestioned until recently, was, as mentioned in chapter one, physicalistic reductionism, which sees the world as a collection of simple entities, each to be treated first as an isolated system and then as capable of forming many-particle systems by the introduction of appropriate interactions with other systems. The habit of mind engendered by this approach has led many scientists to think that a system is completely known once the properties of its parts are known. We have already shown that it is not so, partly because some information is not in the parts (as in the above example of isomers) and partly because much information is latent in the description of the parts (e.g., the rules of valency). Recently, a shift from reductionism to the complementary approach has begun, and a tendency has appeared to look at the whole universe as a single system, whose parts are not treated as nearly isolated systems, but are assumed to be defined through their "couplings," both direct and indirect, to one another. That is to say, the new reference model is no longer that of a group of individuals each on its own, but that of a group of individuals constituting a system which behaves as a whole. This new view is called by some "holism," a name traditionally given to the Scholastic view of man as an integrated unit of body and soul.

The shift from reductionism to holism can be summarized in the statement that the concept of system has changed its reference model from a collection of loosely coupled subsystems or particles to a tightly integrated whole, such as an organism. Thinking in terms of the latter has produced, for example, the description of the biosphere as a "quasi"-organism — the "Gaia" hypothesis mentioned in chapter one — and the objections raised against it.[11] By a different path, even the astrophysicists have come to think in terms of wholes, as is evidenced in cosmological theories and in critical analyses such as those underlying the anthropic principle.[12] One could even say that our philosophy of nature is going back to the Ptolemaic conception, not of course in its geocentric assumption, but in the admission that if everything is not in everything, as the alchemists would have it, at least everything is present to some extent in everything else, so that the fullest reality is the Whole to which everything belongs.

We shall have to say more about mechanism and holism in other chapters. Here let us retain this: the universe should be considered as a complex system made up of complex systems as well as simple ones, rather than a collection of loosely interacting parts. Now, as we have seen, complex systems are capable of exchanging information not only as contact interactions or long range forces, but as messages and operations on one another. The Dance is thus an image hinting at a marvelous, incredibly rich, and continuously changing pattern of relations between its elements.

The path toward this change of reference is by no means a smooth one. An interesting puzzle encountered in the application of the holistic viewpoint to wholes such as a molecule, a cell, a human body is particularly worth discussing in this connection. Science attributes the fact that these objects behave as units to the coherent cooperation of their parts, that is to say, to structure in the case of systems at equilibrium (like molecules) and to organization in the case of systems in a steady state out of equilibrium (like living beings). Each part is involved in the activity of the whole with its specific properties, which are the same as they would be in any other system providing the same environmental conditions; examples are the atoms of a molecule and organs like the heart during transplantation. This seems to imply that the whole *is* the collection of its parts. And yet,

11. J. E. Lovelock, "Hands Up."
12. J. D. Barrow and F. J. Tipler, *The Anthropic Cosmological Principle* (Oxford: Oxford University Press, 1986).

the whole has properties that are not just the sum of those of its parts; indeed, these properties can be completely new with respect to the parts. We have seen with the example of isomerism a hopefully convincing illustration of that. What shall we now conclude if, on closer inspection, we recognize by the same example that there is nothing in the system but its parts with their *in situ* properties, and that the system therefore *must be* the collection of its parts, albeit in a particular configuration?

This is the sort of dilemma which, as scientists, we cannot leave alone. One might object that we are not in Hamlet's situation; why should we care about being or not being, if the dilemma does not impair our ability to predict things and make technological advances? The fact is that, if a solution to the dilemma is not found, the scientists will be pushed back into reductionism, and will continue to look at the parts as if by just knowing them and their laws of interaction they would be able to understand the reasons why the wholes have new and different overall properties and what those properties will be. This seems not to be the case, as biology shows most strikingly: and without understanding there is no designing new experiments or new technical procedures, so that what is branded as progress in science reduces to aimless accumulation of data and conjectures. Fortunately, the notion of information, when completed with the other notion of complexity level, points to a way out of our Shakespearean doubt about being and not being; that is to say, about which description of an object is most faithful to its true nature. We shall make a preliminary survey of this question here, pending a more extensive discussion in the next chapter, which is devoted to the nature of the objects of which the universe is made.

Emerging Information

Suppose somebody asked a scientist to tell what a certain object — a molecule, a recorder, a cell, a cyclamen, a starfish — is. As we already know, unless the asker is prepared to accept useless verbiage (what scientists call "redundancies"), what is required is the shortest complete list of those properties which identify that object unambiguously. That is to say, the what-it-is of that object is a message equivalent to its blueprints, and must contain all the information that is indispensable for identifying that object. According to what we have seen, the string representing that message must have a length l greater than the length l_o of the string describing a juxtaposition of its parts such that no interaction between them is possible. We can also say that, if a system behaving as a whole has properties which its parts cannot have, the whole has a greater information content than the sum of its parts, i.e., new "information" has emerged upon its formation. Of course, this does not imply that knowledge of the parts of a system is irrelevant. It is obviously important to know that a molecule of ethanol is made of two carbon atoms, one oxygen atom, and six hydrogen atoms, or that a man has a brain, a heart, a liver, and so on. Therefore, emergent properties do not replace the information concerning the parts, but enrich it. In fact, a system which is a collection of parts but contains that information depends on how its parts are put together, necessarily behaves as a unit at least in certain respects.

Here comes a difficult point, which is best explained through the example of a molecule, for it is a controversial aspect of research aimed at applying quantum mechanics to chemistry. Physics claims that its theory of quantum mechanics can provide equations (the Schrödinger equation, in most cases) that allow the computation of everything one may wish to know about a given molecule if the atoms forming the molecule are known. This is taken by the reductionists to mean that information about atoms is sufficient to explain everything about molecules. Consequently, they believe that chemistry is but a chapter of physics.[13] Unfortunately, as the eminent mathematician René Thom put it in the title of a book, to predict is not to explain.[14] In the case of molecules, this is borne out by the fact that one cannot extract from the Schrödinger equation certain pieces of information, such as the fact that carbon always forms four bonds, and not more than four bonds, unless one knows what one is looking for.[15] That is to say, to derive from quantum mechanics the quadrivalency of carbon, one must know already what a chemical bond is, solve the Schrödinger equation for the number of bonds of carbon in a lot of molecules, and conclude that the answer is always four.[16] Maybe some day a genius will find a logical proof of this rule. However that may be, clearly the information that can be obtained from quantum mechanics is partly "latent" (i.e., present but hidden) in the equation exactly as it is latent in nature, from which the chemists of the nineteenth century extracted it. One could say that the information about a molecule is there partly as a mere potentiality, like the wealth you could uncover if you knew that a treasure had been buried on your property.

In short, when a physicist claims that if the atoms of a molecule are known all the possible information on the molecule has been given, he is almost right. But a large part of that information is latent, like the fish living in the depths of the sea. It is only when you look at the molecule itself and compare it with other molecules of its kind that you see in actuality the potential information hidden in the information about the

13. M. Bunge, "Is Chemistry a Branch of Physics?" *Zeitschrift für Allgemeine Wissenschaftslehre* 13 (1982): 209–223.

14. R. Thom, *Prédire n'est pas expliquer* (Paris: Champs-Flammarion, 1993).

15. G. Del Re, "Binding: A Unifying Notion or a Pseudoconcept?" *International Journal of Quantum Chemistry* 19 (1981): 1057.

16. B. Nelander and G. Del Re, "Chemical Bonds and Ab-Initio Molecular Calculations," *Journal of Chemical Physics* 52 (1970): 5225.

atoms. So, the phrase "emergence of information" is really well chosen to describe the actualization of new information accompanying the passage from atoms to molecules, from simpler constituents of matter to less simple ones. In the process, all sorts of things that were there, but whose existence had not yet been guessed, have emerged, like fish from the depths of the sea.

That is not the end of the story. A physicist claiming that to know a molecule all one has to know is its atoms is *almost* right, but not quite, because in point of fact knowledge of the atoms does not specify uniquely a molecule. As already mentioned, different *isomers* may be formed by the same atoms; this means that there can be a measure of ambiguity in the information latent in the parts, and therefore that information can be insufficient for a choice among a number of possibilities (say, the various isomers corresponding to a given group of atoms). The example of isomers provides perhaps the easiest argument in support of the claim that the whole is more than its parts. The same consideration applies to genetics: as is well known, part of what an organism is is determined by environmental effects, acting during the expression of the program contained in the genome.

At this point it should be clear that Hamlet's dilemma for complex objects must be resolved in the most Solomonic way. We asked: "which is real, the parts or the whole?" The sciences of complexity answer: "both." We may view a molecule as merely a collection of atoms, with the proviso that most of its information is latent; to actually see the reality of the molecule *as a molecule* we must look at it directly. We may then lose sight of the fact that it is an ensemble of atoms. This apparent contradiction means precisely that the molecule is both itself and a collection of atoms. We can say that the molecule belongs at the same time to at least three distinct levels of complexity: the level of molecules, the level of atoms, and the level of elementary particles. With the exception of elementary particles, each object in the universe can be described as belonging to several levels of complexity. Moreover, the complexity levels can also be treated as *levels of reality*. We shall devote the next chapter to the relation between complexity levels and reality levels because it provides an approach to the multilayer structure of the reality.

Order

The novelties appearing in a molecule with respect to its constituent parts are due to the fact that a molecule has a *structure*, i.e., a specific arrangement of its atoms where each atom performs very small oscillations about "equilibrium" points lying at fixed distances from those of certain other atoms (its "nearest neighbors"), and the lines connecting the equilibrium point of that atom to those of its nearest neighbors form angles that are practically invariable. Structure is thus a special, persisting kind of order which, precisely because it is order, cannot be reduced to the properties of the individual objects that form the set exhibiting it. This example is perhaps sufficient to show why order is so important a concept in philosophical reflections on the way in which science grasps the general structure of the universe.

What is the definition of order? Just try to express in words what you mean in general when you speak of "order" and you will be in trouble. Every time you think you have finally got a definition, your mind (or a friend) will point to an example which does not fit in your definition. The best way out may be to follow the ancient procedure of beginning with everyday examples. Think of a library, an archive, a group of children in school. From these examples you see that in current language order is simply an arrangement of different objects, each of which is assigned a place or number uniquely associated with one of its distinctive properties.

Take the example of a library. A librarian might order books in descending rows, from left to right, according to their weights; while this is not a very clever thing to do it certainly leaves little doubt as to where each book goes. The improbable case of two or more books having exactly the same weight might be handled by placing them one after the other according to the third letters of their authors' names. If those letters also turned out to be identical, the librarian could use the fourth letters of the titles, the colors of the covers, and so on. The kind of order realized in this way would certainly give cause for firing the librarian. Yet, it must be admitted that the *criteria* adopted, however fanciful and impractical they may be, would do the job of assigning to each book one and only one specific place in your library. The librarian has realized order, albeit a meaningless and mysterious one.

Now consider a class of children in school. The children might be ordered according to their family and first names, but that sequence is not enough. They might, as is their wont, start moving around, which would lead to disorder, not order. Each child, therefore, should be assigned a *corresponding* place or number, as the teacher will undoubtedly do.

In short, you may say that order is established when there is a precise correspondence between two sets, e.g., places and schoolboys, and one set (places, in our case) has a known inalterable arrangement: then you know which element of the other set is which. Starting from this conclusion, mathematicians might try to prove that knowing which is which is equivalent to numbering, so that one can always reduce order to numbering — maybe using the continuum of real numbers — but that is another story. As to our project of exploring different kinds of order, there is much more to be said, for order is not just what appears from the above examples.

What if, instead of objects that can be distinguished from each other, we were considering identical objects, say, identical atoms or molecules? Then we should not be able to tell which is which, but we could say that there is order if the particles are so arranged that every one of them is surrounded by the same number of particles at the same distances in the same directions; for example, if each particle lies at the center of a cube (of the same size) whose corners are occupied by eight other particles. This kind of order is found in ideal crystals: their atoms or molecules repeat the same pattern in each direction of space, although different patterns may be associated with different directions. In a *real* crystal order is incomplete for there are "defects": limiting surfaces, atoms or molecules different from the majority ones, and so on. But that concerns the question whether or not order can be perfect, which does not matter here; what matters is that ideal crystals provide an example of "order" where nothing changes if you take two particles and interchange them.

This feature tells us that we are now calling order something that is completely different from what we had before: with books, a different *ordered state* (as a scientist would say) is obtained if two books are interchanged, in an ideal crystal interchange of identical atoms yields the same state. This means that a perfect crystal does not possess a maximum of order in the sense we have adopted so far for this term; indeed, it has a very high measure of "disorder," for there is an incredible number of ways in which its constituent particles can be interchanged so that no one would be able to tell the difference. The confusion arises because we are wont to use the word "order" to indicate the existence of a regular pattern, which we certainly have in the case of a perfect crystal. There is no harm in using the term "order" in either sense, provided one does not conclude that a living organism or the souk of Marrakesh are disordered simply because they do not possess any regular pattern.

Even crystals are not the end of the story. Two of the arrangements we have considered show no special tendency to change or decay, at least within human observation times. Books will not move spontaneously out of their places, nor will the atoms of a crystal at absolute zero leave their places. As for children, we were thinking of their assigned seats in the classroom. Imagine instead that we had considered the same children lining up according to their heights. Imagine, too, that the teacher turns to speak to somebody; suddenly, what was a nice slightly-descending line of heads is at best a broken line, going up and down, left and right at random. This hints at the existence of cases where order is perhaps less strict, but far more interesting, because it is, as it were, alive; it can appear, change, and vanish. To grasp why we speak of order in these cases, let us work the other way around, and try to decide first when there is complete *disorder*.

How can you have complete disorder? Think of a sealed vessel full of the molecules of a gas at a fixed temperature. That chapter of science which Sir James Jeans called "the dynamical theory of gases"[17] states that the gas molecules zigzag at random across the vessel, changing their directions every time one of them collides with another. Their motions are completely random. Precisely because of their randomness, there are, on the average, equal numbers of molecules moving in any given direction at any point in the vessel and during any interval of time. Their velocities are distributed about a mean value, which depends only on the temperature. The average number of molecules whose velocities are lower or higher than the mean by a given amount is also determined by the temperature of the gas. Thus, if we have complete disorder, i.e., a real random distribution of particles, we have a situation where the average properties of the ensemble are the same regardless of the place and time we consider. By contrast, we may call ordered a situation wherein two parts of the vessel are at different temperatures, so that each part can be described as a random distribution of molecules, where the velocities of the molecules of, say, part A are distributed about an average greater than those of part B. In this case further "randomization" can take place. The thermodynamicists say that "entropy" increases, entropy being a physical quantity which, at microscopic level, is essentially a measure of disorder.

And here we are, at last, with the famous story of the decrease of order in the universe. The second principle of thermodynamics, which may be called the principle of universal decay, states that any highly ordered situation, if left alone, will act much like the children standing in a row of decreasing height; it will decay — physicists would say that it will relax — more or less rapidly, until complete disorder is reached. In other words, the overall *entropy* of a closed system tends to increase on the average as transformations take place in that system. The running down of the universe is just this: the molecules of gases will mix so that their average speeds and directions of motions will be the same everywhere, liquids will freeze into crystals which, in spite of their regularity, are in fact highly disordered, as we discovered a few paragraphs ago. Universal decay is not exactly the same thing as the second principle of thermodynamics, because it remains to be seen if the latter applies to the universe as a whole; but there seems to be no doubt that in every spontaneous transformation the overall balance between order increase and order decrease is in favor of the latter.

Let us now return to order. We have seen an example of dynamical, nonpermanent order in the gas contained in a vessel at a given temperature. But the most impressive example of such order is always with us: the human body. It is ordered not because it is beautifully symmetric (inside, we are just a mess), but because the various parts can be labeled,

17. J. H. Jeans, *The Dynamical Theory of Gases* (4th ed., 1926; reprint, New York: Dover, 1954).

and they always stay in their places — or, to put it better, they always stay in the same relation to one another. You would not expect that, on examining the inner disposition of your body, a physician would find on different occasions different situations, the heart directly connected to the lungs one time and to the liver another time, the intestine at the end of the digestive tract one time and between the esophagus and the stomach another time, and so on.

The order inside a living being is not so much an order of place as one of connections, required because each organ is assigned a unique role in the coordinated and integrated activity that keeps that living being alive, and, indeed, gives it its specific and unique identity. It is a very special kind of order, for it depends on the very functioning of each organ, and does all it can to resist agents trying to destroy it — time, diseases, drugs, weapons — although it will eventually yield to them. Moreover, our organs cannot rest even a few seconds, lest their ordered cooperation break down.

All this amounts to saying that, technically speaking, we human beings are steady-state systems out of equilibrium, incredibly more complicated but basically similar to those short-lived whirlpools one can see in certain streams. Some disturbance in the flow gives birth to them, they grow while moving around, collect insects and dead leaves, and eventually die off; their brief existence is marked only by small heaps of leaves and wood somewhere on the bottom and, if you could see it, by the detachment and displacement of tiny bits of rock or clay. Living beings differ quantitatively and qualitatively from whirlpools, first, because they do not persist by a sort of inertia, but rather because they continuously exchange energy and matter with the outer world; and, second, because they interact much more intensely with their environment. Human beings, in addition, can choose — albeit within limits — how to act on their environment, and, alas! even what to do with themselves.

In conclusion, what we have called order in a living being is so much more complicated than order in a library that it deserves another name. It may be called "organization."

Organization and Life

Organization is the concept around which all studies about the nature of life revolve. It is the general property of what we have called systems in the strong sense, whose behavior (or activity) essentially consists in processing input signals to yield output signals, in virtue of an internal structure capable of a dynamical activity. We have seen that organization is close to order. Some scientists even claim that organization is merely a preferential configuration of particles or other elementary components of a system, e.g., neurons, and in fact the word "structure" is often used as a synonym for it. A more elaborate concept associates order with coherence — the harmonious concord of parts which characterizes the Great Dance — but that is still far from corresponding to organization in living beings. In their case — and to a lesser extent in artificial control systems — the two notions of structure (even if coherent) and of organization are distinct and play different roles in their scientific explanation.

As we have done for order, let us start with an example taken from ordinary life.[18] Consider an airline, which we will call XX-AIR. It begins operating with one plane and two pilots, accepting passengers as they come at a given airport. So far, it has neither structure nor organization, because one plane with its crew is not an airline system. But gradually XX-AIR becomes one of the leading airlines in the world, with a hundred planes and crews including stewards, ground personnel, and employees. That makes something we might call a structure, although it is not something rigid. But then, XX-AIR establishes regular flights between given points. Here organization comes into play. The aim of the company is to provide as good and reliable a service as is possible. The quality of the service, however, is not ensured just by timetables and personnel; the staff has to face all sorts of unexpected difficulties. One day, at 8:10 in the morning, the telephone operator at the airline offices of airport Y receives a call informing that the pilot of flight 71, due to leave from that airport at 9:30, has a sudden attack of flu. She immediately calls the traffic director, who makes a call to an incoming plane to find out if its pilot can replace the sick one. The answer is negative, but further inquiries yield the good news that the pilot of flight 55, which is due to land in five minutes at airport Z, twenty minutes of flight away, could do the job. The traffic director then calls headquarters to find out if a service plane can be sent to Z to get the pilot to Y. Headquarters calls a third airport where a plane is available for hire and arranges the trip. Meanwhile, the passengers are informed that flight 71 will have a ten minute delay. The pilot arrives at 09:10 and at 09:40 flight 71 is off to its destination.

Real situations, of course, are often more difficult than the one I have described, if nothing else because costs are a serious limitation. But for our purposes the above example should be sufficient to illustrate the essential point that organization is a dynamical cooperation of parts aimed at performing a given task. If the people involved had not known what to do in an exceptional situation, if there had not been the right competencies and powers of decision at the right places, the existence of a structure

---

18. The following two or three paragraphs are a modified version of a text first printed in the Proceedings of the 1992 Plenary Session of the Pontifical Academy of Sciences, B. Pullman, ed., *The Emergence of Complexity* (Vatican City: Pontifical Academy of Sciences, 1996).

consisting of different elements differently distributed according to a precise scheme would have been useless. But what was the essential reason why organization was required? Simply that, like a living organism, an airline is a unit composed of many elements, and is expected to perform as a unit a specific task in a variable environment. What task? We may call it ensuring self-survival, or more generally protecting its own identity — which coincides with its very unity — in the face of a changing environment, by adjusting all the time to external (and internal) fluctuations and disturbances. More precisely, the airline tries to assure its service as scheduled on its entire network, because that is the very reason for its existence.

The application of this example to living beings and sophisticated machines should be evident. Imagine a person in a dangerous situation. As soon as the danger is apparent, the brain calls the adrenal glands, located on the kidneys, to send an overdose of a hormone called adrenaline into the bloodstream. Adrenaline has a triple role: it causes an increase of the blood supply to organs important in response to an emergency, e.g., the heart, the muscles, the brain; it reduces the blood supply to the digesting organs and to the skin; and it enhances the chemical reactions needed for the production of energy. Thus, the body is brought to a fighting condition. Other chemicals (endorphins, GABA, etc.) are also released in the blood vessels, especially those of the brain, to perform a temporary modification of its functioning, e.g., to bring about the suppression of anxiety during a fight, or to improve the speed of response and reduce sensations such as pain, which would distract attention from the task of self-defense. Much is still uncertain about these processes, but what is known is sufficient to confirm the analogy with the airline example, and at the same time show that a living body is immensely more complex than any social organization.

Organization thus appears to be a necessary condition for the result-oriented behavior of a system acting as a whole in a variable context. As we have already seen, it is that kind of interdependence of the parts of a whole that makes it possible for the given system to adjust its behavior and/or its internal activity to changes in the environment (as revealed by external stimuli or input) as well as (within limits) to internal changes, so as to ensure self-preservation in the case of living beings, or the execution of a pre-established program in the case of artificial systems. In organisms and other possible systems of the same kind the required interdependence of the parts in ensured by full *integration*.

All we have seen so far is now recognized as part of the foundations of science, even if some time ago it was called "natural philosophy." This can be taken to mean that the advances of science have forced scientists to suppress the frontiers between science and general reflections on nature and man, which is precisely what natural philosophy is or should be.

The Laser and the Market

I am now ready to disclose the secret of the Souk. To place it in the right perspective, however, let me return to coherence, the most general concept, at least in the sense given to it in the preceding chapter, in the line of thought we are pursuing here.

Coherence is rigorously defined in the study of light (which in modern physics can also be seen as a collection of particles called photons). First consider "ordinary light," such as that emitted by the gas contained in neon lamps. Photons come from single atoms emitting as light the excess energy they possess because, for example, of preceding collisions with electrons. According to our present knowledge of such things, an atom emits light in the form of a monochromatic flash — that is to say, in the form of a pure sine wave beginning at a certain instant of time and ending shortly thereafter, say, 100 nanoseconds later.[19] This means that, in the vacuum or in air, where the speed of light is approximately 0.3 meters (1 foot) per nanosecond, the flash — the photon — is a "wave train" 30 meters long, which moves in a certain direction, and oscillates between a maximum and a minimum as it moves. Now consider two photons, possibly emitted by the same atom. In general, they are *incoherent* because they are emitted with slightly different frequencies,[20] and travel in different directions. Moreover, even if they happen to be identical with regard to these two characteristics, they are usually different because their max-min-max cycles are displaced with respect to one another in such a way that one of them has all its oscillation maxima before or after the other — a relation technically called a "phase difference." All this is expressed by saying that, in general, two photons, even emitted by the same atom, lack coherence in frequency, direction, and phase.

Until 1963, all specialists agreed that coherent light could only be obtained by producing many similar photons and by filtering out all those which did not possess practically the same frequency, direction, and phase. Such a filtering was possible, but even with the brightest light sources the filtered light would be extremely weak. A revolution took place in this field with the invention of the laser by Schawlow and Townes. Coherent light could be produced with such an intensity that a 1 mm beam aimed at the moon would arrive there with a diameter of 1 meter (a widening of one part in 389,000,000) and come back with an intensity sufficient to be detected by ordinary instruments. Other actual and potential applications of the laser are even more extraordinary, although by now the consideration that *quod quis crebro videt non miratur*[21] has become applicable.

19. A nanosecond (ns) is a billionth of a second.
20. The frequency is the number of complete max-min-max cycles per second.
21. What is often seen is not cause of wonder (Cicero, *De Divinatione*, 2).

In perfectly coherent light, all the photons are identical, and therefore behave in the same way. If you apply this view of coherence to the situations we have discussed in the preceding chapter, you will find that they qualify as highly incoherent, which is not surprising since those examples always involve different objects, not particles of the same nature. But we can extend the notion of coherence to a set of objects of different natures by noting that what really matters about coherent light is that if a photon does something the others do the same. We can thus say that a complex system is coherent if its components are so interrelated that each component's behavior is tuned to the behavior of the others.

Now think of the Souk of Marrakesh. The rat you saw flashing between two dark corners had a good reason to move, for it had seen some interesting food, maybe dropped by a man selling sheep-milk cheese; nor was the latter's presence just a chance, for he was there to make a little money. There is a similar network of relations in time and space for every object or being in the Souk. Chance events can occur, but they are of the kind described by Aristotle, who gave the example of a horse trader going to the market to sell his horses, and meeting a debtor of his who had gone to the same market to buy a horse. Such an event is certainly not determined by some single cause, and it can well be considered as the result of chance; but it really is but a special aspect of the general coherence reigning in the market, because the occasion for it has been provided by the market itself. Moreover, that chance encounter is interesting because the creditor and the debtor had had a business relationship in the past, and their actions beginning with the encounter are determined by it. This means that a chance event is not an element of disorder, but the beginning of a new melodic line prepared by the preceding part of the Great Symphony; and, as we have already remarked, a new melodic line cannot be out of tune with what came before and what is going on when it is born.

I can now, at last, put forward a paradox I like very much: the Souk is much more orderly and coherent than the Quelle. You may declare that you prefer the Quelle, because there you do not risk disease or theft, and you know exactly what you are buying and its price. I am inclined to think the same; but I must admit that, at least as far as I am concerned, that is because of my lazy, unheroic side, which makes me prefer situations where everything is safe and predictable. The real point is that the Quelle is a mechanical machine, where everything and everybody is preordained to be and to behave in a certain way. Things do not depend on each other; there is no "if . . . then" sequence worth mentioning, because not even a single customer's choice between buying and not buying, which is unpredictable for the Quelle, can change the functioning of the system. Only if, say, two rats decide to invade the Quelle store, creating two centers of screaming women, cleaning staff vainly pursuing the invaders, customers crowding here and there, shoplifters becoming active everywhere — is there a situation where things, events, and processes are interdependent. Then the store ceases to be an artificial mechanism to become a system where everything has its natural place and role, where inherent coherence has replaced an order imposed from outside.

One must thus admit that actually the Quelle store, for all its apparent artificial and machine-like nature, is a genuine complex system in the sense given above. This is proven by the very fact that it reacts quickly and efficiently to disturbances, and promptly resumes its role of providing the customers with the goods they seek. The difference with the Souk is that the latter is a *self-organized* system, i.e., one whose organization is just the result of the interrelated activities of its parts. In short, the secret of the paradoxical superiority of the Souk is this: it is a market because people go there to buy and sell of their own accord, not because the company management has decided that it should be one.

It would be quite a nice and useful exercise to go on trying to apply the notions discussed in this chapter to our example. But that may be left to those who hopefully will use the hints given here for further progress on the whole line. Within the scope of this book, we must be content with having gained some familiarity with certain key concepts, and having thus in mind the tools for understanding a lot of things, from economy to the ABS systems of cars. Not only do those concepts make it possible for science to describe *how* the universe is made, but they (and the reality they refer to) are the common denominators of natural sciences and the sciences of man. As we shall see, in virtue of them the latter (e.g., social sciences) are being accepted at last as parts of science with full respect of their fields of application, their specific methods, and their criteria of truth.

We want now to reflect on the nature of the beings and objects with which science populates sensible reality — we want to know *of what* the universe is made, according to today's science.

Chapter 3

The Structure of Sensible Reality

*Until recently, most scientists believed that only elementary parti-
cles are real. Yet our very sense of reality has its roots in the world
which we perceive directly, where a star is a star, a man is a man,
and so on. Today's science is inclined to admit that both represen-
tations are valid, indeed, that the whole "reality" of objects and
beings should be looked at as a set of different levels, differing by
complexity and size. What are these levels?*

About the Use of Ontology – Reality According to Science – A
Discussion on Ontology – Pascal's Two Infinities – Complexity and
"Real" Objects – The Whole and Its Parts, Again – Identity and
the Environment – The Role of Size – Toward Infinite Sizes – Paths
from Elementary Particles

In natural science we are concerned ultimately, not with convenient arrangements of observational data which can be generalized into universal explanatory form, but with movements of thought, at once theoretical and empirical, which penetrate into the intrinsic structure of the universe in such a way that there becomes disclosed to us its basic design and we find ourselves at grips with reality.... We cannot pursue natural science scientifically without engaging at the same time in meta-scientific operations.
— THOMAS F. TORRANCE[1]

About the Use of Ontology

Let us quickly review what we have seen so far. In the first chapter, we considered the metaphor of the Dance and outlined its scope, showing that it applies to objects of the most diverse kinds: electrons and molecules, meteorites and galaxies, daisies and elephants. We have adopted the view that all these objects, living and nonliving, are essentially what our intuition tells us, distinct entities which can be viewed as independent, though interacting, wholes. Some of them are indivisible by nature, like electrons traveling alone in the desolation of deep space, but most of them are composite systems: some are made of moderately interacting parts (which can be either elementary particles or composite systems themselves), while others are made of parts so strongly "coupled" to one another (e.g., the organs of our body) that they have no autonomy at all, so that the whole behaves as a single object or being. We have named "systems in the strong sense" the systems of the latter kind.

In the second chapter we have explored order, static and dynamic, which is the basic general feature which makes systems accessible to science. We have seen that order can take the form of organization. In systems in the strong sense (particularly living organisms), which are special sets of subordinate systems (their parts), organization is extremely effective, the parts being distinguished by their specific role in the dynamical cooperation that imparts to the whole complete unity, with characteristics that cannot be traced back to any single part.

It is in the course of our second chapter that we have come up with an "ontological" dilemma: is an object or being just a collection of elementary particles, as many physicists would have it, or is it what it appears to be as a whole? We have already briefly hinted that the answer

1. T. F. Torrance, *Divine and Contingent Order* (Oxford: Oxford University Press, 1981), 3.

is "both," but we should now pause a little longer on that answer. The reason for doing so is that the picture of sensible reality emerging from the most recent advances of science, particularly of cosmology and of biology, hinges on it. In terms of our guiding metaphor, we could say that we cannot really enjoy the glory of the Great Dance if our minds have no notion of who and what the dancers are. Is a human being nothing but a special association of electrons and nuclei? Is a gigantic galaxy what really matters on the scale of the universe, so that a tiny planet like the earth is important only to us men, actors passing on the stage and then disappearing? Science cannot tell directly how important something is, because it only tries to discover the nature of the physical world. But it can help us to see things in the right proportion, and to establish a foundation for a sensible assessment of that "ontological" question before possible answers are examined. Some of the social changes, not always positive, of the last few decades have resulted from ideologies claimed to conform to science. This was the case with the school reforms, which have swept the whole Western world since the end of World War II: it is difficult to suppress the feeling that those reforms have ultimately reduced the task of school education, in the name of science, to the preparation of as docile consumers and electors as possible. This is but one step in a process that originated long ago,[2] encouraged by the cheap scientism of the media. Now at last the advances of science — which hopefully will reach in due course the opinion makers — are suggesting more and more strongly that the ideas underlying school reforms are not warranted by a genuine scientific mind.

Reality According to Science

Let us pause briefly on the word "reality." The time when logicians of different species — Russell, Wittgenstein, Quine and others — dominated the scene with regard to reflections on science is now over, but in its wake there are still scientists who feel that science has nothing to say about "what there *is*"; those scientists also feel that if science accepts the idea that something exists, then it is not concerned with *what* that something is. The difficulties which the logicians hoped to overcome by a sort of logical surgery were stated very clearly by an enemy of all beliefs, Bertrand Russell, albeit within the limits of his own background and personality. Russell, a world-known logician and a Nobel laureate for literature, was very influential in the Anglo-Saxon world during his long life (1872–1970).[3] The following passage interests us here:

2. C. S. Lewis, *The Abolition of Man* (London: Collins, 1944).
3. J. Passmore, *A Hundred Years of Philosophy* (London: Penguin, 1968), ch. 9.

Let us take first the belief in common objects, such as tables and chairs and trees. We all feel quite sure about them in ordinary life, and yet our reasons for confidence are really very inadequate. Naïve common sense supposes that they are what they appear to be, but that is impossible, since they do not appear exactly alike to any two simultaneous observers; at least, it is impossible if the object is a single thing, the same for all observers. If we are going to admit that the object is not what we see, we can no longer feel the assurance that there is an object; this is the first intrusion of doubt. However, we shall speedily recover from this set-back, and say that the object is "really" what physics says it is. Now [modern theoretical] physics says that a table or chair is "really" an incredibly vast system of electrons and protons in rapid motion, with empty space in between. This is all very well. But the physicist, like the ordinary man, is dependent upon his senses for the existence of the physical world.... He thinks that the sensation you have when (as you think) you see a chair has a series of causes, physical and psychological, but all of them, on his own showing, lie essentially and forever outside experience. Nevertheless, he pretends to base his science upon observation.[4]

The role of observation in science became a dramatic issue in the years when Russell wrote the above lines, in connection with the uncertainty principle and the particle-wave dualism in quantum mechanics,[5] and is still a hot issue because of the famous question of nonlocality, which arose around 1975.[6] However, that is not really relevant to the problem raised by Russell in the preceding quote, because he is thinking of ordinary objects, which obey the laws of classical physics. Therefore, he gives a correct account of the state of matters in his time when, after a few lines, he continues as follows:

The physicist believes that he infers his electrons and protons from what he perceives. But the inference is never set forth in a logical chain, and, if it were, it might not look sufficiently plausible to warrant confidence. In actual fact, the whole development from common-sense objects to electrons and protons has been governed by certain beliefs, seldom conscious, but existing in every natural man. These beliefs are not unalterable, but they grow and develop like a tree. We start by thinking that a chair is what it appears to be, and is still there when we are not looking. But we find, by a little reflection, that these two beliefs are incompatible. If the chair is

4. B. Russell, *An Outline of Philosophy* (1927; reprint, New York: World Publishing Co., Meridian Books, 1960), 4f.
5. S. Toulmin, ed., *Quanta and Reality: A Symposium* (London: Hutchinson, 1962).
6. See e.g., B. D'Espagnat, *À la recherche du réel* (Paris: Gauthiers-Villars, 1979).

to persist independently of being seen by us, it must be something other than the patch of colour we see, because this is found to depend upon conditions extraneous to the chair, such as how the light falls, whether we are wearing blue spectacles, and so on. This forces the man of science to regard the "real" chair as the cause (or an indispensable part of the cause) of our sensations when we see the chair. Thus we are committed to causation as an *a priori* belief without which we should have no reason for supposing that there is a "real" chair at all. Also, for the sake of permanence we bring in the notion of substance: the "real" chair is a substance, or a collection of substances, possessed of permanence and the power to cause sensations. This metaphysical belief has operated, more or less unconsciously, in the inference from sensations to electrons and protons. The philosopher must drag such beliefs into the light of day, and see whether they still survive. Often it will be found that they die on exposure.

Our previous discussion on Hamlet's doubt referred to molecules; Russell's considerations move along the same line, and show that that discussion also applies to a chair. He raises two questions: the real nature of what we see and the reality of what we infer from observation. As to the former, science has made great advances since the time when Russell wrote the passage reported above; and in this chapter we shall explore precisely those advances. As to the relation between direct observation and "real" things — a problem beautifully presented in Plato's *Theae-thetus* twenty-four centuries ago — it was thought to have been solved by modern science with the distinction between "subjective" and "objective" points of view. As a matter of fact, as has been shown by Thomas F. Torrance,[7] the new physics, particularly field theory and relativity theory, has changed the status of the subject-object distinction. What is at stake is not so much "causation" (without which science would be impossible) as the dualistic view that properties are either subjective or objective. The recent advances in the neurosciences[8] and the work of eminent scientifically minded psychiatrists and psychologists[9] have shown that the boundary between what is subjective and what is objective is essentially determined by the context in which the distinction is made and by what is known about the psycho-physical mechanisms of perception. For example, one cannot simply say that color is subjective and light absorption is objective, because the stage at which a really subjective factor comes

7. Torrance, *Transformation*, ch. 1.

8. See the editorial article, "Reductionists Lay Claim to the Mind," *Nature* 381 (1996): 97; D. Chalmers, *The Conscious Mind: In Search of a Fundamental Theory* (Oxford: Oxford University Press, 1996); K. R. Popper and J. C. Eccles, *The Self and Its Brain* (Berlin: Springer International, 1978); and other works of J. C. Eccles.

9. Particularly C. G. Jung, and, more recently, C. A. Tart (cf. chapter twelve).

into play in color perception is when the free judgment of the subject is called upon; before that, the personal history of the observer, his mental structure, and the environment — physical and psychological — most probably act according to precise though partly unknown rules, so that, in principle, it should be possible to determine objectively the relation between the color a given "subject" has seen and the event or process that has brought about the color sensation.

I am mentioning the intricate question of the relation between the subject and the object, the observer and the observed, not in order to enter a long philosophical analysis but to avoid one, i.e., to justify the following tentative proposal: We shall say that a thing perceived by our five senses exists as such if it appears to be independent of our choices or states of consciousness, i.e., if we cannot act or communicate in a coherent way without assuming that it is there and interacts with other objects or beings independently of our perceiving it; we shall say that things beyond the reach of our senses exist if there are facts perceived by our senses which cannot be explained without assuming that they exist in the same sense as things directly accessible to our observation.

A logically minded philosopher would probably find much to criticize in this formulation of the basic tenet of critical realism. But then — although there is much truth in the ancient maxim according to which *vivere est philosophari*, to live is to practice philosophy — probably ordinary people should not be expected to devote himself or herself to philosophical speculations, which tend to become exercises in logic, the more so as they can only prove that even in logic one might implicitly choose one's standpoint on reality on grounds other than logical.[10] Nevertheless, a somewhat deeper reflection on the naïve principle of realism just stated is advisable.

A Discussion on Ontology

Most Europeans and more than a few Americans know the little Italian town of Rimini, the most important center of an uninterrupted line of sea resorts on the Adriatic sea. When they hear the name of Rimini, their minds are filled with images of a bright sun, golden sand, a blue sea, and an incredibly dense crowd of human bodies exposed to the sun or swimming or walking in the streets or filling restaurants and hotels, depending on the hour of the day. I wonder how many of Rimini's visitors have ever thought of those places when autumn comes, and the vacationers are gone. I can tell. The hotels are closed, the beach sunshades are folded and their colors faded, the beaches are moist, grayish, and lonesome, and

10. W. van Ormand Quine, *From a Logical Point of View* (Cambridge, Massachusetts: Harvard University Press, 1961).

one can at last experience also on the shores of the Mediterranean what a poet wrote about the American coast of the Atlantic:

> The sea is the land's edge also, the granite
> Into which it reaches, the beaches where it tosses
> Its hints of earlier and other creations:
> The starfish, the horseshoe crab, the whale's backbone;
> The pools where it offers to our curiosity
> The more delicate algae and the sea anemone.
> It tosses up our losses, the torn seine,
> The shattered lobsterpot, the broken oar
> And the gear of foreign dead men.[11]

Yet, on closer inspection, one realizes that a few hotels and a few coffee shops are still open. The fact is that groups of people who like a quiet, inexpensive place where they can meet for a weekend of discussions go there, and divide their time between attempts to grasp the deepest truths and contemplation of the sea. And they have the time to realize that they and the sea exist, no matter what the philosophers say.

I was once a member of one of those groups, which met to discuss the relation between science, philosophy, and religion. Our discussions led to a "declaration," which I liked very much: the search for truth — the humble though critical acknowledgment of facts or statements which are so and cannot be otherwise beyond any reasonable doubt — must have absolute priority even in religion, regardless of one's own convictions. Subsequently, a lively discussion took place mainly between Father Alberto Boccanegra, a metaphysician, and Professor Sergio Galvan, a logician. The former claimed that ontology — that part of philosophy which discusses what there is — is the only field of inquiry that rests on an evident truth. His declaration surprised us, because it had been made clear in the meeting that even the basic principle of realism proper, the view that there is something knowable outside our minds, was neither evident nor logically provable, although it made more sense than the opposite view. Boccanegra was now claiming that ontology has a single evident starting point: "Being cannot be nonbeing. What could be more obvious?" But Galvan pointed out that the apparent obviousness actually rested on our innate belief in the principle of noncontradiction, according to which a statement and its contrary cannot be simultaneously true. Neither party won its argument.[12]

You might comment that, instead of discussing such idle questions, we should have put our time to better use if we had taken a walk on

---

11. T. S. Eliot, *Four Quartets*, "Dry Salvages" I. 15f.

12. A concise but clear indication of the importance of this problem in philosophy can be found in R. Audi, ed., *The Cambridge Dictionary of Philosophy* (Cambridge: Cambridge University Press, 1995), s.v. "metaphysics."

the beach. I shall not answer that the weather was miserable because that would be a lie; indeed, I would agree with you were it not for one thing: the discussion showed that man cannot dispense with adopting a number of logically unproved fundamental beliefs or principles. That was admitted — though quite against his desires — even by the enemy of beliefs that was Bertrand Russell; and he was right in demanding that those beliefs should be made explicit, carefully chosen, and as few as possible. There is more to that, however. Even the "free man" Bertrand Russell, in ordinary life, took certain things for granted, for example that the chair on which he used to sit would not grow spikes on its sitting surface. There are "ultimate beliefs," which no one really questions even if, as Russell rightly suggested, philosophers are right in trying to dig them out of the unconscious. As Torrance explains,

> [these ultimate beliefs] are irrefutable and unprovable on two grounds: (1) because they have to be assumed at rational proof or disproof; and (2) because they involve a relation of thought to being which cannot be put into logical or demonstrable form. Ultimate beliefs, then, are to be understood as expressing the fundamental commitment of the mind to reality.[13]

An ultimate belief of all human beings appears to be precisely the content of the declaration of adherence to realism given above, namely that there are things that exist independently of us, and that they can be known as they are by a careful logical processing of our sensations. It would be a waste of time to try to prove its validity. At most, on hearing certain people say that no precise knowledge of the reality "out there" is possible, because scientific theories are too idealized to refer to real facts, one could answer by the following question: suppose an engineer designs, using the theory of electromagnetism, a dynamo, which produces a voltage of three thousand volts; and suppose that, having had the dynamo built, he asks you, who think that scientific theories are arbitrary constructions of the human mind, to hold the two terminals with your bare hands when the dynamo is tried; are you sure you would not refuse? More explicitly: whatever certain philosophers say, science works because it deals with what is "out there," not with conventional pictures of our sensations.

We have probably dwelt long enough on the proposal for a realist's creed given in the preceding section. To reformulate it in connection with knowledge, we shall say that it is a built-in principle of the human mind that there is something other than ourselves, and that, if we are careful

---

13. T. F. Torrance, "Ultimate Beliefs and the Scientific Revolution," *The Maxwell Cummings Lecture* (Montreal: McGill University, 1978); reprinted in *Transformations*, ch. 5.

enough, we can learn something about it as it is, although we cannot hope our knowledge to be exhaustive.

Since we now know where we stand, we can now apply with more confidence what we have seen in the preceding chapters to explore the general structure of sensible reality, such as it reveals itself to today's science. Let us start again by consulting the ancient masters, as Chinese wisdom (and the virtue of humility) recommend.

Pascal's Two Infinities

It is typical of truths that are in contrast with man's desire to believe that he is the greatest of all beings that they were announced several times in history and soon forgotten. Such was the fate of the lesson in humility drawn from the Copernican revolution by one of the makers of modern science, the great French mathematician and physicist Blaise Pascal. In a famous reflection of his, he wrote:

> Here is where the knowledge we are gaining about Nature is leading us. If it is not true, then there no truth in man; if it is, man should find in it a great source of humility, since he is obliged to acknowledge that one way or the other he is lower than he thought.

> And since man cannot subsist without believing in it, I hope that before entering grander researches on Nature he will pause to reflect on it seriously and calmly, and that he will look at himself — in order to judge by comparison if there is any proportion between him and Nature.[14]

This, after the collapse of the medieval picture of the universe, should have been the high priority task facing the cultivated people of the seventeenth century, to whom the method of Galileo, applied to the interpretation of observations obtained with the microscope and the telescope, was disclosing a hitherto unsuspected, almost infinite wealth of insights into the secrets of nature. And here is what those people and their successors should have realized:

> Let man contemplate Nature in its full and entire majesty. Let him stop looking at the lowly objects which surround him. Let him behold that extraordinarily brilliant star placed as an eternal lamp to illuminate the region of space in which he lives, and the Earth will appear to him as a tiny dot compared to the immense orbit described by that star, and the orbit of that star will appear as a tiny dot with respect to those of the stars of the firmament. But let our

14. B. Pascal, *Pensées*, ed. L. Lafuma (ca. 1660; reprint, Paris: Éd. du Seuil, 1963), no. 199–72.

imagination extend beyond what our sight can reach: it will sooner be tired of conceiving new things than Nature of providing them.

The whole visible world is but an imperceptible dash in the wide bosom of Nature. No idea can approach its immensity; however much we inflate our conceptions we do not produce but atoms, compared with the reality of things. It is an infinite sphere whose center is everywhere, the surface nowhere. It seems that it is the grandest sensible manifestation of the omnipotence of God that our imagination should lose itself in this thought.

Back to himself, man should consider what he is with respect to everything else, and he will feel lost, and will learn, from this little corner where he happens to be in the Universe, to assign the right value to the Earth, the nations, the cities, the houses and himself.

What is man, in infinity?

But to find another equally awesome prodigy, let him search in what he knows the most delicate things, and a mite will offer him in the smallness of its body incomparably smaller parts, legs with their joints, veins in its legs, blood in its veins, different liquid parts of this blood, small corpuscles in these liquids, structures in these corpuscles. Let him further analyze these latter things, and let him go to the end of what he can observe, and let us take this as the referent of our discourse. He might be tempted to think that he has reached the extreme limit in the smallness of Nature. In fact, that will be but the beginning of the descent into an abyss of even smaller objects.

Pascal mentioned at this point the possibility that every atom would turn out to be a universe in which there would be atoms and so on toward the infinitely small: a sort of fractal universe *ante litteram*. What physics has found in the three centuries since Pascal is not what he expected, but it gives even better support to his argumentation. Nature seems to have proved — think of the dramatic difference between the electrons in an atom and the planets orbiting around the sun — that she does not repeat her patterns when objects of widely different sizes are concerned. Indeed, she offers all the time new and more difficult challenges to our ingenuity; science has reached down below the diameters of atomic nuclei (of the order of 10^{-13} cm) to mysterious particles, which are so small and so strange that the very notion of size loses a precise meaning.

And here is Pascal's conclusion:

Man will then be astonished on finding out that his body, which had seemed an imperceptible dot in the immensity of the Universe, now appears as a giant, a world or rather a universe with respect to the nothing which cannot be reached. One who looks at himself in this way will be full of awe, and, realizing that he is suspended in the body Nature has given him between the abysses of infinity and of nothingness, he will tremble at seeing those wonders; and perhaps, his curiosity having changed into admiration, he will be more disposed to contemplate them in silence than to investigate them with presumption.

We have in these passages an example of the prophetic nature of the intuitions of the greatest thinkers. After Pascal, there were innumerable scientists and philosophers who believed, at variance with him, that man was the master; some even went as far as claiming that it is "human reason" that establishes the laws of nature. In short, they rejected that humble approach which is a foundation of wisdom.[15] And yet reminders to the contrary were frequent and well known already in the nineteenth century, as is shown by Thomas Carlyle's famous passage:

> And what is that Science, which the scientific head alone, were it screwed off, and (like the Doctor's in the Arabian Tale) set in a basin to keep it alive, could prosecute without a heart, but one other of the mechanical and menial handicrafts, for which the Scientific Head (having a Soul in it) is too noble an organ? I mean that Thought without Reverence is barren, perhaps poisonous; at best, dies like cookery with the day that called it forth; does not live, like sowing, in successive tilths and wider-spreading harvests, bringing food and plenteous increase to all Time.[16]

Science has had to wait for a strong lesson from facts before genuine scientists — unfortunately not popularizers of science — began to discover again the sense of awe which the unfathomable variety and order of nature should excite even in an atheist. That lesson has come with the realization of the existence, beyond the space dimensions, of three dimensions of reality not given the attention they deserved by physics, the science *par excellence* of the nineteenth century, before the second half of the twentieth century. One is time, stretching before and after the present, no longer seen as the passive flow of all things. History has been found to play a fundamental role in thermodynamics and in theories of evolution, as well as in the science of materials. Even nonliving things have a more or less rich "memory" of what happened to them in the past, although science is still struggling to understand the mechanism by which even simple crystals retain traces of their past history. Time is, as T. S. Eliot wrote, "time the destroyer and time the preserver"; it has a

---

15. J. M. Templeton, *The Humble Approach*, 2nd ed. (New York: Continuum, 1995).
16. T. Carlyle, *Sartor Resartus* (1838; reprint, London: Dent, Everyman's Library, 1973), 51–52.

direction and even as it were a creative power, which is manifest in the successive appearances of new species along the history of the earth.

The "fifth dimension" is complexity, discussed in the preceding chapter. Its introduction as a fundamental feature of reality leads to a notion we briefly mentioned in that chapter — levels of complexity as levels of reality of a system or being. The next few sections will be devoted to these levels, because, as we have already cursorily seen, they give a fascinating answer to the Shakespearean dilemma of our science: is a complex system such as a living being merely a collection of elementary particles or is there more to it than the particles it is made of?

The "sixth dimension" is size. It emerges in its whole import from Pascal's remarks — the enormous variety of the sizes of the objects constituting the universe. One might think that size is related to complexity because the latter increases with size. That is the case if one compares a higher animal with a protozoan, but there are examples pointing to the opposite conclusion. A cell, for all we can tell, is much more complex than a mountain. Mites are complete insects as complex as a black widow, but the smallest ones are a tenth of a millimeter in diameter, and can only be seen under the microscope. On the other hand, ostrich eggs, despite their size, are single cells. These examples show that complexity and size should be regarded as independent features of the objects making up the universe, at least within certain limits. What science tends to exclude is the existence of objects as small as an atom or as large as a star and yet having the degree of complexity of a living being.

One might also think that size is not so important from the standpoint of science. After all, one might say, what Pascal insisted upon was the significance for man of the existence of extremely small and extremely large objects, not their qualitative differences. Actually, radical qualitative differences have been found to appear when objects with sizes much different from what human beings can directly perceive are considered. The particle-wave dualism of quantum mechanics is a dramatic revelation of such differences, but less evident ones exist also at the other end of the size scale.

Size is related to our ability to perceive objects. We can see a cell only if magnified, we cannot see objects smaller than the wavelength of visible light, although we can in some cases have indirect "pictures" of them (e.g., with scanning tunnel microscopy); and we can touch those objects only as constituents of normal-size ones. As to large objects, we can see them only if they are far away, and in that case we cannot touch them. If they are close, we can walk on them, we can operate on them, but we cannot see them as wholes. Just think of the Milky Way, our galaxy, which we could only see from outside if we were able to build real starships capable of reaching places outside it in a time of months or years — which is forbidden by the present form of Einstein's theory.

The size dimension of sensible reality thus deserves a separate examination. We shall devote to it the last part of this chapter, after we have discussed complexity levels.

Complexity and "Real" Objects

We have already pointed out (in the section on unity of chapter two) that the whole reality of a thing cannot be understood unless it is admitted that the thing is at the same time a collection of elementary particles, a collection of nuclei and electrons, a collection of atoms, and so on up to a structured whole. This conclusion can be generalized and enriched using the already introduced notion of complexity level, dear to Edgar Morin.[17] A thing can be described in different ways, in terms of many simple particles with few properties, in terms of fewer parts with more properties, or as a single unit. We call each description a level of complexity, which is also an aspect of what that object really is. Each level differs by the number of parts and the nature and importance of "latent" information. The deeper levels, those which physics studies, consist of many parts with few manifest properties, and the properties of the whole are largely latent; higher levels consist of few parts, and fewer latent properties, which are partly properties of the whole, and partly properties of the parts belonging to lower levels.

An object is thus, as it were, a stack of levels of complexity. Its whole reality is not just one level, but the whole stack, up to a certain "height," which depends on how complex the object is. However, we must grant to biologists and anthropologists that, when one considers an object as a pawn of a greater game, only the topmost level matters. For example, in studying the wolf as a factor in the ecological equilibrium of a region of the earth, one wants to know what a wolf is as a whole, or maybe a little about its organs — teeth, intestines, etc. — but certainly not its quantum mechanical description. Indeed, for the sake of conciseness, one can say that the topmost level is the wolf's *level of reality*, because it is there that all those otherwise latent properties which make it a wolf, indeed that particular wolf, are actualized. This, however, does not mean that the lower levels are unimportant; quite the contrary is true, because in many cases those lower levels allow science to determine the *mechanism* by which certain characteristics are realized at the higher level.

---

17. Levels of reality are discussed in N. Hartmann, *Neue Wege der Ontologie (1942)* — *New Ways of Ontology* (Stuttgart: Kohlhammer, 1949); cf. Aristotle, *Meteorology*, 12. Also S. Alexander (1859–1938) has realized the importance of this concept. As to the expression "complexity levels," cf. M. Ceruti and E. Morin (eds.): *Simplicité et Complexité* (March 1988 supplement of *50, rue de Varenne* (Milan: Mondadori, 1988) and particularly therein: Basarab Nicolescu, "Complexité et niveaux de réalité," 38–43.

Let us try to express these novel and central ideas of the new science in somewhat different words. The number, nature, and configuration of the elements constituting a complex system (at the deeper level, the elementary particles) is certainly the necessary condition for it to be what it is; that condition is also sufficient up to a number of options, as illustrated by chemical isomerism.[18] Because it focuses attention on comparatively simple systems, physics tends to resolve all complexity into elementary units with as few internal degrees of freedom as possible, so that the variety of properties of a whole arise as a consequence of the multiplicity of possible motions of a large number of mutually interacting elementary particles. Why should one question the assertion that this procedure, which is so fascinating and has been quite successful and fruitful, provides a complete *understanding* of the complex reality of, say, a living organism or even a large molecule? The answer is that, as long as they are latent, the novel properties resulting from the structure and organization of an actual complex system and especially the rules governing them, although to a large extent predetermined by the number, nature, and special arrangement of its constituents, can only be automatically predicted without additional information, if their existence is already established. Indeed, the very existence of those properties cannot be guessed from the properties of the particles and the equations governing their mutual interaction — except perhaps in the way in which a genius would discover a new theorem in mathematics. Moreover, the same collection of elementary particles can give rise to completely different systems, depending on the choices imposed by the environment in which the system has been formed. Let us recall again the case of most molecules, for which a variety of possibilities (isomers) is compatible with the elementary constitution, so that no prediction is possible as to which isomer one will be dealing with in a particular instance unless the way is known in which the pertinent chemical substance has been prepared.

When it comes to living beings, the emergent characteristics that are undetermined at the lower levels may be numerous and far remote from those of the ultimate constituents. As mentioned, a level of complexity is the lower the larger the number of similar parts and the smaller the number of different properties to be attributed to those parts. For example, a low level of complexity of an organism is that of its constituent atoms: a very large number of atoms of hydrogen, carbon, nitrogen, oxygen, phosphorus, sulfur, iron, and a few others, with ten or so properties each, are all that is needed to describe completely an organism at the atomic level; but at that level, of course, even such relatively simple properties

18. Concerning complexity levels in chemistry cf. J. Schummer, *Realismus und Chemie* (Würzburg: Königshausen u. Neumann, 1996), 103ff; G. Del Re, "Ontological status of molecular structure," *Hyle (Karlsruhe)* vol. 4 (1998), 81–103.

as the capability for self-replication of DNA would be unconceivable if not known beforehand. Moreover, there is an astronomical number of possible arrangements of those atoms, and there is nothing in the information we have about them that would allow us to tell which one will make up a living organism.

Thus, the atomic level does not represent the whole *reality* of any given living being. If we move to the molecular level much more can be understood and discovered; we are dealing, therefore, with a higher level of complexity. However, as I have already recalled, there is a sort of *a posteriori* explanation which may be important and which reference to a lower level makes possible: that "vertical" explanation by which one says, for example, "this molecule is particularly heavy because it contains an atom of ruthenium"; or "the X-ray spectrum of this molecule shows a line corresponding to a sodium atom." One refers then to an additive property (mass) or to a property of the atoms (X-ray spectra) not much affected by formation of chemical bonds. Also when one says, "this molecule forms a hydrogenated cation because it contains a nitrogen atom with a lone electron pair," one is descending to the lower complexity level, because, although the notion of lone pair belongs to molecular structure, one is referring to atoms. In the same way, molecular biologists try to explain many properties of living matter in terms of enzymes — the tiny "robots" that take care of the individual chemical transformations of which life consists; enzymes, therefore, are the "elementary objects" of the complexity level of molecular biology. Of course, one can also explain why they behave the way they do at the biological level by considering their molecular structure; but one cannot explain in terms of the latter why a certain enzyme is present in one organism and not in another.

As one climbs the ladder of complexity levels, one gets to properties like consciousness. There, *a posteriori* explanations in terms of much lower levels are still important — just think of tranquilizers, which act as single molecules — but they are hardly sufficient to account for facts. We shall consider these points when we come to the mind-body problem.

The emergence, at higher complexity levels, of new properties which at the lower levels were not only latent but partly undetermined is also why the levels of complexity are levels at which the reality of an object — the "real" chair in Russell's example — is so to speak present in a greater and greater measure. Let us think again about the structure of a complexity level. At that level, we describe certain systems in terms of certain "elementary objects." If the systems we consider cannot be decomposed into fewer parts having a complexity intermediate between that of the "elementary objects" and that of the wholes, then the complexity of the latter is that of the level under consideration. For example, the atoms as originally described by Mendeleyev's Periodic Table

Table 1: Complexity Levels Studied by Biology[a]

Levels	Examples
Communities	Anthill
	Gaia
Multicellular organisms	Man, wolf, ant
Unicellular organisms	
Organ systems	Root system
	Circulatory system
	Digestive system
	Nervous system
Organs	Stem
	Taproot
	Kidney
	Heart
Tissues	Xylem, Phloem
	Blood
	Smooth muscle
	Bone
Cells	
Corpuscles in cells	Cell nuclei
	Mitochondria
	Chloroplasts
Macromolecular complexes	Ribosomes
	Enzyme complexes
	Membranes
Macromolecules	Proteins
	Starch
	Lipids
	DNA, RNA
Molecular building blocks	Amino acids
	Nucleotides
	Sugars
	Fatty acids

a. Cf. David Layzer, *Cosmogenesis* (New York: Oxford University Press, 1990), 213. This table includes communities as the topmost level, but note that communities are not as tightly bound together as organisms or molecules. This complication is discussed below.

---

of the Elements are the "elementary objects" of the complexity level of molecules. Enzymes are extremely complicated molecules, but they are also the elementary objects of the level of complexity studied by molecular biology; this level comprises systems not necessarily endowed with a great measure of unity, but consisting of several enzymes and not susceptible of decomposition into individual enzymes. One can continue toward living beings, as illustrated in Table 1.

Now take the most complex system we know of, the human being. A thing, as we have seen, is at the same time what it appears to be at one level and at another; its entire nature — its τὸ τί ἦν or "what-it-is," as Aristotle called it — cannot be described merely in terms of the objects typical of one level. In particular, a human being is a collection of molecules, but that is not its entire reality, for a human being is by far more than a collection of molecules. The molecular level is a low level of complexity (or of reality), and there are higher ones. One can give a less incomplete description by considering fewer parts, each much more complex than a molecule, for example by treating a living being as an organized assemblage of organs. Then one is dealing with a higher level of complexity. On climbing the ladder, one comes to the level that has been the object of studies by philosophers and thinkers of all ages: the level where one considers as "parts" the mind and the emotional psyche, the νοῦς (nous) and the θὑμος (thymos). But that too falls short of completeness, because from the interaction of emotions and cold logic a whole new set of properties and activities of human beings emerges: think of poetry, think of what is revealed about man's reality by the very existence of works like Dante's poem and Shakespeare's plays, or of Herman Melville's *Moby Dick*.

We thus come to the uppermost level of complexity, where we speak only of man's characteristics or properties, where we look at a man as a fully integrated whole, as a unit. This is the level at which we must place ourselves if we wish to deal with what human beings actually are; this is the level referred to by the wise drunkard in Chesterton's novel, *The Ball and the Cross*, when he staggered away from the two men who had asked him what was a man, while repeating to himself as in answer to an insult: "I say a man's a man; that's what I say. If a man a'n't a man, what is he?"[19] Long before the advent of modern psychology, this point had been emphasized by many thinkers, and evil ensued whenever it was neglected or denied, as recent history teaches. This too is scientific evidence. Much has been gained by science in recent times also in this connection, for we now know that complete knowledge of man (or, for that matter, of any object in space-time) requires consideration of all the pertinent levels of complexity.

The Whole and Its Parts, Again

If we try to extrapolate what we have seen so far to systems larger than human beings — and perhaps including human beings — we shall be in trouble. As I have already pointed out, with regard to the complexity

19. G. K. Chesterton, *The Ball and the Cross* (London: Wells Gardner, Darton & Co., 1910), 141.

dimension what matters is individuality, i.e., integration of the parts into a whole with new properties of its own, and that — as far as is known — attains its maximum in man. A system that is a part of a system in the strong sense is wholly dependent on the environment provided by the other parts for its proper functioning, and therefore it cannot be said to have an individuality of its own. Think of an animal's heart. It will function when separated from the body to which it belongs provided the precise conditions under which it functions in that body are reproduced; this is why heart transplants are possible. But the heart is not a system capable of any activity of its own in a variable environment; in our metaphorical language we could say that, at variance with, for example, a loose stone, an organ of a living body is not a dancer in the Great Dance, because it belongs to that body, and follows strictly what that body does.

The example of the heart emphasizes that complex systems having a high degree of unitariness are indeed made of complex systems — their parts — but the latter may have no right to the status of individual objects; on the other hand, when we speak of the things and beings forming the universe we are not thinking of the parts of an organism. Therefore, there should be intermediate situations — systems intermediate between, for example, a horseshoe crab, which is a complex system in the strong sense, and interstellar gas, which is practically a collection of free molecules exceptionally undergoing collisions. We have already seen one such system, the earth according to the Gaia hypothesis, or, if you prefer, the earth's biosphere; an illuminating aspect of it is given by the mangroves of the Everglades Park in Florida and the horseshoe crabs that can be seen moving slowly on the bottom of the clear low waters in which the mangroves grow, and all the other animals living in that strange and fascinating habitat. It is easy to find more examples of the most diverse sorts. One is given by plasmons, groups of electrons which behave all in the same way under certain conditions;[20] another is given by cell colonies, e.g., colonial flagellates, which are apparently individual living beings, but actually consist of undifferentiated cells cooperating with one another rather than organized to form a whole; still another is a beehive; another is a human tribe; and so on.

Each of these systems offers a fascinating subject of study, but what interests us here is that the limited specialization of the components makes them intermediate cases. In the case of an organism, we can speak of *its* heart, *its* tissues, and so on; nature confirms this way of speaking by the well-known phenomenon of rejection, which occurs when a biologist tries to replace even just one cell of a higher organism with one belonging

---

20. It is to coherent systems of this kind that many physicists refer when they use the terms "complexity" and "organization."

to another organism. On the other hand, in the case of systems having a limited and flexible measure of unity and coherence the parts have indeed special properties, but are individually on their own, i.e., independent, mobile, and capable of playing a variety of roles. In those systems there is room for novelties, for new creations, as T. S. Eliot would say.

At this point we are finally ready to answer explicitly the all-important question: what objects in the universe make up the coherence and harmony that is the Great Dance? To put it less poetically: when we think of the universe as a great system in which processes take place that lead to new order and new beauty, what objects should we think of? Should we think only of elementary particles, or of elementary particles and of complex systems that are parts of other systems? The answer has just been given: no, we should not. We ought to look at the physical world in a way that is closer to an ordinary person's outlook. A picture of the universe as a collection of distinct entities should not include those objects which are integrant parts of complex systems in the strong sense, because those systems have already reached their maximum of integration into wholes. We shall not consider hearts, for example, as objects participating in the Great Dance, however noble they may be; nor shall we assign that role to the electrons of a crystal, even though we admit that there may be in the depths of space free electrons which participate in the Dance on their own. One way to express this idea is to say that to be qualified as a significant participant in the Great Dance an entity must have at least a measure of unity and independence; in other words, it must have an identity of its own as an entity *per se*, in addition, of course, to participating in the coherent evolution of the whole that is the universe itself.

Identity and the Environment

To gain better insight into the significance of complexity as the "fifth dimension" of the universe we must thus consider intermediate systems, like Gaia (chapter one), and have another look at the relations between objects of all sorts.

Those who have a strictly scientific training may never have heard of the German philosopher Georg Wilhelm Friedrich Hegel (1770–1831). In intellectual circles he is both famous and infamous, for he was a great thinker, but his philosophy (so some say) inspired famous destructive ideologies. Be it as it may, he is reported to have said: "If reality does not conform to my philosophy, so much the worse for reality." Apart from that, he claimed (as Bocheński, an eminent Polish historian of logic, put it) that:

> all the relations of a thing are inherent to it in the sense that it cannot subsist without them. In other words, a thing gets to be

what it is through its relations; they constitute its essence. They are all necessary, inner relations.[21]

Now, Hegel's basic views are contrary to realism, so that we might be inclined to disregard what he said on the grounds that we stand for realism. But that would be a mistake. As the ancient Romans would say, *fas est ab hoste doceri*, it is right before the gods to be taught by the enemy, which is a strong way of saying that one ought to have a measure of humility even when he thinks he is right and the other is wrong. In this case it is evident that there is some truth in what Hegel says. Just think of the anteater, whose very name tells us that it is what it is at least partly because of its voracious disposition toward ants. Thus, Hegel is right to some extent, but to what extent? Let us listen to what Bocheński has to say:

> Other philosophers think that there are indeed some such essential relations — for example a sense organ is what it is because of its relation to its object, e.g., hearing in virtue of its relation to sounds; but there are also inessential, not constitutive relations. Thus, say those philosophers, it is not essential for a man whether he is sitting or standing — he remains a man — or, to put it differently, he is *first* a man, and *only after* does he enter such different relations.

The founder of structuralism, Claude Lévi-Strauss (cf. chapter one), rediscovered as a sociologist Hegel's views. Let us not pause here on his disconsolate conception of man, but let us appeal to the physical sciences and common sense to solve the dispute. Think of a radio transceiver. It is a device capable of transmitting and receiving signals, and that is the only thing which justifies its existence: but no one would really believe that, if it did not keep transmitting and receiving all the time, it would "suddenly and softly vanish away," as did the Hunter of the Snark.[22]

On the other hand, consider Prigogine's fundamental contribution, which consists in the realization that the most important objects in the universe are steady-state systems out of equilibrium, subsisting by continuously exchanging with their environment matter, energy, and, through them, information. Prigogine's contribution might seem to bring grist to Hegel's mill, but there is a difference: the environment does not determine what the system out of equilibrium is, it only provides the conditions for it to subsist. Take, for a concrete example, an amoeba. It will die if the water in which it lives is cleaned of all nourishing materials, and will at least change to some extent some of its properties if its environment

21. J. M. Bocheński, *Wege zum philosophischen Denken* (Freiburg i. B., Germany: Herder, 1959), 101.

22. L. Carroll, *The Hunting of the Snark* (1876; reprint, London: Chatto and Windus, 1941).

changes; but that does not mean that the main characteristics of that amoeba as a microorganism are determined by the existence of certain materials in water. All we can say is that whatever is present in the water affects the amoeba, and the presence of the amoeba will modify the conditions existing in the water and possibly the life conditions of other microorganisms in it. This can be generalized to suggest that all objects in the universe — stars, planets, meteorites, living beings, and so on — interact in some way with their environment; nevertheless, they are individual objects with at least some basic properties of their own, which make what was once called their "essence."

The Role of Size

If, instead of complexity levels, we think of size levels, then the story no longer concerns single systems in the strong sense, particularly organisms, but more or less loosely connected sets of them. In the examples discussed at greater length so far, the lower complexity levels are characteristic of objects having in general sizes smaller than those of higher complexity levels lying above them. Indeed, there are examples of increases in size that lead to the emergence of new properties of objects of a given class, and therefore involve a step up to a higher complexity level. Such is the case, for example, of polymer molecules ("macromolecules"). They are but very large molecules, and yet have such novel properties that Hermann Staudinger, the man who gave them their name in 1922, fought for decades to get his most famous colleagues to accept the notion that they were molecules and not aggregates, and only in 1953 did he receive a belated Nobel prize.[23]

It is also quite probable that, in the history of life on earth, colonies of unicellular animals evolved into organisms. Thus, increase in size may involve (in the long run) a change from a set of weakly interacting individual systems to a single fully integrated unity. However, as long as that is not the case, the parts of the weaker system (call it a community) should be looked at as systems *per se*. This is where the size dimension comes into play. Before discussing it in general, let us consider a few concrete examples.

Consider again colonial flagellates. They are "protists" (formerly called protozoa), i.e., organisms consisting of single "eukaryotic" cells, which form either temporary or permanent aggregates called colonies. All the individuals composing a colony are structurally the same and physiologically independent; however, the colony is capable of collective action, such as swimming by the combined action of the flagella of its

23. R. Olby, *The Path to the Double Helix* (London: Macmillan, 1974).

components. Some of the most beautiful green algae present various gradations from small groups of individuals, in structure quite similar to those of closely related noncolonial species, to complex colonies of thousands of cells. The several species of the green algae *Gonium* form square, platelike colonies from four to sixteen cells, usually in a gelatinous matrix, while the colonies of *Pandorina* and *Eudorina* consist of spherical groups of sixteen or thirty-two cells similarly embedded. All the cells have the same structure and are capable of asexual and sexual reproduction. But a differentiation of somatic and reproductive cells (0.005 mm in diameter) appears, for example, in *Volvox* green algae because the cells are often connected by protoplasmic strands and form the surface of a protoplasmic sphere with a diameter of 0.5 mm, possibly containing daughter colonies having diameters five to ten times smaller, which appear as denser green spheres containing one or two thousand cells.

Some protists form colonies with cells so specialized and diversified in their functions that scientists doubt if in point of fact they should not be considered organisms rather than colonies. This is not surprising, because it is often the case that distinctions generally valid become fuzzy in particular instances. The interesting point is not the existence of uncertain situations; it is that complex organisms (the cells) may participate in associations that are not much more complex than they are, that indeed respect the identity of the participants. This is an important fact from the point of view of the "what-it-is" question, because the full individuality of an autonomous object also lies in its ability to participate in those associations. For example, the cells of *Volvox* are special inasmuch as they form colonies, while those of other protists do not. In this sense, and only in this sense, is Hegel's idea that a thing is defined by its relations acceptable in the frame of a scientific outlook on reality.

Coming back to the question of size, at first sight it would seem that there is nothing in the example of the protists that really authorizes us to distinguish between a large colony and a single cell on the basis of size. Indeed, certain microorganisms that help (or attack) mammals, e.g., *E. coli*, form associations with systems billions of billions times larger than themselves. Actually, however, their mode of operation stays at their own level of size or below, because they produce or modify molecules or macromolecules, which are the vehicles of the interaction. Moreover, as far as science can tell, the world in which those beings make their choices — what to eat, what to avoid, and so on — only includes objects they can recognize at the scale for which their input-output devices are designed. If, anticipating a discussion we shall make in the chapter on communication, we apply the notion of "meaning" to all processes involving systems with a minimum of ability to process information, then we can say that objects (or parts of objects) meaningful to a protist cell must either be of a similar size or be the seats of processes taking place in parts of them having a size not much larger than that of the protist cell itself. Nor is a much smaller size meaningful. For all science knows, a cell is sensitive to chemicals, whose molecules are far smaller than the cell itself, but that is only because, just like you and I, it usually deals with lots of molecules of each type at the same time. Its enzymes, which are molecules, will deal with individual molecules, but responses like motion toward a place where there is a certain useful substance or away from a poisonous one will take place in the presence of a sufficient number of molecules of that substance.

Thus, it would seem that in general there is compatibility between objects of similar size, although they may have different degrees of complexity. We can speak of "size levels" in the universe just as we speak of complexity levels; a size level, seen from the standpoint of a being belonging to it, may be called its *direct-access level*. The difference between the two sorts of levels is great. Complexity levels are, as it were, an internal affair of single systems, while size levels involve the environment as far as it is *directly meaningful* for a system.

The next question is, of course: what about human beings? Well, the size of a human being is nothing compared to the size of the earth and huge compared to the size of a microbe. Therefore, also in the case of human beings, just as for any other living being, there is a direct-access level at which each individual interacts with its environment without the help of science and technology. The peculiarity of man's case is that his direct-access level is just a starting point. Our ability to use imagination, reason, and tools, including extensions of our senses such as the telescope and the microscope, make us capable of reaching higher and lower size levels, to explore them, and, if we are wise, to wonder. Man's direct access level is the level of our everyday existence, from which science starts and to which technology applies; it is the source of metaphors and analogies; it is the reference level of our thinking, the plane of reality where we live and die. Our senses are tuned to it and provide information without the help of instruments or theory. At its frontiers there are microscopic beings and the nearest celestial bodies. The former were unknown before the invention of the microscope, and at the direct-access level they appear as "influences," which still in the eighteenth century were held responsible for epidemics, among other things; the latter can only be reached with the help of the most sophisticated technology, which uses properties of matter of no direct significance for our senses. On the other hand, mass-media and fast travel are *amplifications*, not extensions, of the ordinary activities of human beings, and therefore should not be seen as beyond direct access.

Most often, and especially when reflecting on science, we shall use the expression "direct-access level" with implicit reference to man. We have the ability to travel with our imaginations and our tools to other size levels, so that, as poets or scientists, we can, as it were, live in them; therefore, it is sometimes necessary to specify the level to which a consideration refers. To better show what I mean, let me refer to chemistry. At the direct-access level a chemist filters, boils, distills, crystallizes, and so on, until he gets what he considers to be a pure substance, perhaps the sugar called fructose, which you might buy if you were on a diet; but then he leaves that level by imagining a process of indefinite subdivision of its tiny crystals ending at the size level of molecules; there he starts working at the hypothesis that certain special molecules are the systems responsible for the properties of fructose. Thus, he establishes a correspondence between the direct-access level and the size level of molecules, a correspondence, which, by the way, also establishes the complexity level at which chemistry studies matter.

Toward Infinite Sizes

We can thus think that there is a rough parallelism between size levels and the complexity levels of the most complex beings belonging to them, at least below the direct-access level of man. Since there are uncountable size levels above it, does this imply that there are material entities larger and more complex than human beings? Or are there higher size levels that do not involve entities with higher levels of complexity? It would seem that, if by entities one means systems in the strong sense, the answer should be negative. Indeed, the solar system is quite accurately described in terms of sums of the properties of the planets and of the sun; similarly, galaxies appear to form clusters, but so far there is no indication that those clusters have any emergent property with respect to the component galaxies. However, there is coherence, though in a more free or temporary form; indeed, coherence is typical of certain associations of objects having sizes larger than those directly accessible to the senses of man.

Already local biological equilibria on the green hills or in the blue oceans of earth give rise to large systems where there is organization, neither so tight nor so specialized as in a living being, but, precisely because of that, open to novelties, including emergence of new order. Human communities too are systems with a measure of unity, where indeed full unity can arise at least temporarily, as when a large group of honest men becomes a crowd capable of lynching an innocent. True enough, a member of a crowd of that sort has lost his individuality, nay, his humanity; but if you look at the group the entire time it lasts, not just when it forms a beastly crowd, then you can see that it has emergent properties in addition to those of the individuals. Moreover, the latter draw the nourishment of their personalities from belonging to a group, as we all know from the daily observation that loneliness is an unhealthy condition for a human being.

The associations we have just mentioned are the smallest systems human beings perceive and in which they operate *from within*. Mountain ranges like the Himalaya and immense expanses of water like the Pacific Ocean are at the limit of what we can directly interact with; but just when we think of a solitary line of mountaineers toiling in cold unbreathable air toward the top of Mount Everest, and you will admit that there are indeed limits to man's direct access to these systems. The mountains and the seas are objects too big for us to see in their entirety. It is a wonder that before air and space travel, human beings could draw in almost perfect detail, piece by piece, the shapes of such large objects as great mountain ranges and continents; they would miss, anyway, details like the remaining traces of ancient roads, which were discovered only by aerial surveys.

And that is only the beginning. There are systems of which we are aware, but whose scale is beyond all we can really grasp. Can we really imagine how big the sun is with respect to the earth? Can we get a feeling for a distance of just 90 million miles, roughly the distance between the earth and the sun? And what about the distance of the stars closest to the sun, the red Proxima Centauri and the twin stars Sirius α and β, a brilliant white star and a white dwarf, four to nine light years away? Consider what is observed in interstellar space. On the one hand, the very fact that astronomers speak of planetary systems, galaxies, and clusters of galaxies shows that some principle of order and unity, e.g., the attraction of the central sun, is at work even in those immense systems. On the other hand, cosmology is not yet able to cope with the subtle threads that connect celestial bodies separated by light years or the beings living on them, but, as we have seen in the first chapter, they are there.

To give the reader a feeling of what there seems to be in the remotest parts of the universe accessible to our observation, I shall report here the first group of questions proposed for discussion in a meeting of astrophysicists in 1987:

1. What is a good description of the 3-dimensional structure of the Universe for expansion velocities larger than 10,000 km/s [distances larger than $\approx$ 100 Mpc, or 20,000 billion times the Earth-Sun distance]? And at larger distances?

- What is the convincing evidence that some structures are strings, chains, filaments, sponges, bubbles, sheets, voids?

- Do structures exist which exceed 100 Mpc?

- What is the amplitude of structures on the largest scale?

- Did these structures originate in the very early Universe?[24]

24. V. C. Rubin and G. V. Coyne, eds., *Large Scale Motions in the Universe* (Vatican City: Pontifical Academy of Sciences, 1988).

On reading the astronomers' reports, one finds that at those unimaginable distances they have detected collective motions, for example currents of uncountable galaxies streaming toward a point called the Great Attractor, located somewhere near (on the astronomical scale) our galaxy (and the few others which constitute the "Local Group") in the direction of the Virgo constellation.[25] There are no words to describe the sizes of these objects. "Huge" is certainly far from enough. Just consider that the astronomers are speaking of objects which a beam of light, if it did not lose all its energy on the way, would reach in millions of years. Yet, the astronomers speak of the Great Attractor and of the related "Virgo infall" with the same sense of reality as a poet recalling the "whisper of running streams, the wild thyme unseen" on mountains.

What these observations tell us is that the correlations implied by the Great Dance image, though fine and not easily perceptible, concern classes of single bodies (from stray molecules to planets and stars), planetary systems and the like (e.g., double stars), star clusters, galaxies, galaxy clusters, and superclusters, which constitute higher and higher levels of size. We have seen in chapter two that the unique quality of living beings, which indicates that their level of complexity is the highest possible one, is their *dynamical unity*, i.e., their ability to preserve their identities by acting on their environment. But there are objects that have a unity of their own, at an unimaginably greater scale, a unity whose properties and nature science has not yet fully grasped, for example that very galaxy in which we happen to find ourselves, we who live on a planet so tiny that a dust particle would be in proportion a giant. They are objects which, like molecules and smaller objects at the other end of the size scale, cannot be seen even with the help of instruments; they must be photographed, and their properties inferred — or rather guessed — from indirect evidence.

The structure of the reality science investigates thus appears to be characterized by size ranges, which define the boundaries between which entities can have direct experience of the totality of other entities, and complexity levels, which correspond to the degrees of individuality and unity of objects. As we have seen, the full reality of the tiniest part of the universe can only be grasped by considering all the levels of reality, those which can be detected by looking at that entity alone, and those at which that entity is part of more complex systems. But this is only one of the considerations that make it possible for us to get to know the cast of the Dance of the Cosmos. Let us try to outline the whole picture.

25. S. M. Faber and D. Burstein, "Motions of the Galaxies in the Neighborhood of the Local Group," in Rubin and Coyne, *Large Scale Motions*.

Paths from Elementary Particles

If we are not too fastidious about fundamental physics, we can review the conclusion of this chapter starting with electrons, nucleons, and photons rather than with "fundamental particles" (quarks and company). That, roughly speaking, is the stuff of which the stars are made. The sun, in fact, does not contain much but protons, neutrons, electrons, and radiation quanta; but some protons and neutrons are only virtually there, because they are assembled in drops of nuclear matter, the nuclei of light elements, mainly helium. It is possible, as is well known, to use the same ingredients to describe all that is called "ordinary matter." A carbon atom is just a cluster of six protons and six neutrons, which have coalesced to form its nucleus, plus six orbiting electrons. You, *"hypocrite lecteur, mon semblable, mon frère,"*[26] are a collection of atoms and quanta. The galaxy clusters which, according to certain astronomers, stream toward the Great Attractor at unimaginable distances from us, are supposed to be mostly made of ordinary stars, that is to say, nucleons, electrons, and quanta. But these particles are only, as we have seen, the *ingredients* of material reality. To stop at them would be the same as saying that the three fundamental colors, red, blue, and yellow, are all there is in the most beautiful paintings, from the frescoes in the prehistoric caves of Altamira to those of Sistine Chapel.

In fact, there are two major paths to beauty and wonder, which start with elementary particles. Let us call the first one "the Path of the Giants," which, despising detail work, has produced those immense objects that men only know as lights in sky, and about which, despite such technological wonders as the Hubble telescope, we still have only hints and guesses; I mean, stars and galaxies. They are objects about which theories have been built, but so vastly different in size and remote from all we can reach directly or indirectly that no theory of science is really sure to be a description of what they are. The Path of the Giants took just one turn close to us, when it left a yellow star, the source of all motion and life, in this corner of the universe. Observation of the sun — patient observation — and brilliant intuitions have provided such magnificent discoveries as the life-cycle of a star. But we should not be misled by these achievements: if the science that has discovered the nature and the development of stars is valid, no human being will ever get to verify those theories even from such large distances as the earth-sun distance, for relativity theory forbids it. Those jewels in the sky, Betelgeuse the red giant, Sirius the white with its dwarf companion, Bellatrix the blue, and all the others seem to be there mainly for us to dream of impossible voyages; and the majority of stars we cannot even see. Nevertheless there is one

26. "Hypocrite reader, my like, my brother"; so T. S. Eliot quoting Baudelaire, qualified his readers in his famous poem *Wasteland*.

thing we can say, according to science: protons, neutrons, electrons, and other elementary particles are not the whole story. A star, though held together not by organization but by the simple force of gravitation, is an object which participates on its own in the history of the universe; and the particles of which it is made have the same restricted reality as a brick in a wall, unless they happen to get free and fly into space, where even a single neutron could have a role to play. The lights in the sky are stars, and scientific thinking would never be able to describe and rationalize the reality of a star, for one thing by trying to explain how it is formed from individual particles, if it did not take for granted that the real object to be studied is a very special cluster of particles.

We have already mentioned galaxies, clusters of galaxies, and super-clusters. They are most probably associations or "communities" of stars, maybe just held together by gravitational attraction. They are so far from our direct and indirect sensible experience that they would almost be mere mathematical objects, only perceived by the minds of the scientists, were it not for the fact that they leave marks on photographic plates. The mystery they offer for our meditation and our research seems to deserve a qualification I have already borrowed once or twice from T. S. Eliot: they seem to be "hints of other creations," for they do not seem to fit with anything that makes sense to us. Yet, as has been mentioned, a strange and mysterious relation between the very existence of mankind and those swarms of billions of stars at the limit of the observable has been rec-ognized — the anthropic principle. That principle should be treated with great humility and caution; but the very fact that it has been proposed and found compatible with all the rest of science suggests that also the Path of the Giants, from fundamental particles to galactic superclusters, however mysterious and alien to us, is part of the choreography of the one Dance of the Universe.

The other path from elementary particles may be called the Path of Man. Protons and neutrons form nuclei, nuclei and electrons form atoms, atoms form molecules and crystals; and, as we have seen, the structure of molecules, which reveals a regularity of nature emerging from the depths of particle interactions, is the first significant manifestation of complexity in systems that are stable under ordinary conditions in a variable envi-ronment. We know the rest: from small molecules large molecules are formed, then macromolecules, which may act as enzymes; and so on, along the ladder of biological organization. At each level there may be associations of entities, in which the participants do interact but retain essentially their independence, i.e., at least their ability to survive, so to speak, in an environment that is variable at random within certain lim-its. We may thus have the integration of entities into wholes capable of doing what a single individual cannot do, but always as an extension of the individual and — in the world of life — for the benefit of the individual. There is, however, a sort of tendency to integration, at least as long as the conflicting influence of size does not interfere. Even living beings, though capable of a high measure of independence, actually depend on their environments for their survival and play a role in those environments by interacting with the other entities, of the same or of another kind, which form that environment. It is this sort of coherence that science has discovered along with organization; it might be seen as a more flexible sort of organization, in which all components participate without losing their autonomy.

Other entities on the Path of the Giants as well as on the Path of Man deserve a special discussion, for they are not "objects" in the usual sense of the word. The most important ones are fields. Very rightly T. F. Torrance pointed out in several papers that the discovery of the electromagnetic field by James Clerk Maxwell[27] has opened a new perspective not only to science, but to our culture. Entities which belong to a distinct category, and are being recognized by science not without resistance, are relations, whose importance is the *leitmotiv* of this book. We shall turn to them and to fields after we have examined becoming and time, the fourth dimension of our universe. Let us keep in mind that, in the musical language of the Dance, order in space corresponds to harmony, and order in time corresponds to melody, indeed to the numberless melodies which are born and which may eventually fade away, thus signaling certain dancers that their parts are over.

---

27. T. F. Torrance, *Transformation*, ch. 6.

Chapter 4

Time and Becoming

The time patterns of events are arranged in processes, which are the object of science. Processes were once supposed to be essentially causal, but many of them have turned out to be largely "stochastic," i.e., probabilistic, and hence associated with break of full regularity. Is that not in conflict with intelligibility, and with the unceasing enrichment in beauty and harmony of the universe?

Middle Earth and History – The Role of Time – Becoming – The Time of the Dance – Processes and Processing - Deterministic and Stochastic Processes – The Experimental Method, Reversibility, and Irreversibility – Oblivion of the Past and Uncertainty of the Future

A tormenting thought: as of a certain point, history was no longer real. *Without noticing it, all mankind suddenly left reality; everything happening since then was supposedly not true; but we supposedly didn't notice. Our task would now be to find that point, and as long as we didn't have it, we would be forced to abide in our present destruction.* — ELIAS CANETTI[1]

Middle Earth and History

So far, we have placed emphasis on order and coherence in space rather than in time. True enough, we have discovered that the coherence of the Souk of Marrakesh has its roots in the past history of each object or being in it, but this was not the main point of the whole discussion. The relations we were considering were similar to those between the individual notes in a chord in music — several tones played at the same time, giving a harmonious result if they are chosen in a certain way. Even when it came to universal decay, the order we were speaking of did change in time, but it was not the order of events in time. And yet, the reality science studies includes beginnings and ends, events and processes — in short, order in time.

Have you ever asked yourselves why Tolkien's masterpiece, *The Lord of the Rings*, rings so true to most of its readers, despite the fantastic creatures which people it? It should be impossible to accept it as anything but mere invention, and yet, until recently, a large "Frodo lives!" was painted on a parapet of the Mazzini bridge in Rome, a city where every stone is a relic of our "real" history. What makes Tolkien's novel ring true is not so much the story as the world of Middle Earth in which it is set. There are many reasons for the feeling that it is a real world. The peoples of Middle Earth have their own tongues, their own countries; and, what is more significant, they have a history; indeed, even the stones carry the traces of past civilizations and events. Do you remember Frodo and Sam at the Cross-Roads?

> There, far away, beyond sad Gondor now overwhelmed in shade, the Sun was sinking, finding at last the hem of the great slow-rolling pall of cloud, and falling in an ominous fire toward the yet unsullied Sea. The brief glow fell upon a huge sitting figure, still and solemn as the great stone kings of Argonath. The years had gnawed it, and

1. Quoted by J. Baudrillard, *L'Illusion de la fin: Ou La grève des événements* (Paris: Galilée, 1992). Translated by Charles Dudas, York University, Canada as "Pataphysics of the Year 2000" (internet text at www.CTheory.com).

violent hands had maimed it, its head was gone, and in its place
was set in mockery a round rough-hewn stone....

Suddenly, caught by the level beams, Frodo saw the old king's
head: it was lying rolled away by the roadside. "Look, Sam!" he
cried, startled into speech. "Look! The king has got a crown again!"

The eyes were hollow and the carven beard was broken, but
about the high stern forehead there was a coronal of silver and
gold. A railing plant with flowers like small white stars had bound
itself across the brows as if in reverence for the fallen king, and in
the crevices of its stony hair yellow stonecrop gleamed.

"They cannot conquer for ever!" said Frodo. And then suddenly
the brief glimpse was gone. The Sun dipped and vanished, and as
if at the shuttering of a lamp, black night fell.[2]

You see? Memories of a remote past carved in time-worn stone and
desperate faith that the future will bring the dawn of a better day are what
produces that depth in time which makes Middle Earth real. Perhaps
those memories arouse an echo in our minds. However that may be, the
case of Tolkien's Middle Earth shows that the human mind accepts as
reality things and events which extend in time, which have a past and a
future. We may call this extension in time the "diachronic" dimension of
reality. Now, as we have seen, we cannot situate ourselves with respect
to the reality in which we are immersed unless we detect some kind of
order in it. We have discussed so far "synchronic" order, i.e., the mutual
ordering of things one with respect to the other at a given instant of time.
That may be seen as order in space, as long as we consider things and
beings belonging to the material universe. Order in time is another story.

The Role of Time

As I mentioned before, the clockwork image still holds for one particular
aspect of the universe: its limited but probably valid analogy with a computer at work. The idea that there is an invisible intangible built-in clock
which forces the whole system to go on and on toward an unimaginable
future provides an answer of a sort to such questions as: Why do events
follow one another? Why does the machine of the universe not stop? Or
is the "whole show" just a delusion? If so, is it not necessary to explain
why we have the sensation that there are a past, a future, and a present?

These, and similar questions, had been in the minds of the ancient
Greeks since the time of Homer, the singer of the war of Troy. Parmenides, the great philosopher of circa 500 B.C. whom we shall meet

---

2. J. R. R. Tolkien, *The Lord of the Rings*, part 2: *The Two Towers* (1965; New York:
Ballantine 1973), 395.

again later, declared that what really exists cannot change, because being is permanent, and therefore time and change are mere delusions. In the famous Bhagavad Gita, the sacred poem of India which speaks of reincarnation and of duty to God in a fascinating though often perplexing way, some commentators have found the idea that even life and death are delusions. This is one way of declaring that there is something absolute in control of everything. What has science to say about that? Indeed, has science anything to say about that? It has, because it is (or is intended to be) a set of methods and data concerning change. Therefore, if science has discovered anything unchangeable which underlies all change, we should consider it very seriously.

In the very foundations of today's science there are time invariants, for otherwise it would be impossible to guess anything about the past history of the universe. Just consider the principle of conservation of energy. It is true that it holds as long as a system can be treated as isolated, but such a situation may last a long time in interstellar space. During that time the energy does not change. One could even pretend that the energy of the whole universe is an absolute time invariant. A different sort of permanence is that of the electron, which is believed to have a lifetime longer than the probable life of the universe.

But there is another aspect of fundamental science that is not a matter of invariance in time, for it goes beyond time, and that is relativistic space-time. If Einstein's project of treating matter as an aspect of space-time is ever completely realized, then space-time should be seen as something underlying material entities just as we observe them: material objects are like vortices in space-time.[3] As Torrance pointed out, science has discovered, mainly through James Clerk Maxwell's and Albert Einstein's work, "the indissoluble unity of structure and substance, or of form and being, and not least the primacy of the inherently invisible, intangible structure of the space-time metrical field."[4] Time cannot be separated from space, and even in cosmological theories, particularly the Big Bang theory, where the universe is assumed to evolve in time, the space-time structure is actually assumed to be a feature of the universe; time, in particular, conforms to the definition Aristotle gave of it, since it turns out to be the "measure of change." This definition makes it acceptable that astrophysicists should speak of "the first 10^{-40} seconds" in the life of the universe.

These fleeting remarks concern an extremely complicated scientific and philosophical problem regarding the existence of a basic texture of the universe which is both time and space, and is therefore neither time nor

---

3. For details and references cf. G. J. Whitrow, *The Natural Philosophy of Time* (Oxford: Clarendon Press, 1980).

4. Torrance, *Transformation*, 234 and passim.

space; indeed, this texture is not directly observable or measurable as such. When we say that the "world distance" *s* between two events A and B is the square root of their space distance *r* squared minus the square of the distance *ct* light would cover at its velocity in vacuum *c* during the time interval *t* separating A and B,

$$s = \sqrt{r^2 - c^2 t^2},$$

we are also saying that there is no way to measure directly (i.e., to compare using a standard ruler) a world distance, because what we really have to measure are a space distance and a time interval. This is what Torrance means when he says that space-time is beyond direct sense detection. But that is precisely the point: Parmenides would say that what we detect by our senses is not actual reality — reality is an underlying foundation only accessible to the intellect. Science would contradict itself if it denied the reality of observed facts; however, with space-time science seems to have come up with a result in line with the ideas of Parmenides, and it has been forced to admit that there are aspects of reality that the senses cannot perceive as such. We have seen another all-important example in the preceding chapters, namely organization. Both space-time and organization open the way for science to admit that there may be entities that are not sensible in the ordinary sense, but whose existence could even be scientifically assessed.

The coincidence with the views of Parmenides, however, is only partial. One cannot conclude from the theory of relativity *sic et simpliciter* that space and time, taken separately, are not real. In fact, in relativity theory the fourth coordinate is qualitatively different from the three spatial ones — as even those readers who are not familiar with that theory may have realized by noticing that $c^2 t^2$ in the above equation carries a minus sign. Whereas two points in space may be anywhere, two events with a cause-effect relation follow one another in the familiar order, the cause before the effect, even for observers moving one with respect to the other, who will measure different time intervals between the two events.

Therefore, apart from the opening of science to the "inherently intangible and invisible," the conclusion that change and time need not be the fundamental properties of the universe is not implicit in the recognition of the "substructure" that is space-time. That recognition is at most one aspect of the general problem of time, for there are arguments in favor of the view put forward by another ancient Greek philosopher, Heraclitus (ca. 500 B.C.), who believed that the only reality is change, and hence the flow of time. Heraclitus's view is so appealing that it has had many avatars, with modifications and improvements, during the twenty-five centuries since its first formulation; the most recent ones being the philosophical schemes proposed by Bergson at the end of the nineteenth century and by Whitehead a few decades later. Within science, the temptation toward a radical stand in this sense has arisen with the discovery of universal irreversibility, which suggested the title of the famous book by Ilya Prigogine we have already had occasion to cite — *From Being to Becoming*. In fact, that title refers specifically to the transition from the view of change based on the classical mechanics of one- and two-body systems to that based on the mechanics of many-body systems and on statistical mechanics. According to the former the past and the future of every thing are contained in its present, at least for a sufficiently powerful mind; according to the latter, the sheer number of particles constituting most systems is the cause of a behavior that is best described by saying that a system may well *forget its history*, so that its present is only partially a consequence of its past, and its future is unpredictable. We shall dwell on these points later in this chapter; here let us go back to being and becoming. Despite his insistence on "creation of information" and irreversibility, Prigogine did not mean that there are no persistent entities; indeed, he admits the existence of things endowed with a measure of permanence, like living beings.

Thus, the position of today's science is closer to a position of compromise, as was proposed, precisely to solve the Parmenides-Heraclitus controversy, by Aristotle. We shall see details later, but the fact that being and becoming are not alternatives must be acknowledged before continuing the present discussion of time, in order that the claim that time and becoming are essential features of the universe and of all that it contains should not be mistaken for a philosophical standpoint on the being-becoming conflict. Summarizing what we have seen and anticipating what we are going to see, let us start from the following list of basic points:

- There is in the universe an observer-independent structure involving space and time together, with respect to which the quantitative separation of two events is the same for all observers.

- The fundamental principles of physics, particularly the mass-energy conservation principle, are valid with reference to space-time, and as such they are beyond time.

- Nevertheless, time itself has absolute characteristics inasmuch as, if for a given observer two effects are related to one another in time, e.g., one is the cause of the other and therefore precedes it, then the same relation in time must hold for any observer. It is the measurement of the pertinent time interval that will be different for observers in motion with respect to one another, not the past-future relation.

- In the sensible universe all that is becomes, and becoming implies a privileged universal role of time.

- Nevertheless, there are permanent (or at least persistent) entities, e.g., living beings; with the discovery of the role of DNA in cells, science has recently been able to establish the characteristic property which corresponds to each cell's identity.

Becoming

The novelties introduced by the theory of relativity in connection with the scientific notion of time, and the accompanying fascinating subjects — from the paradox of the twins to black holes — have been beautifully analyzed in several books since the publication of Max von Laue's classic textbook on the subject in 1922. In 1995, Paul Davies's book, *About Time*, offered a nontechnical presentation of the conceptual aspects of time seen from the perspective of a physicist.[5] Since the perspective of this book places emphasis on ordered structures and organized systems rather than on fundamental physics, I think it is not reasonable to try to review here the topics covered by Davies's book and the others referred to above. The aspect of interest here is rather the relation between time and *becoming*, which is a property of individual things and beings and of their associations. Becoming, according to current cosmology, is also a property of the whole universe, and it is then related to a special sort of time, cosmic time, which may be seen as the specific time of the universe as such.

A famous physicist and astrophysicist who took becoming into serious consideration was Sir Arthur S. Eddington, the creator of the theory of star evolution. We can perhaps grasp some of the deepest implications of that concept by reflecting on a few of Eddington's reflections. The first consideration points to the fact that,

> Unless we have been altogether misreading the significance of the world outside us — by interpreting it in terms of evolution and progress, instead of a static extension — we must regard the feeling of "becoming" as (in some respects at least) a true mental insight into the physical condition which determines it.[6]

Eddington was writing before the boom in general interest on becoming, which took place under the combined action of the rise of biology and advances in the thermodynamics of systems out of equilibrium. The most influential personality at the beginning of the boom was Prigogine, whom we have already mentioned; he proposed a general scientific theory of becoming, showing in particular why increase in order, as observed

---

5. P. Davies, *About Time: Einstein's Unfinished Revolution* (New York: Schuster/Viking, 1995).

6. A. S. Eddington, *The Nature of the Physical World* (1935; reprint, London: Dent, Everyman's Library, 1947), 95.

in living systems, is perfectly compatible with the laws that govern non-living matter and is not in contradiction with the second principle of thermodynamics (the principle of universal decay; see chapter two and below). Yet, it was Eddington who appeared to be most keenly aware of the double problem becoming poses: its scientific status and the relation between human experience, which always has a subjective side, and what is supposedly objective inasmuch as it is scientific.

This problem has many facets; here we need only consider a few of them. First of all, how can becoming be objective — which implies at least comparison between what different observers experience — if time is relative? The answer is to be found in the concept of proper time (also called local time), which is little discussed in many books, perhaps because it belongs to our ordinary experience. The point is the following. If the world distance s of two events (cf. formula above) is divided by the velocity of light c, one finds that its spatial part yields the time (r/c) a light ray requires to cover the spatial distance between the places where the events take place. If that time is negligible, then the absolute value of s/c is practically identical to the time interval between the two events. This is tantamount to stating that all events taking place in a region of space small enough to be crossed by light rays in a negligible time have a common time, to be called proper or local, which is the time measured by an observer at rest or moving very slowly in that region of space.

Since, in addition, the condition that the cause precedes the effect has universal validity, two conclusions may be drawn:

- in reflections on the experience of becoming the ordinary separation between time and space is all right, because it always concerns an observer, the objects sharing his local time, as well as the local images of distant objects;

- at least up to suitable quantitative corrections, becoming can be scientifically compared and assessed even when it is the object of the experience of different observers moving with respect to one another at speeds that are significant fractions of that of light.

Thus, we can forget about relativity in discussing becoming, except in the case of quantitative comparison of observations made by observers moving at high speed with respect to one another. For example, the great wonder that is the development of intelligence in a baby, as experienced by its parents and relations, does not require Einstein's theory. Parents on earth and parents traveling in a starship at a speed close to that of light with respect to earth would have the same experience, including the ages at which the baby starts, for example, to recognize its mother or make conscious choices. Only if the parents were somehow to keep people on earth informed of their experience would there appear a discrepancy, for it would turn out that their baby is still, say, three months old when a child born at the same time on earth is six; but that would change nothing of the experience itself. This brings us back to the question of a universal clock, which is the metronome of the Dance. In a textbook of philosophy, the answer would require a complicated analysis.[7] For our purposes, however, it will be enough to say that any given elementary manifestation of becoming, say a certain enzymatic reaction or the rusting of iron, proceeds everywhere at the same rate, provided the rate is measured by a local observer practically at rest with respect to the system where that process is taking place. In this sense at least there is a universal time, and we can call it "the time of the Dance."

The Time of the Dance

The idea that an observer's proper time is a manifestation of an "essential" time, which belongs to matter anywhere, implies two fundamental premises, which have been gradually discovered and finally accepted formally by today's science, namely that

- time is, like becoming, an inherent feature of the sensible world itself, not just a "form of understanding," a frame imposed by our intellect on chaotic sensations arriving from outside;

- any observer anywhere in the universe sees in the same way the flow of time, which governs the universal Dance, in accordance with the *cosmological principle* on which today's cosmology rests.

These points allow us to claim that what we see on earth and from earth is the real Dance of the Universe.

Now consider the more specific question: what is the essence of becoming? The answer is contained in two different points.

- In general, things or beings in the material world do not remain exactly the same in two successive instants; there is a sort of driving force, like the voltage of the battery of an electronic watch (or the potential energy of the spring of a mechanical one), which, as it were, forces every system to "move in time" from what we call the past to what we call the future.

- Becoming assigns an "arrow" to time, because the succession between past and future is common to all systems and is *irreversible*, for the past is the realm of all that is unchangeable, all that is a fact, whereas the future is the realm of possibilities and of choices.

7. A brief introduction to this problem has been given by Davies, *About Time*, ch. 5.

It sounds almost unbelievable that, as has been mentioned, until the middle of the nineteenth century the standard interpretation of mechanics — the reference discipline of classical science — had it that a sufficiently powerful mind could deduce the past as well as the future of the universe from knowledge of its state at a given instant. With the work of the Austrian physicist Ludwig Boltzmann (1844–1906) irreversibility was granted citizenship in fundamental science by attributing it to the random motions of enormous numbers of particles, but even so it was not accepted as a feature of material reality as such. Even more unbelievable is that most Christian scientists did not see anything perplexing in the deterministic view, which substantially denied any objectivity to free will. Today's science is far wiser, for it admits precisely that the future is open — and in that sense the allowance for random events has a very positive significance; we shall see that it has a great value for an opening to the possible existence of a spiritual dimension of the world.

In this connection let us reflect on Eddington's suggestion that becoming, and hence the arrow of time, is an indication of the mind's ability to have a direct insight into certain features of sensible reality. Because of this and similar statements, Eddington was considered by some philosophers an idealist, for whom matter is "mind-stuff."[8] Those criticisms were perhaps necessary to show that certain statements of his which bear on philosophical problems are to be taken *cum grano salis*, for they are perhaps phrased in a form which to a philosopher means something other than what is really meant. However that may be, I think we need only retain Eddington's point in the sense that nature and our minds run on parallel rails, or, if you prefer, that there are ultimate structures of reality common to the sensible reality "out there" and to our minds. These ultimate structures make possible what is called the intelligibility of nature; if they are received from outside, then they are not mediated by the senses. Personally, I prefer the notion that they are structures of the mind, similar to Jung's archetypes, very close to the ultimate beliefs we have seen in the preceding chapter; but the point of interest here is independent of the interpretation chosen.

In sum, time has an arrow, that is, the past is qualitatively different from the future, so that the direction of time cannot be reversed even at the most idealized level of science; and we *know* that there is such an arrow, although no experiment reveals it directly to our senses. With this premise, let us see how Eddington handles the scientific side of the story:

> The curious thing is that, although the arrow is ultimately found among the messages from outside, it is not found in the mes-

8. L. S. Stebbing, *Philosophy and the Physicists* (Harmondsworth, Eng.: Penguin, 1944).

sages from clocks, but in messages from thermometers and the like instruments which do not ordinarily pretend to measure time.

From the point of view of philosophy of science the conception related with entropy [a physical quantity strictly associated to temperature] must I think be ranked as the great contribution of the nineteenth century to scientific thought. It marked a reaction from the view that everything to which science need pay attention is discovered by a microscopic dissection of objects. It provided an alternative standpoint in which the centre of interest is shifted from the entities reached by the customary analysis (atoms, electric potential, etc.) to qualities possessed by the system as a whole, which cannot be split up and located — a little bit here, and a little bit there.[9]

Thus, reflection on becoming led Eddington to realize that through entropy science was discovering the limits of reductionism, on which we have dwelt in the preceding chapter and on which we shall pause again.

Processes and Processing

In a sense, the very notion of time implies order of a sort, for non-simultaneous events can always be classed according to their succession in time. Time has an "arrow" — past and future cannot be interchanged; therefore, in a set of nonsimultaneous events one can always tell which comes first, which comes second, and so on. This kind of ordering is basic to understanding. The behavior of a person or the foreign policy of a country cannot be explained without recourse to the previous history of that person or country. The same is true of all physical systems but the simplest ones. For example, the strange phenomenon of "fatigue" in materials — the sudden breaking down of a material that has withstood for years stresses far below its yield stress — is certainly the result of memorization of strains, although the details of how it comes about are still unclear.

However, knowledge of the order in time of a given set of events is not sufficient for understanding. You have to consider the right sequence, select the events relevant to the situation you want to understand, and look for a more sophisticated sort of order, which does not reduce to labeling events according to their order of appearance on the stage of reality. Like the attitudes and postures of the dancers in a ballet, the events in question must be parts of a particular movement of the dance, extending over a certain lapse of time. They are ordered not just because they follow one another, but because they tell a story or build a picture

9. A. S. Eddington, *Nature*, 105–107.

at a certain time, or yield a certain end result. The Great Dance is composed of movements of that sort. Accordingly, the whole universe is the interplay of ordered sequences of events, that is, *processes*, which in turn combine into higher level processes, and so on. Think of the formation of the galaxy, the solar system, the evolution of the individual planets, the emergence of life on the earth, the appearance of man: they are processes within processes or including processes, like the Chinese boxes that were so popular around 1930.

This intertwined network of processes is perhaps what inspired the mathematician Alfred North Whitehead, who turned philosopher when he was sixty-three, to propose around 1920 a "process philosophy."[10] Perhaps this is also why certain philosophers of science were always so attached to the notion that the universe is but a set of "events and processes."[11] These are extremely interesting and illuminating views; but to preserve one's sanity, one should perhaps keep in mind that, unless one calls "processes" what ordinary people call "things" or "beings," no philosopher would really deny that there are things — from electrons to cows — which either retain their identity for a certain time and are so to speak actors of processes, or are pieces of material being processed to make some object — e.g., a lump of clay made into a pot. Otherwise, the word "process" may still be used to qualify a thing, but it is then a technical word used to signify a certain way of looking at reality.

Within science, as far as I know, a process should be seen as a sequence of transformations of a certain component of reality — a collection of particles, a living being, a galaxy. These transformations may well cause entity A to become entity B, or to lose its identity altogether to the profit of other entities, but if there were somebody who claimed that *therefore* it makes no sense to speak of an entity A or an entity B, then an ordinary person would be permitted to ignore him. We all know that a dog or a horse answer to their names until they die; this shows that they have a sense of individual identity; how can we accept the idea that they are merely sequences of events, however logical that claim may be? Imagine that you photograph your dog Snoopy every tenth of a second from the time it is a puppy to the time it is old. I am sure that, given enough time to carefully inspect the pictures (a tedious task, by the way) almost anybody would say that they represent the same dog. Even if somebody said that the photographs represent the process by which a puppy becomes an old dog, he would still think that the puppy and the old dog are the same being. The more so if they knew the real dog. To get an "event and process" picture of a thing one could perhaps have recourse to the

10. A. N. Whitehead, *Process and Reality: An Essay in Cosmology* (New York: Free Press, 1978). Actually, the term "process" as used by Whitehead appears to refer to the embodiment of eternal ideas in matter.

11. Popper and Eccles, *The Self and Its Brain*, 7.

general theory of systems,[12] and point out that the identity of a system in the strong sense may well be ensured by processes taking place in it; but even so the main point remains unaffected: because of "homeostasis," the characteristic ability of such a system to retain its identity in a changing environment (cf. chapter two), those processes give rise to a persistent entity like your dog Snoopy.

This is a point we want to dwell upon. Suppose we speak, for example, of "the process of growing" of a living being. Then we presuppose a certain permanence of that living being. Do you remember the old man who caused the perplexity of his son in quest of wisdom, as reported by Alice to the Caterpillar?

> "You are old, father William," the young man said,
> "and your hair has become very white;
> and yet you incessantly stand on your head —
> do you think, at your age, it is right?"[13]

Well, despite his white locks, one would say that father William was undoubtedly the same person as when he was a child; the process of aging, however unpleasant it may be, respects to some extent the identity of the being or object undergoing it. That is why the ancient Greeks were so puzzled by change; they kept asking one another: how can a thing change, and still be the same? After Parmenides, who denied the reality of change, and Heraclitus, who claimed that everything flows (πάντα ρεῖ = panta rhei), came Aristotle, who pointed out that things do have a measure of permanence, but — in addition to being susceptible to forced change — they have a tendency to change, each in its own way, and that tendency is most manifest in living beings. His great discovery in the philosophy of nature was that as long as something has an identity of its own, that identity is made up of what that thing is and "what it can become because of its own nature." It has taken twenty-three centuries for science to find out again that selfsame thing, albeit in a different and richer language, with Prigogine's notion of steady-state systems out of equilibrium, already often mentioned in this book, and with the discovery of the genetic programming of living beings.

After the above commentary on what has been called a process in a very philosophical sense, let us consider the questions: what are the typical processes science has discovered in nature? Or are processes and processing related to technology? The answers are not obvious because most sequences of events which might be called processes, when they are not sequences of technological operations, are often called "mechanisms"

12. L. von Bertalanffy, "General System Theory: A Critical Review," *General Systems* (1962) 1–20.

13. L. Carroll, *Alice's Adventures in Wonderland* (Cleveland: World Publishing Co., 1963).

by scientists. For example, the process by which certain animal species evolved from a single ancestor species might be called "the mechanism of speciation," even though a mechanism really tells something about the rules that control the determination of successive events in a process — in the case of speciation, for example, Darwinian selection or what have you in its place. Undeniably, not having to be fussy about distinctions is a pleasant thing; however, in this chapter it will be wise to be. Therefore, I suggest that we retain the term "process," even when ordinary usage would have "mechanism," for a chain of successive transformations, regardless of whether they are spontaneous or are due to external causes (as in technological processing).

With this premise, let us consider first of all changes brought about by external actions. We say that "something is being processed" to mean that it is the object of a sequence of operations aimed at transforming it into some final product. This sequence of operations is the process to which the initial material is submitted. The verb "to process" is rather new, but the reality to which it refers has been around for a long time. Thus, pot making — the world's most ancient craft — could be described as the processing of a lump of clay which yields a pot or a vase. The most recent application of the word "processing" is perhaps to information, but there too it is a word made necessary not so much by the novelty of the notion as by the novelty and variety of ways in which input data are transformed into output data. Think of image processing, from, say, a photograph to a computer file. It certainly is a good example, but it refers to a form of processing that leaves the initial information "as is," *viz.* simply made acceptable for a detector other than the eye by some sort of translation.

Genuine processing is not confined to translating into another language. An example is provided by character recognition (OCR) computer programs, which from the image of a text tell a computer "this is an *a*, this is a *b*," and so on. As to that processing which makes an image significant to us — the subconscious or conscious description of it — it must still be made by the human brain. One could imagine a machine endowed with a much greater recognition range than just alphabet letters. Then it could perhaps describe a landscape. But how would it go about it? In what order would it list the elements of the landscape? The recognition program will include some ordering criterion, e.g., listing the objects according to their distance from the observer. But there is a danger: the landscape — maybe one of those beautiful landscapes seen in the backgrounds in Perugino's paintings — becomes a mechanical list of objects: on the left the descending slope of a hidden hill, in the form of an arc of hyperbola close to its asymptote, then meadows in the shape of a trapezium, then a two-story house in the form of a parallelepiped surmounted by a triangular prism, with ochre walls and a red roof, a square stable, and, behind them, three roundish green shapes which partly hide a long blue stripe. Compare such a description with those of Tolkien, apparently so rich in details: they only tell you what is significant, and in the order of significance. The significance, in turn, is determined by the context, by the message the writer wishes to convey, and by the reader's personality — so much so that there are persons for whom Tolkien's descriptions have no appeal at all.

The process by which an image becomes significant is genuine information processing. It consists in a sequence of mental operations of three types: recognition ("this is a house"), selection ("the color of the house is not relevant to the present context"), and translation into a language (possibly the very language of the brain). Its end result is then presented to one's consciousness, which responds to it by certain emotions or feelings as well as by rational judgment and action.

Between the extremes mentioned here, the processes familiar to most of us as well as those only familiar to scientists (microphysical, chemical, biochemical, geological, etc.) can take many forms. They all have the following features in common:

- they are sequences of modifications (events or groups thereof leading to a transformation of the object or material undergoing the process or being processed);

- these modifications are time-ordered, because no two of them can be interchanged in time;

- the individual modifications include genuine change, reordering, and even suppression of parts, leading to a precise end result;

- the transformations of the material may be the result of the very nature of the object being processed (like growing), so that the object does not lose its identity; or they can make the object into something else, as is the case with prolonged heating of clay or decay of a biological tissue.

Deterministic and Stochastic Processes

A process can be either deterministic or stochastic. A deterministic process is one in which an event is "forced" to occur by the event preceding it and has characteristics uniquely determined by the preceding event. The end result of the process is a necessary consequence of the situation at the beginning, for a yes-or-no law controls the process. In principle, if that law is known, the sequence of events constituting the process can be predicted with absolute certainty from the initial conditions, for instance by solving an appropriate set of differential equations.

Stochastic processes are defined as sequences of random events (in mathematical form as "one-parameter families of random variables"). Each successive event may or may not have the characteristics needed to transform the system in a certain way. If it has, the system becomes susceptible of further transformation as a result of another event of the right type, if and when it takes place. Thus, in stochastic processes the end result is not certain. This is why they are said to be "ruled by chance," as if chance could rule anything. More correctly, they are sometimes called "probabilistic." They might be strictly random sequences with all possible outcomes equally probable, e.g., the sequence of the collisions of a molecule in an ideal gas at thermodynamical equilibrium, in which case they produce or preserve the conditions which make the miracle of appearance of order possible. They are particularly important in the treatment of universal decay (chapter two) at molecular level.[14] However, most stochastic processes involve physically different outcomes with different probabilities. They are not completely random because they are selection controlled and result oriented. This means that:

- comparatively few events, with different probabilities, are allowed to follow a given event ("selection" rules);

- the event actually realized determines the probabilities of the allowed events immediately following it; therefore, it controls to some extent how the process is developing ("result orientation").

Let us examine an example. First, suppose our process consists essentially of two steps, with the following tree: A branches out to B, C, and D with probabilities of 20, 30, and 50 percent; B branches out to E, F, and G with the same probabilities; C branches out to E*, F*, and G* with probabilities of 15, 25, and 60 percent; D branches out to E**, F**, and G** with probabilities of 5, 15, and 80 percent. The overall probabilities are given by the following table.

E	F	G	E*	F*	G*	E**	F**	G**
3	5	12	4.5	7.5	18	2.5	7.5	40

The conclusion that the process A-D-G** is by far more favored is trivial, but this does not mean that it is not instructive. The higher probabilities of the outcomes D and G** mean the following: "D is more likely to be the event following A than the two others; and, *if D happens to be the actual outcome* of the first step, then G** is most likely to be the outcome of the second step." The interesting fact is that, when we speak of probabilities, we usually think of repeated trials. But in each process it is the actual outcome that matters, and that is determined in succession

---

14. Jeans, *The Dynamical Theory of Gases*.

by the actual outcome at each step. This is what we meant by saying that the process is "result oriented," an expression which also takes into account a concrete feature of stochastic processes in nature: the fact that the probabilities and even the very events which can follow a given event, say D, often depend on the effect of D on other processes going on in the environment, so that the probabilities associated with the entire process cannot be predicted at the beginning.

The example given illustrates the point that in selection-controlled processes each event opens up a number of possibilities, which are like branches of a tree. A tree has many buds which can become branches, but usually only a few of them do; which branch will pass from potentiality to actuality rather than die depends on external circumstances or inherent rules. There may be an external ordering force, like a continuous flow of energy in a certain direction, or laws like those of chemistry, which, though exerting no direct action, rule out all the possibilities but one or a few. This is why we are speaking of control by selection. If we consider just one initial event of a certain type — say, a single collision between two molecules — then in this type of process the final event is never uniquely determined. It is unpredictable, though only within the limits set by the selection rules, and, if we like, we may say that it is realized at random out of a number of possibilities, that it happens "by chance."

As a second example, let us take the concrete case of spontaneous ordering in magnetic materials. When a crystal of iron is heated above 770°C (its "Curie temperature"), it loses its ferromagnetism (i.e., its strong response to the presence of magnets), and becomes weakly magnetic. On cooling, it becomes abruptly ferromagnetic as soon as the temperature of 770°C is reached again. On the atomic scale, the following process is believed to explain this phenomenon. At temperatures below its melting point, iron is crystalline, and below approximately 900°C its atoms occupy equidistant positions 0.256 nm apart,[15] forming a face-centered cubic lattice. For simplicity, let us suppose that the atoms are tiny magnets free to rotate about fixed centers. If there were neither an orienting external force nor a strong *coupling* between them, they would be subject to thermal motion, and would rotate at random in all directions, with rotation velocities determined by the Maxwell distribution law, i.e., oriented indifferently in any direction and with values distributed about a certain average with smaller probabilities the more they differ from that average. The latter would be the lower the lower the temperature.

Of course, temporary parallel orientations of the atomic magnets would be favored by a lowering of the temperature, which measures thermal agitation at the microscopic level. At first sight, this is not suf-

15. nm stands for a nanometer, i.e., a millionth of a millimeter.

ficient to explain the abrupt change in magnetic properties at a certain temperature, because the increasing alignment on cooling is expected to be gradual. Yet, precisely this alignment is the key to the puzzle. When the probability and lifetime of an aligned pair of atomic magnets reach a certain value, a pair has time to induce alignment of a neighboring atomic magnet, forming a three-magnet cluster; its field is then enhanced, and the alignment grows explosively to form a domain, which ceases to grow only when it meets another domain whose "seed" was formed more or less at the same time as the first one, and may have a completely different orientation.[16]

The example given shows why it is reasonable to say that stochastic processes realize order out of disorder. This statement certainly holds for the end result; as to the process itself, however, it is an oversimplification. This should be already clear, but let us try to be more concrete and explicit. In practice, one always deals with two kinds of real situations. If one is actually studying a "macroscopic" process, say the emission of light from a gas, then at the atomic level one should be dealing with many events of the same type, and the end results will be distributed about some predictable average. There is, so to speak, determinism in the mean. For example, an atom that has some excess energy because it is in an "excited" state may at any time get rid of it by emitting a suitable photon; but if there are many atoms in the same excited state, then after a well-specified time practically all the atoms have made the transition to a lower-energy state. The physicists would express this by saying that the average lifetime of the excited state under consideration is predictable. Thus, the macroscopic process under consideration is essentially deterministic; in this case randomness is actually *irrelevant*.

The other case where ordering factors are present despite randomness is when there is some sort of "Darwinian" selection — i.e., a process in which, after each operation on the object being transformed, a test is carried out by the very environment in which the process takes place, to ascertain that the result of that step fits it (whatever "fits" may exactly mean). This kind of selection can be invoked not only for biological evolution, but for chemical reactions. Actually, "determination by selection" is involved in both the examples already given, and we shall have to consider it later on; however, a chemical example will be useful here.

Take two chemicals capable of reacting with one another to form other chemicals, e.g., methyl chloride and hydroxyl ions giving methanol and chloride ions. The process yielding the end products involves collisions between water and methyl chloride molecules, which form a temporary

16. Cf., e.g., D. J. Epstein, "Ferromagnetic Materials and Molecular Engineering," in *Molecular Science and Molecular Engineering*, ed. A. R. von Hippel (New York: John Wiley and MIT Press, 1959); L. L. Landau, E. M. Lifshits, and L. P. Pitaevski, *Statistical Physics* (Moscow: MIR 1976), sec. 151.

unstable molecule (the activated complex), which then collapses, giving either the initial molecules or the end products. The collisions are random events; but the formation of the products is absolutely certain. Moreover, there is no significant formation of other molecules, say ethanol, formaldehyde, and so on, even though that would be compatible with the laws of chemistry. The reason is usually given in terms of thermodynamical quantities, such as free energy. But that kind of explanation is a justification in terms of general laws holding on the average; it is not a description of what actually happens. What happens is that, if other activated complexes are formed, they are extremely unlikely to collapse into anything but the original molecules; and if they do give other molecules, these have very few chances of survival, for they are extremely likely to break down spontaneously or upon collisions, yielding either the original molecules or the expected new molecules. Thus, the game proceeds toward the accumulation of the two new chemical species, methanol and chlorine ions, and every other type of molecule is eliminated or limited to a few individuals. When the new molecules are sufficiently numerous — i.e., as the chemists would say, when their concentrations are sufficiently high — collisions between the new molecules may give back the original molecules, so that equilibrium is finally reached.

Thus, a vessel where a chemical reaction takes place is much like a simplified version of an ecosystem where there is competition between new species and those which gave rise to them. Many species may not be fit for survival either because they are inherently weak or because they succumb in the competition. The species that survive are the only ones that somehow or other continue to be formed in spite of losses by spontaneous decay ("death") and by back-transformation into the old species. Of course, molecules are not living beings, so that the analogy must be taken *cum grano salis;* but it shows that selection-controlled processes are stochastic processes always having the same outcome, and thus, if sufficient information is available, they are determined by their outcome.

Perhaps the best designation of result-oriented processes would probably be "finalistic processes," were it not that a number of scientists and philosophers of science think that finalism is something good for religious assemblies, and therefore is not acceptable in honest-to-God scientific explanation. After Barrow and Tipler's successful discussion of the anthropic principle and related topics,[17] a more tolerant attitude has emerged. But the real point is that inherent finalism and intentional design realizing some aim of the designer are two different things — and this is perhaps a good reason why "result-oriented" is more acceptable.

17. Barrow and Tipler, *Anthropic Cosmological Principle.*

The Experimental Method, Reversibility, and Irreversibility

One cannot understand why irreversibility is such a hot topic in today's reflections on science if one does not tread again the path in time that has led to the present situation. That path started from my compatriot Galileo Galilei's work. There seems to be no possible doubt that he was the founder of modern science. And it is said that he founded modern science by introducing the experimental method: all the statements of science should be based on facts, and verified by producing new facts. One should know the kinds of arguments that made up the science of the Aristotelians of Galileo's time to realize how great an innovation it was. Yet, Galileo's fundamental contribution to mechanics — on which Newton based his work — is by no means a verifiable statement. It is a principle, the principle of inertia, according to which every body not subjected to external actions will remain in the same state of uniform motion (or rest) until such external actions take place. Now, the absence of external actions can perhaps be realized in space (although that is not certain); but, were it only because of weight, it cannot be realized on earth. Moreover, no situation where friction and/or air resistance are absent can be realized on the earth — nor, if you consider the presence of interstellar dust, even in deep space. Thus, contrary to current belief, Aristotle's physics was in better agreement with immediate observation than was Galileo's, when it claimed that every motion requires a mover. The great innovation, Galileo's principle of inertia, was the result of an idealization of actual situations. You can progressively reduce friction by lubricants, and then try to imagine what would be the situation if you possessed the perfect grease; you could experiment on a horizontal plane, so as to neutralize weight, and then generalize the result to free motion in space. Thus, the reason why Aristotle did not discover the principle of inertia was not, as certain popular books have it, because he did not care about facts; that, as I have already mentioned, was the feat of his self-appointed seventeenth-century followers. He did not discover it because he was a biologist, and his mind was, therefore, less prone to certain types of idealizations than Galileo's.

Reversibility belongs to the same class of conceptual tools of modern science as the principle of inertia. It is a characteristic of idealized processes that they are never completely realized in nature; on the other hand, they are extremely useful for the establishment of new laws and for the explanation of observed facts. In the nineteenth century, the science of heat transfer, production, and transformation into other forms of energy — thermodynamics — made extensive use of idealized experiments, precisely of the type which had allowed Galileo to state his fundamental principle. Later, Einstein did the same in several fields of physics, and called those idealized experiments *Gedankenexperimente*, experiments in thought. The *Gedankenexperimente* of thermodynamics are those where reversibility and its contrary appear most clearly. Let us consider them.

Imagine a cylinder and a moving lid, like the piston of an automobile engine or the lid of a modern wine butt. Now suppose you want to study the transformation of heat into mechanical work. You fill the cylinder with some gas (or leave in it the air it certainly contains), make sure that the piston or lid makes the container perfectly tight, then place a weight (say, *n* kg) on the piston. The latter slowly goes down and reduces the volume available to the gas contained in the cylinder. The pressure of the gas increases, and there comes a moment when the piston stops. The whole process is a thermodynamical transformation, but not the one of interest here, for the time being. What you want to observe comes next. Suppose the cylinder is at room temperature (say, 25°Celsius), and you start heating it. The pressure of the gas inside increases, and the weight is slowly pushed up. If you have some way to measure the heat, Q, you have administered to the vessel, and you know the displacement, d, of the piston, you can easily compute the "work," W, done by the gas which corresponds to that quantity of heat, and thus find the "mechanical equivalent" of heat: you multiply the weight by g (the acceleration of gravity) and by the displacement, d, and that will be $W = ngd$, which also measures the mechanical energy into which Q has been transformed by the process just described.

It stands to reason — as some friends of mine would say — that, if you divide W by Q, you get the famous "mechanical equivalent of heat," i.e., the mechanical work you can get from one unit of heat, say a kilocalorie. But, if reason has anything to do with this conclusion, then reason should be more cautious before drawing conclusions. Was the whole heat supplied to the vessel used to lift the weight? What about friction? What about the kinetic energy of the piston and of the weight? Or, for that matter, what about the weight of the piston? If reason does not answer such questions, then your equivalent may depend on the specific experimental setup used to determine it. The general answer is that the points to which the questions refer do not matter in an ideal experiment. Our mechanical equivalent of heat will be indeed independent of the experimental conditions, because in its actual determination we have carried out a number of real experiments enabling us to estimate with great accuracy what would be the outcome of the ideal one. In the latter, the heat absorbed by the cylinder, the piston, and the gas is negligible and all the heat supplied goes to the system; there is no significant friction, and the piston is weightless. What is especially important here is that, in addition, the whole process (the "thermodynamical transformation") is assumed to proceed so slowly that *at every instant the system could be considered at rest*. This means that the piston and the weight absorb no heat in order to gain kinetic energy. It also means that at each instant the situation is such that the sense of motion of the cylinder could be reversed, with the system retaining no memory of the positions, volumes, and temperatures it had had in the forward transformation. That is to say, the transformation we have imagined is such that every instant of time is an end and a beginning, and the driving force that decides which way it will proceed is infinitesimal. It is such a transformation that we call *reversible*.

In the example given, reversibility is a property only present in an ideal situation, never to be completely realized. Thermodynamics recognized this fact in the first decades of the nineteenth century, mainly with the work of Sadi Carnot (1796–1832) and his famous cycle. The second principle of thermodynamics states that — at least if large numbers of particles are involved, as is the case with the vast majority of natural and artificial systems — no real process leading to transformation of energy from one form to another is reversible. If it takes place in a closed system, energy is conserved, but part of it is anyway downgraded; it is heat at a comparatively low temperature, which in further transformations will perform very poorly. This fact implies that after a number of such processes most of the energy will be accumulated as very low-grade energy. This consideration, if applied to the whole universe, leads to that principle of universal decay which we have already encountered: the universe is slowly decaying toward a state in which all its energy will be stored in matter at the lowest possible temperature, and therefore no further transformation will be possible.

Today, what with the expansion of the universe and the special laws of quantum mechanics, the gloomy picture of a slowly dying universe is no longer so popular among scientists. But irreversibility, the basic property of all ordinary transformations, remains a fundamental aspect of the physical world. The paths of time are all one-way streets, and, as we have seen, "becoming," the central problem of the Greek philosophers of twenty-five centuries ago, is being recognized again as a central problem of science. One should say "is being recognized" because there are still many scientists who, as did the physicists of the beginning of the nineteenth century, hold a view which denies that irreversibility is an essential feature of nature. Despite difficulties that have arisen within physics itself, they still follow that extreme form of determinism which claims that, if our minds were strong enough to master a scientific description of facts where the tiniest parcels of matter are treated one by one, then the laws of physics would enable us to tell the state of the universe at any instant of time, past or future, from its state at one instant. This is tantamount to claiming that statistics, uncertainty, and irreversibility are not built-in features of nature, but features of science due to the limitations of man's ability to cope with the enormous complexity of reality.

The grounds for this obstinacy are not to be found in blind conservatism. What is at stake is the belief that nature is regulated by rigorous laws matching those of logic. The consequences of rejecting this belief would be dramatic, especially for popular views of God, which are naïve, but serve as guidelines to many people. The unexpressed argument behind those views runs as follows. The laws of nature are laws in the same sense as ethical or juridical laws; therefore, if nature does not follow rigid laws, and if those laws are not of the same type as the laws of logical thought, then God the Creator is not the almighty mind we expect him to be. But there is a flaw in this argument: what scientists call "the laws of nature" are generalizations of observed regularities, not, as human laws, rules imposed on responsible people. Nor is the fact that they can be expressed in our language in the form of logical *if . . . then* statements a necessary consequence of the fact that nature is the work of a supreme mind; why should that Mind work merely like a logician and not also like an artist? Why should its creation be fully understandable — "intelligible" — by lower minds, such as ours? We may well agree with Einstein's remark that "God is deep, but not devious," meaning that we must have confidence that we shall understand nature if we try hard enough, but then we must also agree with Einstein that the most unintelligible fact of nature is that it is intelligible.

Thus, no matter what our religious ideas are, we must be prepared to face facts that cannot be fitted into our own views of how nature should work. Irreversibility is a case in point. Whatever the determinists say, once a pack of cards has been shuffled, no memory remains of its previous order. Eddington expressed the significance of this point as follows:

A reversal of the time-direction which turns shuffling into sorting does not make the appropriate transformation of their causes. Shuffling can have inorganic causes, but sorting is the prerogative of mind or instinct.[18]

The two clauses of this statement are worth a brief discussion. The first one is the formulation of irreversibility as the fact that causes and effects cannot be interchanged: if a state A of a physical system is followed necessarily by a state B, this does not mean that if state B came before it would (or could) be followed by state A. The second clause is no longer acceptable *sic et simpliciter*, because spontaneous appearance of order is now admitted, as we shall see presently. That is why we have chosen to write "no memory remains of its previous order" before quoting Eddington.

A complete or partial loss of memory in natural transformations is the general property of nature to which the term irreversibility refers —

18. Eddington, *Nature of the Physical World*, 99.

although, to be honest, the existence of "thermostat assemblages," i.e., ensembles of particles with no memory of their past history, is actually suggested rather than proven by experiment. However that may be, it is interesting to read what Edwin Kemble of Harvard wrote on this matter in a comprehensive treatise of quantum mechanics:

> Experiment shows that the statistical properties of a large assemblage of independent identical microscopic, or macroscopic, systems which has been "aged" in a thermostat [i.e., a device capable of maintaining it as long as required] at a definite temperature T for a sufficient length of time usually become constant and independent of the initial state of the assemblage. The ultimate state is then defined as one of thermodynamic equilibrium at the temperature T. By erasing all vestiges of the initial state the thermostat acts as a history-destroying device. To be sure there are numerous cases in which this function is imperfectly performed.[19]

Oblivion of the Past and Uncertainty of the Future

We have already seen that, as illustrated by the clockwork image, the science of the latter half of the eighteenth century and the first half of the nineteenth century was dominated by mechanistic determinism, according to which all processes are continuous cause-effect chains governed by inviolable laws, so that past and future are all contained in the present. The past could be reconstructed and the future predicted with absolute rigor from the equations of mechanics by a sufficiently powerful mind. Although it diverged from everyday experience, that belief was supported by many great successes, especially in astronomy, and it continues to have many successful applications today. Just think of the well-known prediction of solar eclipses and of the less well-known determination of the precise times of past eclipses, which has found confirmation (as well as applications) in the ancient records. For example, according to J. K. Fotheringham, the Chinese Book of Poetry *(Shi King)* "contains a lamentation caused by an eclipse of the moon, followed by an eclipse of the sun. The dates are clearly defined and are found to agree with the lunar eclipse of Aug. 21 and the solar eclipse of Sept. 6 in 776 B.C."[20] Yet, our discussion of stochastic processes shows that the picture about predictiveness and retrospectiveness of science has changed dramatically. The most recent development is associated with the popular topic of deterministic chaos (cf. chapter five).

---

19. E. C. Kemble, *The Fundamental Principles of Quantum Mechanics* (New York: Dover, 1937), 433.
20. *Encyclopædia Britannica* 1960, s.v. "eclipse."

The state of our reflections at this point can be summarized with reference to predictability and order. Noting in particular that retrospective predictability is equivalent to what we have called "memory," we can consider four scenarios:

- two-way predictability: the present contains information sufficient in principle to reconstruct in all details the past and to predict in all details the future evolution of a system;

- forward predictability: the present contains information sufficient in principle to determine the future evolution of a system;

- backward predictability: the present has a complete memory of the past, i.e., contains information sufficient in principle to determine the past of a system;

- unpredictability: the present does not contain information sufficiently accurate to allow accurate and complete predictions in either sense.

These four scenarios could be further split into "sub-scenarios" if a distinction were made between unpredictability and *partial predictability*. However, since otherwise science would be impossible, a measure of predictability must be characteristic of reality. Moreover, science has discovered that, depending on the field of inquiry under consideration, the four scenarios coexist in varying proportions.

The above fourfold subdivision also applies to order, because order includes as an essential feature that of obeying precise laws, and hence of having a fully deterministic evolution. Noting that the whole distinction hinges on the information contained in the present, we can build a list parallel to the one above as follows:

- stable order: the present is made of ordered structures in the same number and of the same degree of complexity as in the past and in the future;

- "chaos": the present is less ordered that the past;

- formation ("creation") of order: the present is more ordered than the past;

- disorder: it is not possible to make any statement about the relation between the degree and nature of order in the present and that in the past or in the future.

As in the case of predictability, it would seem that the actual case is one where each of the four scenarios is a correct but partial description of reality: there is a measure of permanent order which makes science possible, but there is also a drift toward disorder, particularly the possible branching out of ordered situations into new situations to which no unique order parameter can be assigned beforehand ("chaos"); there is a tendency to the emergence of new ordered structures, and there is a "noise background," which is entirely beyond the reach of our science, so that we cannot even know if it could generate or destroy order.

Armed with these precisions, the reader is now invited to explore two elementary mathematical illustrations of the above considerations: deterministic chaos and Conway's world.

Chapter 5

An Interlude on Chaos,
the Game of Life, and Chance

*Two computer simulations of real processes help us to understand
the role and significance of chance in the Universe. Deterministic
chaos shows a special form of disorder: long term unpredictability of events obeying full determinism. Conway's game of life,
supplemented by a simple additional rule, shows how simple selection rules make it possible for a random set of objects to evolve
with formation of order. Does that provide an illustration of the
"creativity" of chance?*

Deterministic Chaos – The Emergence of Order – Conway's World
– Chance and Appearance of Order – About the Role of Chance –
Chance as Cause

There are an infinity of machines which are completely equivalent to the universal Turing machine, and hence can emulate any other machine. Dozens of those machines have been described in the technical computer literature, but here I will mention only two: the billiard ball computer and the Game of Life. — FRANK J. TIPLER[1]

Deterministic Chaos

Another feature of the development of processes in time is the possibility of "chaos" — deterministic chaos and quantum chaos. The word "chaos" has done much to make that feature popular, and certainly partakes more of poetry than of science. Its introduction could be branded as advertising; but the advertised product is certainly worth great attention, and thus — except for its indirect contribution to the current very sloppy use of words — that advertisement is an honest one. What "chaos" actually means in this context is "unpredictability" of the evolution in time of processes governed by a certain law, particularly a deterministic law, which leaves no room for randomness.[2] Thus, clearly, this sort of chaos has little to do with disorder. Let us look at the question in more detail, using a standard example, an example which also proves a very important point about science: that problems need not be complicated to be interesting.

Let us imagine a population of x living beings — say, bacteria or human beings — per square kilometer and try to predict its evolution. We can assume that, in a certain period of time, the net increase (births minus deaths) of that population is proportional to x by a factor k, so that it is multiplied by a factor $\mu = 1 + k$ at the end of each period of time of the same length. This reminds us of the popular notion of population explosion. However, we can also expect that, as the density x becomes larger and the space at each individual's disposal becomes smaller, the birth rate will decrease and the death rate increase, possibly because of easier diffusion of diseases.[3] Thus, k must be multiplied by a factor

---

1. *The Physics of Immortality* (New York: Doubleday, 1994), 37.
2. For a concise but comprehensive presentation, cf. R. V. Jensen, "Chaos," in *Encyclopedia of Physical Science and Technology*, 1990 yearbook (New York: Academic Press, 1990), 47–75. The story of chaos has been told in a popular form by J. Gleick, *Chaos* (New York: Penguin 1987). For a more technical, but beautifully illustrated presentation, see H. O. Peitgen and P. H. Richter, *The beauty of Fractals: Images of Complex Dynamical Systems* (Heidelberg and New York: Springer 1986).
3. To bypass equations, skip to the last clause of next paragraph.

$1-\alpha \, (x - x_{lim}) \, / \, x_{lim}$, where α is a small number such that, for example, when x doubles k is multiplied by $1 - 0.1 = 0.9$ (i.e., it is reduced by 10 percent); and x_{lim} is an ideal population around which the density effects are negligible. If we call x_n the population at a certain time and x_{n+1} the population after, say, one year, then we can write the equations:

$$x_{n+1} = \mu x_n \left[1 - \alpha \frac{x_n - x_{lim}}{x_{lim}} \right], \text{ if the result is} \geq 0,$$

$$x_{n+1} = 0 \text{ otherwise.} \tag{1}$$

Let us consider a few cases when the growth rate is fixed at 2 percent ($k = 0.02$, $\mu = 1.02$), the damping factor α goes from 0 to 3, and the population x_{lim} for which there is no crowding effect is the population at the beginning of the first period of time (which we may call "year" for simplicity). Let the initial population be 1000 individuals (Table 1).

A net yearly growth of twenty new individuals in a thousand — which is the case in our example in the absence of crowding effects ($\alpha = 0$) — would be quite large for many large-mammal populations; just think

Table 1

year	$\alpha = 0$	$\alpha = 0.1$	$\alpha = 0.2$	$\alpha = 2.0$	$\alpha = 2.5$	$\alpha = 3.0$
0	1000	1000	1000	1000	1000	1000
1	1020	1020	1020	1020	1020	1020
2	1040	1038	1036	999	988	978
3	1061	1055	1049	1021	1037	1063
4	1082	1070	1060	997	959	878
5	1104	1084	1068	1023	1078	1223
6	1126	1096	1075	996	885	413
7	1149	1107	1080	1024	1163	1163
8	1172	1118	1084	994	704	606
9	1195	1126	1087	1026	1249	1349
10	1219	1134	1089	992	480	0
11	1243	1142	1091	1028	1126	0
12	1268	1148	1093	990	787	0
13	1294	1154	1094	1030	1230	0
14	1319	1159	1095	988	533	0
15	1346	1163	1096	1032	1179	0
16	1373	1167	1096	985	666	0
17	1400	1170	1097	1035	1246	0
18	1428	1173	1097	982	488	0
19	1457	1176	1097	1038	1135	0
20	1486	1179	1097	979	767	0

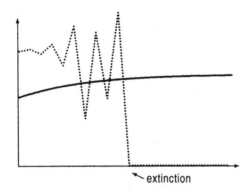

extinction

Figure 1: Trends in "population" change for $\mu = 1.02$ (individuals *vs.* years). Full line: $\alpha = 0.1$; dotted line: $\alpha = 3.0$ (cf. Table 1).

that, at the beginning of the twentieth year (penultimate line in table 1), it would amount to 1457 individuals (second column of the table). Things being what they are, diseases and violence eliminate an increasing number of individuals as the place becomes more and more crowded. In a very healthy and nonviolent population, the ideal yearly growth is reduced by 2 percent after the fifth year, 14 percent after the fifteenth year, 21 percent after the twentieth year, and so on. If the effect of crowding is more severe, it may happen that the population rapidly attains a zero growth rate. This happens if the yearly losses rise to 3 percent, 19 percent, 26 percent, respectively (third column of the table).

Then, at the end of the twentieth year, the individuals lost are more than a quarter of the population: that is the price paid for zero growth. If the crowding effects are extremely severe, the population is doomed to extinction; in the last column of our table, it becomes extinct after nine years. Let us resist the obvious temptation to use the above figures to prove or disprove arguments about overpopulation and species extinction on our planet. For that, an exhaustive discussion of the validity of the approximate equation used and of the nature of the factors determining k and k' would be necessary, and such a discussion is outside the scope of this book. Let us rather consider the strange behavior of the population numbers in the fifth and sixth column of Table 1. In the fifth column, the population oscillates in a very curious way. In even years, it is above the initial value, reaches a shallow minimum and then rises again; in odd years, it is markedly below the initial value, reaches a deeper minimum, but then starts rising again. After a while the cycle is stabilized, as can be confirmed by computation of the figures up to one thousand years.

With $\alpha = 1.9$ (not included in Table 1) we have another surprise: the behavior of the results is the other way around, for at the start they oscillate wildly, but later they calm down, and finally they settle at 1010. On closer inspection another feature appears: the same values are repeated 1, 2, 1, 2, 2, 3, 3, 6, 9, 18, times before a stable value is reached.

These things are intriguing, because after all one would expect that such a simple formula as equation 1 would show a simple behavior — in this case a rise at the beginning and then a decline. In fact, the oscillatory behavior we have found is just a hint of a quite unexpected phenomenon. To see what this phenomenon is, let us first remark that equation 1 represents the law of evolution of many different processes, and the parameters μ and α can take values that could be quite unrealistic in the description of the growth of a population of large living beings, but would be required in the description of other processes. Let us take, first of all, $\alpha = 0.01$ and let us drop x_{lim}. The simplified equation

$$x_{n+1} = \mu x_n \left(1 - \frac{1}{100} x_n\right) \tag{2}$$

represents a special form of equation 1. Let us now consider values of μ larger than 3. This choice may be required to describe, for example, multiple amplification of a signal, obtained by feeding the output signal back to the input port a large number of times (say, eight thousand). In this case the variable x need not take only integral values. In general, application of the new equation shows the same trend as above, i.e., expansion, stability, or decline. But on closer examination a very exciting phenomenon appears. Suppose our equation describes the output-input relation in a control system, and consider an input signal of intensity 80 (in certain units), whose output will be fed back as an input eight thousand times, and then utilized. Also suppose that we have a slight inaccuracy in our input, say, of the order of 10^{-8}, that is to say, a few parts in *one hundred million*. As long as $\mu < 3.4$, the result is as expected, for the slight differences in the initial value of x are reflected in the output (beyond the fourth decimal figure). If the amplification factor is increased, but does not exceed a certain threshold ($3.4 < \mu < 3.57$), those differences do not affect even the fourteenth decimal figure: the device behaves as a perfect signal stabilizer. But beyond the 3.57 threshold something extraordinary happens: the final output signal is completely erratic, even for changes in the initial signal that are essentially negligible. Table 2 shows what happens; it is the simplest example of deterministic chaos I know of.

Compare for example the first and the last column of the table, and look at the effect of changing the initial x from, say, 80.000001 to 80.000003 — just 1 part in 40 million. This difference is what Lorenz, one of the founders of research on "chaos," would have called the wing beat of a butterfly in Florida.[4] One would think that it could not change things much. Yet, if the signal it sends is processed according to the law

4. See Gleick, *Chaos*.

Table 2

initial x	$\mu = 3.56$	$\mu = 3.58$	$\mu = 4.00$
80.000000	37.3814	35.9285	35.2163
80.000001	37.3814	37.8904	90.7073
80.000002	37.3814	35.8722	30.5397
80.000003	37.3814	38.4649	1.2112
80.000003	37.3814	33.8810	77.4860
80.000004	37.3814	37.9366	99.7604
80.000005	37.3814	34.3293	85.6966
80.000006	37.3814	34.1008	19.2086
80.000007	37.3814	38.7474	83.9889
80.000008	37.3814	34.7590	0.3304

we are examining, and if μ happens to be 4, then after eighty periods (which could be a few hours, depending on the length of the period), that tiny difference could give a final signal which is either very close to the input signal or practically nothing. If the output were related to the air pressure in Canada, one might or might not have a storm there depending on which of the two practically identical initial values has been, so to speak, activated by the butterfly's wing beat. If one has even closer initial values, the end result will be of same kind, provided one waits long enough. Apart from storms, imagine what the instability associated with equation 2 could mean if that equation really described a control device, e.g., a device expected to keep an input signal below a certain value in order to prevent an explosion.

One might find many arguments to suggest that the laws 1 and 2 are far too simple to describe real situations, and therefore the chaotic behavior they give rise to may be just a curiosity. Actually, our simple example illustrates a situation that arises in many real problems. In addition to climate and control devices, it can be predicted and observed in celestial bodies. Since it can typically occur in phenomena governed by systems of three or more differential equations, the motions of certain planets and planetoids (e.g., the small bodies circling Jupiter) can be chaotic, and such appears to be the case. Imagine the problem this could be for a space probe or even a spaceship crossing a region where that unpredictability arises.[5]

What is especially striking about "deterministic chaos" is that it is deterministic, i.e., that the process by which it arises is by no means ran-

5. P. H. Richter, "Harmony and Complexity: Order and Chaos in Mechanical Systems," in *The Emergence of Complexity*, ed. B. Pullman (Vatican City: Pontifical Academy of Sciences, 1996), 103–123.

dom, for each step completely determines the next step. The point is only that, if one is dealing with a process which, in principle, should repeat itself regularly, but the values of the "parameters" (in the above case, μ, α, x_{lim}; in other cases the masses and average distances from a heavy body of a number of small masses, etc.) are such that "chaos" is possible, then the slightest imprecision in the completion of each cycle may cause a completely different and unpredictable evolution of the next cycle. Now, tiny imprecisions are unavoidable and random, so that the evolution of such a process is also random and therefore unpredictable, despite the fact — let me say it again — that the laws governing the process under consideration are rigorously deterministic and perfectly known.

The implications of this discovery for science in general are dramatic. It shows that science has no way to predict the evolution of certain processes, at least under certain circumstances. Nature, even when it appears to follow laws that can be understood and translated into mathematics by human scientists, admits disorder along the time axis in the form of deterministic chaos. Luckily enough, as appears from our example, deterministic chaos is confined to certain values of the parameters. This means that it depends on instabilities which cease to be such if a disturbance arises that is large enough to remove the input signal or the amplification factor or the damping term from the danger zone. This is why, after all, scientific predictions work. The lesson in humility, however, should be kept in mind by every scientist, especially those who brand as scientific any fashionable prediction based on trends observed on a few cycles or for a few years.

The equations of quantum mechanics can give rise to "chaos." But in that case randomness is — within certain limits — a built-in feature of the reality described by the theory, and therefore it is less surprising. We shall not dwell on it here.

The Emergence of Order

Do you remember the learned Roman who believed that love of truth, justice, and beauty — what the Romans called *honestas* — was the only thing that could make life worth living? His name was Cicero, he lived between 106 and 43 B.C., and was killed by Antonius's cut-throats in one of the most beautiful corners of Italy, the coast around the bay of Formia, eighty miles south of Rome. To be sure, Cicero was not above all criticism, and was involved in the violent political vicissitudes of Rome before, during, and after Caesar's dictatorship; but his belief in *honestas* was genuine, and is witnessed by a number of books whose sincerity is unquestionable. It is in one of them that he wrote that famous remark I have already quoted in a short form, a remark more topical today than it was in his time:

Quod [quis] crebro videt non miratur, etiamsi cur fiat nescit.

(What a man often sees is not cause of wonder, even if he does not know why it happens.)

This holds particularly for order and disorder. That particular form of disorder which has been poetically called "chaos" is fascinating to both scientists and laymen because it is unfamiliar and unexpected. The much greater wonder of increasing order around us, challenging the second principle of thermodynamics, passes unheeded simply because it is too familiar; for that increasing order mainly appears as life, especially intelligent life, and its creations — from beavers' dams to man's tools, materials, machines. What general laws of nature lie behind the unceasing increase in order and complexity of nature, and how can it be reconciled with the law of general decay? We have already seen many facets of this question in our general discussion on the nature of order, but it is now time to recall certain points and to pause a little longer on the processes which lead to order along the dimension of time.

According to everyday experience, one would expect that matter, left to itself, would fall into disorder and decay. That experience has been translated into a fundamental principle of science — the second principle of thermodynamics. Yet, the birth of the tiniest unicellular algae in the sea plankton or in a forest — and, in the nonliving world, the birth of a star from a gaseous nebula or the birth of a planet by accumulation of cosmic dust or wandering rocks — are episodes of nature's unyielding effort to maintain a harmonious balance between order and disorder, indeed to form new order. The Great Dance includes death and disorder, for the dancers will leave the stage when their time comes; but it is largely creation of order against disrupting forces. This creation of order from disorder mostly takes place by stochastic processes; but can we say more about the trick by which disorder is made into order, the trick by which nature repeats every day the miracle, as it were, of "unshuffling" the cards of a pack? Hints at the answer have been already given. Let us make another step toward it, in preparation for the intriguing topic of autopoiesis, the spontaneous formation from scratch and the growth of structured and organized systems.

In many cases, the nature of processes leading to order in space and time is evident. For example, a planet might be formed from small rocks by the following process. Two rocks collide by chance, and under the heat of the impact they melt together; then another rock collides with the newly formed, bigger one. Then, the size of the rock is sufficient to attract by gravitational attraction the smaller rocks wandering about. The resulting mass attracts bigger and bigger rocks, and after every impact the temperature increases because of the transformation of kinetic energy into heat, until at last all the rocks wandering near enough to the big, roundish cluster of fused rocks that is the newborn planet have been collected and melted together. Then, because of the high temperature which keeps everything liquid at least inside the planet, the metals and metal salts present in the original rocks migrate according to their densities and fluidities, so that finally no memory of the original rocks is left, and the recycled-rock planet is like new.

In other cases, no orienting forces such as gravitation are involved, and order resulting from the operation of "self-amplification of fluctuations" is made possible by the operation of the built-in selective properties of matter. We shall presently begin a more systematic exploration precisely of that basic feature of the universe, the spontaneous appearance of order from disorder. But now, while we still have "chaos" in mind, let us begin by illustrating its constructive counterpart, using another simple mathematical model.

Conway's World

The model in question became popular among computer addicts around 1970 under the name of Game of Life; it was invented — as far as I know — by J. H. Conway, who published it in 1969 in *Scientific American*.[6] The idea is very simple. We take a matrix (not too small, say 40×40), whose elements are ones and zeros and perform on it the following operations:

- if an element is 1, change it to 0 unless it has exactly 2 or 3 neighboring elements equal to 1;

- if an element is 0, change it to 1 if it has exactly 3 neighbors equal to 1,

- repeat *ad libitum*.

This is considered to be an ultrasimple model of life processes because, if a nonzero element is supposed to represent a cell, then the "cell" may die if the number of neighboring "cells" is not right — as might happen in a cell colony — and a new cell may be born if three cells surround an empty space.

What is very amusing — and full of meaning for those who try to look under the surface of things — is that, depending on the initial matrix, in certain cases the ones grow in number and change their distribution without end, while in other cases they reach a fixed number and a stable or oscillating configuration. In yet other cases the matrix will become empty, a matrix of zeros. A rather general example is given in figures 2

---

6. Conway's game has been discussed in connection with computer theory by Tipler, *Physics of Immortality*, 37.

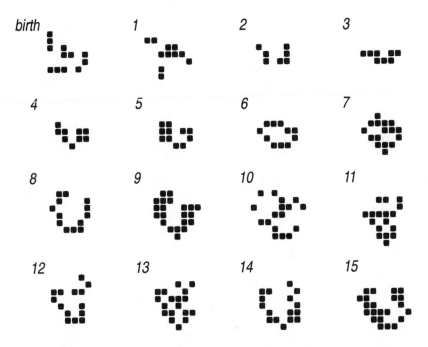

Figure 2: Evolution of a "colony" of 12 cells according to the Conway rules (cf. text). The figures give the five-generation cycles to which each arrangement corresponds. Subsequent cycles are shown in figure 3.

and 3. An initial irregular group of twelve cells (divided into four islands) reduces to seven units after ten "generations"; then the "colony" starts thriving, reaches twenty-one elements after eighty cycles, then attempts to divide into two "colonies" (between 80 and 110 "generations"), then unites again, reaching its apogee (a compact group of twenty-five individuals at the end of 115 "generations"), then separates again and starts to dwindle, until its dies at the 150th "generation." Note that one could illustrate the rise, decline and fall of an empire on the diagrams obtained by the simple Conway rules; one would merely treat the different islands as nations. Conway's model tells us that the Great Dance may well follow extremely simple rules, which are nevertheless creative, and generate extremely rich patterns.

A related remark of quite a different kind (to be considered again in the next chapter) is that, when we say that the sequence of figures 2 and 3 reminds us of the history of an empire, we are assigning to each diagram a *meaning*, suggested by familiarity with the history of mankind, and possibly prompted by a desire to understand the human condition. Now,

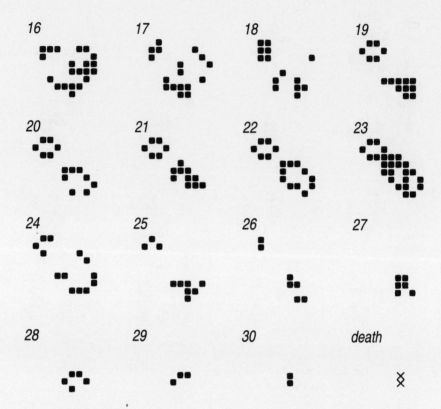

Figure 3: Decline and extinction of a "colony" of 12 cells according to the Conway rules (cf. text). The figures give the five-generation cycles to which each arrangement corresponds, cycles 16 to 31. The Conway rules (cf. text) imply that an isolated pair of cells cannot survive; therefore, cycle 30 (150th generation) is the last one in the life of the "colony."

moved by the historical suggestions, one might think that the twelve cells just examined simulate the rise and decay of organization. Actually, that is not the case, because Conway's world is not designed to include dynamical interdependence.

Yet, Conway's world can help us to grasp more clearly the mechanism of the emergence of order. Let us consider the case shown in figure 4. It converges to a combination of two distinct sorts of symmetry. The six-cell ring remains unchanged; the three-cell bar oscillates between the vertical and the horizontal position. This situation is a very simple form of *diachronic order.*

One can find many examples of the same kind by changing the initial number and configuration of cells. It would seem that, in Conway's

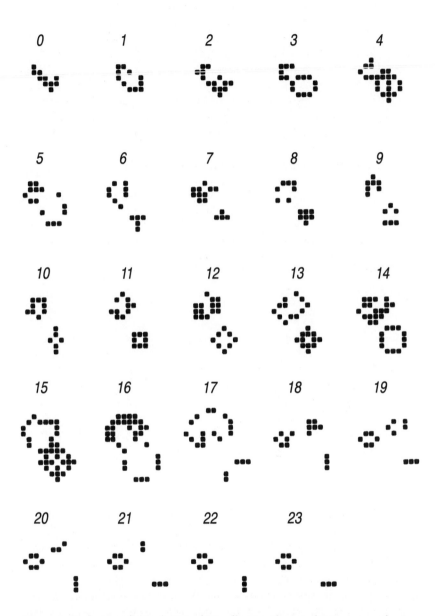

Figure 4: Evolution of a "colony" of 10 cells according to the Conway rules (see text). The figures give the "generation" number. Starting with the 22nd generation the population becomes stable, but its space distribution oscillates between the two last configurations.

world, a cluster of objects capable of death and birth has three possibilities open; to die, to reach an invariable symmetric state, or to survive indefinitely by performing the same cycle between two or more configurations. To be sure, this is little more than a guess, which would have to be proven by a serious mathematical demonstration, for no amount of computer evidence can exclude cases like oscillating expansion beyond any limit or deterministic chaos; however, it can be accepted if Conway's game is taken as a model of the kind of process we are reflecting upon. The question we want to consider is: What is there in Conway's rules that leads from relative disorder (in figure 4, an asymmetric arrangement of ten cells) to a system that is highly ordered in two different ways — stable symmetry and oscillation between two equivalent images?

The answer, of course, must be found in Conway's rules as listed above. But if Conway's world must match some basic features of our world, we have to consider two points:

- there is a clockwork that inexorably leads the cells, at regular intervals, into evolution channels leading each to a distinct new state (birth, survival, or death);

- the channel selected for each "cell" depends on the latter's situation, and admits of no exception.

This is an entirely deterministic process, but it is based on a way of looking at things that is completely different from the usual Newtonian approach, where situations are modified by forces. There is no force here, unless one considers a force the universal effect of the time of the Dance, but every object is forced to pass as it were through a sifting system, i.e., is subjected to *selection rules*, which uniquely determine its next state. On the whole, the selection rules act in such a way that only ordered arrangements will survive.

Chance and Emergence of Order

As long as the rules valid in that simple world are those listed above, one cannot really say that a completely random distribution of cells can evolve into order, albeit of that limited kind of order which is possible in Conway's world; after all, at least three cells in a very special arrangement must be present before a new cell may be born, and even then the cluster will be rather uninteresting, because it will either freeze into a square or die altogether. A simple new rule, however, is sufficient to make Conway's world include spontaneous emergence of order from a random distribution so as to model the emergence of order from chaos (in the standard sense, not in the sense of "unpredictability" used by the discoverers of deterministic chaos). We must assume that, if in our limited chessboard there are only a few cells, then a fourth evolution channel is open: a new cell can appear *at random* in the immediate neighborhood of any existing cell; and the probability that this will happen is high, say 70 percent, if there are one or two cells, but then it decreases, say to 65 percent, when there are three cells, 60 percent when there are four cells, and so on; so that after a certain threshold no new cell will be accepted by the cluster. This decrease in probability models a property we attribute to a cluster capable of surviving, namely the ability to reject or even kill foreigners. In our own world this is a well-known phenomenon already at the level of multicellular microorganisms, which produce chemicals inhibiting the addition of extra cells beyond a certain limit; this is something like the immigration quotas introduced by certain countries after a period when frontiers were completely open.

We have thus introduced into Conway's world the possibility of a chance beginning of the "creation" of order closely matching what is considered a plausible hypothesis for the appearance of that extraordinarily rich form of order that is life. The whole process modeled may be called "self-organization" or "autopoiesis," and will be examined in the next chapter in a more general context. Here, let us retain the essential point that it consists of two phases:

- the formation by chance of a cluster capable of growing and of dying;

- the actual evolution of the cluster thus formed.

The reader can already guess that selection rules operate in either phase. Try now to answer the question: are we entitled to summarize what we have discussed by the statement that chance has *created* the evolving cluster?

About the Role of Chance

To answer this question, let us anticipate here a number of considerations whose full significance will become clear when we have examined autopoiesis in connection with the origin of life.

As will be seen in the next chapter, the arguments for the emergence of life by a sequence of chemical reactions and associations from a completely disordered "primeval soup" appear to be scientifically plausible; albeit amidst a lively debate, supporting evidence obtained by *ad hoc* experimental studies is gradually accumulating. Nevertheless, in view of the high selectivity of the processes leading to the emergence and growth of order and organization, it is perfectly legitimate to be perplexed by the notion of chance as used in hypotheses about the origin and evolution of life. Confusion between metaphysical and scientific issues has even brought about unjustified emotional overtones, despite the fact that the spontaneous appearance of living beings from nonliving matter was considered an unquestionable fact all through the Middle Ages, when the existence of a Creator was accepted almost universally. It was Francesco Redi (1626–1698), a doctor and poet at the court of the Medicis in Florence, who first gave evidence that the worms typical of rotting meat are not generated by it, but by the eggs deposited on it by flies; and it took another century before the notion of spontaneous generation was finally abandoned.

We shall explore the return of spontaneous generation "by chance" from nonliving matter in the next chapter. Here let us return to considerations made in the preceding chapter on the formation by chance of an ordered structure, with particular emphasis on the claim by certain physicists that a spontaneous process could never yield such a complicated ordered system as the most elementary DNA-like molecule. Let us review their argumentation on the chemistry involved, keeping in mind the example of methyl chloride already discussed in chapter four.

Suppose you have the appropriate atoms and small molecules — essentially ammonia, methane, hydrogen, water, and maybe carbon dioxide — moving randomly inside a closed vessel. What is the probability that by a random collision they will form in a reasonable period of time an organic molecule of interest for the construction of living organisms? The answer is: nil. You can see that on the example of glycine, the simplest amino acid. For its formation, a methane molecule, an ammonia molecule, and a carbon dioxide molecule (CO_2) are required. The ammonia molecule (NH_3) must hit the methane molecule (CH_4) in such a way that two hydrogen atoms are expelled and a bond is formed between carbon and nitrogen (thus giving a more or less stable "complex," say the methylamine molecule NH_2-CH_3): then a carbon dioxide molecule must hit the resulting molecule so as to capture a hydrogen atom linked to carbon and replace it, so that finally H_2N-CH_2-$C(=O)$-OH is formed. Of course, the whole process might take place by a simultaneous collision of the three molecules, rather than in two steps, but a three-particle collision is far less probable than a sequence of two, as can be easily realized by thinking of a soccer game. As to the stepwise process, suppose the ammonia-methane collision has a probability of one in a million per second. The probability that the collision will take place in the direction and with the energy required to bring about formation of a "complex" capable of reacting with carbon dioxide will certainly be something like one thousand times smaller. Thus, you have to wait something like thirty years before you are sure that a single molecule of your first "complex" has been formed. The next step is by far less probable, because a carbon dioxide molecule must hit with the right energy and in the right way that particular molecule out of hundreds of millions of billions of billions.

You might think that one could wait until many molecules of the first "complex" are formed. But that would not work, because that complex may break down in the meantime because of a further collision, even if the favorable general conditions persist long enough.

If this is the situation for a simple molecule such as glycine, one can easily see what the situation will be like for a very large molecule (at least hundreds of times as large as glycine) such as is required for the self-reproductive behavior of a primordial quasi-living object, a protobion. Thus, the argument that life cannot have emerged by chance seems unassailable. The famous experiments of Oparin and others, which proved that glycine is formed when sparks are produced in a gas having the composition mentioned above, support that argument by suggesting that it would have taken violence to force the formation of glycine (and other amino acids); and violence is certainly the least indicated procedure to form much more delicate molecules, as should be present in a protobion. Life, as we all know, wants very mild and stable conditions.

Thus, common sense and the calculus of probabilities would seem to concur to make the hypothesis of spontaneous emergence of the supermolecules of life, let alone that of living beings, a science fiction theory. But the everyday experience of the chemists offers evidence that there must be something fishy in the above probability argument. Every chemical synthesis relies on chance encounters of molecules. Complicated supermolecules have been produced by self-assemblage in recent times.[7]

The physical reason why certain improbability arguments are mistaken is that they ignore the role of concentration, i.e., of the number of molecules per unit volume. In a chemical vessel — or, for that matter, in the primordial earth's atmosphere or in one of the droplets in which life might have first emerged three and a half billion years ago — there are billions of billions of molecules of each type. If the first step (say, formation of methylamine) takes place with a probability of one in a million seconds when there are but two candidates for the required collision, then in a droplet a thousand billion "complexes" may well be formed in a fraction of a second. Even if only one out of a million of them is successful in the next step, a million glycine molecules will be formed in a second. Of course, a million molecules is not too much, for they would weigh approximately 0.7 billionths of a billionth of a pound (12.5 10^{-17} gms); but if rather long times were available then larger quantities could be produced.

Another objection could be raised at this point. According to the example just given, starting from grams of the various ingredients, only extremely small quantities of the final product would be obtained. Now,

---

7. Cf., e.g., E. C. Constable, "Molecule, Assemble Thyself," *Nature* 362 (1993): 412–413.

literally thousands of successive steps of the same kind would have been necessary to yield a molecule resembling possible precursors of the simplest living systems. Under these circumstances, how can one believe that even an extremely simple life-like system could be formed? The answer is that the prevailing conditions on the earth in a certain period of its life were such as have to be assumed for the whole process to take place, and lasted long enough; indeed they were changed precisely by the appearance of life. We shall pause on this point in the next chapter, when we try to give a more detailed account of the whole topic. Here, let us go back to the question of chance.

Chance as Cause

A curious but popular conclusion often drawn from the formation of order "by chance" is that chance plays a creative role in the evolution of the universe. What we have seen might make one think that it is so: is it not the fortuitous meeting of two molecules with the right velocities and orientations that generates from chaos such an ordered structure as a molecule? Well, the answer is: no, it is not. We already know what it is that the question ignores. That particular happy meeting is only a condition for the rules of chemical valence to operate. The latter are "selection rules," because they do not force the collision complex to become a new molecule, but simply express the fact that, for a molecule to be stable, nature requires that it should obey certain construction rules, e.g., that a carbon atom should form four bonds with well-specified characteristics. True enough, there are cases where more than one molecular species is allowed; but then the possible molecules are limited in number and will be formed in precise ratios.

If you think about it, you will probably agree that the word "chance" stands for "absence of causes." Yet in everyday language we treat chance as the cause of certain events. For example, a friend of mine once objected to the claim that chance cannot cause anything by pointing out that we know of people killed by chance because a roof tile fell on their head exactly at the moment they were passing. I felt disarmed by that objection. I should have known better. There are in that case two events, one following the other. The falling tile may or may not collide with the head of a person. That is one event. The breaking of a skull is a different event, and is not the fact of chance. Had the victim worn a steel cap, that person would still be alive. What was random was the encounter of the tile with the head, not the ensuing cerebral commotion.

Thus, saying that, in the case of chemistry (or, in general, in the production of ordered systems), chance is creative is more or less like saying that chance makes choices because, when a sieve is shaken, only particles below a certain size will find by chance holes allowing them to go through. The main difference between the two statements is that in the latter case you have to have a sieve and shake it, whereas in the former case the "sieve" is provided by nature itself in the form of selection laws, the shaking by the thermal motion of molecules. One could say that anyhow the right collision might or might not take place. Let me say it once again: in processes of the type of chemical reactions the numbers of candidates for useful collisions are so huge that if there is enough time the result is virtually certain.

Concerning in general the claim that chance creates order, those who make that claim should also explain what the word "creation" means in this context. If it has its primary philosophical meaning of "something appearing out of nothing," then it would seem that the claim in question is worse than false, it is absurd. If "creation" means that order appears out of disorder, then the statement is not absurd, but it is false on two accounts. First, chance is not a force, it is the *absence* of a force. Second, what creates order is the selection rules, the laws governing the evolution of the cluster. The ancient Greeks and Romans did have a goddess who impersonated chance, but then it was she who took decisions based on dice throwing or something similar; nowadays those who assign to chance a creative role would feel insulted at the innuendo that they believe in any god whatsoever, so their point seems to be untenable beyond any possible doubt.

In short, all we can do with chance is to declare that — because it is chance — the germ of the cluster (in the example of Conway's world) might never be formed, just as a bingo number might never appear. But if it does, the cluster will follow a path which — at least in Conway's little world — has no bifurcations. It must die or be stabilized, so that, if many germs are formed, after a time all the cells will have formed permanent frozen or oscillating colonies. All this, let me say it again, if the *right* bingo numbers appear — i.e., if the growing germ is enriched by the arrival of a sufficient number of immigrants. If that is ruled by chance, it might never happen; but the probability of it never happening would be as high as that of the number three not appearing at least twelve times if bingo numbers are drawn a few billion times (putting them back each time). That is possible in principle; but would you really believe that it is a possibility to be taken seriously?

Chapter 6

Birth of a Voice

*The Great Dance evolves toward a richer and richer structure as
new order and hence new objects emerge from the universe's immense reservoir of hardly differentiated matter — from interstellar
gas to the primeval soup. Harmony in time implies a measure of
continuity: there would be a dissonance of a sort if evolution by
"complexification," which appears to be a fact in the history of
life as well as in that of the universe at large, did not apply to the
transition from nonlife to life. Can the difficulties arising in this
connection be overcome, not least the fact that the sciences of life
require that finalism should be admitted in science?*

Self-organization, Autopoiesis, and the Origin of Life – Science and
Religion on Life – The Case for Finalism in Science – Nature as
Intelligible Reality – Explanation, Predictiveness, and Openness –
Causes and Ends – A Dream of the Far Future – Finalized Behavior
and Coherent Evolution – The Universe and Its Teleonomy

One of the fundamental properties which characterize all living beings without exception: that of being objects endowed with a project, which at the same time they represent in their structures and realize in their performances (such, e.g., as the creation of artifacts). — JACQUES MONOD[1]

Self-Organization, Autopoiesis, and the Origin of Life

We have seen two aspects of order, order in space and order in time, and how they develop and evolve from disorder, against the general tendency to decay, by amplification of random fluctuations and by feedback stabilization. The most highly ordered forms known to science, those complex wholes with a specific identity that are the living organisms, are ephemeral, for they last from minutes to centuries. So far, science does not seem to have any hint that there can be organized forms similar to living beings surviving for millennia or millions of years, like the artificial star being Vanamonde imagined by Arthur C. Clarke.[2] Nor do the other ordered structures, e.g., the stars, live indefinitely, as far as science can tell. Yet, it is ordered structures that make the universe what it is, a dynamical unit full of beauty and wonder.

In Conway's world, we have seen order arise from chaos; but the kind of order we have been able to consider has been just permanence or oscillation. We have seen a process apparently modeling more closely the evolution of life forms, including their decay and death, in the case of twelve "cells," which could simulate not only the complete life cycle of a cell colony, but the historical cycle of an empire. Actually, in the latter case and more so in the simulation of the life cycle of an organism, the system must be assumed to have that sort of coherence which we have called organization or dynamical interdependence, whereas in Conway's world such a kind of relation does not exist; in that world order is only symmetry in space and time. If it were possible to introduce organization, then the properties of the "colonies" — clusters of cells in contact — derived from the twelve-cell initial colony would be those of single units, so that the analogy with, say, one or more countries or even with an organism would be better simulated, albeit at an extremely simple level.

1. J. Monod, *Le hasard et la necessité* (Paris: Seuil 1970), 22. – "... *l'une des propriétés fondamentales qui caractérisent tous les êtres vivants sans exception: celle d'être des objets doués d'un projet qu'à la fois ils représentent dans leur structures et accomplissent dans leur performances (telles, par exemple, que la créations d'artefacts)."*
2. A. C. Clarke, *The City and the Stars* (New York: Harcourt, Brace and World, 1953).

The evolution of a system up to the formation of a single larger unit could simulate the growth of a living being. Include in the process the random formation of the initial cluster as discussed in chapter five, and you then have a model of *autopoiesis*.

The sort of process which bears the name of autopoiesis — a word meaning something like self-making — has attracted particular attention in relation to chemical processes, because it is those processes that are assumed to have led to the spontaneous formation of the first living structures — the "protobionts." With chemistry in mind, Simon Hadlington explained the basic notion as follows:

> The term "autopoiesis" was coined in the mid 1970s to characterize a "living" system as a structure defined by a boundary within which occurs a series of interdependent reactions that regenerate the boundary and its components, which then assemble in the structure itself. By this definition autopoiesis is broader than simple self-replication, and none of the earlier systems could be classified as autopoietic.[3]

In agreement with its etymology (creative "activity" indicated by "poiesis," and reference to the very system that is being formed indicated by the prefix "auto"), the new word thus designates the spontaneous formation and development of a complex object having some kind of autonomous behavior (otherwise the prefix "auto" would not apply). Its meaning is close to that of "self-organization"; indeed, in the case of life, it can be identified with it. It is a scientific notion because science nowadays accepts the view that ordered structures and organized systems can emerge from chaos and "grow," at least under certain conditions, without the aid of external factors.

The concept of autopoiesis has been applied to the way in which our ideas become organized, thus forming knowledge,[4] as well as to material objects, particularly the first elementary living beings. In the case of material objects, its mechanism can be thought of as spontaneous assembling consisting (at least in the first stages) in the repetition of two steps (cf. chapter five):

1. the random encounter of two parts (say, molecules) A and B having certain properties;

2. the establishment of an interaction between the two parts resulting in a unit AB capable of forming a more elaborate assemblage upon casual encounter with a part C of a type in general different from A and B.

3. S. Hadlington, "Autopoiesis: Living Micelles," *Chemistry in Britain* 28 (1992): 10.
4. Cf., e.g., C. A. Skarda, "Understanding Perception: Self-organizing Neural Dynamics," *La Nuova Critica* (Rome), N. S. 9–10 (1989): 49–60.

These steps are followed by the encounter of AB with part C and by step 2, and so on. Similar steps also apply to the formation of a crystal from a solution; however, if the product shares at least some characteristics of life, at each stage the structure formed will actively participate in orienting and promoting development toward a system that will not be at equilibrium, but in a steady state dependent on incessant exchange of energy and matter with the environment.

With an appropriate chemical composition and under appropriate conditions, repetition of the above steps could give rise to extremely complicated units, provided the same conditions persisted for a sufficiently long time and there were no tendency to disruption of the units formed. In fact, the inevitable existence of some tendency to disorder will put a limit to the increase of order by the above steps. At a certain stage, further development of a unit formed by successive random encounters with suitable parts must take place by some more elaborate mechanism not relying on chance at all, such as the growth of a living organism. This later stage may include interaction with the environment that will favor growth until adjustment to the environment has reached an optimum.

Reflection on this stage of self-organization requires a discussion of evolution and of environmental equilibrium, in particular competition between individuals of different species. There are, of course, factors acting against the construction of order, particularly competing processes in the environment and the spontaneous tendency to disruption of coherence. These factors can explain why natural organized systems reach a certain degree of complexity and stop there, or indeed begin an inverse process of decay, such as aging. In this respect, the ideas of Manfred Eigen (a Nobel laureate for work on chemical reactions) concerning the mechanism by which, after the steps listed above, nonliving matter may have given birth to the first most elementary living structures, are especially interesting for the general theory of complexity. Before attempting to summarize the main conceptual lines of Eigen's ideas, let us take a brief look at the scenario to which they apply.

The first assumption is that, in the reducing atmosphere of primeval earth, electric discharges catalyzed formation of amino acids and purines, the fundamental building blocks of living matter. Solutions of those primordial chemicals were formed in water accumulated in small recesses in the rocks (possibly near hot sources on the bottom of the seas), and were thus protected from the violent temperature changes taking place in the open air, particularly those between day and night; these changes would not reach those natural reaction vessels with their full strength, and would cause them to heat up or cool down by at most a few degrees Celsius, enough to speed up certain chemical reactions and to slow down others, but not enough to bring about dramatic changes in chemical composition. Thus, the conditions were realized for the spontaneous formation of chains of small molecules, which in the long run would yield self-catalyzing or self-replicating systems, possibly contained in droplets capable in their turn of spontaneous multiplication. The self-replicating systems would be large molecules or groups of molecules of a very special type, carrying a highly specific and comparatively large amount of information, such as the length of the chain, the nature of the atoms forming it, and the number and arrangement of atoms and bonds. Their ability to catalyze the assembling of copies of themselves meant that they would hand on to other groups of atoms the information they embodied, and that that information would "survive" far beyond the limits of their natural lifetimes. If they could do so despite disturbances capable of disrupting the ideal incubation conditions in which they had been formed and despite the inevitable replication errors, then they would constitute the first timid premonition of life, the *prebiotic* molecules. Eventual formation of more and more complicated molecular and supra-molecular systems having the same characteristics would then lead the way to the appearance of life proper.[5]

The scenario just outlined is of course largely conjectural, but to most experts in the field it seems consistent with all that is known about the history of the earth, and deserves systematic assessment. Its substantiation according to the usual procedures of science is in progress, and, if it keeps its promises, it will constitute a great advance in man's grasp of the spatio-temporal order of things. One of the most important points to be clarified is the mechanism by which a self-replicating "prebiotic" system would be formed and the persistence and enrichment of the corresponding information ensured.[6] This is where Eigen's ideas come into play.

To simplify matters, think of those molecules, such as purines, phosphates, and sugars, which could be the building blocks of the simplest self-replicating molecular systems, as letters, and of the resulting systems as words. Any chemist would expect that many different sorts of "words" could be formed with the same "alphabet." Why is biological information only contained in "words" made with a limited number of the available "letters," arranged according to very strict rules, namely self-replicating molecules of the DNA type? To answer this question, Eigen assumed that in fact a variety of self-replicating systems (the "words" A, B, C, . . .) was formed in the primeval soup, but a sort of Darwinian selection operated. Consider for example the population of words A. This

5. For a recent discussion of the *status quaestionis* cf. A. Lazcano, "Chemical Evolution and the Primitive Soup," *Journal of Theoretical Biology* 184 (1997): 219–23.

6. The comparatively novel notion of molecular self-replication has been briefly reviewed by L. E. Orgel, "Molecular Replication," *Nature* 358 (1992): 203–209.

population would increase as a result of spontaneous formation,[7] faithful replication of A, and errors in the replication of other words; it would decrease as a result of spontaneous dissociation and errors of replication of A. Therefore, under steady external conditions, the various populations would change until equilibrium concentrations were reached. With appropriate parameters, the system of differential equations describing the approach to equilibrium admits a solution where only one "word" has a significant concentration.

Thus, although a number of important questions remain open, it would seem that a mechanism has been found to explain why — despite its appearance out of a chaotic situation — the molecular basis of life is the same for all living matter, at least on earth. However, there is a crucial objection, which Eigen and Schuster pointed out and attempted to overcome by the "theory of the hypercycle."[8] The objection is that the number of errors of replication would increase with the size of the replicating system, so that Darwinian selection could yield significant concentrations of one or a few comparatively short "words," but would not lead to the formation of self-replicating systems much richer in information. Eigen and Schuster's hypercycle can be illustrated by considering five "words," A, B, C, D, and E. Suppose that the system of these words is self-replicating not (or maybe not only) because each word is self-replicating, but because A catalyses the replication of B, B that of C, C that of D, D that of E, and E that of A. Then a steady state can be reached in which a particular "sentence" ABCDE is dominant and capable of self-replication. Thus, by a very simple model, Eigen and Schuster have shown that the gradual "complexification" (a new technical word for "appearance of greater complexity") of living matter starting from a chaotic mixture of its nonliving components is perfectly compatible with the laws of nature; indeed, it may correspond to a potentiality present in nonliving matter such as it is at a certain stage in the history of a planet. Of course, there is a large gap between the presentation of the outline of a possible mechanism and the proof that things actually happened that way, but work is being done in that direction.[9]

Let us now briefly review again the two basic objections raised against the whole picture, keeping in mind what we have seen at the end of the preceding chapter. One objection, which curiously convinced even eminent scientists, has been already discussed there. It consists in the consideration that the simplest imaginable replicative structure is so

7. Here "spontaneous" refers not only to successive random collisions between smaller systems, but to the action of external factors, such as γ rays.

8. M. Eigen and P. Schuster, *The Hypercycle: A Principle of Natural Self Organization* (New York: Springer, 1979).

9. For a commentary on the state of the problem, cf. R. M. May, "Hypercycles Spring to Life," *Nature* 353 (1991): 607–608.

complicated that its formation by random collisions is enormously improbable. This objection assumes that all the elementary constituents must meet simultaneously, which is not the case in the proposed scenarios. Moreover, in the situation described above, the formation of protobionts would take place in solutions of the required chemicals containing numbers of molecules of the order of the Avogadro number $(6 \cdot 10^{23})$, the same as happens in the reaction vessel of any chemist. The magnitude of that factor, the stepwise nature of the proposed mechanism, and the high probability that the conditions favorable to the appearance of life would remain so as long as necessary all concur to make what seems at first sight a terrific degree of improbability into a reasonable degree of plausibility. Indeed, from the point of view of a chemist — whose everyday operations, if the "simultaneous and unique" scheme were valid, would be next to impossible — the only possible doubts actually concern the correct choice of pressure, temperature, and concentration of the components.

The other most important — and undoubtedly more serious — objection comes from certain biologists. One of them, a distinguished molecular biologist originally trained as an organic chemist, once declared that he could not really believe that the theoretical schemes and fragmentary evidence presented so far could really account for the spontaneous emergence of such incredibly complicated objects as even the simplest virus; and yet viruses may be looked at as beings intermediate between living and nonliving, because they depend for their reproduction on host cells. In other words, even granting that the right environmental conditions could be present, the progressive emergence, complexification, and self-organization of molecular systems is not likely to have reached spontaneously the stage of living matter; for the way would have been so long, and the intermediates so frail and sensitive to the slightest changes in environmental conditions, that it is not reasonable to believe that, barring some sort of miracle, the end result could be reached.

This objection results from a personal evaluation, and one might be tempted to dismiss it *sic et simpliciter* on the ground that it is not "scientific." That, however, would be a mistake, for it is an objection coming from people who have a direct professional experience of the intricacies of molecular biology. The best answer cannot be more decisive than the objection itself, and is only a plea for a more optimistic attitude. As to present viruses, their simplicity is deceptive: their dependence on specific hosts proves that their very existence *presupposes* the existence of genuine living beings, which means that they cannot be similar to "prebiotic" or "protobiontic" molecular systems; of those, none has been found so far, perhaps because they were not compatible with fully blooming life. As to the general point, no genuine scientist would claim that the chemical origin of life has been completely proven, nor would he or she claim that there is much hope to bridge the gap between simple models and the incredibly complicated network of chemical structures and reactions in actual living beings. But it is not in human nature to give up so easily the quest for a more complete understanding of the operations of nature; the same sort of argumentation could have been applied in 1897, thirty years after James Clerk Maxwell's discovery of electromagnetic waves, to the possibility of remote control from the earth of objects like the 1997 Mars Sojourner.[10] One point in the objection under consideration has been already dealt with at a preliminary level by the hypercycle idea, which suggests a way in which complex molecular systems could be stabilized. Other aspects are being tackled by supramolecular chemistry, a field of chemistry devoted to the design and realization of molecular devices, i.e., systems made of molecules fitting one another as the parts of a machine and capable of performing a "function" — say, that of an automatic switch. But the way is indeed long, and no wise person would bet on the possibility that we shall ever be able to reproduce in the laboratory, starting with simple molecules, the whole itinerary of the emergence of life. The work under way seems to be making a slow progress toward a *plausibility* assessment of an assumption that would fill a gap in our understanding of the universe, and would also provide guidelines for guesses about several mysteries — for example, the possibility of life in other places in the universe. The feeling that even such a limited task may prove impossible is by no means foolish; but it cannot and should not stop us if our search for knowledge is a humble attempt to situate ourselves better and better in the universe in which we have been born.

Science and Religion on Life

In short, the evidence and theories we have seen are part of a *plausibility* study, nothing more. Only hints and fragments of proofs have been collected so far. The perplexity of certain biologists concerning the gap between what would be reasonable proof and what has been found is fully justified, and only people not familiar with distinctions between facts, conjectures, working hypotheses, and so on could claim that all major doubts have been removed. It is even reasonable to expect that — given for one thing the extremely long time the actual process must have taken, if it took place at all — it will never be possible to do much more than make the plausibility argument stronger. Let us pause a little longer on the reasons why science is nonetheless so keen on defending the notion of the spontaneous origin of life.

First, unless, contrary to the evidence found so far, nature is a chaotic mixture of occasional regularities intertwined and entangled with one

10. The tiny fully automatic vehicle sent to explore Mars by the Americans.

another in a multitude of useless duplications, science can only be a faithful description of reality if it satisfies two general conditions, economy of thought and internal consistency. That is to say, science should avoid duplication of theories and laws and should reject, in addition to contradictions, also not indispensable discontinuities. Now, the idea that the sensible world should be divided into an "inorganic" kingdom where the formation of order is spontaneous though limited, and an "organic" kingdom where unknown and possibly unknowable additional causes are at work appears to violate both conditions. In fact, it would require two systems of fundamental laws, which is against economy of thought and inconsistent with the scientists' basic conviction that nature is simple and unitary.[11] Moreover, it would involve no lesser difficulties were science to deal with the connections and interrelations between the two kingdoms. Scientists now know with a significant degree of certainty that all the most complicated processes in a living organism are chemical reactions obeying the same rules as those performed in the laboratory; they know that even the transmission of hereditary characters is entrusted to a macromolecule (DNA) whose constitution and structure is known or knowable (at least in principle), and obeys the standard rules of chemistry; they have confirmed, albeit without the slightest intention to do so, that Aristotle was right when he saw in integrated dynamical organization (chapters two and twelve) the difference between what is living and what is not. Therefore, plausibility arguments such as those we have outlined above (and if possible stronger ones) are what is needed to ground the belief that there was no discontinuity in the history of the universe when life appeared, and that a process of "complexification" (as some call it) has been taking place in the universe since the time when all that existed were independent protons, electrons, photons, and other particles at an incredibly high temperature.

Secondly, the enthusiasm of some and the correlated perplexity of others seem to stem from considerations unjustified from the point of view of science as well as from that of metaphysics. The enthusiasts claim that the spontaneous origin of life is a proof against creation — and indirectly against the spiritual nature of man — but they mistake the scientific reconstructions of the past for a description of how God may or may not have proceeded in creating the world. The perplexed, who are often afraid that belief in creation by God is incompatible with the spontaneous emergence of life, probably do not consider that, for those who believe

11. Cf., e.g., H. Poincaré, *Science and Hypothesis* (1902), trans. W. J. G. (only initials given) from French (New York: Dover, 1952), 145. The English translation is accompanied by an introduction by the eminent British physicist J. Larmor. We have detected a few imprecisions in the translation, and therefore we shall often refer to the original text: H. Poincaré, *La science et l'hypothèse (1902)* (Paris: Champs-Flammarion, 1968). References to the French original will be identified by the French title.

in creation by God, "spontaneous" means here "developing from nonliving matter without ad hoc interventions as far as the laws of nature go." Now, who established the laws of nature? By not considering that the God in whom they believe is the master of everything, including space-time and the laws of nature, they are paradoxically telling God that He should have created life in a way not susceptible of scientific description in terms of the very laws He himself has established. As to concordance with the sacred books, if the Greco-Roman and Judeo-Christian traditions have any right to consideration, truth cannot be in conflict with truth; therefore, in case of apparent incompatibility between *ascertained truths* in science and religion, the problem for those who accept both is to humbly look for the misinterpretations that must be the cause of that disagreement. Even the famous condemnation of Galileo was justified at its time with the claim that Galileo's proofs were not sufficient, not with a choice in favor of religious truth against scientific truth.[12]

The same sort of antagonisms and misunderstandings arise in connection with another problem, which we are now in a condition to tackle: the existence of finalism (also called, following Aristotle, "internal teleology") in the sensible reality. Mechanistic determinism held that science could only accept "efficient causes," i.e., causes such that the past determines the future. We have seen, both in dealing with predictability and appearance of order and in discussing the selection rules of Conway's world, that this is not so obvious in today's science. Let us take up the question in a systematic way.[13]

The Case for Finalism in Science

When one considers organized systems enjoying at least a minimum of freedom of action, post-Galilean science is confronted with a completely new perspective. Until about 1970, when Jacques Monod published the swan's song of positivism (cf. next paragraph), the stage was held by the hard-core determinists, those thinkers who claimed that freedom of choice is an illusion, not only as regards "nonhuman" animals, but as regards human beings. They would say that belief in personal freedom is an illusion, and if perfectly known, a person's history and the history of the environment in which that person lived up to the time of any particular

12. Cf. W. Brandmüller, *Galilei e la Chiesa: Ossia il diritto ad errare* (Galileo and the church: The right to make mistakes) (Vatican City: Libreria Editrice Vaticana, 1992). A paradoxical but suggestive analysis of the reasons which led to Galileo's condemnation has been given by P. K. Feyerabend, "Galileo and the Tyranny of Truth," in *The Galileo Affair: A Meeting of Truth and Science*, ed. G. V. Coyne, M. Heller, and J. Ziciński (Vatican City: Specola Vaticana, 1985).

13. A quite exhaustive analysis of finalism covering several aspects of the following discussion and providing a wealth of references is given by Barrow and Tipler, *Anthropic Cosmological Principle*.

choice would prove that the decision made was the only possibility. Many books have tried to support or demolish that argumentation.[14] Perhaps the best rebuttal is simply that there are choices which cost us an effort, in some cases a fight against our primary instincts; and our inner experience tells us that these choices can be good or bad, and that the choice is up to us. Moreover, those organisms which, though not free in the moral sense, are active participants in the Great Dance, also make choices, which we would describe as actions chosen in view of certain ends. According to our common sense, a lion does not kill a zebra because a sequence of causes and effects has led it to do so, but, rather, it kills the zebra *in order to* get food. That is precisely the difference between a lion and a mechanical system.

Let us go back to the case of Jacques Monod. He was a great scientist and a representative of positivist scientists, who refuse belief in anything they do not consider "scientific." Monod's case goes back to the decade ending with 1970, when, with his book on chance and necessity,[15] he shook the world of culture by explaining that, despite the presence in every organism of some kind of project, life consisted in a sequence of physicochemical processes ruled by the special determinism of chemical transformations. According to this view, which we have already had occasion to mention, each tiny step of that intricate network of processes which ensures the unity and the activity of a living organism is a chemical reaction between molecules of one species with molecules of another species, resulting in the production of molecules of one or more new species. The resulting new molecules, under the conditions in which the reaction takes place, are always the same — which is why one speaks of determinism both in ontogenesis and in phylogenesis. The determinism in question is very special because it admits exceptions, in the sense that, at least under special circumstances (say, the presence of radioactivity), molecules of unexpected species may be formed in very small numbers. These exceptions are the product of chance.

In the light of what we have already seen about evolution, it is easy to understand that those exceptional molecules will be a disturbance because they do not fit in the complicated reaction network that makes a living organism live. The same consideration applies to reproduction. This is why Monod spoke of "necessity": one cannot expect a living being to follow an unpredictable pattern in its development (ontogenesis), or a species of living beings to undergo all the time random changes in characteristics. There is, however, a tiny possibility that the molecular species produced by a random error will fit in the life processes of the living being in which it has been produced. In that case, the being will

14. Cf., e.g., C. Lamont, *Freedom of Choice Affirmed* (New York: Horizon, 1967).
15. Monod, *Le hasard*.

be different from all the others; if the change (or mutation) concerns its germinal cells, it will start a new strain of beings. It seems likely that only extremely small changes would be possible in this way; but they are known in individuals, and are the essence of the current explanation of speciation, i.e., the multiplication of living species. It may be admitted that the accumulation of mutations in one species will eventually give rise to a new species, a strain of living beings that cannot interbreed with those of the original species.

The possibility and role of constructive mutations as a result of random exceptions to the rule of necessity is what Monod meant in the very title of his book. Unfortunately for his argument — and being an honest scientist — he could not avoid one pitfall of determinism as applied to life: the fact that, as we have seen in chapter two, organization is always finalized. To overcome this difficulty, he introduced the notion of "teleonomy." In the passage partly quoted at the beginning of this chapter, he wrote:

> One of the fundamental properties which characterize all living beings without exception [is] that they are *objects endowed with a project*, which they represent in their structures and realize in their operations — e.g., the creation of artifacts. Instead of refusing this notion, ... we ought to recognize it as essential to the very definition of living beings. We shall say that the latter are distinguished from the structures of all other systems present in the Universe by this property, which we shall call *teleonomy*.[16]

Thus, guided by his scientific honesty, Monod affirmed from the beginning of his book that scientific explanations in biological matters cannot dispense with ends, with internal teleology. The discussion of chapter two should suffice to show that mechanism is not entirely applicable to living beings, and in general to organization, full as well as partial. Consider again the example of an airline (cf. chapter two). You could try to explain its behavior in an emergency as just a cause-effect chain, but then you would miss an essential point: the choices. You can say that the news that the first pilot was sick *caused* the telephone operator to do something, although I am not even sure of that; but the decision to call headquarters is the operator's. You might say that the operator had been instructed to do so; but, if so, I do not doubt that the instructions relied on his or her ability to make choices depending on the nature of the emergency. Do you not think that the operator would have called an ambulance or a doctor, had the problem been the health of a passenger? In short, the operator selected the action that corresponded to the aim of the company, the service which justified its very existence. Had the

16. Monod, *Le hasard*, 22.

operator been a computer instead of a human being, it would have contained a program with choices to be made by following a particular path in a tree of "if-then" options. Ultimately that would have amounted to the same thing: the "if-then" options are selection rules, and the choice is programmed in view of an end result. Finally, had the operator been a member of an ecosystem faced with a novelty — say, a crocodile realizing that what it is pursuing as Captain Hook is really an unpalatable robot — it would have followed its "instinct" depending on the analysis its primitive brain would carry out: if the chase was intended to free the terrain from enemies, maybe it would continue; if the chase was aimed at providing food, the crocodile would start looking or smelling around (whatever it is that crocodiles prefer) in search of its favorite prey.

Thus, finalism — what I have called "result-oriented behavior" — appears to be a fact of nature, recognized by scientists with the rise of organismic biology. It goes together with chance, for we have seen that the trial and error procedure, which nature appears to follow in stochastic processes, involves selection rules, which preserve a measure of determinism — and hence intelligibility — though making room for creative novelties in the harmonious many-voiced development of the Great Dance.

We have thus come to one of the central points in our review of the foundations of science, a point which is not so welcome even to genuine biologists who in practice adhere to Monod's view of the world. Let us take the bull by the horns and try to show somewhat systematically why finalism is an essential ingredient of scientific explanation, i.e., of nature as intelligible reality, and why, as Jacques Monod himself pointed out, the notion that finalism is a sort of nonscientific intruder appears to be untenable.

Nature as Intelligible Reality

Recent epistemology, even when it recognizes the built-in realism of science, still seems to question Galileo's image of "the book of nature":

> Science is written in that Great Book which lies open to our eyes, —
> I mean the Universe. But we cannot understand it unless we first
> know the language and learn the letters in which it is written. It
> is written in mathematical language, and its letters are triangles,
> circles, and other geometrical figures without which it is impossible
> to understand one single word of it.[17]

As with all analogies, whether one accepts the book image or not depends partly on basic issues and partly on personal semantics, i.e., the personal shade added to the meaning of words. I believe the basic points Galileo was trying to drive home were:

---

17. G. Galilei, *Il Saggiatore*, translated in an excellent collection of reflections by O. Pedersen, *The Book of Nature* (Vatican City: Vatican Observatory, 1992), 62.

(i) nature exists and is independent of us;

(ii) nature can become known to us provided we observe it with

(a) humble awareness that we are usually biased by preconceived schemes;

(b) complete readiness to treat those schemes just as working hypotheses;

(iii) the process of understanding requires detection of inner relations and regularities, which our mind perceives as logical relations and rules.

Thus understood, Galileo's analogy applies to all branches of science; indeed, it is a way of defining the program of science — the general targets of scientific inquiry — which is valid even today, and, more important, is valid not only for mechanics, the science "created" by Galileo, but for chemistry, biology, paleontology, even psychology. These sciences may well be only partially or not at all susceptible of formulation in terms of equations and/or geometrical relations, but they are attempts at rationalization according to point (iii) above.

An all-important implication of the "book of nature" analogy is that intelligibility is an intrinsic property of nature, which we study when we analyze "scientific explanation." That is to say, scientific explanation is simply the realization by our minds of relations which actually hold between entities, events, and processes in nature. As we have seen in chapter three, this aspect of realism is now accepted by most scientists under the impact of the realization that mankind can only grasp a tiny fraction of all there is to understand, and that faithfulness to reality is the only way we have to check the validity of our scientific results.

Explanation, Predictiveness, and Openness

The above interpretation of Galileo's "book of nature" implies belief in the possibility of identifying distinct objects in nature, and of establishing the relations among them in terms of spatiotemporal order. Indeed, in the light of modern science, in particular of what we have seen in the preceding chapters about the constitution of the universe from quarks to galaxies, Galileo's points can be restated as follows:

(i) there is a reality independent of us;

(ii) that reality is a multi-level collection of "quasi-independent" spatiotemporal objects;

(iii) at each level space-time objects are related to one another in some "order."

Intelligibility then means that a mapping of space-time objects and of their relations onto elementary propositions and theorems of a logical structure in our minds can be realized, and any amount of information beyond a minimal threshold admits one and only one optimal such mapping, subject to improvements and expansions as new information comes in. Such a mapping is what we call a theory or explanation applying to facts, although it is "open" in the sense that it may have to be extended to accommodate new facts.[18] In other words, the existence of an external intrinsically ordered reality reflects itself in two properties of our scientific theories:

- predictiveness: we have no choice in the logical description we give of what we have discovered about a certain reality, so much so that, once a certain amount of information has been collected, we can tell something about features of reality yet to be observed;

- openness: there are far more (knowable) features of reality than we have discovered at any instant of time.

The expression "logical description" deserves a brief comment. It is considered here equivalent to "scientific explanation" because, in agreement with views initially proposed by Hertz and others,[19] and later supported by Einstein's work on relativity, temporal relations are not formally different from spatial relations, and therefore something like a "causal explanation" is not different from, say, the description of a shape. Of course, the four causes of Aristotle are still important, especially efficient and final causes, but in science they may be treated as a convenient terminology for relations in space-time that are actually necessary and/or sufficient conditions. The history of the idea that explanation is but an ordered description is the history of the bright side of the epistemological views inspired by Ernst Mach, who laid the groundwork for the age of Einstein in science.[20]

Causes and Ends

A discussion of intelligibility and explanation thus reduces to a discussion of the relations of events with one another, more precisely of order in space-time. We have already seen that, although the time separation and the distance in space of two events are observer-dependent, there is a fundamental qualitative distinction between time and space, which holds for all observers; we are therefore justified in sticking to that distinction

18. Concerning scientific knowledge we follow here to a large extent the analysis carried out by Torrance, *Transformation*, ch. 2, 3.

19. Cf. H. Poincaré, *Science and Hypothesis*, 167.

20. Passmore, *A Hundred Years of Philosophy*, 320ff.

on a universal scale. In a general sense order in space, discussed in chapter two, may be called "structure" (sometimes "syntax"); order in time, discussed in chapter four, may be called "causal determination" to the extent to which future "states of the universe" can be explained in terms of (i.e., depend on) past ones, and "final determination" if future states ("results" or "effects") provide an explanation of (i.e., are a condition for) the specific character of the present state. To make things clearer, let us formulate the types of general questions demanding explanations of the two kinds:

- causal: are there past events that had to occur necessarily for the present state of the universe to have its specific features?

- finalistic: is there a future state of the universe that requires that the present situation should be what it is and not different?

Here by "state of the universe" we mean all the events which an observer perceives at a given instant of time.[21]

Many points should be discussed in connection with the above distinction. Are both sorts of explanations scientific? Are they mutually exclusive or compatible? Are there situations where both explanations are indispensable? Is it possible to explain observed facts completely one way or the other?

Before examining these questions it may be useful to consider again the two terms "mechanism" and "determinism." Strictly speaking, they are not synonyms. Mechanism is the viewpoint according to which processes in nature are either random sequences of events or cause-effect chains of the same sort as are realized in mechanical machines by levers, gears, pulleys, etc. Determinism is the belief that no choice or randomness is admitted by nature in its basic processes. It is possible to admit in mechanism a measure of randomness, and it is perhaps possible to consider a nonmechanistic deterministic process. However, in current usage determinism and mechanism stand for "mechanistic determinism," which corresponds to the clockwork image of the world, and assumes that *every* process in the physical world conforms to a mechanical scheme. We shall try to follow current usage unless there is the danger of confusing the issues.

After this premise, let us note first of all that classical mechanics, inasmuch as according to it the state of a system at any instant of time contains all information about its past and future, should allow a free choice between either explanation. In fact, with the above definitions, finalism is already present in it. The famous principle of least action is

21. Cf. G. Del Re, "Cause, Chance, and the State-space Approach," in *Probability in the Sciences*, ed. E. Agazzi (Dordrecht: Kluwer, 1988), 89–101.

an example. A clearly finalistic formulation of this principle was given by Arthur G. Webster in his classic treatise on dynamics:

> Nature tends to equalize the mean potential and kinetic energies during a motion.[22]

Webster, however, made a passing disparaging reference to the "philosophical and metaphysical arguments" which led Maupertuis to propound them. If there are unbiased historians of science, they ought perhaps to investigate this possible case of interaction of metaphysics with science. Passing to thermodynamics, where irreversibility is taken into account, we find an example of a law by which the "result" conditions the phenomenon in the principle of Le Chatelier, which is similar to the principle of least action, but has no clear-cut causal equivalent. It states that every physical system will respond to external actions tending to modify its state so as to minimize their effect; for example, as a response to the application of pressure from outside, the moving piston of a cylinder containing a gas will move so as to increase the pressure the gas exerts from the inside, by reducing the volume of the gas.[23]

Despite the central role of these principles, the dogma that classical mechanics excludes finalistic explanations is saved by use of the words "as if" in finalistic principles, and by proofs of "equivalence" between those principles and principles stated in terms of efficient causes (forces). Yet, no specialist could find a scientific objection to a reversal of the formulation, e.g., as follows:

A. least action (finalistic explanation): every natural motion takes place so as to minimize the *resulting* time mean of kinetic and potential energy;

B. cardinal equations (causal explanation): every natural motion takes place *as if* the external influences (external forces and momenta) determined at every instant the future change of total linear and angular momenta.

Ordinarily, as mentioned, the "as if" limitation is assigned to the least-action principle A. Two points should be retained in this connection:

(i) the equivalence between A and B is obtained at the price of the introduction of ad hoc quantities such as forces;

(ii) even if predictive equivalence is granted, the question of explanatory equivalence remains open.

22. A. G. Webster, *The Dynamics of Particles* (1912; reprint, New York: Dover, 1959).

23. O. Costa de Beauregard, in Agazzi, ed., *Probability*, reports considerations to the same effect by the great American chemist G. N. Lewis (1930).

Point (ii) can be rephrased as follows: are we sure that an explanation is not richer if it contains the finalistic alternative, even when the latter adds nothing to predictive power? This question raises the semantic aspect of scientific explanation, rigorously set aside by thinkers for whom philosophy of nature reduces to conventionalist epistemology.

We have already touched upon point (i). The introduction of field theory and its developments, in particular general relativity theory, have confirmed that forces are not only nonobservable, but superfluous in scientific explanation, being replaced by concepts such as information, contiguity, and algorithmic determination. Consider a simple two-dimensional two-particle space-time, i.e., a universe where the events are points in a plane characterized by a position coordinate x, which is the position of particle 2 with respect to particle 1, and a time coordinate t, measured by a clock located at particle 1. The possible "configurations" of the universe (events) are specified by (x, t) pairs. Other characteristics of an event (say, internal changes of the particles) may be summarized by a parameter p. We express the causal relation between two *events* $A = \{x(A), t(A), p(A)\}$ and $B = \{x(B), t(B), p(B)\}$, with A preceding B in time, by saying that if A is observed, then B will be observed, and there exists an algorithm whose application to information about A yields all possible information about B. Thus, even though a dependence of the position and state of one particle on the other is introduced, no entity such as a "force" is required. Forces, of course, retain some validity as *entia rationis*, i.e., fictitious entities used by reason to set up logical arguments, since mathematical quantities which can be interpreted as forces (or as the effects of forces) appear in formulas such as Newton's fundamental equation of dynamics, $F = ma$; but it should be kept in mind that those equations actually describe the way in which the properties of space-time at the site of a certain body change because of the presence of other bodies.

A Dream of the Far Future

Concerning point (ii) of the preceding section, an ad hoc version of an example given many times can perhaps clarify matters. Two alien scientists from the van Maanen star, having discovered how to overcome the light-velocity barrier, land on Mars, and find a Planet Exploration Module at work. They study the object and soon ascertain that it is a completely autonomous system taking photographs and analyzing the Martian soil. At last, the first scientist says: "We now know everything there is to be known about this object. Let us continue our exploration." "What about its origin?" asks the second scientist. "You are right, we should investigate how it came about. But we have no clues to that, for the moment," answers the first scientist. "And as to its purpose?" says the second scientist. "That is a false problem: once we know how it came about, we shall know that it had to be what it is and do what it does. Otherwise it was the result of chance. Purposes are fictitious constructions," replies the first. "I am not fully satisfied," says the second. "It seems to me that to really know something about this object we have to find out what role it plays, what place it has in its environment. I agree that the word 'purpose' may be misleading, but 'role' and 'place' also refer to an end." "Ends are outside science," says the first. "Let us rather continue our exploration."

The reader certainly knows better than that. You know that, even if the two aliens had found out everything about the origin of the module, and how it was built, still they would not know why it took its photographs and analyzed the soil. They would still miss the most important piece of information about the module — the fact that it is a tool. You might be tempted to yield to the authority of those philosophers of science according to whom nothing significant can be derived from facts of this sort, but you should resist that kind of temptation. Expand the example and imagine that the beings who had designed the module were only driven by the need for energy sources and habitable space — as evolutionary pragmatists would claim of human beings. In that case there would be no need of thinking minds and even less of free wills, but we would have introduced purpose anyway as a feature of objective reality, and hence to be taken into account in any complete explanation. In other words, as the second scientist pointed out (and will be discussed in more detail presently), use of the words "purpose," "aim," and "end" does not imply here the intentional design of some engineer, but simply allows reference to a possible function or role of the module in ensuring some general end result; knowledge of the function would make it possible to situate the object under consideration — the module — in the context to which it belongs, the solar system with its inhabitants. Whereas, before discovering the use of the module, the scientists from elsewhere would have only known how it worked, knowledge of its function would have allowed them to discover its relations with other objects in the solar system, and to guess something about the complexity level of the animal species inhabiting that system, independently of their self-consciousness and free will. In other terms, "purposiveness" may be seen as an inherent feature of sensible reality strictly connected to the inner and outer coherence of the systems that make up the universe.

Finalized Behavior and Coherent Evolution

The example just given shows that finalism and functionalism are not to be confused with the possibility that one or more free intelligent agents have brought about the particular configuration of parts that has been recognized as a planetary exploration module. Whether that configuration appeared by chance or by virtue of the intentional design of some intelligent being is not essential for our present argument — although, to be sure, it does suggest extra-scientific questions bearing on the spiritual dimension of reality.

Let us next consider the typical case where the insufficiency of the causal conceptual dimension is most striking, that of a living being in its environment, say a wolf. The very name of the animal makes us think not of how it works, but of its dynamic relation with the environment in which it lives — that is to say, of its function in maintaining the ecosystem in which it lives in its steady state. In other words, the wolf is an animal such that it can occupy a specific ecological niche, "the wolf's niche," i.e., contribute to the general aim of maintaining the equilibrium of the ecosystem to which it belongs, particularly by reducing the population of herbivores or eliminating carrion. Of course, mechanistic science will object that

(a) the emergence of the wolf in the world has been the result of a spontaneous trial and error procedure,

(b) the steady state of the ecosystem is the result of mutual adjustments of functions.

Such objections actually miss the point, because points (a) and (b) are not in question; what is being emphasized is that a *complete* scientific explanation of the wolf requires taking into account an aspect that focuses on potentialities in the future rather than on actualities in the past and present.

The case of the wolf shows something Monod failed to emphasize in connection with the existence of a project (although he did mention it), but is now a central point of environmental science. In looking for the aims of the "project of a living being," the great French biologist was reduced to begging the issue by identifying that project as

making the "dream" (F. Jacob) of every cell come true: to become two cells.[24]

Actually, as we have already seen, the "project" serves a more complex purpose: making a living being capable of preserving its identity and producing its likes *so that* there may always be a sufficient number of beings performing its particular function, a function which is indispensable for the coherent operation of the whole ecosystem to which it belongs. As a matter of fact, taken in this sense, a project can be expected for every object in the universe. What is typical of living beings is that

---

24. J. Monod, *Le hasard*, 32. François Jacob was another influential French biologist of Monod's time.

their "project" includes an active and multiple-choice interaction with the environment, so that their identity is preserved despite incessant participation in the dynamical coherence of their environment. As we shall see, this association of seemingly incompatible characteristics reaches its maximum in the case of human beings, because only humans — as far as is known — can tamper with the most delicate operations of nature. And science has acknowledged that the peculiar characteristics of human beings are a fact of nature, indeed something fully compatible with the laws it has discovered.

Keeping in mind that our considerations apply to what is susceptible of a scientific explanation, it would seem that finalism in nature can be defined by the following alternative (but equivalent) statements:

A: the characteristics of the eventual result are essential for understanding most (although not all) of the processes by which the observed reality is what it is and not otherwise (e.g., the fact that on earth there seems to be only a two-legged rational being and not a four-legged one); or:

B: most (if not all) of the processes taking place in nature include trial-and-error steps whose issues can only be explained in terms of selection rules, which guide an overall process toward its eventual result.

It is explicitly recalled here that there may be processes that — although they are always susceptible of a finalistic explanation, as mentioned in connection with the principle of least action — are not only determined by the history of the system under consideration, but do not require any additional teleological consideration; there are other processes that admit a mechanistic (cause-effect) explanation starting from a given initial state, but whose initial state is the result of a selection; there are processes that are completely result-determined, and there are processes that are simply result-oriented. All this was mentioned at some length in the preceding chapter. It is also important to keep in mind that what is called here "eventual result" may be intrinsic to the system under consideration (e.g., equipartition of energy among its degrees of freedom), but may also be environment-dependent, as in the case of a biological "function."

Let us now complete our argument by a general example. Following a curious custom of mediaeval philosophers, we shall let Socrates stand for "a given human individual," and build an example on his case. Everybody knows who Socrates was, but it is useful to recall something about him. He lived between 470 and 399 B.C., and, instead of writing big books, used to discuss with the young, carrying out with them what is now called "concept analysis"; the idea he put forward was that the noblest activity is the honest and humble search for truth, and that one ought to shun obsequious, servile acceptation of current doctrines — I mean conformism — even when those doctrines are sound. Woe betided Socrates because of that. His nonconformism became in the long run intolerable to the establishment. A man preaching revolution plays the ordinary game, and counterattack is possible, but Socrates had high moral standards and never attacked traditional customs; yet, his love for truth, if spread around, would end up by exposing hypocrisy and false myths. Thus, in accordance with a typical procedure of human societies, he was declared guilty of corrupting the young and sentenced to death. It was understood that Socrates would be unofficially allowed to flee abroad; but, after explaining to his friends that the laws are there to be obeyed, he drank the poison prepared for him.[25] The end of the story is not reason for wonder, but the very appearance and activity of Socrates on the stage of Athenian society is, because evidently that society made room for him and gave him time, indeed encouraged him to become one of the greatest thinkers in the history of mankind, and one who stands alone as a philosopher-teacher. In short, the mystery about him is this: why did a unique philosopher like Socrates appear in that particular time and place and why has such a philosopher never appeared again? One could say that Socrates was the result of a unique combination of genes, but that does not sound sufficient. In a different social context that same inquisitive boy that became Socrates could have become an engineer or a farmer or a doctor, though perhaps not an athlete or a hunter: Socrates grew to what he was to fill a need of the social and cultural context of Athens in his time. Consider what modern genetics teaches us, that the "expression" of hereditary characters recorded on a DNA double helix depends on the environment (particularly the material in the egg), which not only provides the means for transcription, but affects the choice of the gene to be read next. By analogy, one could say that our Greek friend developed precisely into Socrates because the social conditions were "ripe," and played an active role in orienting his personality toward a particular role. His development could then be envisaged as a stochastic process, each step being accepted for continuation by an "interactive" selection — a selection performed by what the social environment had become because of its own evolution and because of Socrates' very presence. The selection corresponded to filling a vacant position on the stage of that society. Thus, an explanation of the reason why a man called Socrates became Socrates the philosopher is incomplete if we just say that he had the qualities for that role; we should also say that his qualities were oriented

25. Beautiful considerations which apply to the topic we are discussing were made by Socrates while he was waiting for the poison; cf. the epigraph of chapter twelve.

by the environment *so that* he could fill a vacant role on the stage of Athenian society; as he grew, that society could begin a change in a certain direction, the direction of better adherence to the immortal ideals of knowledge for its own sake, work for justice, and contemplation of beauty.

At this point, the objection could be raised that the example of Socrates points to a crucial flaw in our case for finalistic explanations of natural processes within science (i.e., without calling free wills into play). "Ha!" could one say. "You are forgetting that Socrates was eliminated by the Athenian society in much the same way as an organism rejects a cell that does not belong to it. How can you speak of the role of Socrates as society's purpose in orienting him toward becoming a philosopher?"

That is a good question, and here is a possible answer. First, the Athenian society gave Socrates time until he was seventy before deciding to get rid of him; second, human society is notoriously plagued with lust for power, envy, and what have you; therefore, the apparent contradiction is removed by the consideration that there is in human society what certain philosophers might call evil and certain engineers might call malfunctions of control mechanisms. Science might be facing here a problem it can state, but not tackle, because it bears on the free will of human beings. However that may be, the changes initiated by Socrates were the germs of new ideas, which fructified centuries later, only to be wrecked after two millennia of glory on the gloomy shores of hedonistic utilitarianism.

The example of Socrates applies to any object that is at the same time itself and a member of a larger unit. Therefore it also illustrates the claim that a complete understanding of observed facts can only be obtained if it is admitted that both "because" and "in order that" correspond to genuine features of reality, and therefore should be recognized as equally necessary for complete knowledge of it. In other words, in order to explain a fact so as to make it part of our store of data to be classified as "acknowledged, understood and declared faithful to reality," we want both an idea of the circumstances and entities that started it — how and why it came to be what it appears to be here and now — and of the future to whose realization it is concurring by evolving in that way and not otherwise.

But this is not the whole story. The scope of finalistic explanations only appears in its full import if two points, which may have got mixed up during our discussion, are emphasized:

(i)   an object evolves according to its own nature either because of built-in programming (as in the case of living beings) or simply because the general laws of nature impose that pattern of evolution (as in the case of a star);

(ii) the nature of an object usually leaves it open to adjustments to the environment, so that what the object is at any instant of time also includes those adjustments.

Point (i) implies an *intrinsic teleonomy* or finalization toward an aim, which consists essentially, as we have mentioned several times, in the conservation or even defense of the identity of an object or being in the presence of a varying environment. Point (ii) implies an *extrinsic teleonomy*, i.e., finalization of a given object in favor (as it were) of its environment and conversely. Survival of the species and the search for food are typical examples, but the behavior of certain nonliving steady-state systems can be interpreted in the same way. One can then think of a common finalism of an object and its environment.

But what could be the common goal, which the system "object plus environment" pursues? If the environment is in general what the Athenian society was for Socrates, if something (or somebody) is what it is and not something else not only because of its inherent characteristics, including its own teleonomy, but also because of the function it is destined to perform in its environment by the very nature of the environment, then one should perhaps find the aim of the evolution of every object belonging to a complex system in perfect tuning to (i.e., coherence with) its environment. This conclusion applies even when — as we are assuming after the "ontological" discussions of the preceding chapters — we only consider systems whose components are themselves objects or beings, inasmuch as they retain a measure of autonomy.

The Universe and Its Teleonomy

Let us now consider that the complex system "object plus environment" will have itself an environment, and so on. This means that we must accept the idea that everything is what it is both because of its own nature and of its belonging to this universe. Let us therefore turn to the latter. The universe is a peculiar space-time object, because it cannot be observed from outside and can only be defined in terms of its constitution — the individual space-time objects in the ordinary sense. Nevertheless, it can be described by analogy with objects belonging to it, provided that only inner properties be considered, i.e., by means of the so-called "models of the universe." Any attempt to get such a description leads, at least in the view of contemporary cosmology, to the conclusion that the universe shares with all other space-time objects the property of "becoming." Now, this becoming is different from that of all other space-time objects because by definition it cannot be oriented or affected by the interaction with other objects: within the natural sciences, the physical universe is what it is and changes the way it does only because it obeys the general laws of physics, and has neither an external (physical) cause nor a function. Yet, the more we study it, the more it appears to resemble a complex system endowed with a great measure of coherence and evolving along a unique line. Is it really legitimate to claim that, at variance with all other objects, it has no intrinsic teleonomy, no inherent program, no end point for its evolution?[26]

Of course, science can only ask the question. As scientists, we can admit that the logical consistency of the whole picture would be improved if a unitary design and project were postulated, but we have no way to test the truth of such a postulate. As thinking human beings, we have the right to ask: is it reasonable to refuse the idea that coherence in time and space and creation of information are the work of a free intelligence whose conscious deliberation and action has produced everything? To come to terms with the mystery of reality we should perhaps open our perspective beyond science, and accept Eddington's remark:

> There is a side of our personality which impels us to dwell on beauty and other aesthetic significances in Nature, and in the work of man, so that our environment means to us much that is not warranted by anything found in the scientific inventory of its structure.
>
> There is much to be said for excluding the whole field of significance from physics; it is a healthy reaction against mixing up with our calculations mystic conceptions that (officially) we know nothing about. I rather envy the pure physicist his impregnable position. But if he rules significances entirely outside his scope, somebody has the job of discovering whether the physical world of atoms, aether, and electrons has any significance whatever. . . . Am I to tell [my audience] that the scientific world has no claim on their consideration when the eternal question surges in the mind: what is it all about?[27]

We shall come back to that eternal question in our concluding chapters. In the meantime, let us move to facets of science that widen the picture by telling us how coherence and variety combine in the Cosmic Dance.

---

26. Cf. J. M. Templeton, ed., *Evidence of Purpose* (New York: Continuum, 1994).
27. Eddington, *Nature of the Physical World*, 111, 113.

Chapter 7

Regularity, Variety, and the Unity of the World

How is the ever changing variety and coherence that is the essence of the Great Dance ensured? Einstein said that "God does not play dice"; but dice-throwing, if rightly understood, might model nature's method of obtaining variety and diversity.

Chance and Fate: Another Face of Stochasticity – Chance and Variety – Wastage and Dice-Drawing – The Value of Individuals – Chance and Necessity, Again – The Epoch of Galaxy Formation – The Anthropic Principle – Ways Away from Wisdom – Fields and Space-Time Continuum – Knots in Space-Time – The Ship's Bearings

The question, whether it is Chance or Fate that rules the Universe, has occupied me a lot these last few weeks," he quietly commented. "I am almost beginning to incline for Fate: How powerful and unimaginable must the One be who has the threads in his hands." — CLARK DARLTON[1]

Chance and Fate:
Another Face of Stochasticity

The introductory quotation of this chapter is from a German science fiction series whose hero is Perry Rhodan, "the heir of the Universe." His adjunct and friend, Atlan of Arkon, a man from a galactic empire of the past, makes the above consideration when, as their great starship crosses a remote star cluster, he realizes that they have unexpectedly arrived close to the capital planet of an extragalactic empire menacing the galaxy. I wonder if, in the last few years, Perry Rhodan and Atlan have remained faithful to the assignment they had in the 1980s — to represent genuine human persons, who, despite their enormous power and quasi-immortality, retained a profound sense of responsibility and dedication to peace and justice. That noble conception of what a man should be is probably the better part of the Western tradition, going back to Greece and Rome. Terence (185–159 B.C.), a slave native of Carthage who was probably the playwright most admired by the educated Romans of the time of Caesar, summarized it in a famous apothegm, *nihil humani a me alienum puto* — "I do not consider alien to me anything worthy of a man." Dante, Shakespeare, Pascal, Goethe owe their immortal fame precisely to that ideal. Yet, it was an ideal that began to decline in the middle of the nineteenth century, when (as some believe, not without evidential support) obscure forces and secret international connections took control of the vague humanitarian theorizing of many intellectuals and the thirst for justice and freedom of the poor. Lust for power always bears monsters: those forces or connections led humanity, probably out of mere indifference to long-term consequences, to the first world war and the October revolution, and left the psychological climate which made possible the horrors of the second world war. The horrible

1. *Perry Rhodan: Das Mutanten Korps*, ed. W. Voltz (Rastatt, Germany: Moewig, 1979). "Die Frage, ob der Zufall oder der Schicksal unser Universum regieren, hat mich in den letzten Wochen sehr beschäftigt," gab er in ruhigem Ton zu. "Fast beginne ich, dem Schicksal die größeren Chancen einzuräumen. Wie gewaltig und unvorstellbar muß jener sein, der die Fäder in der Hand hält."

success of the "logic of power," however, would not have been so extensive had the cultural situation of the West been different: the decline of humanities and the rise of an arrogant science and technology created the conditions for that success. In fact, five years before the outburst of the second world war an American historian of philosophy had clearly identified what proved to be its socio-cultural root:

> Greek philosophy leaped on to heights unreached again, while Greek science limped behind. Our modern danger is precisely the opposite: inductive data fall upon us on all sides like the lava of the Vesuvius, we suffocate with uncoordinated facts, our minds are overwhelmed with science breeding and multiplying into specialistic chaos for want of synthetic thought and a unifying philosophy. We are all mere fragments of what a man might be.[2]

At first sight, the situation is not much better after sixty-five years. Truly enough, things take time, and perhaps today's teenagers will effect a recovery; but the immediate present is not happy. I must confess that, when I want some light reading, I only buy the reprints of Perry Rhodan issues that are at least several years old, lest I should discover that the better part of the German tradition also has yielded to the spirit of the age, whose symbol is the turbosex offer appearing on one's monitor in response to an innocent Internet search by a none-too-discriminatory search engine. However that may be, the Perry Rhodan stories, intended for readers having more or less the same educational background as the readers of the 007 stories, represented until recently an attempt by a team of writers to counter at least in fiction the realization of a prophecy by an eminent American historian:

> An age without great men is one which acquiesces in the drift of history. Such acquiescence is easy and seductive; the great appeal of fatalism, indeed, is a refuge from the terror of responsibility.... Let us not be complacent about our supposed capacity to get along without great men. If our society has lost its wish for heroes and its ability to produce them, it may well turn out to have lost everything else as well.[3]

The reader might feel that this question of what a man should be is a digression from our main theme. It is not, for two reasons. First, it concerns the relation between science and the spiritual side of man; second, it concerns chance, seen as a scientific notion laden with moral and philosophical implications. If English "fate" means the same as *fatum*,

---

2. W. Durant, *The Story of Philosophy* (New York: Simon and Schuster, 1934), ch. 2, 9.
3. A. M. Schlesinger, Jr., "The Decline of Heroes" in *Adventures of the Mind*, ed. R. Thruelsen and J. Kobler, first series (New York: Vintage Books, 1959).

its Latin origin, then it is the word of the gods. In this sense Atlan looks at fate as an alternative a responsible man ought to consider when confronted with the unpredictable, with a novelty which might be either just a random drawing of nature's dice or a decision of the Maker of the universe. Now, as we have already seen, *by its very nature* chance is not and cannot be that force of nature some hasty people would like it to be. Indeed, it is present but irrelevant in processes where a great number of identical particles is involved; but if there are otherwise instances of random events on which the future really depends, then science, though incapable of answering, poses precisely the question posed to Atlan of Arkon: are those events the proof of a structural irrationality of nature, or are they a suggestion that there are events whose causes lie beyond the reach of science?

Chance and Variety

Let us first of all see if the possibility of *relevant* random events is founded on facts. Single stochastic processes are essentially result-oriented, and thus determined, but their initial event might very well never take place. As we have seen in chapter five, in the case of the supposed origin of life, as in the case of any sequence of chemical reactions, the huge numbers of identical trials involved would make the right initial event practically inevitable, and the resulting process would yield a precise end result because of "Darwinian selection." But when you come to processes like the generation of a single living being, then the situation is different.

Given a large number of human couples, science expects the birth of at least a few human beings, certainly not dragons or dinosaurs. But human beings are so complex, and have so many different characters, that no two of those new human beings will be exactly equal; even single-egg twins will be different because of slight differences in the conditions of expression of their identical hereditary characteristics. A human being — science admits, though not with a will — is a unique unrepeatable entity. That unique entity, so far as today's science can tell, is the result of chance: either of the gametes[4] that combined to yield the new being might have met any other partner, or might have died without meeting any. Moreover, those particular parents who generated, say, our friend Socrates, met because of circumstances that were largely casual: they happened to live in the same town, their parents happened to have some common acquaintance, and so on. C. S. Lewis pointed out that even the whole historical process that culminated in the birth of Jesus Christ was a stochastic process guided by selection, which operated on individuals

4. This biological term, curiously enough not explained in certain concise dictionaries, stands for either of two sex cells which on meeting may yield a fertilized egg.

or groups of individuals whose emergence was — so far a science goes — a random event, and therefore could not be attributed scientifically to natural causes:

> After the knowledge of God had been universally lost or obscured, one man from the whole Earth (Abraham) is picked out. He is separated (miserably enough, we may suppose) from his natural surroundings, sent into a strange country, and made the ancestor of a nation who are to carry the knowledge of the true God. Within this nation there is further selection: some die in the desert, some remain behind in Babylon. There is further selection still. The process grows narrower and narrower, sharpens at last into one small bright point like the head of a spear. It is a Jewish girl at her prayers. All humanity (so far as concerns its redemption) has narrowed to that. Such a process is very unlike what modern feeling demands: but it is startlingly like what Nature habitually does.[5]

I think no one would say, regardless of his attitude toward religion, that the birth of Jesus Christ was irrelevant for mankind. Some theologians like to claim that Jesus was "just" one of many founders of religions. Personally, I do not think that, even as a mere student of facts, one could consider the founders of religions as more or less equivalent members of a class; not even the Mr. Minit shoe repairers in supermarkets are equivalent. At any rate, most people would probably agree that the founders of the great religions of the world were all exceptional men. But even granting that, is it really scientific simply to say that the birth of Christ *just happened?* One should at least apply the sort of considerations made about Socrates in the preceding chapter, but then one would have to explain the ability of a religion "based on fear" (according to a curious belief of Bertrand Russell's) to conquer the world, to appease the uncouth warriors invading the Roman Empire, and much later give a moral reference to the pioneers of the American West. One could generalize the idea that somehow such a religion was required at a certain moment of history by the conditions of society; if so the need for a religion, indeed for a religion having certain characteristics, is a fact any scientific description of human behavior ought to take into account.

Wastage and Dice Drawing

There is another general point which even C. S. Lewis could not clearly see, for he lived before the recent great advances of biology and cosmology had become known to all interested intellectuals: the principle of universal coherence — as we may well call it, now that we know what

5. C. S. Lewis, *Miracles* (London: Pan Books, 1947), 120.

coherence is — implies that every object or event in the universe should participate in the general harmony. Nature must have a reason for every apparently useless operation she performs. Selection rules make certain events unproductive in the long run, as in the typical case of mutations realizing a being incapable of surviving for a reasonable time in a given environment. Yet those events must have a role to play, because they are notes in the Harmony of the World, gestures in the choreography of the Great Dance, and even a single note or a single gesture may be necessary for perfection. This is the general reason why I am inclined to think that C. S. Lewis was unjust to nature, when he wrote:

> Selectiveness, and with (we must allow) enormous wastage, is her method. Out of an enormous space a very small portion is occupied by matter at all. Of all the stars, perhaps very few, perhaps only one, have planets. Of the planets in our own system probably only one supports organic life. In the transmission of organic life, countless seeds and spermatozoa are emitted: some few are selected for the distinction of fertility. Among the species only one is rational. Within that species only a few attain excellence of beauty, strength, or intelligence.[6]

There is no denying that in nature, especially in connection with living beings, many facts throw doubts on the existence of a general law of harmony and economy. The most serious doubts are those that derive from the "problem of pain": why is there so much suffering among living beings? One may perhaps dispose of this question in the case of lower animals by claiming that, to them, what would be pain to a being with a high degree of consciousness is not necessarily more than an automatic reflex, a signal alerting the organism against some attack. One may extend this consideration — though against the feelings of many — to all animals, on the grounds that they do not fully "realize" what is happening to them. Unfortunately, whatever we may say or think about animals, with which humans cannot really identify, there are diseases and accidents that kill people in the most atrocious ways — and they are not necessarily the punishment for violations of the law of God by the victims or by their parents, as many Jews of Christ's time believed:[7] a simple and comforting theory, were it true. Thus, suffering is a mystery, which neither science nor philosophy can solve; it is a mystery which only religion can solve, and the solution depends on the religion. The most abominable ones, like that of the Aztecs of Mexico, were indeed based on the idea that physical pain deliberately inflicted on innocent victims is the only way to satisfy the gods. I for one prefer to believe in a

6. Ibid.
7. Cf. Luke 13:1–5.

God who is the source of all that is good, and that the presence of pain inflicted by nature (and of evil) is part of a mysterious plan of his; as we shall see, the *Weltanschauung* science offers to us goes in that direction.

If such is a reasonable stand on the problem of pain, why then, when it comes to that other apparently unjustified aspect of nature which looks to us like wastage, should one not agree with Lewis that it belongs to the method of nature? The problem is not whether there is wastage or not, for science is far from knowing everything, but whether what looks like wastage to us is really so. One should probably take into account that people are accustomed to think in terms of human engineering abilities, labor, and capital costs, and therefore somehow feel that (for example) not to put to use such a marvelous biological machine as a gamete is a waste of time and energy. But to nature a gamete costs even less than a single electron, and if it is not used, not much is lost, provided that anyway one gamete pair out of a large number produce a new being; the rest will be recycled.

The psychological bias of the very term "wastage" applied to the operations of nature appears more clearly if one looks at its possible alternatives. Imagine that all the seeds produced by a single plant were needed to give origin to a small number of new plants: who would dare to tell nature it could have done better had it asked for advice from the scientists, who would have shown it that it could do with just one seed per seedling? Probably only an old-style worshipper of science, because present science has learned a few bitter lessons from attempts to improve on nature. The DDT story has proven to us that whatever kills insects is a poison for any living being, and one can at best rely on differences in lethal doses; the disastrous consequences of indiscriminate use of plant hormones and pesticides are well known; the mad-cow crisis of 1996 seems to be the latest consequence of interfering with natural equilibria, if it is true that it has grown into an epidemic as a result of feeding cows, which are herbivorous, with proteins from sheep or other cows. These, and many other cases, have shown scientists and people in general that they should be extremely cautious when it comes to tampering with nature, except when required by emergencies, as in case of famine. This is why I expect that, if nature used all the seeds of a plant to make new plants, all scientists worth that name would be content to admire the marvel that would be the combination of hundreds of seeds to form a single plant. Now comes the point: Why then are we surprised that nature should use a large number of seeds to produce just one seedling, not by combining them together, but (in addition to forestalling losses) to provide an opportunity for the new being to be different and unpredictable, albeit within the limits of one and the same species, possibly with mutations opening the way to new species? The same holds for human beings: if no room were left to chance in the meeting of human gametes, there would be rigid rules which would determine *a priori* all the characters of each human being: no individual would any longer be a unique unrepeatable object. In fact, even recent attempts at cloning higher animals suggest that such a dubious practice would anyway yield individuals that are not strictly identical, let alone the differences that would be brought about by the environment during early life.

Thus, neither reasons of economy nor reasons of efficiency really apply to nature's methods. Simply put, nature uses chance to get variety — what nowadays many call "diversity" — and variety is an essential character of the beauty of the Great Dance, particularly of the Music it embodies. A similar argument also holds for stars and galaxies. We shall get to that side of the story in a couple of sections; before that, let us see what a great art expert, John Ruskin, had to say about the relation of variety (or diversity) to beauty:

> Consider the different ways in which change and monotony are presented to us in nature, both having their use as darkness and light, and one incapable of being enjoyed without the other, change being most delightful after some period of monotony, as light appears most brilliant after the eyes have been for some time closed. I believe that the true relation of monotony and change may be most simply understood by observing them in music. We may therein notice, first, that there is a sublimity and majesty in monotony that there is not in rapid and frequent variation. This is true throughout all nature.... [Yet,] the talent of the composer is not in the monotony, but in the changes. He may show feeling and taste by his use of monotony in certain places or degrees, that is to say by his *various* employment of it. But it is always in the new arrangement or invention that his intellect is shown, and not in the monotony which relieves it.[8]

Let me add that not only nature as we contemplate it when watching a sunset or a stormy sea, but the universe at large is beautiful precisely for the reason given by Ruskin: science discovers the monotonies and regularities of the universe, but in the attempt to describe the whole reality it studies it is forced to accept variety in the form of random events ultimately leading to new unpredictable wonders as well as increased coherence.

The Value of Individuals

Another point is worth emphasizing. Although gametes are nothing particularly costly for nature, which ensures diversity by producing so many

---

8. J. Ruskin, *Unto this Last and Other Writings*, an anthology ed. by C. Wilmer (Harmondsworth, Eng.: Penguin, 1985), 94–97.

that the pair that will actually yield a new individual is chosen at random, it does not follow that in human communities the victims of diseases and wars, the babies which died at birth or shortly thereafter, handicapped people, and so on, just represent the expendable pawns of nature's selection game. The reason lies again in the distinction between objects having at least a measure of autonomy and ability to influence (and be influenced by) their environment, and objects existing solely in view of a precise function, e.g., the parts of an organism. Gametes are often mobile bodies capable of surviving for a while under appropriate conditions; but they have no function whatever in their environment except pairing with a gamete of the opposite sex to produce a fertilized cell. Therefore, they are not even indispensable for the integrity of an organism, as its parts are. Moreover, they are produced automatically almost as a byproduct of the life activity of the parent organisms; they are in a sense like integrated circuits, whose cost is small, and would be nil if the materials and the machines were anyway available, and no workers or technicians were needed. Thus, to say that nature's method of producing many gametes to get one fertilized cell is really no wastage sounds correct.

On the other hand, a fertilized cell is something else, at least in the case of higher animals. First of all, it has taken two parents to form it; secondly, it immediately starts to interact with its environment — think of the change in the hormone equilibrium of a mother starting with the very conception of her child; thirdly, it has since the beginning its own identity; fourthly, it takes a lot of time and effort by other individuals to bring it to maturity, and during that whole time it plays an evolving role in its environment. A fertilized cell is not just a note, it is a *voice* in the symphony embodied in the Great Dance. When it comes to a fertilized human egg, then the investment nature makes in it, and the return nature expects is really great: it includes a variety of actions, from influencing hormone release and interplay in its mother to forcing certain patterns of behavior in its parents, from being the object of its teachers' care to affecting college and university staff by questions and subject choices. Try to apply this consideration to artificial fertilization, and you will realize how dubious, even from a merely scientific standpoint, is the practice of keeping fertilized human eggs as a reserve for repeated attempts to graft an egg in a woman's womb. In general, as far as science goes, nature has a place for every being; a place which science cannot fully establish because of the extremely complicated network of relations in which it participates, but which science has come to appreciate well enough to lead people to campaign for biodiversity and for animal rights. Excesses and contradictions such as considering the starvation of third world peoples less important than biodiversity or the life of a dog more important than that of a baby should not obscure the fact that there is a genuine scientific basis in those campaigns: nature is (or tends to become) a harmonious whole where each individual object has a role to play, however short or long, however high or low.

Chance and Necessity, Again

The above view of chance applies particularly to speciation. Not only is "dice drawing" the method by which nature realizes diversity and beauty within a species, but it also makes a random exploration of all the creative potentialities of life possible as time goes by and the conditions of the biosphere change — it makes evolution, indeed complexification possible. At the same time, there are rigorous deterministic barriers to novelties, precisely as in music the rules of harmony and melody are respected even in the works of the greatest composers — although they could (and did, in a few instances) take the liberty to ignore those rules. We have seen that there are processes, such as chemical reactions, which are only microscopically ruled by chance, but in fact are deterministic because the individuals involved are identical, and neither "when" nor "where" actually matter, so that nature's method of repeated dice drawing actually realizes a precise and predetermined result. In short, as long as the choice of particular individuals is not relevant, there is a deterministic line in the history of the universe; it even seems correct to say that, given the rules of the game, even such supercomplex systems as human beings were bound to appear, sooner or later, on the stage of the universe. Nature took something like ten billion years to produce a planet where the right conditions for the emergence of life would be present, and four billion more years for the enormous number of "dice drawings" to give the mutation which, according to evolution theory, finally yielded man; but, to a mind knowing all the rules of the game, the appearance of man might have been a predictable event, just as the end products of a chemical reaction are known beforehand to a chemist. On the other hand, stochastic processes involving single individuals, each different from the others, have no obliged issue. The appearance of Socrates (and *a fortiori* of Christ's Mother), technically speaking, was an unpredictable novelty resulting from a sequence of random events, where "random" simply means, to people who humbly accept things as they stand, that they were not imposed by the laws science has discovered.

Thus, within science, "irrelevance" and "novelty production" are the two faces of chance, which coexist when a large enough number of individuals are involved. But science also reaches in this way one of its borders with what "transcends" it. This is the case, let us say it again, particularly when individuals emerge who, like the self-amplified fluctuations giving origin to order out of chaos according to Prigogine's theory, change the history of mankind. The big board signaling the border of science carries in big letters precisely the question posed by Atlan of Arkon:

Zufall oder Schicksal? — "Chance or Fate?" Should one think of events whose realization is merely a possibility left open by the operating laws of Nature as "blind chance," or as that space of intervention which the Being who has made those laws has reserved for himself (and for created free beings)?

If you read once again the passages by Lewis quoted above, and consider our remarks about wastage, you will probably agree that a Supreme Being may well have claimed as a "space of unpredictable intervention" the collection of the events in which novelties are produced. Most of those novelties probably play in the Great Dance a role similar to that of the mutations of Darwin's theory of evolution, but some are known to form precise patterns in the history of humanity, as in the case of Abraham and his descendants. By having to acknowledge the existence of this reserved space, over and beyond raising the question of creation, science strongly hints (which is as much as it, being science, is allowed to do) at some power which is spiritual, i.e., free and not observable, and is interested in human beings as individuals, particularly in that side of "being human" which it is customary to call the spiritual dimension. At the same time, history and historiography appear as a scientific field of inquiry, the science of patterns of development in time of human society, as was proposed by Giambattista Vico (1699–1741).[9]

Chance, in the present context, thus means that one out of several possibilities is either realized spontaneously or chosen by a free agent. Also, human beings are agents capable of altering the "natural course of things" so as to artificially produce novelties. This is made possible precisely by the existence of an undetermined part of sensible reality on which human beings can act. For example, suppose an American on a tour in Peru picks up a few papaya seeds, and, after returning home to the Great Lakes region plants them in a greenhouse, so that after many years the seeds produce lofty trees. Now suppose that the American in this story just happened to choose mutant seeds, which produce frost-resistant trees. Then you have a novelty — papaya trees capable of thriving in free air on the shores of the Great Lakes — resulting from a combination of genuine chance (the mutation), action of a free agent (the American's transfer and planting of the seeds), and natural process (the germination of the seeds and the growth of a tree); this combination would introduce into the Great Lakes district a tropical plant. Now, the actions of the American constitute an unpredictable succession of events, which lie within the scope of science inasmuch as they are *observable;* but then they belong to a very special (and only recently discovered) dimension of science, which concerns the place of man in the universe. We

9. Mainly in his *Scienza nuova* (A new science) of 1725, where he enounced the principle that *verum ipsum est factum*, true is what is made or done.

shall devote to the latter the next chapters. For the time being, let us resume our course and return to the coherence and unity of the universe.

The Epoch of Galaxy Formation

The interplay of chance and necessity along the lines just summarized is an essential feature of the entire description of the world provided by science at the turn of the second millennium, despite the independent origin (and fields of inquiry) of the disciplines involved — physics, chemistry, biology. Physics — more precisely theoretical and particle physics — is involved in the current Big Bang theory of the origin of the universe. We shall not pause on its details, least of all on the famous "first 10^{-34} seconds," not only because the literature on that side of the story is more than sufficient, but because a review of it would not be particularly helpful for the understanding of the main themes of the Great Dance. What is interesting for us is what happened next according to the Big Bang theory. I have found a most lucid summary in a lecture given in 1992 by the distinguished British astrophysicist Martin J. Rees:

> Our universe seems to have evolved, in between ten and twenty billion years, from a dense amorphous fireball to its present state, where its dominant features are galaxies, distributed in clusters. How did the observed structures emerge and evolve? We are forced to suppose that the early universe was not completely smooth and uniform. If it had been, it would still, even now, consist of nothing but smoothly distributed cold diffuse gas. There must, even at very early epochs, have been some irregularities in the density or in the expansion rate. These were of small amplitudes. However, any region that was slightly overdense would have lagged more and more behind the overall cosmic expansion, eventually condensing into a gravitationally bound system: a galaxy or cluster, depending on its scale.[10]

Within the galaxies the same mechanism supposedly gave rise to stars. In some cases stars form clusters, particularly globular clusters, which are among the most beautiful objects that can be seen through a telescope. The globular clusters orbiting the galaxy M31, for example, were photographed in all their glory by the Hubble telescope in 1996. In the long run, however, stars may become lonely jewels in the sky, like the red giant star Betelgeuse. We can only wonder about their role in the Great Dance, but we may be sure they have one, if only because they make us, other participants in the Dance millions or billions of light years away, wonder about them.

10. M. J. Rees, "The Epoch of Galaxy Formation," in B. Pullman, *The Emergence*, 217.

Chance and necessity are the key concepts here too, for what Rees briefly describes in the passage above is again self-amplification of random fluctuations. The other key concept that is feedback enters the story because we have here a case of what some scientists call "the snowball effect." A big snowball rolling down a hill covered with snow will get bigger and bigger, as long as new particles of snow stick to its surface with a strength sufficient to compensate gravity and centrifugal forces, which tend to detach it. The growth phase can be described as an input message — the surface of the snowball — and an output message, the collected snow. Now, the larger the surface, the more snow will adhere to it; the more snow adheres, the larger the surface becomes: there is positive feedback, increasing the size of the snowball faster and faster, until eventually equilibrium is attained because of losses. Similarly, gravitational attraction would make a small irregularity in the primeval gas increase in size and in attraction power until centrifugal and other forces become so important that they overcome gravity: a gaseous nebula is thus born, and within it stars begin to form. The growth stage is controlled by positive feedback, the "input" being gravitational attraction, the "output" partly fed back to the input being mass increase. The interplay of chance and necessity has here both its possible faces: (a), the initial irregularity, as any fluctuation in a gas, is expected to be unpredictable, but the succeeding snowball effect is deterministic, and can be described by means of mathematical equations; (b) during the time the right conditions of temperature and density persist, the number of fluctuations capable of self-amplification will be so high that a number of galaxies and stars will certainly be formed. But whether or not a particular star, e.g., the slowly pulsating red-orange giant Betelgeuse — a globe with its surface at 3000°C, as large as the solar system well past the orbit of Jupiter, as rarefied as extremely high altitude air on the earth, shining from about 600 light years — would appear in due course with its particular light spectrum, its precise mass and size, its particular position with respect to its neighbors and to the earth, that is a question for which — according to the present state of the art — science has no answer, except the general consideration already made: that where and what it is must make a difference if the universe is a coherent whole.

This consideration holds *a fortiori* for the quasars, those mysterious objects, several hundred billion times brighter than any star, which dwell in galaxies billions of light years away from our galaxy. Is it possible that they are really part of a coherent system in the same way as human beings and blackcaps?

It might sound strange that science should be involved with such general and apparently vague questions, but a positive answer is a corollary of a strange and perplexing aspect of reality, which has emerged from the new science of the second half of the twentieth century: it is the anthropic principle, which we have already had occasion to meet.

The Anthropic Principle

The anthropic principle,[11] formulated by B. Carter in 1964, has such far-reaching implications that it was a hot subject of debate for several years. The general public's interest has now subsided, and it has become (in its weak, more genuinely scientific form) part of the accepted basic aspects of science. For one thing, that principle provides an answer to Lewis's implicit question about the large number of stars that are apparently necessary for the production of just one inhabited planet.

In agreement with my commitment not to dwell too long on questions to which other, excellent books have been devoted,[12] we shall confine ourselves only to what interests us here. The whole story can be summarized as the following "syllogism."

First premise: Our present view of the history of the universe (*viz.* cosmology) is based on the accepted general laws of nature.

Second premise: Those laws involve precise universal constants, i.e., special values of certain physical quantities.

Third premise: If any one of those universal constants had a value slightly different from the one it has, then

a. the processes which have produced the chemical elements necessary for life such as we know it would not have taken place, at least within the estimated life of the universe;

b. even if they had taken place, evolution would not have had the time to produce *Homo sapiens*.

Conclusion: Therefore, the very existence of human beings implies that the general laws ruling the universe must involve precisely those particular values of the universal constants that are derived from observed data on the expansion of the universe, the formation of galaxies and stars, in short all the processes in matter, in the microscopic world and at the remotest distances from Earth.

The above conclusion is called "the weak anthropic cosmological principle." I for one should not like to transform it into the "strong" anthropic principle, which claims that the universe was made in such a way that human beings would appear. That would probably be an unlawful intrusion of belief in God into a merely scientific argument. To be

11. Barrow and Tipler, *Anthropic Cosmological Principle.*

12. In particular, see Barrow and Tipler, *Anthropic Principle,* and D. Layzer, *Cosmogenesis* (New York: Oxford University Press, 1990). An extensive critical review of many other useful books is given by J. M. Templeton and R. L. Herrmann in *Is God the Only Reality?* (New York: Continuum, 1994).

sure, reasons for believing in God the Creator do emerge from what we know about the universe; indeed, we shall have to make a short digression on spiritual matters presently. Here, if we stay within science, the point to be emphasized is different: it is that, according to the anthropic principle, cosmological studies also support the notion that the universe is a coherent whole, so that the number of stars in it, its size, its age are all related to one another and to the existence of man, even though none of those characteristics is the cause, the "reason why" the others are what they are. Let one example suffice: the age of the universe is the time that was necessary, according to the Big Bang hypothesis, for the universe to produce a star such as the sun, for the sun to produce a planet like the earth, and for the earth to produce Homo sapiens; it is also the time that was necessary for the expanding universe to reach its present size.

Of course, neither the Big Bang nor the precise mechanisms of the origin and evolution of life are yet proven beyond any possible doubt; but even so the coherence between the general structure and evolution of the cosmos and a local event in its history — the appearance of man — is more than astonishing: it feels incredible. This is especially the case if one considers that aspects related to one another were discovered and studied within independent theories belonging to different branches of science (physics for the general laws, chemistry for the origin of life and for the transmission of hereditary characteristics, biology for the evolution of the species). We may even be tempted to extrapolate the anthropic principle to the general rule that every local structure or organized system is what it is and evolves the way it does because the universe is what it is, and, were that local detail not so, then everything else in the universe would have to be different. This extrapolation would be a scientific version of the ancient belief that *tout est dans tout* — everything is in everything; it is probably exaggerated because it is difficult to believe that one star more or less would make a difference, for stars appear to be formed in enormous clusters, as do the seeds of a plant;[13] but then stars might participate in the coherence of the universe in some way similar to what we have seen above for the seeds of a plant.

Ways Away from Wisdom

It is now time for the announced digression. The preceding points about chance and diversity, together with the hypothesis of the spontaneous origin of life, have given rise to the well-known debate between creationists and anticreationists. That debate appears to hinge on the belief that,

---

13. An example is provided by the cluster NG1850, recently photographed by the Hubble Space telescope: 20 percent of the visible objects are very young stars, not more than four million years old.

if chance plays a real role in the sensible world, then the existence of an intentional design of the universe is ruled out. Such a belief actually treats God as a sort of superhuman being, as paganism does, and does not apply to what the Supreme Being is thought to be in our culture. In fact, there is a tendency to forget that, since time is a property of the sensible world, a Supreme Being who has created the latter has also created the former. We use the term chance to indicate unpredictability of the future; therefore, it only applies to a being like ourselves, who knows the world by means of its senses, i.e., in terms of "here" and "now."

Augustine of Hippo made this point sixteen centuries ago,[14] when he made it clear that God, if he is really the Creator of everything, has created as it were *tota simul*, everything at the same time, what was, what is, and what will be. God is not an engineer who has set up a mechanism, and possibly modifies and adds pieces to it as time goes by; rather, God has conceived and realized the whole creation by a single act.[15] The history of the physical universe such as is being laboriously reconstructed by science is to us what the description of a line, which we see in its entirety at one glance, would be to a one-dimensional being who advances along the line, and therefore discovers its points one after the other.

In sum, for a metaphysician believing in the existence of a personal God, the very existence of life is sufficient proof that God has chosen it to be; the process by which it has appeared within time is only relevant to human beings — and to God when God deliberately places himself at our level. Therefore, neither creationism nor anticreationism can gain anything by proving or disproving that life has appeared by chance. If anything, one can say that, for those who believe in God the Creator, the artistic side added by the failure of Laplacian determinism to account for the history of the universe makes the new world-view suggested by science more open than before to the Glory of God revealing itself in the physical universe.[16] If, alternatively, one has reasons to reject the existence of God, then it is perhaps sufficient to say that matter has its own laws, which include selection rules acting like a filter, and to admit that science cannot predict everything, particularly the characteristics of new individual beings; to claim that chance is the creator of order and life amounts to assigning to chance precisely the role of the God whose existence is considered superfluous.

14. *Conf.*, ch. 11, 4.6 to 6.8.
15. This does not exclude "miracles," i.e., exceptional interventions of God in space-time: to be above time is not the same as being outside time. Nor does it exclude free will: to have taken our choices into account in the eternal instant of creation is not the same as having determined them. Cf. C. S. Lewis, *Miracles*, 181f.
16. An extremely illuminating passage on this point can be found in C. Journet, *Le mal: Essai théologique* (Paris: Desclée De Brouwer, 1961), ch. 5, sec. 2. See also A. Peacocke, "Science and God the Creator," in Templeton, *Evidence of Purpose.*.

Fields and the Space-Time Continuum

The anthropic principle expresses the unity of the universe with reference to the appearance of life. A completely different approach to that same notion was discovered much earlier by modern science with Einstein's general relativity and unified field theory, which in turn had its roots in the discovery of the electromagnetic field by James Clerk Maxwell (1831–1869).[17]

Although the notion of field has an intuitive quality, so much so that even many healers speak of cosmic energy fields and the like, when it comes to showing what a force field is a physicist is tempted to resort to equations and leave it at that. The reason (at least in the cases I know) is that, when you are being trained in physics, you start with vectors and other simple notions, then you are introduced to position dependent forces and energies, then you grow familiar with the flow of a fluid (which assigns a velocity vector to each particle of a continuous medium, and therefore to each point of a certain region of space), then you are introduced to electrostatics and magnetism — and finally you are shown that electric and magnetic forces can be assigned to the individual points of a certain region of space, regardless of whether those points are occupied by bodies capable of exerting such forces. If at this stage you are still tempted to think that you are dealing with a sort of invisible weightless fluid (the ether), you will be told, in the words of no less an influential man of science than Einstein himself:

> The electromagnetic fields are not states of a medium but independent realities, which cannot be reduced to terms of anything else and are bound to no substratum.[18]

Einstein's point is what makes grasping the force field concept particularly difficult: a field is not, as some would say, just a property of the points of a certain region of space; it is an entity in its own right, which reveals itself through properties of the points of space. Of course, one is always free to think of it as a thin fluid occupying a large expanse of space; but then one should realize that there are essential differences. One such difference is that one cannot take away part of the field (e.g., by filling a bottle with it) and leave the rest unaltered; if energy is subtracted from the field, then the whole field changes everywhere, even at

17. Cf. J. C. Maxwell, *A Dynamical Theory of the Electromagnetic Field* (1864; reprint, with an appreciation by A. Einstein, edited and introduced by T. F. Torrance, Edinburgh: Scottish Academic Press, 1982).

18. In A. Einstein, *Mein Weltbild (The World as I See It)* (1934; reprint, Frankfurt: Ullstein Materialien, 1979), quoted by T. F. Torrance as note 29 to the introduction to Maxwell, *A Dynamical Theory*. That introduction is a very useful guide for those who wish to know more about the origin and the nature of the notion of force field.

distances of billions of light years, though much later; indeed, in the case of the electromagnetic field, precisely that many years later.

There are many sorts of force fields — electromagnetic, nuclear force, weak interaction, gravitational fields. Einstein's hope was to find that universal field which contains as special aspects all the known ones, but a complete unified-field theory, as far as I know, is still under construction. At any rate, the basic steps were made with general relativity and with field quantization in the first half of the twentieth century. A very simple equation based on general relativity theory and describing the general gross behavior of the distribution of matter in space lies at the root of cosmological theories such as the theory of the expanding universe. However, if the view of sensible reality given by science is to be grasped in its full purport, Einstein's basic ideas should be grasped at a more intuitive and accessible level than that of the equations in which they can be expressed for professional applications.

As has been already mentioned in our considerations about time, relativity theory holds that the universe is an invisible and intangible space-time continuum; according to the essential idea of the unified-field theory, that continuum is in fact a force field *sui generis*. What makes it particularly difficult to grasp is that it includes time. All we can do to overcome this difficulty is to rely on analogies — which are, anyway, a perfectly legitimate tool of science, provided their limits are fully realized. As a first analogy, let us imagine that all objects, including ourselves, are denser regions inside a sort of transparent jelly full of defects, and that these denser areas are free to move along special paths (the "geodetics"). We see all objects as distinct entities, which is correct, but the stuff of which they are made is exactly the same as that of which we and the intervening space are made. You may say that the individual objects are lumps of matter immersed in emptiness, but that is not really true; they are better described as denser and thinner regions of the same fluid, moving around and deviating light rays, so that they appear to repel other objects (cf. next section). If you could make a stack of instantaneous images of this strange medium, you would have a description that also extends in time, indeed includes time in such a way that an object is what Eddington called "a four-dimensional worm."

We may call "space-time continuum" precisely the medium that is the stuff of which everything is made. If we also take into account that the past is the realm of frozen, dead, unchangeable facts, the present is the realm of becoming, and the future is the realm of what could be, but is not yet, then we may also think of the space-time continuum as a sort of primeval jelly where, here and there, past realities and future possibilities coexist, and in which material objects are just "knots" of higher density. This, I think, is the best one can do with a general analogy. Ad hoc analogies would be necessary to help in specific problems (see below).

Because it involves time as well as space, the space-time continuum cannot be perceived as such by our senses; it is "invisible and intangible," although it has by no means the status of a "transcendent" reality, of God in the Judeo-Christian tradition, whose presence is manifest rather in the pattern of events that constitute the history of the universe and in the inner experience of man. The space-time continuum is evidence that science has had to acknowledge that the essence of reality lies beyond the direct reach of our senses, indeed of our experiments "in the laboratory." Truly enough, experiments provide indirect information on underlying features of sensible reality, but theory plays a major role in their interpretation, so that we have to rely heavily on our reason. This, as Torrance has shown,[19] is an all-important result of recent scientific advances. Science has had to admit for good that one cannot discriminate between what is real and what is not on the basis of "observability" only. This is true in connection with many fields of physics other than relativity, but the latter, because it concerns the basic categories of space and time, is the field where it is most evident.

Our senses do respond to space-time, but they do so by separating time and space. If you ask Relativity how that can be so, since the stuff of which we are made, with the possible exception of our minds, is precisely the space-time continuum, she will give you the answer we already know: "This is because in your normal environment all objects move with a velocity that is a tiny fraction of the velocity of light; and under these conditions the unity of time, space and matter may be treated as their juxtaposition. Your minds, however, do realize that the situation you perceive directly with your senses is not wholly satisfactory when they try to reconcile the permanence and incessant change of certain entities, e.g., our old friend Snoopy."

In fact, the ancient Greeks had realized that the changes to which material things were subjected, from motion to decay, could not be easily reconciled with the fact that things occupy a specific place at any given instant, and retain their identity at least for short time. To solve this difficulty Plato imagined that what we perceive in our life on Earth is just a reflection of a reality lying beyond our senses as a World of immutable Ideas, where space and time have no legitimate place. Aristotle, on the contrary, unified space and time by affirming that the reality of an entity at any given instant of time is what it is in that instant and what it tends to become because of its structure and its environment. "This," Relativity goes on with her answer, "is the closest science came to the space-time picture before Einstein discovered me; but I add something more. Aristotle assumed that in an entity or being there is a 'nature,' a tendency to evolve in a certain way, which could or could not be actual-

19. Torrance, *Transformation*, ch. 2.

ized, depending on such accidents as sudden death. I add that the entire reality of a thing is its whole history, that it is a four-dimensional 'worm' of which you only see instantaneous sections, and of which you, because you are immersed in space-time, can only guess the future development or past history, if you observe it for a while, with a degree of uncertainty which depends on its complexity and on your science."

The unity and coherence of sensible reality, as conveyed by the Great Dance image, clearly emerges from these remarks, along with the notion, which we have already discussed, that the principle that a cause must precede its effect implies that there is a sort of rubber-like supertime which is common to all things. This way of putting it is approximate, and we should actually speak of the light-cone of relativity separating possible from impossible event chains, so as to ensure that causes will always precede effects, and hence events future for one observer cannot be past for another; but I hope the reader will realize that I am trying to recall the gist of the matter. Paul Davies has presented in an extensive popular book the mysteries of time.[20]

Knots in Space-Time

The idea that a force field could manifest itself in lumps or knots (quanta) which would behave as particles appeared in physics at the end of the twentieth century as a consequence of Max Planck's discovery of quantization, and was mainly developed by Albert Einstein. At that time it concerned only the quanta of the electromagnetic field, the well-known photons, which are very special because they can never be observed at rest, indeed, have zero rest mass. In 1935, the Japanese physicist Hideki Yukawa put forward the idea that the quanta of the nuclear force field could be regular particles with a nonvanishing rest mass, to be called π-mesons. Yukawa's proposal was later superseded by an incredibly complicated zoology of new elementary particles, some of which are clearly established as field quanta. Indeed, physicists not specialized in particle physics have the clear impression that something is amiss in the whole story, because the much advertised quarks are by definition nonobservable, which makes it impossible to ask the fundamental question: are they actual particles or simply fictitious entities? Nevertheless, there seems to be no question that Einstein's basic idea that all bodies are quanta or lumps of quanta of a single universal field — the very space-time continuum with characteristics extended to include the four fundamental interactions — is extremely reasonable, and one day Einstein's dream may come true.

20. Davies, *About Time.*

The following may help to grasp the basic idea behind the assertion that four-dimensional objects are "knots" of space-time. Take for example a star conceived as a solid sphere. It is a region of space-time where the motions of other bodies allowed by the very laws of nature are either curved around the star or end or start at its surface. There is no qualitative difference between what we perceive as free space and what we perceive as a solid body; there is a quantitative difference, namely that in free space the natural motions of a test body are rectilinear, near a star they are such as the law of gravitation would predict, inside the star (as far as the solid-sphere model goes) they simply do not exist. Of course, a real star is much more than a solid sphere; but the picture just given still holds in its essential features, and only becomes much richer in details and distinctions if the fact that a star is a nuclear furnace is taken into account. The idea that a body is just a special distortion of space-time is well explained by an analogy proposed by Carlson, a popular science writer of many years ago. Suppose an alien from space arrives by night in the vicinity of our planet, and looks from a certain altitude at a crowded divided highway whose east and west-bound lane separate to bypass a hill and then join again. It is nighttime, the alien does not see the cars and the road, but only streams of lights flowing for a while parallel to one another in opposite directions, then turning to their right to make a half circle, and then resuming parallel trajectories somewhat later. He might conclude that where the separation takes place there is a center of repulsion which forces the lights away from their natural rectilinear course; we know that there is no force at play, it is simply that the "natural paths" of the "luminous objects" descried in that region are curved around the hill. The latter is the view of general relativity, the former is the Newtonian conception, where the only natural motion is uniform rectilinear motion. It should be noted here, of course, that this analogy belongs to those we make in order to grasp the properties of space-time, a reality actually beyond our senses. With this reservation, it also applies to the fascinating sort of object that is a black hole, for in such a system even the natural paths of light rays would be folded back, so that light rays emitted by the black hole cannot escape from their source; this is why a black hole is not visible, and its presence is only revealed because of the curving natural paths of objects moving in its vicinity, though not too closely.

Consider next the motion or the transformation of a body. All natural paths in space-time change with its changes in location or in properties, at least in its vicinity. That is to say, a change of an object in space-time involves a change in structure of space-time itself. To understand this point think of a motor boat on a perfectly still water surface. Its propeller creates a disturbance consisting of waves which we can consider circular (for simplicity) as long as the boat is still. When it moves, roughly speaking, the waves retain the same shape, but their centers move all the time. If a body in space-time behaves in a similar way, then we can expect that other bodies will "feel" its presence and its evolution, the more so the closer they are to it (in space and in time). The decrease of this effect for increasing distances in space is entirely analogous to the decreasing intensity of gravitational, electric, magnetic attractions and repulsions generated by that body as predicted by classical physics; its decrease in time is analogous to the flattening out with time of waves produced on a water surface.

In terms of the Cosmic Dance image, one could say that the dancer or group of dancers who have started a new figure "signal" their motion to nearby dancers, who follow the new development according to the rules of the Great Symphony. The change in the structure of space-time associated with the change of one body representing a particular theme in the Symphony thus manifests itself also through the bodies close to it. In turn, those bodies modify the structure of space-time around them, so that they as it were relay the initial event. If there is no special mechanism at work, the message will become weaker and weaker as the distance in space and time increases, so that what it produces as long as passive receivers are involved is a sort of local coherence, dying out with distance. This implies that passive bodies at a great distance in space and time are not affected by a particular event at a given point and instant of time. But there are other sides to the story. The most important one is that information processors and amplifiers exist in the form of living beings, particularly human beings. It is true that the light coming from such a remote object as the globular cluster G1 orbiting around the Andromeda galaxy, at about 2.3 million light years from the sun, arrives here so weak that it has taken the Hubble space telescope to obtain an image of it, but we *know* that G1 is there, and this fact may cause effects which, though small, are far greater than their cause. To this selective amplification property of communication to and between living beings we shall devote a whole chapter. But that is not all. To get a feeling for the enormous range of possible repercussions of local events just consider that the space-time continuum might resemble the membrane of a drum. As everybody knows, the slightest stroke on a drum will generate vibrations which propagate to the rim and are reflected back from it. The distance that can be covered by the vibration wave is very large with respect to the region directly hit by the stroke, and could be much larger. Is this sort of phenomenon possible in the space-time continuum?

Other modes of unity, more mysterious though mathematically worked out, include a famous and still unsolved problem raised by the American physicists J. A. Wheeler and R. P. Feynman in 1945. According to electromagnetism, no light source could emit light if there were not, somewhere in space, an absorber capable of absorbing it. But absorbers are far away in the future of the emitter: for instance, the matter that absorbs the radiation of the sun will be reached by the sun's radiation after minutes to millions of years. How is the sun to know that after its emission that matter will be there, ready to receive its radiation, at the time it emits? As far as I know, the Wheeler-Feynman paper was never challenged, but neither was its contradiction with relativity removed — i.e., the restriction that nothing can happen that requires a message traveling faster than light. A mysterious fact of the same sort has emerged out of the recent discovery of apparently nonlocal phenomena. The evidence is still little understood, but certainly opens new vistas on the nature of matter and on the unity of the universe.[21] The main point is that under special circumstances two particles behave as if they could "communicate" instantaneously at large distances, again an event strictly forbidden by the theory of relativity, which sets the velocity of light as the upper limit to the velocity of information transfer. If the evidence cannot be explained in any other way, as a vast majority of physicists seem to believe, this means that the particles in question constitute a unit extending over a comparatively large region of space. That is to say, they normally behave as genuine particles occupying single points of space, but there are circumstances under which they behave as if each particle occupied two or more points at the same time. We are thus confronted with a "nonlocality" property which points to an underlying long-range *synchronic* coherence of the world, whereby a general pattern is ensured at any given instant of time over and beyond the normal operation of cause-effect chains, which is *diachronic* because it concerns successive events.

In short, the notion of a space-time continuum, which is space, time, and matter all in one, emphasizes the unity of the universe. At the same time, however, it seems that novelties appearing in a particular region of space at a certain time can only participate in the *long-range* coherence of the Dance if

(a) some suspected but so far poorly understood "nonlocal" mechanism overcoming the limitations of relativity is at work, *or*

(b) coherence is ensured by information exchange involving highly sophisticated control systems capable of processing and amplifying the information carried by extremely weak messages — that is, living beings, as in the example of the astronavigating blackcap.

The Ship's Bearings

This chapter is in a sense a chapter of odds and ends. It contains a number of points that we had just descried during the exploration made in

21. D'Espagnat, *À la recherche du réel*.

the preceding chapters. What we have seen, however, is far from being a minor addition to the picture we are trying to outline. We have found that, though chance appears to play no significant role in the end result of evolution at large, and in general whenever nature resorts to repeated trial-and-error operations, when it comes to individuals chance is the tool nature uses to produce variety and novelties. That the novelties produced adjust to the universal coherence — as illustrated before in the case of Socrates — is a new version of Darwinian selection which takes nothing out of the element of randomness present in the birth of Socrates or the birth of any other human being. When one considers women and men like the Virgin Mary and her Son, then, apart from religious belief, one feels that individuals so important for the history of mankind reveal the existence of patterns of events which science can only acknowledge, for they appear to lie outside the scope of general laws. The question then is again whether or not the word "Fate" should be used instead of "Chance," meaning by Fate the decision of a Supreme Authority in charge of the universe. At the same time, the existence of patterns of "significant" events, which science (in the ordinary sense) treats as random because it cannot find any law or spontaneous process by which they can be brought about, strongly points to the importance of including in science not only sociology, as is currently done, but the science of history and in general all human sciences, as long as they satisfy the fundamental classical definition of science: *scire per causas*, to know in terms of causes.

Fate and human sciences have thus appeared on the stage of the Great Dance. But in this chapter of odds and ends, we have also spoken of the coherence and unity of the universe. The anthropic cosmological principle has shown us that present science has been led to describe a universe where the most general laws are finely tuned to the very existence of man — an insignificant detail in terms of size and duration. Whether or not our science is final, the behavior of remote quasars is in some way "conditioned" by the fact that the same laws that govern it have the particular form that would make life possible; and that form conceals a mysterious and wondrous unity.

The space-time continuum and the unified-field perspective open another vista on the unity of the universe. The universe might well be a single invisible and intangible whole where matter, space, and time are fused together, and the reality we see might be the manifestation of that unity on the planes accessible to our senses. But then mysteries without end arise, not least the paradoxes of physics at the quantum and classical level, nonlocality and the emitter-absorber puzzle of electromagnetism.

The two parts of this chapter are related to one another in that they show that science is now admitting that it is far from being the source of all wisdom, except in the sense that it opens our minds to the beautiful, the unknown, the free forces of spirit acting in that very universe which it describes in an ever richer and coherent way.

From now on, therefore, we shall have to navigate in different waters, those where man is the center of attention, and the spiritual side of reality surfaces again and again even if one is not looking for it. We shall have to spend a little more time on a particular face of the Great Dance: how is the ever changing coherence that is its leitmotif ensured? Fifty years ago, a scientist would have answered: "by forces and fields." Today, as we have seen, that is not enough: not only has organization been discovered again, but the celestial navigation of the little blackcaps and the lofty music of the pulsars, as we have seen in chapter one, suggest that the glue holding the universe together must be more than electromagnetic and gravitational. We already know that the concept best describing the situation is *communication;* and we have just seen that living beings, especially human beings, are particularly efficient in that connection. This is why our attention, even within the frame of science, must now shift to life and more specifically to man.

Chapter 8

The Place of Man

According to ancient philosophy, man is an animal endowed with reason and capable of making free choices. The claim still exists that science tells a different story, and ethics is only a set of taboos. But, for one thing, can environmental science do without the notion of human responsibility? What new insights do systems theory and machine design provide in this connection, and more generally on the relation between man's strictly biological programming and his insuppressible need of reference to some higher reality?

Prologue – Science as a Tool of Man – Man as a Free Agent – The Foundations of the Science of Environment – The Moral Issue – Biological Manipulations – Ethics and the Theory of Systems – A Summary and Some Questions – Homeostasis and Individuals – The Optimum State – A Supreme Legislator? – The Place of Man – Robinson Crusoe

---

Consider ye the seed from which ye sprang;
You were not made to live like unto brutes,
But for pursuit of virtue and of knowledge.

— DANTE ALIGHIERI[1]

Prologue

Our exploration has arrived at a realization of the greatest importance. Cosmology, chemistry, biology, systems theory all converge to confirm that, after the crisis of the seventeenth century, the picture of the sensible world presented by science is again one of beauty and coherence as it was in Dante's time. But change and innovation are no longer confined to a sphere where evil and decay are free to rage; they are features of a unity, that of a grand and harmonious Dance of all things, tiny or huge, simple or complex. Now, the pattern of the Dance in time and space does obey in its main features laws that science has discovered or at least guessed; certain events, however, particularly the appearance of individual dancers or of extremely improbable fluctuations, are not determined by those laws — although they conform to them. As we have seen, a scientist will say that they are due to chance, meaning that their causes, if any, cannot be found by the methods of science; and this implies that in sensible reality there is room for the spontaneous emergence of novelties as well as for the intervention of free agents.

The latter side of the story was clear to the ancients and should have been made evident to Galilean science at least by the marvels of technology since the eighteenth century. What is technology but the deliberate realization by human beings of situations whose spontaneous realization is exceedingly improbable, but which do not violate the laws of nature, indeed take advantage of them? Thomas Aquinas, around 1260, explained this by a very simple example:

In nullo enim alio natura ab arte videtur differre, nisi quia natura est principium intrinsecum, et ars est principium extrinsecum. Si

---

1. Dante, *Divine Comedy*, "Inferno," 26, 119–120: Longfellow trans.

> *"Considerate la vostra semenza;*
> *Fatti non foste a viver come bruti*
> *Ma per seguir virtute e conoscenza."*

enim ars factiva navis esset intrinseca ligno, facta fuisset navis a
natura, sicut modo fit ab arte ... natura nihil est aliud quam ratio
cujusdam artis, scilicet divinae, qua ipsae res moventur ad finem
determinatum, sicut si artifex factor navis posset lignis tribuere,
quod ex se ipsis moverentur ad navis formam inducendam.[2]

The above quotation can be translated as follows, with the freedom required to make use of current language possible:

In fact, it would seem that the nature of a thing [i.e., its inherent drive to spontaneous change] only differs from technology because it is an intrinsic modifying force, whereas technology is an extrinsic one. For example, if the technical procedures necessary for the construction of a ship were inherent in the materials used to make it, the ship would be made by its nature just as it actually is by artificial means. The nature of things [particularly of living beings] is but the set of procedures of a certain technology, obviously divine, by which those things change to acquire a final shape and structure, just as would be the case if the designer of a ship could impart to the materials entering its construction the ability to move and take the shapes required to realize the ship.

The self-assembling of pieces to form a new structure is now an established fact of chemistry, and is postulated, as we have seen, in theories of the origin of life. Nevertheless, Aquinas's argument still applies, because chemists have to put together the right ingredients, thus creating a highly improbable situation, whereas the theories of the spontaneous origin of life all strive to show that the right conditions were in the order of things at the time when life appeared.

Science as a Tool of Man

The scientists of the eighteenth and nineteenth century (as well as most biologists of the twentieth century) were well alive to an all-important implication of the above consideration, namely that the view of man as a free agent is fully consistent with science. That is probably the psychological reason why some of them tried to turn determinism into a general principle of nature, also applying to human beings, while others, like Jacques Monod, ignored the significance of the manipulation of nature by human beings, and decreed that all that could not be explained by scientific laws was blind chance. Actually, according to the picture of things science has arrived at in the last decades of the twentieth century, the technologist intervenes where nature itself leaves room for interventions, i.e., where, if left to itself, it would either accept passively the situation

2. Aquinas, *In Aristotelis Libros Physicorum*, LII, l.XIV.

it happens to be in or, because of the continuous motion of molecules and smaller particles, would wait for some self-amplifying fluctuation to occur.

Now, human interventions are not necessarily minor happenings in the Great Dance. Even before the great achievements of modern technology there were in history periods when man's technical ability had dramatic consequences, both negative and positive. Just think of the exchange of infectious diseases and the introduction of new vegetables that took place in the seventeenth century between Europe and America because well-built caravels had allowed Columbus to cross the Atlantic.[3] In that century what we consider today an obsolete technology was sufficient to cause planetary changes which natural barriers had prevented for tens of thousand of years.

This means that somehow science has to face the question, far too easily solved by Jacques Monod, of the place of man in the universe; even without invading the domain of spirituality, science cannot afford to leave such an efficient (and dangerous) Dancer out of its analysis of the Great Dance. But then, as we are going to see, the great question of moral values arises on two accounts: environmental problems and the way science can account, in terms of the general theory of systems, for the functions that such a special animal as man has in nature.

These considerations can be rephrased in a different way, which can help us to appreciate their significance under a different perspective. If science is the tool by which human beings establish a cognitive and operative interaction with nature, then mere common sense tells us that the central, albeit implicit, task of science is to situate us as knowing and free subjects in the very picture of the universe we ourselves make, by means of science, for our own use. Indeed, we have started this book by pointing out that the primary significance of science is to provide a critical analysis of sensory experience, which is a necessary condition for applying ethical values to concrete situations. Of course, science is also important because it makes technological advances possible, but that is a secondary aspect; should anybody doubt that this is the case, let that person consider the current passionate debates about many issues of science (e.g., evolution), and the fact that "what science offers for our belief" (in the words of Bertrand Russell) has provided the foundation for scientistic creeds, from Russell to Monod to certain science fiction writers.

As a matter of fact, not only can science throw light on the place of man in the universe, but it can be misused to serve strange preconcep-

---

3. Syphilis was probably imported to Europe by Columbus's sailors. The Europeans exported their diseases, and even attempts at establishing constructive relations with the Indians often failed because the Indians were not immune to European diseases, as is witnessed by the sad remains of the Jesuit mission of "Les Saintes Maries" in Ontario. Among the vegetables introduced in Europe were potatoes and tomatoes.

tions. Consider those popularizers of science (including certain Nobel laureates) who claim that science shows beyond any possible doubt that man is merely an animal like the others. Unless it means what the ancient Greeks stated long before the rise of modern science ("man is a rational animal"), that statement is void of meaning, because animals range from whales to butterflies, from elephants to mites, from amoebas to bees: which of them should man be like? Actually, what the popularizers in question presumably mean is that, since other animals have no ethics or religion, it should be so with humans too. One can contend that, since we have in common with other animals only the fact that we are animals like elephants and flies, and since different animal species have different specific characteristics, it is not against the order of things that man should possess rationality — the ability to think — and freedom of choice. Thus science has nothing to say against moral values and a spiritual reference.

I believe it can be shown that in fact today's science strongly points to the necessity of reference values for the conduct of individual persons. There are, as everybody knows, scientists and writers who, in the name of science, campaign against moral rules. But their crusade seems self-defeating; for they usually campaign at the same time against anti-Semitism, pollution, and so on, and a moment's reflection shows that this is a contradiction: if moral principles are a fiction, why should one expect that human beings should feel bound to precise principles in particular matters? On what grounds should a person who has been told that he should always do as he pleases, and does not feel obliged to respect other people in general, respect those who belong to a particular race or community? The implicitly granted and explicitly denied fact is that, according to what the scientific-technological enterprise has to teach, the Great Dance of the Universe — the coherent becoming of individual systems and beings, all interacting and communicating with one another, and hence all partaking of an overall unity — allows for the existence of animals (the humans) endowed with freedom of choice; and freedom implies the necessity of basic invariable moral rules, one being precisely respect for all other human beings. If such freedom is not granted, then contradictions are unavoidable. Let us see in more detail how this point can be analyzed within the frame of science.

Man as a Free Agent

What we have to reflect upon is the actual and the ideal harmonious relation of a human being with its environment. A complete treatment of this theme would require a preliminary study devoted to the definition of man, and would take us beyond the limits of this book. Nevertheless, as we have just begun to see, in the very course of a reflection on what science has to tell about the interrelation between man and his environment, living and nonliving, one is led to explore certain aspects of human nature. More specifically, emphasis has to be placed on the fact that, precisely because a human being is a rational animal capable of free choices (at least within the limits which we shall determine below), that human being is a person, indeed an "acting person," which only through action comes out of the realm of potentialities to become a reality.[4]

As we said, there have been conflicting views about the actual freedom of man. The determinists claim that *actually* this freedom is just a feeling, because the genes and the personal and social history of any given person actually decide what that person will choose on any given occasion. The application of scientific criteria shows that this argument is flawed, simply because it invokes nonobservable causes. A fine consideration by Heisenberg, one of the founding fathers of quantum mechanics, applies here as to many other arguments based on an unproven and unprovable possibility:

> One should particularly remember that the human language permits the construction of sentences which do not involve any consequences and therefore have no content at all — in spite of the fact that these sentences produce some kind of picture in our imagination; e.g., the statement that besides our world there exists another world, with which any connection is impossible in principle, does not lead to any experimental consequence, but does produce a kind of picture in the mind. Obviously such a statement can neither be proved nor disproved. One should be especially careful in using the words "reality," "actually," etc., since these words very often lead to statements of the type just mentioned.[5]

An observable aspect of important choices is that they very often cost considerable psychological stress and suffering, because the person who has to decide would much prefer one alternative and yet feels that he or she is obliged to choose the other. In this case, feelings are the facts, while the claim that after all the course of action was predetermined can only be defended by saying that "actually" there were other unknown factors at play. Another observable aspect is that in practice most determinists assume that they and their fellow human beings are free, for example by supporting legislation for or against certain forms of behavior. It must be admitted that there are also consistent determinists, those for instance who claim that criminals should not be punished, because the fault is with society and the genes; but that theory is what K. Popper would have

---

4. Karol Wojtyla, *The Acting Person* (Dordrecht: Reidel, 1979). Cf. also M. Blondel, *L'action* (1893; reprint Paris: Quadrige/Presses Universitaires de France, 1993).
5. W. Heisenberg, *The Physical Principles of the Quantum Theory* (Chicago: University of Chicago Press, 1930), ch.1, 15.

termed unscientific, for it is so vague that, if it is false, no one will ever be able to prove that it is, no matter how much evidence is presented against it. As to the consideration that there are inclinations and circumstances which favor, sometimes irresistibly, choices in one or the other direction, we all know by personal experience that, except in conditions of strong psychological unbalance, either fear of consequences or personal moral standards also play a fundamental role.

The reader will certainly realize that the remarks just made concern questions that lie at the borderline between natural sciences and disciplines like sociology and psychology.[6] To remain in the ambit of the natural sciences, we must be content with this practical consideration: whatever the various camps claim, the vast majority of people as far back in the past as historical records go have based their actions on the belief that each human being is a free rational subject — a "person" in the philosophical sense of the term — nor are there any genuinely scientific observations supporting the opposite view. Indeed, especially in the second half of the twentieth century, science has been faced with ethical issues and (despite attempts to assert the contrary) it has to look somewhere else to cope with them. Let us examine this point.

The Foundations of the Science of Environment

Until about 1990, the mass media channeled an enormous interest on environmental problems, and the effects were certainly beneficial, if only because one no longer sees everywhere little streams of water full of the dirty foam of sulfonates. Later, perhaps justifiably, since most citizens were finally aware of the pollution problem, public interest moved to other issues. Nevertheless, a field of inquiry called environmental science has continued to thrive, and, despite the (very human) tendency to brand conjectures or fears as scientific facts, it has gained the respect of the scientific community. This state of things justifies our beginning with a question, which sounds only vaguely related to our present theme: when speaking of environmental science, is one referring to a body of knowledge obtained and developed in the same way as the science of materials, the science of systems, physics, chemistry, and even medicine?

The reason for this question is simple. If the answer is "yes," as some people seem to believe, then man is ruled out: for, to describe the nature and state of environmental science, one need only make a list of problems and of advances made in our knowledge and ability to control

6. An interesting analysis related to this point can be found in an article by U. Görman, "Does Sociobiology Hold Implications for Ethics?" in *The Science and Theology of Information*, ed. C. Wassermann, R. Kirby, and B. Rordorff (Geneva: Labor et Fides, 1992).

our environment by means of practical measures inspired by science, and make a few vague remarks as to the prospects of the human species in the challenge posed to its survival by the very advances of science and technology. If the answer is "no," then one has the unpleasant task of explaining the role of scientific "facts" and "methods" in environmental studies, which nevertheless use the term "scientific" to stress the soundness and certainty of their "data." If the answer is "yes, but...," then perhaps we have a more interesting time before us. Let us examine the three possibilities in succession.

The "yes" answer — the notion that the relation of man to his environment can be considered as the subject of a science of the same type as physics and biology, not involving any metaphysical or ethical issue — would certainly please a number of philosophers and educators of the modern schools (think of the Western branch of materialism, e.g., John Dewey's evolutionistic instrumentalism) because it would be compatible with a relativistic view of truth and ethics. Unfortunately, it is not compatible with the nature of the case: when people speak of respecting nature they are clearly thinking of something independent of them; and if nature belongs to the "otherness," then the sophists of all times will have a hard time justifying their theses.

But neither can one say that the study of such material things and beings as form the environment of man is not scientific; for then one would not know what to do with the role of science and technology in the very origin of the problem. The "no" answer is thus obviously unacceptable. It seems natural to expect that the right answer should lie at the golden mean.

Let us now try to prove that it is not legitimate to declare that our subject belongs to a scientific discipline of the same type as physics, but it is legitimate to consider it the subject of an autonomous discipline of a meta-scientific type. By this I mean that a possible environmental science may have all the attributes of scientificity, which we shall list in a moment, but is certainly dependent for its raw material, as it were, on other disciplines. Physics, chemistry, biology extract from reality their own facts by observation and experiment, classify them, and derive from them a variety of rules and laws, which are all based on those facts, even though, especially in the case of physics, they may be applicable to a wider class of facts. This is not the case with environmental studies. For example, the facts and the theory on which the issue of ozone depletion is based belong to chemistry and to a smaller extent to the physics of the high atmosphere: but the issue itself lies beyond the so-called "universe of problems" defined by the "programs" of physics and chemistry.

Trying to express what common sense suggests, we can probably say that a discourse is scientific if it is based on:

1. Facts ascertained according to criteria ensuring a maximum of objectivity;

2. Unambiguous cause-effect relations critically established by excluding alternatives;

3. Clearly defined assumptions;

4. A careful distinction between conjectures, extrapolations, and facts.

There seems to be no doubt that environmental studies could be scientific in the sense defined by the points above. Whether the current practice of environmental scientists conforms to them is a different question, which does not interest us here. But another question remains: how can we prove that those points refer to a discipline genuinely different from physics, biology, and other traditional branches of science? As we said, the facts on which environmental science is based are ascertained and processed by other sciences. However, what makes a science is not the individual facts, but the questions raised about them, which require precise criteria for the assessment of cause-effect relations. It is as if, given a fabric with threads of different colors and sizes, one person studied the sizes and arrangement of green threads, another inquired about the rules governing the choices of colors, while a third tried to ascertain the role of green threads in the general aspect of the fabric. This example shows that the same observation, possibly processed and interpreted according to the schemes appropriate to a certain class of problems, can be used in a study of an entirely different sort. Think of the mechanisms of cell reproduction: they have been discovered by the application of chemical knowledge, but, by the very nature of the problem, the results belong unquestionably to biology.

Considerations of this kind lead to the conclusion that the necessity of borrowing procedures and interpretations from traditional disciplines is by no means a reason why environmental science should be refused an independent status. The condition for such status is that there should be a specific problem or set of problems, to be treated with ad hoc procedures. If this condition is satisfied, then environmental science may be considered a discipline by itself, in fact a *metadiscipline*, a discipline working with information processed by other disciplines. Consider the general formulation of an environmental problem: "Which facts are relevant to environment pollution and preservation, and why?" This formulation involves several special concepts, in particular those of environment and pollution, which confer its specificity to environmental science. These concepts are used here with (a) reference to human beings or to animals subconsciously treated as if they were human beings; (b) reference to a value scale, by which some facts are "good," other facts are "bad."

If objectivity (according to point 1 above) is a basic condition for the scientificity of environmental studies, then one implication is that what we call the environment of man is actually whatever there is (on the material plane); therefore, by accepting the existence and the "rights" of nature above and beyond our whims, we incorporate realism in the very notion of environmental science. Moreover, if points a and b above are accepted, then humans are considered as free agents responsible for possible "damage" to nature, i.e., capable of choosing between good and evil. Finally, ethical acceptability of an action must have the same status as, say, absolute temperature — it must be independent of the observer.

Thus, from the question of environmental science being a science we reach the conclusion that, when it comes to problems concerning the relation of man to nature, science presupposes an ample *metaphysical* commitment, because it rests on a view of man and of nature characterized by realism, belief in free will, and belief that ethical rules independent of individuals and circumstances are necessary. This is the standpoint we shall adopt in our further reflections.

The Moral Issue

Since we are interested in the relation of human beings to their environment and to life, we can confine ourselves to the choices and responsibility of man in that connection. Our first question must then be: What kind of moral rules should one think of when considering environmental problems? In general, they are those which man should follow if he is to make choices consistent with his nature and his role in the universe. Although belief in a natural ethic is not equivalent to believing in God, there are strong arguments in favor of the thesis that the Ten Commandments as interpreted by Christianity are essentially a concise codification of those rules. Even granting such a claim, however, it cannot be denied that the Ten Commandments were written for a civilization where machines and chemicals were extremely primitive. Therefore, their application to the problems raised by modern science and technology is a serious challenge for moral theologians. More specifically, there are two fields where theologians, philosophers, and scientists have just begun a new systematic reflection: our responsibility toward nature in general and toward living beings in particular — in short, not only environment modifications of our natural environment, but also biomanipulations and biotechnology.

Concerning our relation to nature in general, I think that all those who are sensitive to that problem have one basic notion in the back of their minds: that there is a general harmony of the material cosmos, which is independent of man and which must be respected as *sacred*. I call here sacred, in agreement with the Jewish philosopher Abraham

Heschel,[7] what is accessible to us but is not at our disposal. If this is a correct interpretation of the word and the mental attitude it expresses, it is certainly not surprising that even materialists engaged in environmental protection have a sort of religious attitude toward nature. Nor is it surprising that many Christians, on the contrary, feel that their religion is only concerned with God and human beings; for they take in a modern sense certain expressions of the Scriptures, and do not realize that God's creation must be respected and considered sacred because, although it was left open to human interventions, it was not conceived by man for himself. The presence of this point in the Scriptures has only been recognized by recent exegesis of the Old Testament, in particular of the passages where (in the Book of Genesis) reference is made to man choosing the names of the animals — which is the very action in ancient patriarchal civilizations a man would perform to recognize his son and assume responsibility for his support and education as well as authority over him — and where (in the Book of Job) God himself points out that the material universe is an illustration of the fact that his ways and aims are unmeasurably richer and more complex than man can even conceive. Thus environmental science joins the traditional sciences in adhering implicitly to the Great Dance image, the notion that the universe has an inherent dynamical coherence and harmony. By raising the ethical issue it also raises the question of the principle to which that coherence should be traced back, and hints at the world-view presented in the Book of Job. We shall also see (in chapter ten) that it has also recovered, without realizing it, the alliance between man and nature that was characteristic of "genuine" alchemy.

Biological Manipulations

It is not linguistic coincidence that already in Aristotle's time the word "nature" denoted the external material reality as well as the built-in principle of development and behavior of a specific being or entity, that is, what distinguishes that being or entity from everything else. Now — at least if we confine ourselves to entities not made by man, and more specifically to living beings — the "what-it-is-ness," the "quiddity" of a given entity includes the fact that it is as it were integrated in its environment, albeit with a measure of indeterminacy, what we may call, in the case of human beings, the free-choice domain. Thus, nature may be understood as the integrated set of all natures in so far as they are "spontaneous," and hence exist independently of human will.

Tampering with the mechanisms of life of even one individual is one way, perhaps the most serious way, in which man can violate the sa-

7. A. Heschel, *Who Is Man?* (Stanford, Calif.: Stanford University Press, 1965).

credness of nature. As is well known, reflection on this aspect of man's relation to his environment (including the human body) is made especially difficult by the fact that there are conflicting duties. For example, tampering with the human genome might provide cures for terrible genetic diseases. Another example is experiments on animals, which, in the mind of many a researcher, are indispensable for progress in medicine.

That there are problems is now acknowledged everywhere; for instance, a few years ago the National Institutes of Health of the United States requested a study on the moral aspects of the well known "Human Genome Project" sponsored by the American government. Here I should like to draw attention to two crucial but usually neglected points. One is the *criteria* by which some set of ethical rules is established. The other is the question of *experts*.

Let us consider first of all what is currently understood by "ethics." In expressions such as "bioethics" the word ethics has been downgraded to what until a few decades ago was called "professional deontology," namely the particular rules professionals, e.g., doctors, ought to conform to in their activity.[8] It has been suggested[9] that the identification of ethics with deontology is related to the persistence of a point of view which in the last analysis makes human "reason" (whatever that may be) the ultimate lawmaker in matters of knowledge and decisions. Actually, the observation of the results of the application of that view in certain societies, particularly in the educational system, has persuaded many a sociologist that only a normative ethics involving a clear-cut hierarchy of values can provide the foundations for an ethical system and a deontology really consistent with the nature of man. We shall try to examine this point in greater depth in the latter part of this chapter.

Two values, nature and life, are often said to be provided by science. That should mean that science tells us that nature and life must be considered more important than, say, personal comfort. More important for what and for whom? For the survival of the human species? But, then, do a dog or an ant worry about the survival of their own species? Or do they worry about their environment? And, even if they did, how can science prove than *Homo sapiens* should do so? As to nature, even granting that science can show that it is a value, should its *status quo* be respected more than the right to survival and reproduction of certain human communities? Do scientists no longer believe that the driving force of nature

8. For details on the general meaning of the term "deontology," which essentially applies to the branch of ethics which discusses duties as such, cf. the entry "deontology," by A. Quinton, in *The Fontana Dictionary of Modern Thought*, ed. A. Bullock, O. Stallybrass, and S. Trombley (London: Fontana Paperbacks, 1988), and extensive dictionaries such as the *Random House Dictionary*.

9. E. Agazzi, *Il bene e il male nella scienza* (Good and evil in science) (Milan: Rusconi, 1992).

is precisely the fight of animal species to affirm their own survival and multiplication at the expense of the others?

Perhaps, when certain scientists speak of values derived from science, they really mean that those values can be "founded" on the recognition that the universe is a harmonious whole, whose harmony can be perturbed by man especially if life and nature are not respected. But — unless, as happens in the strange civilization of the West, we consider men (except oneself, I suppose) just an error of nature — it would seem that human beings are entitled to the same respect as any other living species. This reflection raises several problems. For example, imagine that certain primitive tribes live on animals whose species is in danger of extinction, and that you can prevent those tribes from hunting them; on what grounds would you decide one way or the other? Fortunately, given enough good will and love for our neighbors, we have been given sufficient ingenuity to solve such conflicts; but the temptation to avoid difficult and expensive research might induce the false belief that a choice between two conflicting alternatives is actually required. It might even happen that mere guesses about the future, e.g., the possibility of increase in CO_2 concentration in the atmosphere centuries ahead, may be used to defend the anti-human choice while pretending that what is in question is the future of mankind.

It is not as easy to believe that human ingenuity can overcome those conflicts of values which arise when the lives of individuals are at stake. Issues such as abortion are extremely simple at the theoretical level: abortion is the destruction of a human life, and no "but..." can change that fact; moral conflicts may arise in specific concrete cases, each of which will have its own ethical configuration, but specialists of ethics or, for that matter, legislators know that particular cases cannot serve as arguments against that general assertion, because difficulties arising with concrete applications of general rules are there in all moral and legal matters. On the other hand, a general theoretical assessment becomes increasingly difficult as more sophisticated applications of biomedical technologies are considered. For example, the *in vitro* development of a human embryo could be construed as work in favor of life, which is a positive value. The repugnance it inspires is hard to justify, yet most of us are morally certain that there is something wrong in it. Is it because such a procedure would amount to fabricating orphans? Is it because we are sure that technology will never be able to reproduce the physiological conditions of ordinary gestation? We have thus to define carefully the value we have to oppose to the life value; all we know at the moment is that the difficult part of the issue concerns the means as well as the ends. As a matter of fact, here is where the difference between the values "living being" and "human person" seems to be most important.

In general, biomedical technologies are means, and the temptation is great to declare that they are generally wrong because they interfere with the natural mechanisms of life. But this position is obviously too simplistic, for it would apply even to vaccinations, drugs, and ordinary surgery, whose role in reducing human sufferings has been enormous. On the other hand, procedures like the artificial prolongation of life appear to require a serious ethical analysis, for it often seems that there the professional pride of medical doctors is at work rather than the life-value. We touch here a key difficulty in the relation of human society to advanced biomedical procedures, what Paul K. Feyerabend rightly and eloquently described as the *problem of experts*.[10] This problem is most evident in the case of organ transplantation. Let us grant, for the sake of argument, that organ transplantation as such is morally good under all circumstances. But, as is well known, it requires live organs, which may be taken from a human being who is in a state of "brain death." Such a human being is one about whom an expert declares that

(a) brain activity is irreversibly lost;

(b) if the equipment keeping the body in activity were removed, decomposition would immediately set in.

Even among specialists, only a few are considered competent enough to establish that those two conditions are satisfied, and hence the human being in question is actually dead. But consider on what delicate grounds the assessment is made. Condition (a) includes the word "irreversibly," which means: "if one waited, it would not return to normal"; condition (b) contains an explicit "if." Now, it is true that science usually works with predictions, which are invariably realized. But in other cases general laws are involved, and the evidence for their validity is really overwhelming; here only statistical data on a limited number of cases are available. One could say that, after all, doctors always have to certify death; but in case of doubt they can always wait one or two days, and check that decay is actually taking place. That is not possible for brain death declarations, because then the organs would no longer be good for transplantation.

I leave to the reader the problem of deciding what is the right stand in this matter. What is of interest here is that, through laws and public opinion pressures, we accept or refuse the authority of experts in these matters. If we accept it, then we share their responsibility in decisions which might amount to killing a person in order to use that person's organs. If we do not accept it, we end up in the situation we are witnessing with regard to the chemical industry: many people would vote for its suppression all over the world, just to wake up the next day to the hard reality of general starvation and devastating diseases. In sum,

10. G. V. Coyne, M. Heller, and J. Źiciński, eds., *The Galileo Affair: A Meeting of Faith and Science* (Vatican City: Specola Vaticana, 1985), 155ff.

the correct role of experts and public opinion is a first-magnitude sociological problem in connection with biological manipulations as well as with environmental science.

Ethics and the Theory of Systems

Let us now return to the main stream of our reflections on man's relation with nature. We have already shown the fuzziness and contradictions of the statement that man is an animal "like the others." Here we should add that nevertheless such a statement makes sense if it is intended to raise the following question: since animals appear to have specific characteristics, which enable them to fit in the network of relations that is nature, can science tell us something about how the supposed specific characteristics of human beings make the human species capable of a particular biological role? This is a new question. In connection with environmental science we have seen that scientists take for granted that humans are rational and free beings; here we are asking how it comes that nature has produced such beings. If science can give an answer, then we can infer that somehow biology includes information relevant to the existence of a spiritual dimension of mankind.

Although, as I had occasion to mention, ferocious enemies of the notion of function can still be found among scientists, probably no one would deny that statements like "in a biological community ('biocenose') the predators have the function of controlling the population of herbivores" are scientific statements that can be substantiated and made more precise by observation. In fact, the term "ecological niche" was coined precisely to indicate "the role of a species in relation to other species and its physical environment."[11] It belongs to a branch of science that was well established long before environmental science appeared, namely ecology, particularly animal ecology, defined as follows:

> Animal ecology is concerned with the interrelations between animals and their environments. It is a branch of ecology, or that branch of biology which embraces the interrelations between plants and animals and their complete environments. Ecology is a basic approach to the conservation of natural resources, and — together with several other biological sciences, such as biochemistry, genetics, cytology and general physiology — cuts across the sciences of zoology and botany. That is, it is concerned frequently with general principles that apply to both animals and plants.[12]

11. W. K. Purves and G. H. Orians, *Life: The Science of Biology* (Sunderland, Mississippi: Sinauer Assoc., 1987), 1168.
12. Orlando Park, in *Encyclopaedia Britannica*, 1960 ed., vol. 7, s.v. "animal ecology."

The premise above is important to show that the question we want to consider at this point is a genuinely scientific one: "What is the ecological niche of the human species, i.e., its role in relation to other species and its physical environment?" It is a question involving the "general principles" mentioned by Park in the passage just quoted. It is normally given only cursory attention in environmental studies, probably because of the utilitarian bias — and the resulting (unjustified) loss of interest in "understanding" — characterizing most current scientific research. Yet, to give an example, when Dr. Peter Raven, the director of the magnificent Missouri Botanical Garden, once spoke passionately in defense of biodiversity,[13] he did have in mind the belief that the attitudes of human beings in that connection mattered, which in turn means that he attributed to the human species precisely an ecological niche, that is, a specific role in its environment, and moreover a role involving responsibility.

Scientifically speaking, one could perhaps present in the following manner the essentials of the answer to the new question with which we are confronted. The very fact that scientists are human, and hence emotionally involved in the matter, makes a completely objective analysis very difficult; nevertheless, it is clear that science provides no justification for the often heard claim that mankind is but a cause of damage to nature. Those who believe that, if human beings have a role at all, it is a destructive one, and that for nature the only good human being is a dead one are probably well-meaning pessimists who lack the patient courage everybody should have in all aspects of life. In my opinion, the real point is that our species has an extreme adaptability, which implies that it can interfere with the most varied environments; therefore it is expected to find by reason and careful balancing of issues the right action to be performed in each case. Moreover, that right action must be a complicated combination of individual and collective choices. If humility and a deep sense of responsibility are missing, then man's actions can indeed be disastrous.

Let me give an example, which takes us back to environmental science. Probably ignoring an interesting detective story by Edgar Wallace on the same topic, the brother of a friend of mine once decided that to have so many earthworms in his garden was a disgusting fact. He studied the matter, and had the brilliant idea of inserting in the soil two vertical metal plates several meters apart, and then applying a comparatively high voltage to them. The poor earthworms (so he reported) literally squirted out of the soil. They were then collected and disposed of. The success of my friend's brother was such that in a short time the soil became a compact

13. P. H. Raven, "Biological Diversity," in *The Emergence of Complexity*, ed. B. Pullman, 252–265.

mass unsuitable for any vegetation except a few pioneering plants. (If you do not know why, read something about the all-important ecological niche of earthworms.) The moral of this story is that, at variance with other animals, even in a situation of nice ecological equilibrium people can do the craziest things, and one or a few individuals may be sufficient to alter that equilibrium. If they hit on a self-amplifying change (e.g., by introducing a few couples of rabbits in an environment not prepared to deal with rabbits, as happened in Australia) their innovation may spell catastrophe. Of course, nature has its own correction mechanisms, but in the process many species may be lost, vegetation-rich areas may be reduced to deserts, etc., and that might be negative for the human species itself; indeed, it is possible to envision actions that would completely change the face of our planet. Moreover, many scientists (Peter Raven is undoubtedly among them) feel that there is something in nature such as it is now that must be respected regardless of the material interests of the human species, because, as the Pirates of Penzance would sing, "for all our faults, we love the Queen," the queen being here, of course, nature.

From the point of view of animal ecology, examples like that of earthworms as well as general considerations lead to a picture whose outline is as follows. The human species is a pioneering species whose role is to occupy and modify for its own use and welfare even spaces where not only its life, but any life is impossible. Its drives are the same as those of any animal species, survival and propagation, but its survival requirements are very special: the environment should be beautiful, interesting, emotionally balanced, and so on. This is an experimental lesson taught by the complete failure of sociological theories, such as Leninism, which assumed that human beings could be made happy by the same methods as would apply to cattle, and by the diffusion of nervous diseases, drug addiction, dubious religious sects. That a human being wants more than material comfort and freedom from worries about his or her future is an observable fact because an instinctive reaction is slowly building up: more and more people feel that love does not reduce to sexual appetite, that a live sunset may be far more beautiful than a TV picture, that sport is great only if it values the moral and intellectual qualities of the athletes. This feeling is shared even by people who call themselves materialists: they would, for example, gladly eat from hand-painted china plates, sleep between beautifully decorated sheets, open their windows on the most beautiful landscapes. It is true that many people, if offered such luxuries, would manifest what we might consider a lamentable bad taste; but good taste is also a result of education, and it develops by iteration. If one eats from plain earthenware plates, one will appreciate plates with some decoration, though rough; then one will start to distinguish between more and less fine decorations; then one will realize that porcelain is more agreeable than earthenware; and so on. This is how, in the Middle Ages, the people of Florence could make their city the cradle of unsurpassed artists out of simple uneducated artisans, sometimes, like Giotto, children of peasants or shepherds. Nowadays, artisans making fine objects are almost an extinct species; yet the few who are still active and are not afraid of patient work with no assurance of success realize beautiful things and even sell them without any problem.

In short, in its expansion the human species uses the intelligence of its members to realize as far as possible a high *quality* of life. The contemplation and the making of beautiful things, the challenge of problems and the joy of finding their solution, the realization of friendly relations and of social justice are not superstructures, for, even if they were just psychological whims, they would motivate people in their actions. This means that, when certain people speak about, say, biodiversity, they are expressing a characteristic concern of "human animals," who feel that nature, such as they find it in places where other living beings thrive unhindered by human activities, is a desirable environment for the quality of life of their own species. Problems arise, as we have already seen, when the *value* biodiversity is given a higher priority than the achievement of decent living conditions of other human beings (or their survival as an ethos). Respect for nature in general belongs to the same category of values associated with the quality of life; and so do many other values and "taboos."

Why are these "values," though not derivable from biology, a biological necessity? The answer we can give is not final because research has been hindered by that radical reductionism which, lest one should introduce notions which cannot be measured in the laboratory, ignores even obvious facts. It ignores, for example, that love between a man and a woman cannot be just physiological sex, because in humans, as in many higher animals, the bringing up of the offspring requires the collaboration of the parents; and, at least in the human species, collaboration is not possible if there is no reciprocal attachment and willingness to ignore difficult temperamental traits. The general scientific explanation of why values are a biological necessity, as far as I can see, is as follows. Since the human species has an enormous adaptive flexibility, that is to say, is equipped with the means to solve the most difficult survival problems — say, living under the sea — through the development of the appropriate know-how and the accompanying technology, human groups can use that flexibility to realize social conditions that in the long run would endanger the survival of the species. In particular, nature places no immediate penalties on patterns of unnatural behavior, like human sacrifices in certain cultures and cruel slavery in others. Sufferings and serious social problems as well as stagnation and decline will follow, but that will be a slow process, and only after a long time will nature set things right either because populations with healthier social systems will subdue, albeit by violence, the deviated cultures or because a reaction will arise from within. History knows examples of either process. Think of the famous myth of Iphigenia: she was going to be killed by her father Agamemnon to ensure favorable winds for the Greek fleet leaving for Troy when the goddess Artemis intervened to save her. That myth is doubtless a trace of the reaction of the Greeks themselves against such an unnatural action as the sacrifice of one's own child. At the same time, it seems likely (although, of course, not admitted by certain popular history textbooks) that the acceptance of Spanish rule by the Indian cultures of Central America on the arrival of the Conquistadors was favored by the elimination of mass human sacrifices, which were so atrocious that they horrified even a man so accustomed to violence as Fernando Cortés.

The above examples are probably sufficient to illustrate what history appears to teach,[14] namely that human society as a whole is *grosso modo* similar to a control system; a very simple example of which is an airplane in automatic flight. That is to say, if an organized group of human beings — a tribe, a nation — begins deviating seriously from a pattern of internal relations which makes it reasonably fit for survival under the conditions proper to human beings, sooner or later one of two things will happen: either the built-in control mechanisms will succeed in reducing the resulting perturbations to relatively unimportant oscillations about the "normal state" — possibly starting an oscillation toward the opposite extreme — or, because of the frequency and importance of the perturbations, the control mechanisms will fail, and the system will collapse. Historical events — consider wars — suggest that, when it comes to drastic measures for the preservation of a community, the control mechanisms do not heed individuals, and in the attempt to perform their function they will cause sufferings and deaths. Now, according to the feelings of a vast majority,[15] that a sick society will sooner or later be healed or eliminated is a meager compensation for the sorrows and sufferings of the victims of the process. If the sickness is due to external causes, one can only blame nature or declare that it was the will of God; but if it is due to human choices, then one is tempted to join those who think that human beings are an error of nature. Now, also the fact that almost everybody feels that single individuals matter is a fact of nature; science can but acknowledge it, considering, for example, that the earliest human civilizations we know of buried their dead. A tomb with a name or sign referring to the person buried there, or with whatever the

14. It is instructive to interpret on this model the historical analysis of the latter period of the Roman Empire to be found, for all its Voltairean bias, in Edward Gibbon's masterpiece, the famous *Decline and Fall of the Roman Empire* (1776–1794; reprint, London: Dent, Everyman's Library, 1966).

15. The exceptions confirm the rule because they always concern people whose driving force was lust for power, possibly disguised as humanitarianism.

primitives believed the dead needed in their voyage toward the afterlife, is certainly uniquely related to care for individual persons.

A Summary and Some Questions

The "control system" scheme just outlined and the problems it raises are so important that it will be useful to consider it a little longer.[16]

The argument we have developed so far can be restated in a number of points:

a. contemporary science has an operative dimension — experimental research and science-based technologies — which depends on human choices;

b. by introducing environmental science scientists have implicitly accepted that human individuals make responsible choices, and hence must refer to moral values and rules;

c. those moral values and rules cannot be provided by science, which would cease to be science if it went beyond the observation and correlation of facts;

d. on the other hand, it is a task of science to study the "ecological niche" of *Homo sapiens*, and interpret the observed behavior of the human animal in terms of biological and ethological principles;

e. the human species appears to be a pioneering species capable of surviving in environments where no other animal would survive, and of modifying those environments so as to make them suitable for life;

f. this particular role, in the light of the standard principles of engineering technology, is seen to require an enormous measure of flexibility in the responses of human individuals to new situations;

g. therefore, organized human groups (from tribes to civilizations) can be viewed as control systems of a very special sort, i.e., with feedback mechanisms allowing, before they take control, deviations from the natural behavior pattern of members of a group that would be unthinkable for other animals;

h. the price paid for such deviations is suffering and premature death of many individuals, as happens, for example, in a war — a fact which may explain the widespread feeling that those deviations should be avoided;

16. This approach is essentially based on the ideas put forward by von Bertalanffy, "General Systems Theory: A Critical Review," *General Systems* (1962): 1–20 and other works.

i. in fact, modern scientific observation shows that, apart from religious and philosophical considerations, in the human species each individual is important as such. The main points supporting this claim are:

- the ability of human beings to devise and select the procedures and tools required for adaptation to the most diverse environments, which is a result of the fact that single individuals possess reason and the ability to decide even against primary instincts;

- the observed tendency of human communities to modify their environments so as to attain a high "quality of life" for their members, essentially based on the adoption by the latter of the three Platonic ideals of truth, beauty, and respect for the rights of others;

- the fact that the human species devotes a large portion of its activity to the bringing up of its young by developing the personality of each individual;

j. together with other observations, like the role of leaders and heroes, these facts suggest that human groups rely for their efficiency on the cooperation of individuals, each of whom plays an active role, in which he or she is normally expected to make responsible and intelligent choices.

This list is rather formidable, but it is also most relevant to our purpose of seeing how the results and methods of science, first of all the hard facts it has discovered and critically assessed, shape our *Weltanschauung*, particularly in connection with the place of man in the universe and with his insuppressible spiritual aspirations. What the above argument leads to is that a view of man consistent with today's science should include a notion which the science of a few decades ago flatly refused; the notion that, because of the very role of man in the harmony of the world, each individual of the species *Homo sapiens* is a "person," i.e., a free rational being whose behavior is regulated by reason and moral rules.

Homeostasis and Individuals

A fundamental conclusion emerging from the points discussed is that human communities as such are regulated by feedback mechanisms, which sooner or later will restore their normal state, which only allows limited deviations toward patterns of behavior in contrast with certain basic rules. However, such control effects will generally take time, precisely because otherwise the flexibility and adaptability of the human species would be impaired. In other words, just as we have basic instincts in common with all other animals, we also have an instinctive tendency to form groups endowed with a measure of "homeostasis" (as it is called in systems theory), so that regardless of the intentions or choices of the individuals, the survival of the human species with its special characteristics is ensured — unless, as can happen with any other control system, a catastrophe pushes the situation beyond the reach of the feedback mechanisms.

We have said that, at variance with other animal species — at least as far as we can judge from outside — reason and observation suggest that in the human species as distinct from other animal species, each individual is important *per se*. This statement does not contradict the well-known maxim that no one is indispensable, for it does not refer to the claim that one way or the other society will adjust to the loss of any individual; it means that — as illustrated by the case of Socrates proposed in chapter six — each individual has a unique role to play; indeed, in certain circumstances, e.g., in an exploration of the moon, one individual may have to represent the whole species. That individual may be a pioneer, or an explorer, who at least reports to others the results of the exploration, or a leader, charged by the other members of the community to make choices for them; but also, in general, an isolated human being may make a personal choice that starts a self-amplified fluctuation, possibly favored by particular circumstances but nevertheless resulting from his choice. Just think of the one woman in Jericho who, by protecting Joshua's scouts, caused the extermination of the inhabitants of her town.[17] Apart from the religious significance of the fall of Jericho, that episode is one out of a large number of historical accounts showing that the behavior of a single person is important in a society, and may, so to say, cause a harmful instability of the system that is his or her community.

The Optimum State

In all this, of course, there are observed facts and interpretations. The latter are partly just hints, as far as science goes, because further research may be needed to make certain general analogies into rigorous models; but the facts, particularly the relation between an individual and his community, are clearly established, and, apart from the details, their interpretation in terms of general systems theory seems unquestionable. That is sufficient for us, because what we are examining in this book is not the details of science, but the picture science leads to. Indeed, that picture is bound to include inferences from scientific observations and

17. Josh. 6:1ff.

theories that do not belong properly to science. I want to remind the reader of this point because our discourse has now come to the fundamental inference we have to make if we accept point (j) of our list, in accordance with the spirit of environmental science: if the behavior of each individual *Homo sapiens* is significant and must be responsible, it must follow certain rules, and those rules cannot be chosen case by case. The reason is to be found in the control system model of a community. Let us state a general law which that model implies: Since the correct operation of a community requires the free collaboration of all its members, and since each member has a role to play in ensuring its operation, the free choices of each individual must be such as to minimize the risk of deviations from its optimum operational state, which might require the operation of the built-in control mechanisms, accompanied by damage to individual members. If this "law" is accepted, then a major problem appears: how can an individual minimize the "optimum operational state of his community" if he does not know what that state is?

If you think just a moment, you will see that the problem with our society, especially after the rise of the Enlightenment, is precisely that every intellectual has his or her own idea of what that optimum state is, and some of those intellectuals have even succeeded in experimenting with their ideas. The terrible failures of mass centered ideologies (think of Cambodia) and the results of the fight against "taboos" (think of AIDS in the Western countries) show essentially one thing: society is too complex a system, and the role of fluctuations in it too important to justify the application of simple theories or recipes. Simple theories or recipes may be right on certain accounts, but precisely because of that they can be dangerous if applied without great caution.

In conclusion, the optimum-state question, though scientific in nature, seems to be beyond the grasp of human beings, both because of the limitations of the human mind and because people are frequently influenced by superiority complexes and the lust for power and money. Thus, facts confirm that the answer should be sought along the path humble people always tried to tread, though not always with success: we have to search for absolute moral rules[18] given by a Supreme Being, who is the only one who really knows what the optimum state of human society (and of the universe, for that matter) should be. The Hindu sacred book Bhagavad Gita is instructive in this connection, because it presents the same notion in the form of a dialog between Arjuna, a good willing man, and the god Krishna, who tries to persuade Arjuna that a man should not try to choose his moral rules without referring to a higher source, because he

18. Since the time of Voltaire, the term "absolute" has been the target of all sorts of sarcasms and contemptuous remarks, as if it could only be used by stupid or uneducated people. Actually, it simply means the opposite of "relative," i.e., that whatever it applies to is independent of circumstances and other variable factors.

cannot take into account all the intricacies of the relation between an action and its consequences.[19]

A Supreme Legislator?

The question about the "normal state" of society thus becomes: "Since the normal state is likely to be known only to a Supreme Being, has that Supreme Being handed down the rules, or is the human condition a ceaseless groping for guidelines that are forever hidden to us?" This is obviously a question not only outside natural science, but outside philosophy. There is a possible scientific approach through the study of history and the application of statistical evaluations, but the uncertainties and the risks of biased interpretations are so great that research is unlikely to provide reliable answers. Thus, despite the great advances in natural and human sciences, we are still confronted with the need to shift our reflections from the sensible level of observed facts to the level of religion: like Virgil with Dante in his voyage through the other world, the scientific approach cannot take us all the way to the answer we are seeking. Curiously enough, Immanuel Kant, a philosopher who is the fundamental reference for those who stand for the primacy of human reason in all matters, emphasized that the necessity of moral rules independent of personal judgment was related to the existence of God.[20]

One could contend that in practice an individual has to choose a course of action under circumstances that may be highly variable, so that it makes no sense to speak of invariable absolute rules. Let us briefly consider this point. Of course, to make up one's own mind one must analyze the situation and determine what the best behavior will be under the given circumstances; but then there must be some general criteria, some yardsticks playing the same role as the laws for a judge. The most general criterion is the idea that one must choose good and not evil. As the issue is better focused, distinctions appear between immediate personal advantage or satisfaction and good as such. This calls into play the notion of responsibility, for in the last analysis, if the ultimate standard is not personal pleasure, then people must be responsible to somebody or something; some people will say to other human beings, some will say to their own consciences, some will say to God, but all will implicitly admit that if no "external" judge is assumed there is no criterion of choice independent of the person who has to make that choice. There have been attempts to show that an ethic that refuses an ego-centered reference

19. The essential rule proposed by Krishna is related to reincarnation and the justification of the caste system, but it can be interpreted in a more open way, as T. S. Eliot suggested in his *Four Quartets*, "Dry Salvages," III, lines 154–166.

20. Cf. J. H. Brooke, *Science and Religion: Some Historical Perspectives* (Cambridge: Cambridge University Press, 1991), 204ff.

(and thus assigns an important place to altruism) is a mere strategy of the members of the human species in the fight for survival (or what have you) of our species. One could contend that such a standpoint is too radical an attempt to fit facts to a theoretical framework that tries to explain everything in terms of biological evolution of the Darwinian type; however that may be, it implies the recognition that every human being instinctively feels that he has a moral responsibility when he decides how to act. People know that they can damage other things, they know in the depth of their hearts that a conduct involving damage to others or to other things cannot really be advantageous to them, however attractive it may seem at the moment.

The next step in the search for general criteria serving as guides for personal conduct is the actual choice of absolute rules. This is because reason (especially if based on science) tells the ordinary man that neither he nor the greatest scientists can understand or predict everything. He can feel or realize — depending on education — that there are general rules in nature, particularly that any human group, seen as a control system of a given class, must oscillate about an equilibrium condition, which corresponds to the optimum quality of life of its members, who share the same basic needs and desires. An ordinary person also feels instinctively what we have already seen, namely that the behavior of the individual members of a group must stay as close as possible to a golden mean, for the price would be either the extinction of the group or a number of victims. Now, that golden mean cannot be really known, because even statistical studies are limited by the difficulty of collecting significant data; therefore, the only solution is to choose some "preferences," for instance respect for others, beauty, truth, and always act according to those preferences. This is what is currently called "choosing a set of moral values," which are felt to be universal, and which are chosen precisely because they are not dependent on individual judgment. Practical but still general rules follow, for example the Ten Commandments or the famous foundation of Roman law,

honeste vivere, nemini nocere, suum cuique tribuere

live honorably, damage no one, give to everybody what is his.

Once the rules are chosen, the individual will feel responsible for their application, not for their content. Of course, the application is not always easy, as we know from the difficult time judges often have in trying to divide right from wrong.

As an illustration of the points about rules and choice let us consider again, as an example, the defense of biodiversity. That issue is generally considered important, possibly for utilitarian reasons, but also because people like nature as it is. Many feel that they are responsible toward nature for its equilibrium, because it is in their own nature to respect, indeed love nature in its present state. However, when they are faced with a choice, e.g., between carelessly throwing away a piece of plastic or disposing of it so that it will not interfere with natural processes, or between destroying the vegetation of a certain area to make room for cultivated land and insisting that the food to be produced be obtained from other sources, they have to consider also other requirements of the human species, for example its survival. Unless there are absolute guidelines for making a choice, there might be groups for which the sacrifice of an area of virgin forest would benefit strangers whom they do not care much about, there would be others who would emphasize the need for food, and so on. And it is very likely that each group would decide according to its own viewpoint. That does not sound right: if a choice is really necessary, then it stands to reason that one should avoid taking a stand superficially on the basis of personal preferences or traditions or emotions or what you will; one should instead start from certain basic rules, like "do not kill," which require that a solution should be found for those people who might starve if the areas in question are not open for cultivation. Scientific good will and an unbiased study would probably lead to a solution that would satisfy both exigencies. In other words, it would be necessary to exercise what the students of ethics call "the virtue of prudence," which in this case is another name for humility: one should examine the issues, refer to a moral code not chosen subconsciously to please one's unexpressed sympathies and prejudices, consider the hierarchy of values that code proposes, and only thereafter take the responsibility of a decision. This is what science leads us to, although the moral code itself cannot be provided by science as such. There are as a matter of fact scientists who believe they can derive moral principles from science, but it would seem that what they mean is that the only elements they accept in their ethics as independent of their own choice are what they consider scientific facts, and then they construct their set of values so as to make it compatible with those facts. What they ignore is perhaps that subconscious drives are also a scientific fact; and their standpoint exposes them more than others to the action of those drives. This consideration, together with the others already presented, seems to show that a coherent world-view based on science must face the problem of the search for moral values that are not relative to the place, the time, and the individual applying them, while realizing that they should be found outside science proper.

The Place of Man

It is a curious paradox that, having admitted that chance is really chance, *viz.* absence of causes, we have solved a number of strange inconsistencies, particularly the tendency of certain scientists to refuse the human species a characteristic status while requiring that human beings should feel responsible for what they do to nature. Observation shows that not only is man a very special animal, but, despite deviations, the human species is a pioneering one with characteristics implying freedom of choice, ethical rules, and ideals, whose pursuit by individuals is part of the very biological role of the species. To sum it up, let me recall again Heine's poem on the basic existential problems of man.[21] He speaks of a young man watching the stars, and (foolishly, Heine says) expecting from the starry firmament an answer to questions on which people of all ages pondered in vain. The young man was probably mistaken in asking the stars and not, like St. Augustine, going beyond sensible things; but here the interesting point is that Heine adds to the usual questions about man, his origins, and his destiny: *Wer wohnt dort oben auf den goldenen Sternen?* — Who lives up there on the golden stars? That question stems from a dream that has been haunting many human beings since the idea was accepted that there may be inhabited worlds among the stars. That human beings should have dreams of that kind is also an indication that our ecological niche implies a very special role in the whole universe. Science too is largely the outcome of dreams, as the founder of modern organic chemistry, Friedrich A. Kekulé (1829–1896), used to tell his students:

Let us learn to dream, gentlemen, then perhaps we shall find the truth...but let us beware of publishing our dreams before they have been put to the proof of the waking understanding.[22]

This admonishment emphasizes two of the specific characteristics of the human species: imagination and reason. Both are required for scientific research and in general for every specifically human activity; and dreams may be seen as the source of rational thought as well as of action. This is perhaps why I still remember the opening sentence of a sermon by a Lutheran minister on the Bavarian radio, around 1985: "Dreams are the material of which the spirit is made." I hope I have shown that observation and application of scientific information and concepts confirm it, by suggesting strongly (let me say it again) that the apparently "useless" ideals and dreams of humanity are actually manifestations of the task of *Homo sapiens* in the universe: building a bridge between matter and spirit.

21. H. Heine, *Buch der Lieder*.
22. Quoted in D. L. Hurd and J. J. Kipling, eds., *The Origins and Growth of Physical Science*, vol. 2 (Harmondsworth, Eng.: Penguin Books, 1964), 124.

Robinson Crusoe

I cannot close this chapter without recalling Daniel Defoe's masterpiece, a book now relegated among old-fashioned books for teenagers, but really a case-study on the ecology of the species *Homo sapiens:* on the basis (so it is said) of the adventures of a real person, a sailor called Selkirk, it shows how and under what conditions our species plays its role through a single individual. Three facts are particularly significant about this book.[23] One is that it is complementary to Pascal's image of a man abandoned asleep on a deserted island.[24] The second is that it was written at a time when the discovery that human beings can apply their reason and imagination, through science and technology, to improve their material condition had not yet been made into the belief that human reason suffices to guide human actions. The third is that with time such a masterful parable about man and his relation to nature and society became in the popular mind a book for teenagers, while adults reveled in the reading of books by Émile Zola, by D. H. Lawrence, and the like; masterpieces, according to literary critics, but masterpieces that accepted that debased conception of man which resulted in the horrors of two world wars.

Defoe's book has been called an exploration of "the tension between God's purpose and human weakness, making it a moral fable of great literary significance" and "a tale of high adventure."[25] It is probably all that; it is also an instance of the Puritan spirit of its age; but certainly it is more: as I said, it is a study of how a single individual can be fully a member of the human species even in the utmost solitude, provided he or she is guided by ingenuity and reference to a spiritual sphere of reality. In a sense, it should be clear even to an agnostic that Robinson Crusoe was saved by his having God as the referent of his vicissitudes. It was in the last analysis that belief which prevented him from falling into despair and becoming a brute, as was the case with Ayrton, a character of another tale of men on a deserted island: left on a deserted island to expiate his crimes, he had broken down and become practically a brute when he had mistakenly concluded that the promised rescue, which had been his only motive for remaining a man, would never come.[26]

23. D. Defoe, *Robinson Crusoe*, 1719 (London: Dent, Everyman's Library, 1956).
24. Cf. quotation in chapter one.
25. D. Defoe, *Robinson Crusoe*, read by Tom Baker, Penguin Audiobooks, audiocassette, 1992.
26. J. Verne, *L'Île mystérieuse* (The mysterious island) (1874; English translation, New York: Permabooks, Pocket Books, 1961).

Chapter 9

Mechanism, Magic, and How Nature Is One

What about the approaches to the unity of the world — astrology and magic — abandoned in the seventeenth century with the rise of mechanism and now enjoying some popularity? The highly successful mechanistic approach of science is in contrast with the justification of those doctrines in terms of sympathies and correspondences; on the other hand, their resurgence suggests that their global view of the world, in which "noncausal" relations and powers or entities not accessible to the senses are admitted, fills as it were an existential need of the animal Homo sapiens. Have scientists anything to say about this?

How Nature Is One – The Rise of Mechanism – Coherence: A Secret Network of Relations – The Spirit of Alchemy: *Tout est dans tout* – An Intuition of Complexity – Father Marin Mersenne and the Harmony of the World – Sympathies, Influences, and Causes – Kircher, the Wood, and the Trees – Panpsychism Yesterday and Today – Could Magic Work? – About Demons, Fairies, and Other Invisible Beings

*They who believe in the influences of the stars over the fates of men are,
in feeling at least, nearer the truth than they who regard the heavenly bodies as related to them merely by a common obedience to an external law.
All that man sees has to do with man. Worlds cannot be without an inter-
mundane relationship. The community of the center of all creation suggests
an interradiating connection of the parts. Else a grander idea is conceivable
than that which is already embodied. No shining belt or gleaming moon,
no red and green glory in a self-encircling twin star, but has a relation with
the hidden things of a man's soul, and, it may be, with the secret history of
his body as well. They are portions of the living house wherein he abides.*

— GEORGE MacDONALD[1]

How Nature Is One

In his famous reflections on science, the mathematician and physicist
Henri Poincaré (1854–1912), whose genius was also manifest in the
openness with which he looked at science, made a consideration especially interesting for the theme of this book: by comparing the universe
to an organism and then by using the verb "to ignore," he pointed to
the major role of information exchange in the unity of the universe — an
aspect we shall develop in next chapter:

> Let us remark first that any generalization presupposes a certain
> measure of belief in the unity and simplicity of Nature. For its unity
> there cannot be any difficulty. If the different parts of the Universe
> were not like the organs of one and the same body, they would not
> act one on the other, they would ignore one another; and we, in
> particular, would know but one of them. Thus, we do not have to
> ask ourselves if Nature is one, but how it is one.[2]

Also very important in this passage is the remark that the real problem is to understand *how* nature is one, which means, as far as I can
see, both how the unity of nature is realized and in *what* it consists.

---

1. MacDonald, *Phantastes*.

2. H. Poincaré, *La science et l'hypothèse* (1902; reprint, Paris: Champs-Flammarion,
1968), 161. "*Observons d'abord que toute généralisation suppose dans une certaine mesure
la croyance à l'unité et à la simplicité de la nature. Pour l'unité il ne peut pas y avoir de
difficulté. Si les diverses parties de l'univers n'étaient pas comme les organes d'un même
corps, elles n'agiraient pas les unes sur les autres, elles s'ignoreraient mutuellement; et
nous, en particulier, nous n'en connaîtrions qu'une seule. Nous n'avons donc pas à nous
demander si la nature est une, mais comment elle est une.*"

The answer of science to these questions is now slowly emerging from the mists which concealed it before the recent advances of ecology and cosmology. We have explored many facets of that answer in the preceding chapters, and we have seen that, quite unexpectedly, ideas hitherto considered entirely outside science are required, one way or another, to describe the world such as is offered by science for our contemplation and action. Among those ideas are beauty and free will, which are made compatible with science, even necessary, by the need to account for what the scientists call chance, a name which may well be a name for the unpredictable events by which nature (or its Architect) realizes variety and beauty. And there is the rational and responsible nature of the human animal; its admission into the kingdom of science is required by the consideration that human beings can damage nature and themselves if they do not think ahead and realize that they are expected to make the right choices.

If such new and unexpected conclusions are the necessary result of scientific advances, should we not consider the possibility that other notions, sent into exile by the science of our parents and grandparents, could apply for readmission into our culture? We should indeed, the more so as some of them (such as those underlying astrology) are already among us as clandestine visitors; which is not an acceptable situation. With such considerations in mind, it is now time to explore other possible facets of the answer to Poincaré's question about how nature is one. We shall do so by a procedure recommended by the great traditions of the West as well as the East: we shall focus our attention on the past, to see what, without foregoing the scientific mind, we can learn from it about the reasons why in the popular mind science has failed to meet certain human needs, and has produced the current resurgence of interest in magic, parapsychology, alternative medicines, and alchemy.

There seem to be good grounds for tracing the crisis back to the loss of faith in mechanistic reductionism — a gradual loss brought about by field theories, the theory of systems, the recognition of complexity levels, the great principles and ideas of the new cosmology, and also by the breakdown of such "scientific" cures of the ills of society as Marxism-Leninism and evolutionary instrumentalism. When the opinion makers started to have doubts about the omnipotence of mechanistic science, the force of their propaganda weakened, suggesting that perhaps it had no strength of its own; and the dam collapsed that, after the success of their crusades against religion, still protected society from superstition and ignorance. Yet, the mechanistic approach to scientific problems was the tool that made the rise of modern science possible. Therefore, a very important question remains unanswered: where did mechanism fail?

An attempt to answer this question requires the answer to at least five subquestions:

- What circumstances and needs caused the appearance and rise of mechanism?

- What were the conceptual merits of mechanism?

- Why was it proposed as an exhaustive approach to reality?

- Is there really any need to supersede or at least supplement it?

- If it is not abandoned, how should it be integrated without giving up the logical rigor and the scrupulous faithfulness to facts which the methods of science have brought to our culture?

We have directly or indirectly handled most of these questions in the preceding chapters. What remains to be done here is essentially to add a few pieces of information and to summarize the *status quaestionis*, the state of the matter. After that, we will start groping through the forest of strange ideas that mechanism put to sleep in the great century of Galileo, Pascal, Leibniz and Newton. Perhaps we shall thus find ideas that should be recovered for a better understanding of how nature is one.

The Rise of Mechanism

The role of relations in the physical world is one of the reasons why the Great Dance image and its musical implications provide a fecund analogy for a description of the world where exchange and creation of information, mutual compatibility and adjustment, coherence, and a measure of uncertainty or freedom are all acknowledged as essential characteristics. As we have seen already, the clockwork image, which it replaces, was the epitome of mechanism, according to which all relations are in principle of the nature of those between parts of a mechanical device. Mechanism arose as a result of Galileo's fight against the Peripatetics, the men of science of his time; it should be added that the genius of Galileo succeeded because the times were ripe. We saw in chapter two the example of Don Ferrante, the scholar who succumbed to plague because the sort of thing that was plague did not fit into his science. People like Don Ferrante exist in all times. Even today there are people who deny that emotions or the mind are something real on the grounds that they cannot be isolated and studied as such in the laboratory; and there are people who fight against experiments on animals not with arguments over which a serious debate can take place, but with the paradoxical claim that, since the beings which we call animals do not belong to our species, no experimenting on them can be useful to us; needless to say, the names of Pasteur and of Salk and the history of vaccines are unknown to them.

Thus, in every epoch one finds a tendency to transform the science of that epoch into a set of ideological tenets for which facts are irrelevant.

This was the cultural climate at the time of Galileo Galilei, who set fire to the highly inflammable container of questions about nature for which the purely rhetorical science of his time had no significant answer.

An example of the novelty of Galileo's approach should suffice. I wonder if Galileo had a poetical spirit, and if he had ever admired the full moon transforming a landscape into an eerie world of dark shapes crouching on the ground, contorted shadows raising arms to the sky, pale luminous splashes silently appearing and gliding away, white rocks standing out of the dark like bones of a Leviathan, luminescent mists flowing through the jagged outlines of distant woods. It is quite probable that this is not what interested Galileo about the moon; yet he was a dreamer in his own way. Not being able to travel to the moon, he wanted to know as much as possible what it was really like, and whether the image given by a telescope, suggesting the existence of mountains and oceans, was really correct. His reflections in that connection must lie at the origin of a discussion presented in one of his dialogues about the idea that the moon is a polished spherical mirror.[3] The traditional answer was that it must be one, because otherwise it could not reflect the light of the sun; and in support of that claim the scientists of his time offered not only the opinion of the ancient masters, but the fact that a polished metal plate would reflect the light of a lamp. But Galileo had realized that a plane mirror might have properties different from those of a spherical one: he had a spherical mirror made, lit a lamp in its vicinity, and could prove to himself that the mirror did not look bright. He thus showed by observation and experiments on the reflection of light that the moon has a rough surface, and what through a telescope looked like craters and plains must actually be so.

This story shows that Galileo's innovation was not so much recourse to experiment, as the use of experiments as the final arguments for proving or disproving theories. His reasoning thus involved the systematic refusal of explanations based on causes that do not lie within the reach of experimental tests. From this refusal and from the active interest of the men of his time in machines — Pascal, the profound and poetical author of the famous *Pensées*, was also the inventor of the first mechanical calculator — the idea arose that the explanation of observed phenomena was to follow the procedure one would use to find the cause of a malfunction in a machine: look at the machine and forget about external influences, such as jinxes or witchcraft, and determine the chain of actions by contact which would normally ensure the regular operation of the machine; finally, follow the chain in question backward, until the damaged part is identified. Since clockworks were at the time rather sophisticated

---

3. G. Galilei, *Dialogo sopra i due massimi sistemi del mondo* (Florence: Landini, 1632), First Day.

machines built in an incredible variety, it is no wonder that the clockwork image of the universe should, as already mentioned in chapters one and two, become the reference model of science. Its major pioneers were two Frenchmen, René Descartes (1596–1650), a famous philosopher and founder of analytical geometry, and his friend Father Marin Mersenne (1588–1648), a friar of the order of the Minims, founded in Calabria by St. Francis of Paola. Mersenne is particularly interesting to us for he also wrote many books on music and was greatly interested in the "Harmony of the World." Until the time of the English physicist Michael Faraday (1791–1867) and of James Clerk Maxwell (1831–1879), the Scotsman who developed Faraday's ideas and created today's theory of the electromagnetic field, scientists literally believed that things push or pull one another as gears and levers of a machine. We had already occasion to recall how Lord Kelvin reacted to Clerk Maxwell's discovery. After Maxwell, it was admitted that things could influence one another by the more subtle procedure of creating around them "Fields of Force"; but the mechanistic view remained in force, namely the claim that what we have called complex objects are no more than mechanical devices or their chemical equivalents, in the sense that in them each part acts on the other as a part of a clockwork, and a rigid chain of causes and effects connects an event to its past, events not in the chain having no influence on the end result. We have already mentioned that this view has been called "mechanistic reductionism," for it is not confined to the claim that mechanistic explanation is extremely valuable and important, but it claims that *all* we have to know about reality is the individual cause-effect chains, which involve localized actions of the same kind as the wheels of a gearing exert on one another. In this view, no consideration of the whole, let alone a finalistic point of view, is considered scientifically significant, even if the whole has a unitary behavior.

Such was clearly the position of Mersenne. As a Roman Catholic friar, he was certainly well aware of the holistic approach of Aristotelian biology, but he believed, following Descartes, that a science based on mechanics would provide stronger argument for the distinction between the spiritual and the material. Almost paradoxically, as he was discussing "Universal Harmony," he wrote:

> I thus say that the ear does not know the sounds, and just serves as the instrument and organ of their passage into the mind, which considers its nature and properties, and consequently that the beasts have no knowledge of the sounds, but only their representation, without knowing if what they apprehend is a sound or a color, or something else; so that one could not say so much that they act as that they are acted upon, and that the objects make such an impression on their senses that they must of necessity follow them,

as of necessity the wheels of a clock follow the weight or the spring which pulls them.[4]

In Mersenne's mind, mechanism was a weapon for defending the spiritual nature of man, because he considered knowledge as a faculty of the spiritual moiety of man, in agreement with the well-known dualism of his friend Descartes. Unfortunately, his weapon backfired, for mechanism became mechanistic reductionism, opening the way to the various "isms," from rationalism to positivism and finally to scientism, which identified the whole of reality with what the natural sciences could study by their own procedures and schemes, the procedures being observation and experimentation, the schemes being various forms of mechanism.

Mersenne's view of animals was shared in its essential features by the most recent advocates of mechanistic reductionism, biologists probably wary of the risk that otherwise one might admit into science (i) the idea that life is governed by laws other than those which apply to nonliving matter, and (ii) notions which they consider to be theological, particularly finalism. We have already seen in some detail that neither worry is justified. Let us insist here on the main point already made in this connection: life is an organized and finalized activity, but this does not imply that it results from the addition of some separate entity to the processes which make it up; the point is simply that new properties can emerge from a set of mutually interacting parts or coordinated processes: what makes a man a man, for example, is not just the complicated interplay of the physicochemical phenomena that are his body at each moment of time, even though he does "result" from them, but the emergent properties of the whole. Nor does the claim that living beings obey some sort of project imply theological notions, as is clear from the very fact that Jacques Monod, a declared anti-spiritualist, spoke of the teleonomy of a living organism. Prigogine, the eminent physical chemist already mentioned in the preceding chapters, summarized these ideas from a slightly different point of view:

> Man in his singularity was certainly neither called nor expected by the world; on the contrary, if we assimilate life to a self-organized material system evolving toward more and more complex states, then, under well determined circumstances which do not seem to be exceptionally rare, life itself is predictable in the Universe, constitutes in it a phenomenon as natural as the fall of heavy bodies.[5]

4. M. Mersenne, *Harmonie Universelle* (1636–37; repr. Paris: Centre National de la Recherche Scientifique, 1963).

5. Prigogine and Stengers, *La nouvelle alliance*, 192–193. "*L'homme dans sa singularité n'était certainement ni appelé, ni attendu par le monde; en revanche, si nous assimilons la vie à un système d'auto-organisation de la matière évoluant vers des états de plus en plus*

Because of these considerations, at the horizon of science a tendency is appearing to think that mechanistic reductionism should be abandoned altogether, for it ignores essential aspects of today's science, and, inasmuch as it presupposes the existence of separate chains of events, stands in contrast with the "law of universal coherence" expressed by the Great Dance image. Actually, not only is there no contradiction, but the approach of mechanistic reductionism still has an important role to play. In fact, the belief in universal coherence coexisted historically first with the belief in gods governing the affairs of humanity and the events on earth in an unfathomable and often inhuman way, then with a measure of mechanistic explanation of phenomena. At least the latter kind of explanation is compatible with the more general one, because there may be regularities in a temporal sequence of events in a specific region of space which are like single voices in a fugue: each voice has its own law of evolution, even a repeated theme, within a more general scheme of consonances. Moreover, an explanation in terms of local effects is often the only practical one, as when a chemist tries to explain a chemical reaction by considering only two juxtaposed molecules rearranging their bonds.

Indeed, Mach's principle (cf. chapter one) is implicit in a basic tenet of physical sciences, that regularities observed in our region of space-time can be expected to hold at all times and places. In the version I shall adopt here, Mach's principle states that distant parts of the universe have a constant average influence on events in any specific region of space. This implies that those events that might reveal the existence of a more general scheme are discarded as random deviations in science's search for regularities. Now, a principle, especially one that must be adopted before doing science, is neither a proved truth nor a generalization of observed facts; therefore, precisely as in the case of random events, there is no objection from this side to attempts at interpreting events that do not obey known regularities as produced by causes unknown to science. Nevertheless, there are risks that may discommend such attempts because the two essential features of modern science — foundation on observed facts and establishment of cause-effect chains — are today in danger. This is the result of two different factors. First, the initially successful attempts to make science into a sort of religion, such as we have seen in connection with finalism, played havoc with education and social values; second, a tide is rising against misused technology and excessively specialized science. Now, the essential features of science should be firmly defended, for they have given us not only unprecedented living standards but knowledge of some of the deepest secrets of nature,

---

complexes, alors, dans des circonstances bien déterminées et qui ne semblent pas d'une rareté exceptionnelle, la vie, elle, est prévisible dans l'univers, y constitue un phénomène aussi 'naturel' que la chute des corps graves."

such as the transmission of hereditary characters and the nature of the soil of remote planets. These things we should not forget, for it may be necessary to take a stand against the increase in ignorance and superstition that is already resulting from uncritical opposition to the widespread claim that methods based on mechanistic reductionism provide the only true and complete key to the understanding of reality.

In the light of the most recent achievements of science in general, as illustrated in the preceding chapters, the claim that the *only* real relations between events in the physical world are cause-effect relations, to be described in terms of the relative motions of subsystems, possibly elementary particles, appears to be untenable. Nevertheless, in one form or another, the cause-effect explanation of observed facts based on a mechanical analogy should remain an essential demand of the modern mind. This is especially important for a reason we have not mentioned so far, which will be the subject of the following chapter: technology, the application of nature's laws in the free space of action human beings have at their disposal, is made possible by the knowledge of local causal relations, even when, as in last generation machines, communication plays an essential role. Even phenomena pertaining to the unitary nature of a complex whole, like the increase in order and the emergence of new properties, which seem to contradict the principle of universal decay (*viz.* the second principle of thermodynamics), are in fact compatible with mechanistic science.

This takes us back to the main theme of this chapter. The second principle is one of those general laws which, although historically reached by a path rather different from that of the rest of physics, are in complete agreement with mechanistic reductionism. Until the middle of the twentieth century, it was held to imply that the universe tends toward a state where nothing can happen, because a time will come when no special regions of it will exist which can produce work by becoming somewhat more "commonplace." For example, the stars will cool down and their energy will no longer support possible life on their planets. Their "ordinary" destiny would be that of extremely cold quasi-spherical masses of rocks. This gloomy prospect is actually invalidated by the fact that it ignores cooperative effects and self-amplification of fluctuations. Moreover, the universe (as we saw in chapter six) is a very special scientific object, which cannot be treated *sic et simpliciter* as an ordinary isolated system. For example, according to the new science, a dying star can become a black hole or a pulsar, and the casual encounter of two masses of rock, traveling at sufficiently high speeds one toward the other, may yield a new star or a star seed. At the price of an accelerated decay elsewhere, even ordered structures can appear and thrive and reproduce themselves, and can exchange information so as to superimpose a pattern of order and coherence on the general tendency toward darkness and chaos. Even granting that the predicted cold death will come, the question: "How long will such a countertrend last before it has to yield to the rule of chaos?" is an elusive one. The end, if it comes, belongs to so poorly defined a future that it makes little sense to speak of it. Moreover, if our universe is an expanding one, the very principle of universal decay, while holding on a scale large with respect to the galaxy, becomes questionable on a much larger scale.

These remarks remind us that — despite its unquestionable usefulness in the understanding and emulation (or control, as people used to say before ecological disasters) of nature — mechanism should not be expected to lead to full scientific understanding when it comes to unitary complex wholes, and even less when the construction of a *Weltanschauung* is at stake. We have already explored the main nonmechanistic lines of science, and shall now probe into history for hints of possible hitherto ignored lines of the same kind.

Coherence: A Secret Network of Relations

Coherence, a term applied here to the general property of the universe that ensures its unity, is a very general notion. The sort of coherence that is the active organization of different parts realizing the unity of a living whole is so far from the sort of coherence observed in laser light that no specific application to organisms of this concept alone seems possible. Yet, the coherence of light waves has at least one aspect in common with organization: that what happens at one point of space at a certain time is tuned to events at another point at the same or a different time. This is what makes events predictable: it is the foundation of the intelligibility of nature, but need it be limited to the regularities current science has discovered or tries to discover? Are the standard criteria of science general enough to ensure that no other approach is possible to the understanding of nature and to man's relation to it?

François Wahl, quoting the French philosopher Michel Foucault, wrote in 1973:

> the existence of a secret network in which things as it were look at one another in the face, the display or arrangement of things in a table which shows how to go through them, — which is the principle of all knowledge — , and what sorts of relationship rule them, — which establishes their meaning — , here is what constitutes the lines for understanding them. Evidently, this is not possible if the configuration of their relations is not inscribed in some way in every thing; so that to think of one leads to think of the others.[6]

6. F. Wahl, *Qu'est-ce que le structuralisme?*, 19.

Now, relations in space and time are the features of material reality studied by science since the time when Galileo established that a scientist should not *tentar le essenze*, try to understand essences, i.e., "what things really are beyond appearances." The same Poincaré, to whose authority we have appealed in connection with the unity of nature, identified the reality actually described by physics precisely as relations.[7] He pointed out that the same mathematical equations (which are like sentences expressing quantitative and logical relations) are found to describe the most disparate phenomena. Considering that genuine structuralists are akin to logical positivists and language philosophers, in that (as in the above quotation) they do not consider sense or significance as reference to features of a reality independent of the knowing subject, it is not surprising that Poincaré's remarks about relations should have led many philosophers of science, not too familiar with the actual structure of science, to classify him as a conventionalist; in simpler words, they thought he meant that science is an artificial construction of laws decided upon by mutual agreement of the scientists. Such a conception would have implied that such laws as the equivalence between mass and energy, which made the atomic bomb possible, could be just as conventional as the choice of right-hand driving. Now, Poincaré was too concerned with real things, even though he was writing long before atomic energy, not to be aware that the laws of nature are in no way a free choice of man; his point was only that the unity of nature, as far as science is concerned already in its very first stage, classification, is a matter of relations rather than of objects, a coherence based on some fundamental relational standards coexisting with a marvelous variety of objects and beings.[8] In that he was certainly close to the logical positivists and to the structuralists, but he was much too wise to reduce everything to relations, let alone treating those relations as the product of the human mind. Restating what his predecessor Galileo had pointed out three centuries earlier in the light of the intervening advances of science, he only meant that what science is interested in and is capable of descrying in the jungle of reality is patterns of change common to completely different things, say gases and force fields.

The Spirit of Alchemy: *Tout Est Dans Tout*

We saw on several occasions that the very image of the Great Dance, as well as many of the scientific ideas it conveys in the manner of a metaphor, is in fact old. Nevertheless, I think it would be a mistake to treat this recovery of the past as one of the usual cycles of history: it is

7. H. Poincaré, *La science et l'hypothèse*, ch. 8.

8. Cf. G. Del Re, "Poincaré et le mécanisme," in *Philosophia Scientiae (Nancy)* 1 (special issue 1) (1996): 55–69.

something more profound, for today — perhaps as a result of worldwide communications — we are becoming conscious that what happens in a given place is related to whatever happens somewhere else, even far away from us. If we worry about the fate of the rhino or about life in the depths of the oceans, it is because we realize that these facts have something to do with us, that — in dramatic contrast to mechanistic views — *tout est dans tout*,[9] everything is in everything, as we have recalled already, indeed in a much more concrete and observable way than we thought. We are perhaps the first living beings on our planet who can actively participate in a global network of relations, which are at least partly channeled by our own technology; yet we are somehow discovering again what the ancients knew by an instinct as old as mankind. As T. S. Eliot wrote:

And what there is to conquer
By strength and submission, has already been discovered
Once or twice, or several times, by men whom one cannot hope
To emulate — but there is no competition —
There is only the fight to recover what has been lost
And found and lost again and again.[10]

Intuitively, therefore, the ancient maxim just mentioned seems to express a deep truth. But we cannot be content with a very general and vague statement. *Tout est dans tout*, but how? Surely it cannot be taken to mean that an atom literally contains the whole universe, as we have seen in connection with Pascal's reflections on the "two infinities" and his fractal world. That is ruled out. But then, if it applies to an atom, does it mean that somehow the "information content" of an atom is the same as that of any other system in the universe, the earth with its inhabitants, for example? If the atom and the earth were mathematical objects, that would not be impossible, for we know that the points of an infinite line can be put in a one-to-one correspondence with those of a segment. But in the nature of the case we have to think in terms of information bits, and information does not have the power of the continuum. How can less complex objects contain the same amount of information as more complex ones? In real objects there are different degrees of complexity — of information content — and in theoretical schemes there are different proportions of information actual and potential.

Remembering Poincaré's ideas about relations, one might then suggest that the expression in question should be taken to signify that the

9. L. Pauwels and J. Bergier, *Le matin des magiciens* (Paris: Gallimard, 1960). According to a kind communication from Professor F. García-Brazán of the J. F. Kennedy Argentine University of Buenos Aires, this expression was an adverbial locution of late ancient Greek, and is to be found in the Greek original of St. Paul's letter to the Ephesians (1:23). The *Corpus Hermeticum* contains several expressions similar to it.

10. T. S. Eliot, *Four Quartets*, "East Coker," V, lines 11–16.

same pattern is discovered and the same *relational* concepts apply to objects of different complexity provided that only those gross features of the more complex object are taken into account that correspond to the degree of complexity of the less complex are treated. But even this interpretation seems dubious if we compare, say, an atom to a planetary system: in the former, classical mechanics is not even a crude approximation and quantum effects determine its most important features; in the latter the converse is true. For example, we can assign a trajectory to a planet, but not to an electron in an atom. However, as Poincaré pointed out in his time and as was confirmed by later advances of theoretical physics, the equations representing widely different phenomena are similar in structure. According to Poincaré,[11] mechanism can be interpreted as that view which describes all the phenomena treated by science in terms of the basic equations of analytical mechanics, but the variables entering them, which represent measurable quantities, will have a different interpretation for different phenomena. An example is the application of the Lagrange formalism, originally made for point masses, to the electromagnetic field.

This relational perspective, if carried beyond mere mathematical formulations, gives support to the idea that the appeal of the maxim *tout est dans tout* stems from the fact that it is a hyperbolic way of expressing the fact that in everything there is at least one characteristic in common with everything else, its being an element of the Great Dance and therefore in some way tuned to everything else. To say that the pattern of change of the universe is coherent in time and space implies that in everything there is as it were a reflection of everything else, so much so that the same basic concepts and equations describe the *relations* between the parts of any system, including the universe itself.

An Intuition of Complexity

In chapter three we saw that the starting point of experimental science and technology, whatever certain philosophical schools may claim, is a strong realistic commitment, namely the belief that our sensations, provided that they be critically assessed by reason, inform us about a reality existing independently of us. We also saw that in every object — except, possibly, in genuine elementary particles like the electron — there are as it were *layers of reality* corresponding to the different levels of complexity at which it can be described. A vividly colored fish of the Great Barrier Reef is a special configuration of electrons and nuclei, but it is also an organized ensemble of living cells, it is a collection of organs acting together with a finalized organization, and it is a colored fish: the sum of the latent

---

11. G. Del Re, "Poincaré et le mécanisme," and references therein.

and explicit information contained in each description of its reality is the same (at least up to a number of possibilities compatible with any given level), but the fact that it is that particular fish and not any other object or being that could have been made with the same elementary particles is only apparent at the highest level of complexity. The complexity version of realism thus provides a foundation for another possible meaning of our intuitive idea that *tout est dans tout* in the light of the most recent advances of science: after all, it is the nature and relations of the elementary particles making up a body that lie at the bottom of its ladder of reality levels, and that nature and relations are the same for all objects.

Thus, we have two related but different intuitions in the maxim under consideration: that the universe is a coherent whole, in which every object enjoying a minimum of independence is a knot in a network of relations, not necessary causal, as suggested by the Great Dance image; and that every object is a whole whose ultimate parts are the same, with the same properties, as the ultimate components of every other whole. Along this double line we reach a deeper insight, following Poincaré, into "how nature is one." Recourse to the informational definition of complexity (cf. chapter six) allows inclusion in the Great Dance of man and spiritual beings — though on the existence and nature of the latter science cannot tell much. What remains utterly outside a picture of the universe guided by science is either the perpetually self-differentiating matter of many materialists or the eternal infinitely complex and infinitely rich reality of the supreme Composer and Choreographer.

The recognition that the unity of nature implies relations that are not just those of mechanism goes back to times in which magic and astrology were respectable fields of inquiry, and suggests that it may be instructive for us to continue our exploration of the abandoned paths of science with an examination of such strange notions as correspondences, sympathies, and influences, which were derived from the idea of the unity of nature and of the harmony of the world. Let us begin by returning to Mersenne and mechanism.

Father Marin Mersenne and the Harmony of the World

The idea that things are somehow present in one another was essential to the rather confused theories of magic. This is why, despite the limitations of mechanism, one should take sides, as it were, with Father Mersenne, in his dispute in favor of mechanism with the Oxonian Rosicrucian Robert Fludd (1574–1637). Mersenne did believe in the harmony — and hence the unity — of the universe, but for him the latter implied coherence only inasmuch as it was the necessary consequence of the unitary design of the Creator:

by the very idea of Universal Harmony — the title of a famous book of his — Mersenne denotes a *providential* correspondence of proportion in all parts of Nature,

writes Stefano Leoni, a historian of music.[12] Now, as Leoni points out, Mersenne fought a victorious battle against the naïve animism of Fludd, who sought in the Kabbalah the principle of medicine and astrology; and against the doctrine of correspondences that is the essence of the Kabbalah, according to which

the stars, the elements, the parts of the body, just as they *are* each a number and a letter of the Hebrew alphabet, are also notes of the musical scale.

An impressive illustration of the nature of the explanations in which Fludd believed is offered by Brooke on the example of the weapon salve, a balm supposed to heal a wound by application to the weapon which had inflicted it; according to Fludd, the healing

was effected by a sympathetic power transmitted from the blood on the weapon to the blood of the afflicted.[13]

This example probably suffices to show that Mersenne's fight for reason and lucidity should find an ally in every educated person; but, as we have seen, that fight should not degenerate into arrogant nothingbuttery; that is to say, one should not dismiss certain ideas just because they appear in contrast to mechanism. The real problem with Fludd was not his ideas, but the fact that he did not apply a basic rule of science, which the founder of structural chemistry, Kekulé, expressed much later by saying that scientists could (and maybe should) take their dreams seriously, but only provided that they submitted them to a severe trial by reason and experiment.

The "principle of correspondence," which we shall see in more detail and perhaps in a less negative light in the next two chapters, was the foundation of magic. Roughly speaking, it purports that if something happens to an object it will happen to every other object placed in "correspondence" with it either by nature, e.g., because of similarity, or (by means of certain magic words) by a magician or sorcerer. A familiar example is the belief that by transfixing a photograph with a pin and pronouncing certain words a specially endowed person can kill the person in the photograph. Taken in this sense, it involves a sort of primitive animism, which assumes that the photograph contains a part of the "soul" of the person it represents. In another less primitive but equally uncritical sense, it implies that images and words can produce effects on

---

12. S. Leoni, *Le armonie del mondo* (Genoa: ECIG, 1988).
13. Brooke, *Science and Religion*, 120.

inanimate objects. We shall see in the chapter on communication and symbols that there is a particular context, information transfer, in which this sense is compatible with science; but the claim that the principle of correspondence is a law governing nature in general sounds extremely difficult to prove, to say the least, to a scientist of the twentieth century. Therefore, Mersenne was certainly right in his remark that

> *nemo sanae mentis dixerit imagines vim habere; non ita inhaeren-*
> *dum esse numeris ut rem eo modo se habere [credant], quo numeros*
> *esse viderint, quippe qui nihil ad vim musicae faciunt.*

> no sane man would say that symbols can influence things, nor should one be so attached to numbers that he would believe that a thing behaves according to the properties of a number, for numbers do not confer to music its strength.[14]

However, the mechanistic concept of force (which, as mentioned in a preceding chapter, is anyway questionable in the light of relativity theory) cannot cover coherence, even in such simple cases as the coherent light of a laser. Coherence might be destroyed by a perturbation, but, as long as it is there, it is simply a fact; no force is exerted by light waves in one region of space that causes light waves in another place to adjust to whatever change takes place in the former, even though they maintain the same relations of frequency, direction, and phase. More generally, Mersenne's objections to Fludd are valid, but the existence of a network of noncausal relations, which ensures the unity of nature might justify the notion of correspondence, and, as we already know from the case of the little blackcaps (cf. chapter one), might even have a role in events involving living beings.

Sympathies, Influences, and Causes

Let us now try to assess the possible status of the doctrine of sympathies and influences in the general frame of contemporary science. The mechanistic conception, even when it accepted chance and irreversibility, only considered individual processes one at a time; it had the truth of a description of the Adagio of Beethoven's Ninth Symphony considering one melodic line and one instrument at a time. It grasped something of reality and of its structure, but it missed, as it were, the orchestra and the harmony: that is why it was incapable not only of explaining (we are still to some extent in the same quandary), but of admitting that *an explanation was needed* of the fact that certain instruments would play together all of the time, others would be heard only for short periods, and

14. M. Mersenne, *Quaestiones in Genesim* (Paris: Cramoisy, 1623).

the drums would mark by soft, isolated beats the presence of a mysterious power timidly but gratefully accepting the joy of the great company. For similar interplays of events and processes in nature mechanism could only invent a general pseudo-cause, namely chance, to conceal as it were its limitation to chains of efficient causes. Truly enough, the first violin, the bassoon, the cellos know from the score when and what they have to play, and that is all *they* need; but the composer felt, so to speak, that he had no choice, that those were the time and the theme and the instrument required by the symphony taking shape in his mind.

As mentioned in chapter one and above in connection with the Mersenne-Fludd dispute, the relations on which astrology and magic were based were correspondences, similarities, affinities, influences, sympathies involving objects or entities as disparate in nature as words, numbers, metals, and stars. Their origin is actually ancient and noble, for they can be traced back to the associations between words and things typical of the Ancient Testament and to the Pythagorean and Platonic belief in the significance of numbers and geometrical figures. Under the Roman Empire, in the Greek-speaking part of the Empire, those two traditions melted together, and gave the fascinating analogical interpretation of the Ancient Testament by Philo of Alexandria and the famous treatises of Hermes Trismegistos, on which we shall pause in next chapter. The basic idea is well illustrated by music: since a piece of music has a profound emotional effect on us, there must be something in common between it and us; since a metal string can be made to emit certain musical notes, there must be something in common between it and music; since the musical notes have frequencies that stand in simple ratios, they must have something in common with numbers; and so on. Indeed, by a sort of transitive property, one could claim that if numbers are the foundation of music, and if music influences the mood of human beings and animals, then numbers can influence human beings and animals. A similar argument served to justify astrology: since the constellations have different positions in the sky in different seasons, and since the rhythms of life follow the seasons, then the constellations, indeed even single "stars" (the planets) influence events and things on the earth. A theoretical foundation of a sort was thus given for the so-called "influences," particularly of the stars. By the same token, since widely different objects or processes could appear to be subject to the same influences, one could speak of "sympathy" (which, as mentioned in chapter one, is the Greek word συμπάθεια, "undergoing together"), meaning what we said about correspondences, that objects in correspondence, particularly similar ones, have as it were a parallel evolution or history.

Several treatises on the "science" of sympathies and correspondences explicitly included in a theory of the harmony of the world were bequeathed to us by the intellectual melting pot that was the seventeenth century. A concrete example of the kind of considerations made in them is provided by the work of Athanasius Kircher, on which we are now going to pause.

Kircher, the Wood, and the Trees

From what we have seen so far, the active aspects of correspondences that are influences and sympathies might contain at least a grain of truth if, as MacDonald emphasizes in the epigraph to this chapter, they are associated with emotions aroused in a living being by the sight or contact of an object or a material. But if we go further, and consider inanimate objects, we find at least three difficulties: the apparent arbitrariness of the associations, a large measure of confusion between symbolic function and physical nature, and the practical impossibility of specifying interactions precisely enough for any verification. These difficulties clearly emerge from the correlations proposed as the "World Harmony of Sympathies" by the German Jesuit Athanasius Kircher (1602–1680) in the epoch of Fludd and Mersenne. First, he establishes a sequence of ten Enneachords:

> *Mundus Archetypus* (God, pure spirits)
> *Mundus Sidereus* (Stars & Planets)
> *Mundus Mineralis* (Minerals)
> *Lapides* (Stones)
> *Plantae* (Herbs)
> *Arbores* (Trees)
> *Aquatilia* (Aquatic Animals)
> *Volucria* (Birds)
> *Quadrupedia* (Quadrupeds)
> *Colores varii* (Colors).[15]

The criterion followed in choosing this sequence is less arbitrary and primitive than it looks at first sight. Two notions seem to be involved. One is a sort of temporal and causal succession: God and the angels preceded the creation of earth, minerals came before plants, plants before animals, and colors, the appearances of all things, emerged from the very existence of those things for the benefit of humanity, not included in the table. The other notion is complexity, that is to say the number and degree of interdependence of the parts that constitute an entity. It is difficult to see how this notion would apply to colors, but we can think either of a corpuscular theory of light or, once again, of the complexity of human beings, the external observers.

---

15. A. Kircher, *Musurgia Universalis* (Rome: Haer. Franc. Corbelletti, 1650).

Next, Kircher lists, for each Enneachord, entities corresponding to the musical intervals, from *Diapason Ditonus* to *Tonus*. In the line corresponding to *Diapason cum Tono*, he puts:

Cherubs
Saturn
Lead
Topaz
Hellebore
Cypress
Tunny
Owl
Donkey and Bear
Dark Brown.

The arguments for this particular sequence were often suggested by rather superficial considerations, such as the fact that the owl is a symbol of wisdom, and hellebore was long believed to cure madness.

From the case of Kircher one can judge the mixture of profound intuitions and uncritical beliefs that characterizes all students of the doctrine of sympathies, down to Aleister Crowley, an occultist and tarot student of our century. Kircher was undoubtedly one of the most serious thinkers in the field, and grasped the double face of complexity, material complexity and informational complexity, which is the central point of the now reemerging view of the world. But his classification also demonstrates that affinity or sympathy as such can have no direct action, and are not the same as a force like gravitation, unless new laws of nature, those of magic, are proved to work. Those tempted to revive magic and its laws (possibly in the form of telepathy, telekinesis, auras, and the like) would point out here that absence of evidence is not evidence of absence; and, if a person trying to work magic (or its equivalent under a modern name) failed, they would say that special personal characteristics are necessary. But this only means that even if we were prepared to grant that there are real magicians, we should look at magic as an art belonging to the realm of special hardly learnable parapsychic or "mental" abilities (much like the musical ear), not as a technique based on laws of nature independent of the person observing or applying them.

Let me add one more remark about Athanasius Kircher. The end of the sixteenth century was a branching point in the development of natural philosophy. With Kepler and Galileo, the tendency of Western thought to focus attention on the detailed quantitative description of the space-time structure of things triumphed over the other tendency, that of looking at things as wholes, as integrated units interacting as such with the outer world. The real novelty of that time, namely emphasis on the critical assessment of facts, was accepted, of course, by those who shaped modern science (not last Marin Mersenne), whereas the reductionistic mental attitude, which consisted in explaining away every whole by describing its parts, was adopted by all scientists and natural philosophers, and resulted in a generalized reductionism with positive and negative sides. Kircher himself (judging from the lists reported above) is a good example of the negative sides of reductionism: his view of music lost sight of coherence, and focused attention on musical intervals and accords — he missed the forest by too much looking at the trees. The major feature of the very metaphor he was studying, the Symphony of the World, is its unitary spatiotemporal nature; but his approach was that of a student of the theory of music who would try to understand the marvelous discovery of beauty and serenity expressed by the first movement of Beethoven's Sixth Symphony by studying which instruments, scales, and accords were chosen for that purpose. The idea that those choices were by no means accidental is entirely correct; but their analysis has a meaning only if their role in making up the whole is clearly understood.

It must be conceded, however, that, if Kircher's approach looks as reductionistic as that of his critics, this was not just because of the mental attitude of his time, but because Kircher tacitly assumed that the unity of the picture he was setting up would be ensured by referring every detail to man. This too is a point where our science has room for greater humility, and therefore for a better understanding of reality. The popularity of the anthropic principle,[16] which sees the size and age of the universe related to the very existence of humanity as a consequence of the universal constants of physics having precisely the values they have, is proof that human beings cannot be kept out of the picture. Indeed, the most important fruit of the emerging view of man, whose scientific side was beautifully presented by Prigogine and Stengers as a "New Alliance" between man and nature,[17] is that it allows us to distinguish between objects perceived as mere facts and objects (or signs) that play the role of symbols without eliminating one of the terms. This distinction will be dealt with in chapter eleven. Here we just record it and proceed in our exploration.

Panpsychism Yesterday and Today

Even in the golden times of magic and astrology, many eminent thinkers were much more cautious than the average scholars. In the fourth century A.D., for example, Saint Augustine expressed disapproval of the "mathematicians," *viz.* the astrologers. In contrast, the impressive comeback of astrology in our society — which, according to many a scientist, should

16. Barrow and Tipler, *Anthropic Cosmological Principle*.
17. Cf. the passage quoted above.

know better — shows that, if there has been any progress during the last few millennia, it has not concerned certain basic intuitive ideas. A plausible explanation of the belief in influences and sympathies may be found in a built-in tendency of human beings to animism, i.e., to attribute a rudimentary "soul" to everything. Now, nonconformist but respectable thinkers of our time, particularly the Jesuit priest and paleontologist Pierre Teilhard de Chardin[18] and the German zoologist Bernhard Rensch, proposed that a "psychism" should be attributed to all objects in the universe; thus, not only is animism, a characteristic of primitive societies, well alive in our consumer society, but it has received some support by respected scientists. We shall see in chapter eleven that current science, if one succeeds in crossing the barriers between disciplines, can provide a convincing explanation and interpretation of these views; for they can be recast in terms of the concepts of the science of communication, and then the strictly animistic implication that there are intelligent spirits animating rocks, plants, and animals can be removed; and belief in spiritual realities, required, according to many thinkers and scientists, to ensure the coherence of the world-view offered by today's science, can be given a more serious foundation.

What seems to be valid of the notions on which magic and astrology are based is that certain distant and physically unrelated objects — say, a planet and a bird — could affect by their presence and changes, in a way not covered by mechanism, other objects that are capable of modifying their properties in response to signals coming from their environment, and could therefore influence through them in a similar way, in virtue of positive feedback and amplification, the state of the part of the cosmos to which those objects belong. This consideration, as mentioned, is related to the concept of *communication* (information transfer) and to its role in the evolution of the universe. In this way, the difficulties arising when influences and sympathies are treated as forces disappear. In particular, the limitations otherwise imposed by energy requirements are definitely not in question. Consider an example. One might include among influences the relation of the astronavigating blackcap to the stars. Now, it is true that the little bird receives energy from the stars which guide it, because vision requires energy. However, only a few photons are necessary, and they carry an extremely small amount of energy and momentum. The astronomers do measure those quantities by highly sophisticated instruments, but they confirm that no significant force is associated with them. Mersenne was right when he said that in such cases no *"vis"* should be invoked. The process by which the blackcap orients itself is due to another property of the light coming from the sky: the "information" it

18. P. Teilhard de Chardin, *Le Phénomène humain* (Paris: Seuil, 1955); B. Rensch, *Das universale Weltbild* (Frankfurt a.M.: Fischer, 1977).

carries. Exchange of information does require energy, but just enough to be felt by the sense organs. The latter amplify the message, transmit it to the decision centers, and the little bird changes its course accordingly. It is the same as when your car radio tells you that the road you are on is barred a mile ahead: the resulting detour is not caused by a force, but by a piece of information, a message, causing you to make a certain decision. Also pain is a message: it tells the brain that the condition or situation of a particular part of the organism is not normal, and should be given priority over other motives of action at a level depending on its intensity.

It would seem that we should classify long-range interactions in the universe into two types: direct ones, which are mediated by actual forces, and indirect ones, which are mediated by information processing. The former bring about, for example, the tides induced by a celestial body on another not too distant celestial body (say the moon on the earth). As to the universe at large they are certainly of little import for events on our earth, but they do exist, and may shape history at the million-year scale, because the whole solar system is subject to gravitational forces produced by the rest of our galaxy, and other galaxies exert some gravitational action on ours. Indeed, within the general trend of the so-called Hubble expansion, nearby galaxies appear to move toward accumulation centers, for instance the Great Attractor in the region of the Centaurus constellation in the southern hemisphere. A very special form of direct interaction between bodies in the universe is the arrival (or departure) and the possible impact of meteorites, comets, and asteroids in the solar system. An enormous meteorite may have caused the extinction of the dinosaurs: where was it from? It could come from the permanent asteroid reservoir of the solar system, but it could come from outer space as well. The meteorites that should cause the end of mankind according to prophecies may well have been already traveling millions or billions of years toward their destination. In the light of unifying principles such as the general laws of physics, the anthropic principle, self-amplification of fluctuation, such catastrophes too are part of the Great Dance.

The interactions of the second type have little or no direct effect, as a rule. Consider the light arriving to us from the depths of space. It does not carry sufficient energy to bring about any significant direct effect. It is, however, rich in information; it may therefore induce significant changes at the receiving end whenever suitable information processors, in particular human beings, are available. Consider as an example the effect of the sight of the starry sky on a person. It consists in a subtle change in mood and way of thinking about nearby things, which in turn may induce actions that would otherwise not take place. And since, as Dante would say,

Poca favilla gran fiamma seconda

a little spark is followed by a great flame[19]

it may rightly be expected that the starry sky, especially in those seasons when it is brightest and purest, would "influence" the conditions on the whole earth.

The above is an extreme example illustrating the general point that changes in the moods of animals, their migrations, hunting expeditions and reproductive seasons are determined through information processing by a number of external factors which include the constellations. The effect of nearer objects, even when it is only psychological, is of course even more important, from the sight of the moon by a wild dog to the odors which may determine our choices without our realizing the cause, and finally to affinities of ideas or sensations. Whether transmitted over a large distance or not, indirect interactions seem to provide a reasonable scientific counterpart of notions such as sympathies, affinities, influences, etc.

In conclusion, reflection on the theoretical background of magic and astrology confirms that it is not right to think of relations as if they always implied that type of interdependence which is called in mechanics "strong direct coupling." Two systems are coupled if changes in one of them affect the other; they are directly coupled if their coupling does not depend on third parties; they are strongly coupled if events affecting one affect the other almost to the same extent. In contrast, although similarity also is a relation, we do not consider it in any way as a sort of interdependence. As an example, let us consider the pentacle, which magicians considered a powerful symbol, capable of trapping demons. Those magicians were most probably mistaken, but, since their brains worked as well as ours, the idea that a geometrical drawing can exert a power cannot be discarded merely on the grounds that magic does not work. The point, as we shall see in chapter eleven, is that a pentacle is a symbol, i.e., a sign which the minds of intelligent beings associate with an inaccessible reality and which they may interpret as prompting or interdicting action; therefore, it might establish a measure of interdependence inasmuch as it can *indirectly* affect material reality through (and only through) direct coupling to minds.

Could Magic Work?

As we said, people seem to be getting interested in magic again, especially when it comes disguised as a superscience with no technicalities,

---

19. Dante Alighieri, *Divine Comedy,* canto 1, l. 34. Longfellow translation from ILTweb, Digital Dante Project, Columbia University.

and hence open to everybody. A bestseller on imaginary illuminations and colored auras,[20] which tells of a community whose members help plants to grow in perfect health by the energy fields their illuminated minds irradiate, is a typical example of magic recast in a pseudoscientific language: it is appealing to many people because technology has become too difficult, and they feel happy at the idea that they could control nature in a much simpler way in virtue of unknown innate powers of the human mind. People more familiar with science and philosophy are of course somewhat skeptical, but open-mindedness demands that we try to answer the question: are we really sure that magic cannot actually work? A discussion of this question is also important in view of another fundamental question, which has been haunting even the minds of the most radical materialists for several decades: to what extent and in what sense does a *Weltanschauung* built on the more recent advances of science require the existence of a spiritual dimension of reality? We have already found hints useful for an answer in the preceding chapters; but we have still a long way to go. An open point being the existence of nonmaterial entities, an examination of magic is an interesting way to get acquainted with the problems involved in the acceptance of that existence.

In its practical aspects, magic is based, so to speak, on a cause-effect interpretation of the correlations of the Great Dance. The difficulties are of two orders. First, a person's will can perhaps interfere with correlations dictated by information processing, but that will generate a *statistical fluctuation* in what is a general order. With such fluctuations, as we recalled on several occasions, the outcome is never certain. Most of the time, like sparks falling on a heap of materials mostly wet or fireproof, they will be reabsorbed by the whole before anything special happens. In certain circumstances, like sparks hitting an inflammable spot, they may start a sequel of extraordinary events: but where and when and how large and how lasting the latter will be cannot be predicted, partly because then the "magician" should have a detailed knowledge of the situation, partly because there could be a case of deterministic chaos — that is to say, a situation whose long-term evolution is unpredictable even if only strict causality of a known type applies (cf. chapter five).

The second order of reasons why magic is not expected to work is that we have no idea of how *our earth* could influence the stars. As to nonliving matter, the earth is too tiny to affect in any way bodies even a few light years away. As to living beings, experts tend to think that life (not to speak of intelligence) is unlikely in our planetary system except on earth, and extremely rare in the universe; anyway, extrasolar life would not be affected by the presence of the earth in any way our science can

---

20. J. Redfield, *The Celestine Prophecy* (New York: Warner Books, 1993).

imagine, for the earth does not even send enough light to the stars to play a "visual" role.

Therefore, nearby as well as distant objects, as far as we can tell, cannot be acted upon by information exchange in a way our science can conceive on the basis of known facts. It would seem that any belief in the efficacy of magic rests on belief in the existence of a set of rules we cannot trace back to ordinary experience, as is the case with the laws of science, but only to some inexpressible intuition, and on the notion that the human mind can affect matter directly, without the intermediation of the body. That is to say, one could believe that operating rules exist such that a whole chain of events will obey the will of the magician if they are applied; then the problem would be to find those rules, and, as is well known, people claiming to have found them are not so rare. One could also decide that there are spiritual beings inhabiting and controlling trees, springs, stars, and that the human mind has the power of communicating with them, indeed of forcing them to act in specific ways. The practices of shamans are partly based on this sort of doctrine, which is obviously a corollary of animism, but monotheists like Marsilio Ficino (1433–1499), a famous scholar held in great esteem by the Medicis of Florence, had the same beliefs regarding the stars.

All this sounds quite naïve to scientists who know that even vitalism — the notion that a special organizing force is at work in living organisms to keep them alive — introduces a redundant explanation for the fact that living organisms are obviously highly organized units capable of defending their identities. Why should there be powers of the mind that can be used at will to perform deeds that our limbs and our instruments (including space probes) already perform? And — in an evolutionary perspective — why should there be powers whose survival value is zero?

About Demons, Fairies, and Other Invisible Beings

The special kind of animism that is typical of magic admits the existence of invisible mediators between symbols and reality, i.e., being endowed with some sort of ability to give symbols a particular meaning and to act in accordance with the specific characteristic of those symbols. Such, for example, are the Elementals of the Tarots, workmen of the shop of creation, who would obey orders given through a ritual using the Tarot cards, producing soil out of nowhere or starting terrible storms.[21] Supposing that such intermediate creatures exist, words and signs could serve as symbols having a tremendous power; the most familiar example being perhaps the evocation and confinement of a demon within a pentacle by a Word of Command.

21. C. Williams, *Trumps.*

Belief in demons, Elementals, and other invisible beings capable of controlling the forces of creation and of obeying orders of intelligent beings is a fascinating kind of animism. Perhaps its appeal stems not only from the archetypal nature of animism, but from the feeling it breeds that man's relation to the forces of nature is not that of a helpless though proud creature carried and eventually crushed by the unrelenting march of a mindless power, but rather that of an intelligent being who, by discovering the right symbols and rituals, can establish contact with the invisible beings who rule those forces, and even impose its will on them. It remains to be seen whether such beings exist, if they are simply the angels, the souls of the dead, and the devils of the Judeo-Christian tradition, or if they include the spirits of the plants, of the rocks, of the planets, as in the Greco-Roman tradition and in the religions of the American Indians. One point, at any rate, is clear: symbols and signs only become capable of action if the Great Dance involves beings capable of a minimum of abstract thinking and free will, that is to say, beings endowed with something like a mind, albeit of a rudimentary kind compared with ours.

An example will help us. It is taken from fiction, but we can treat it as a real story, because it matches closely what ancient peoples and magicians would accept as true. In Tolkien's *Lord of the Rings*,[22] the Fellowship of the Ring attempt to cross the great mountain Caradhras. When a terrible snowstorm forces them to give up, Gimli the Dwarf growls: "Ah, it is as I said. It was no ordinary storm. It is the ill will of Caradhras. He does not love Elves and Dwarves, and that drift was laid to cut off our escape." Here there are two points, which Tolkien had certainly transferred to his book from his studies of Medieval literature and folklore. Caradhras is attributed a will moved by hate and love, and storms are classified into "ordinary" and intentional ones. This gives us a picture of the kind of being that Caradhras is. It is endowed with some freedom of choice, though not with intelligence. It is like a brute, capable of liking and disliking other beings, and of acting accordingly with its own specific means — wind, snow, stones. Those are, as it were, the tools of its ordinary activity, but they can be used against anything that has roused its aggressiveness. An analogy with which we are all familiar is that of a dog, which can use its teeth not only to feed itself, but to attack human beings, animals, and even inanimate objects which for some reason it considers enemies.

If Gimli were willing to discuss such matters, he would probably say that a mountain has a "soul" (in the Aristotelian sense already recalled, and discussed in chapter twelve) of a very simple kind. It is normally inactive, and the mountain behaves just as science expects it to. But it will be aware of unusual events such as the presence of foreign living beings,

---

22. Tolkien, *Lord of the Rings*, part 1: *The Fellowship of the Ring*.

and may even consider them enemies if it feels that they are capable of damaging its integrity — for instance if their likes delved into it or used its stones to make buildings, thus destroying plants and dens of animals, or even just changing the beauty of parts of it. Gimli would also explain that the spirit of the mountain cannot even imagine matters that do not concern the mountain directly: in that sense, it is less complicated than the "soul" of a simple animal; indeed, it could be compared to a computer-controller with a very limited program. Yet, precisely like an animal or a computer, it remembers and has inclinations. It may be "evil," if to it beings not belonging on the mountain are *ipso facto* enemies to be expelled or destroyed.

The objection immediately comes to the mind that an animal is an organism endowed with the ability to learn (at least to some extent) and to adjust its behavior to a changing environment, while a mountain is essentially a huge heap of stones. To the modern mind, that is a decisive objection. But an individual of another culture, indeed of the culture now taking shape on the debris of physicalism, could give an answer worth some reflection. With time, because of gravity, of water accumulating in it, of plants growing on it, a heap of stones might develop some sort of identity, manifesting itself in a measure of unitary active behavior. In fact, a mountain range has a specific interaction with the atmosphere, a specific climate, a specific role in determining the weather hundreds of miles around it. Now, science would work on the assumption that what is active is the atmosphere, not the mountain, and it will consider the latter simply as an enormous obstacle with a complicated shape lying in the path of the winds. Very probably that assumption will be enough. But is the distinction really so clear-cut? Why cannot we say that the mountain "acts" on the winds so as to change their velocity and direction? The reason is the old principle called Occam's razor in honor of its discoverer, William of Occam (1290–1349), nowadays called by some the principle of parsimony: if the (avowedly simplified) model of a mountain as a passive obstacle on the path of winds explains everything there is to explain, all the known facts, why should we complicate matters by additional fanciful assumptions? Well, it is possible, for example, that minor changes in the temperature of rocks should affect the microclimatic conditions on it; and those minor changes might in turn switch on a self-amplified chain of events; but that a few men walking on the mountain should disturb its equilibrium to the point of letting loose a big snow storm sounds quite implausible.

A measure of uncertainty anyway remains, and scientists have discovered why it cannot be removed: there are phenomena which science cannot account for or rule out in all their details. We discussed this problem in chapter five in connection with stochastic processes and deterministic chaos. In the case at hand, the point is that the present theories of science can explain storms and other features of weather *in principle*, but they have to deal with so many variables that they can predict the number, strength, location, and duration of possible storms only in terms of probabilities. That is to say, they tell you what a storm cannot be or do, and the short-term probability that there will be a storm under given circumstances, but nothing more, because they have to deal with situations where only averages over long periods of time and large geographic areas show a measure of order. In fact, even in circumstances when the probability of a given atmospheric event is judged small — say, excellent weather with low humidity and high pressure — a tiny "statistical fluctuation," that is, a small occasional ripple in the even course of events, might be amplified rather than die off. This is especially possible on high mountains, where currents of warm and cold air move all the time up and down the slopes, forming whirls as they meet rocks or trees. Then the weather will become unstable, and eventually a storm may break. Who causes that fluctuation? Nobody, says science: the appearance of spontaneous fluctuations is in the nature of things. Gimli would see it differently: he would say that the sleeping soul of the mountain has awakened and brought about the fluctuation, for example by causing a piece of rock to fall and thus produce a suitable movement of air.

Of course, maybe Gimli's language was just metaphorical, in the sense that what he meant when speaking of the mountain was actually invisible beings, such as the Elementals, controlling events on the mountain. But that does not seem to change the essential question: is it really possible that a great mountain should have some ability to learn, to remember, to attack? I for one would answer "no, there isn't," but then, if I found myself in the terrible storm described by Tolkien, I would instinctively feel that the mountain is treating me like an enemy. There is something funny in our psychology in this connection. Carl G. Jung (1875–1961), as is well known, made up a theory in which he assumed that the human mind has built-in structures that determine what I have called the "instinctive" responses of a person to given circumstances.[23] We could state his idea (albeit with no guarantee of faithfulness to his thought) by simply saying that we humans tend to treat analogies as reality especially when we are under stress, as when we curse a tool that does not work as it should. This is one way of reconciling the conflict between our experiential responses and our cold logic. For the sake of intellectual honesty, however, it should be added that the "analogical" explanation just given might be applied as an easy (but reductionistic) argument against the existence of spiritual entities. In fact, as we saw in chapter six, science such as it has become in the last few years has recognized that there are un-

23. C. G. Jung, *The Role of the Unconscious* (1918), Collected Works 9 (Princeton, N.J.: Princeton/Bollingen, 1959).

predictable events; they are attributed by a trick of language to a cause called chance, but chance is actually a name for the absence of causes that can be detected by scientific methods. When we swear against the unexpected behavior of an object it is because we are faced at the personal level with the same situation science faces with regard to random events. At variance with science, however, we want a cause at all costs, and find it in a sort of malevolent free will of the offending object. Such a response is certainly a merely emotional one, but on what proofs do we base our certainty? One proof is that no structure has been found in a mountain that would correspond at least to a primitive nervous system, and science does not know of any case of awareness and emotions not associated with a nervous system; another is that, as Occam's razor requires, *entia non sunt multiplicanda praeter necessitatem*, entities should not be multiplied beyond necessity, and, provided chance is accepted as an explanation, the psychological effect of analogies accounts for everything without introducing ad hoc entities.

Although — shall I say it again? — I for one do not believe that a mountain can have emotions or act willfully against anybody or anything, it is amusing and instructive to note that there are weak points in both negative arguments. One is that scientists actually know of systems similar to a brain that might be mistaken for stones — integrated circuits on silicon chips such as are used, for example, in computers. Now, it would seem that computers cannot show emotions, but all depends on what we mean by emotion. Reactions like those Gimli attributed to Caradhras can be classified as responses to a perturbation that tends to modify the state of a system; now, responses of that kind can be programmed even in the ROM of a computer. If we say that somehow Caradhras reacted on behalf of other powers, then we can think of a computer participating in a network and responding to a certain perturbation because of the danger not to itself, but to the network. I know that the idea that a mountain can be a computer in a network is quite farfetched, but I suppose the point is clear: it is one thing to exclude a possibility by common sense, it is another thing to do so because current science could not take it seriously.

As to the second weak point, it is somewhat less of a science fiction scenario. We suggested that Occam's razor should be applied because the analogies accounted for everything; but we should have specified "everything for which science can account"; and that changes the whole perspective. As is now well known, science can only account for trends and produce probability estimates when it comes to storms and other events that result from amplification of random fluctuations; an explanation for the fact that a certain storm took place at a certain time in a certain place with a certain intensity is not superfluous. Therefore, the Occam-razor objection should be completed by a proof that the coincidence of the attempt to pass the mountain by the Fellowship of the Ring and the terrible storm in which they were taken can only be a coincidence; but how can we be sure? In real-life coincidences of the same kind, a religious person would see the will of the Providence, possibly acting through minor spiritual entities, the angels. As an alternative, the anti-spiritualists offer belief in "blind chance," as did Monod,[24] i.e., the belief that if something happens for which science cannot find a necessary cause in the material world then that event has no cause at all. As discussed in chapters five and six, this leads to a paradox, because even the tests of scientific predictions are the result of "arbitrary" choices of the scientists, whose interventions are causes not predictable by science.

All this leaves many questions open. The major underlying problem is the following. Supposing there are pure spirits and that they can act on matter, has science anything to say about how they do so? We shall return to this problem in chapter twelve, when we speak of "downward causation," a fact with which science has to cope. In particular we shall explore a view that belongs to the history of mankind at least since the dawn of civilization, and arrived to us through Plato and Descartes, down to the eminent Australian brain scientist John C. Eccles: the idea that the human being is a combination of two separate entities — the body and an immaterial principle, called the "soul," the mind, or the self depending on the thinker. The general problem of the possible action of spirit on matter might be clarified if there were some idea of how an immaterial mind could act on the brain. The other view, that the spiritual dimension of man is a feature of the highest complexity level of our whole reality, goes back to Aristotle, and is held by the main stream philosophy of the Roman Catholic Church, combined with belief in the immortality of the soul (see chapter twelve); and this is sufficient proof that it leaves room for spiritual realities.

In sum, there are in magic many intriguing and possibly useful ideas; but it seems clear that both in Fludd's and in Redfield's form it is quite disappointing as a supplement to the mechanistic approach to the nature of the relations between objects and beings in the universe — in short, to the question "how nature is one." Nevertheless, George MacDonald's general consideration quoted in the epigraph to this chapter applies: there must be something in magic, if it reappears again and again in the history of mankind. We can perhaps disentangle this skein, but it will be better to do so after pausing on alchemy — which is quite a different story, though often put in the same heap as magic — and briefly touching upon astrology, whose success can be easily traced back to the parallelism between the apparent motion of the constellations and the seasons on the earth.

---

24. J. Monod, *Le hasard et la necessité* (Paris: Seuil, 1970); published in English as *Chance and Necessity*, trans. Austryn Wainhouse (New York: Knopf, 1972).

Chapter 10

Alchemy and Technology:
From Wisdom to Know-How

Despite the influence of beliefs similar to those ruling magic, alchemy was based on observed, reproducible facts. This is why a review of its double face, which was at the same sapiential and operational, opens new perspectives on the present plight of the technological dimension of the scientific enterprise.

Alchemy and Chemistry – The Origins – Alchemy as Science – The Spirit of Alchemy – A Path to Wisdom – Analogies, Allegories, Correspondences – Alchemy, Mysticism, and Ethics – About Spiritual Standards

Follow the way of the Ancients
And you will know the eternal essence of the Principle.

— Lao-Tzu[1]

Alchemy and Chemistry

In the examination of magic, we reached the conclusion that it did not really concern nature, that, if anything, it concerned the immaterial dimension of reality; for it was expected to allow control of lesser spiritual entities (or, in its modern version, hidden powers of the mind), which in turn could act on nature. What about astrology and alchemy, two other abandoned lines of research, also related to magic? Well, the former was based on the dubious belief that the positions of the stars in the firmament influence a person's temperament and history, and even the history of mankind; we have already seen that whatever may be valid in that idea should probably be rephrased in terms of mere parallelism: e.g., climatic influences on moods, which are a fact, depend on the seasons, and the seasons are parallel to particular arrangements of the constellations, because both depend on the position of the earth on the ecliptic.

Alchemy, on the other hand, was an experimental discipline trying to establish cause-effects chains leading to repeatable experimental results; indeed, its aim was the kind of knowledge that would allow man to reproduce in the laboratory the most mysterious operations of Nature. Therefore, although it relied on a general world-view that was abandoned in the seventeenth century, alchemy was closer to modern science than magic and astrology long before it gave birth to chemistry. Indeed, an attempt to understand what it was and why people were so interested in it will open an illuminating perspective on the nature of science and give material for reflection on the present plight of technological research. In point of fact, there was a great difference between it and astronomy, the science from which present physics originated. Astronomy was concerned with observations and tried to find a representation of the universe in terms of geometrical figures — circles, ellipses, hyperbolas, and their focuses — capable of explaining them; alchemy aimed

1. Lao-Tzu, *Tao-teh-Ching*, poem 14. Translated into Italian with an introduction and notes by the philosopher J. Evola (Milan: Ceschina, 1959). We refer to Evola's work because, as is well known, the translations of Chinese texts are actually interpretations, and many of them are so full of inconsistencies that they are unlikely to correspond to the intentions of Lao-Tzu.

at discovering how operations such as calcination (which takes its name from the process in which limestone is changed into lime) can be used to imitate and emulate the transformations of materials performed by nature in volcanoes or in living beings. It is precisely because of this practical approach to knowledge that since its beginning alchemy was close to what technology in general is today; for technology is not just the production and improvement of tools, which help ordinary people in their ordinary operations, but the design and realization of devices, processes, and materials that — in addition to making it possible for human beings to do what by nature they are not capable of doing, e.g., to speak to one another over distances of thousands of miles, or to fly by mere muscular strength — allow them to "understand by doing." In fact, the slightest modification in technological design or production method involves some degree of understanding of new aspects of matter's actualities or potentialities. Examples of the scientific nature of practical applications are provided not only by the history of science, but by the fundamental conceptual contributions of technology to present science, such as the introduction of the notion of feedback and of information content.

The transition from alchemy to chemistry took place in the seventeenth century, as did the move from Aristotelian physics to Galilean physics; nevertheless the former presents itself in a much different way. As we have already recalled, pre-Galilean physics and astronomy gave priority to mathematics and measurement, and for them the observer was, so to speak, like a person watching from a window the action in the street below; alchemy, in contrast, involved the researcher in a system of mystical theories, which required spiritual commitment as well as physical activity. The deliberate obscurity of many texts and the number of charlatans and mountebanks who practiced it was so large that laws against it were promulgated in various times and places. Sir Thomas Edward Thorpe, a distinguished British chemist and brilliant writer, gave in 1894 a lively description of that dark side.[2] Therefore, it might be cause of wonder that, among the great men who took an active interest in it, there were such diverse personalities as the German Dominican monk Albertus Magnus (Albert the Great, 1200–1287), teacher of Thomas Aquinas and a rigorous thinker, the French scribe-notary Nicolas Flamel (1330–1417) and his wife, serious experimenters with empirical and mystical minds, and even Isaac Newton (1642–1727), the very man who, by founding modern mathematical physics, masterfully completed the affirmation of Galileo's approach to the study of nature.[3] What we want to do here is

2. T. E. Thorpe, *Essays in Historical Chemistry* (1894); we have been able to consult this work only in an Italian translation by R. Pitoni under the title *Storia della Chimica* (Turin: STEN, 1911).

3. C. Gilchrist, *Alchemy* (Longmead, England: Element Books, 1991).

to understand the reasons why alchemy appealed to them, and to show that there was a substantial scientific continuity between alchemy and chemistry. This is important for our exploration of what modern science suggests or hints at beyond experimentally observable facts. If alchemy had a mystical dimension and yet was a science in the modern sense, then maybe that lost dimension, considered an unforgivable fault in the age of rationalism and positivism, might offer a gleam of hope for the present plight of science. For it would seem that ecology and bioethics are bound to remain at the stage of good intentions if they do not recognize that man's scientific and technical activity cannot be treated as if it did not engage his whole physical and spiritual reality; alchemy might provide the blueprints for such an urgent task.

The Origins

Alchemy is so old that there is disagreement as to the origin of its name. According to some authors, it is a derivation from the Arabian translation of a late-Greek word, according to others it is a toponym from al-Ham, i.e., Egypt, the biblical land of Ham, son of Noah. In fact, it is quite likely that alchemy was first practiced extensively in Egypt, possibly coming from Mesopotamia, the great plains between the rivers Euphrates and Tigris, where the first great empires of the Near East flourished more that ten thousand years ago; it was certainly also practiced in ancient China, and there are historians who think it was first born there.[4]

However that may be, it stands to reason that alchemy appeared soon after the discovery of fire. It probably took our early ancestors a long time to tame fire. Eventually they did so, but their relation with it was always that with a friend-enemy; fire helped them in many things, to get light and heat, to make certain foods eatable, to reclaim land, and yet it could not be touched, and if left to itself it could cause disasters and suffering. It is not surprising, therefore, that it should be considered in a way sacred, something of which humanity could not freely dispose. The myth of Prometheus, the giant who stole fire from the gods and was cruelly punished, reveals that mankind, in its mythopoeic age, was already conscious of that double nature of fire, and feared the consequences of using it against the will of the gods. This feeling of strangeness was reinforced by the realization that fire opened the way toward the knowledge of the most recondite secrets of nature. As with astronomy and astrology, the very first origin of alchemy should perhaps be looked for in the world of the shepherds of Mesopotamia, after the discovery of fire. Perhaps it

---

4. A detailed discussion, albeit slightly biased in favor of the gnostic-esoteric face of alchemy, has been given by one of the best students of alchemy as distinct from chemistry, the Swiss T. Burckhardt, *Alchemie: Sinn und Weltbild* (Olten, Switzerland: Walter, 1960).

was born when, in the frosty nights of those vast plains, they would sit in silence around the bonfire lit to cook foods and to provide heat. Perhaps it was they who, in the morning, while looking at the remains of the fire, would sometimes find that the stones that had been most intensely exposed to heat had changed their color and consistency, and perhaps had produced small shining spheres, gray or reddish in color: new materials, sometimes very beautiful, had mysteriously been formed. Further observations followed. People realized, for example, that ash had the power to scour tissues, and that certain stones, after calcination, would heat water while changing it into a strange mineral milk.

This was how chemistry was born.[5] But it was a very special chemistry, because the people of those times would not make the rigid distinction between matter and spirit, between outer and inner experience, which was introduced in the seventeenth century, and produced both the great successes and (in the long run) the antihuman tendencies of modern science. In those very ancient times there was indeed a separation, but it was between the secret recipes that artisans had developed for dyeing tissues, preparing materials for building, tanning skins, etc., and yet more secret studies, aimed at penetrating the secrets of the gods, and therefore considered as belonging to the sphere of religion. Those researches, by which man proposed himself as the apprentice or the competitor of the gods, were what was called alchemy. It was not just a science, therefore, but also a collection of rituals with the purpose of partaking with the gods (indeed with God, in Christian and Islamic alchemy) of the power to act on matter to transform it. The foundations of this religious dimension do not seem evident today, possibly because we have lost the ability to appreciate how marvelous the chemical transformations of matter appeared even to the people of the nineteenth century. We modern men, even when we know very little chemistry, think of atoms as tiny balls, which unite to form extremely complicated molecules, and learn from the "experts" that the rules of construction and destruction of these edifices are known, or at least will be known as research goes on. In short, we believe that the methods of science will allow us to know or discover without the help or the permission of anybody what nature can and cannot do, how it can do something or why it cannot do something else.

Actually, a simple experiment suffices to remind even the specialist of the marvels and mysteries to be found in the simplest chemical transformation. Buy some copper sulfate, such as is used in vine growing, and some middle-size iron wire. Fill a glass jug with water in which you have dissolved as much copper sulphate as necessary to make a light-blue solution. With the iron wire make a small tree, possibly with a clay base to

5. A brief but rich description of the chemical processes known to antiquity can be found in the already cited book by T. E. Thorpe.

make it stand upright, of a size such that, when placed in the glass jug, it will be completely covered by the blue solution. Then, if you have the patience of a true alchemist, sit down and silently watch nature at work. For a few minutes nothing seems to happen. But then a tiny copper-red spot appears somewhere on the little wire tree. After a few minutes more such spots appear. An attentive eye realizes that the ultramarine blue of the liquid is taking on a faint green shade. As time passes, the spots grow into little rhomboidal leaves of copper, while the liquid turns decidedly to green: the "tree of Venus" of the alchemists has put forth its leaves. At this stage you should choose. Either you banalize the whole thing, and say to yourself that after all there is nothing strange in what has taken place, for the difference in electrochemical potentials causes iron to displace copper in the solution; or you can listen to your sense of wonder, which tells you that you are watching an operation of nature which, though very simple and easily accessible, is similar to those that take place in the womb of a volcano or in living matter.

The alchemists made the latter choice. One might say that it was only because they lacked rigor and a critical mind; yet, truly speaking, even if they had known the explanation in terms of electrochemical potentials, it is likely that they would not have found that explanation satisfactory. The tree of Venus is never the same: imperceptible variations in the reaction conditions suffice to change the number of leaflets, the times, and the quantity of copper powder that settles on the bottom of the vessel. To the attentive observer of facts, the mystery surrounding the details of that particular process is not greatly reduced by the knowledge that there is a general rule telling which metals displace which from their solutions.

This example probably suffices to show why alchemy had a religious dimension — emphasized, of course, by the fact that before the invention of the microscope it was not easy to treat as real a world of objects so small as to be invisible. The philosophical framework (and hence the theory) of alchemy therefore started from a conception of the animistic type founded on the four-element doctrine and on gnostic views of Pythagorean and Platonic origin. That general approach to the relation of man to nature and to supernatural realities was initially the only theoretical foundation of alchemy, although, unlike magic, little or no place was granted to demons and Words of Command. Thus, as we said already, alchemy was essentially an empirical exploration, and experience in the laboratory had a prominent place; at first sight, it would seem that the alchemists did not feel the need for general rules in the sense of modern science, and that the rational fabric of chemistry was born only when the Galilean revolution restored the priority of facts. Yet, the doubts expressed above remain: is it possible that there should be no scientific spirit in a science which counted among its students Albertus Magnus and Isaac Newton?

Alchemy as Science

In order to proceed we should perhaps first answer another question: what was really alchemy? What were the alchemists looking for? No clear-cut definition, as far as I know, is available, the more so as the secrets of the alchemical art were jealously guarded by those who had discovered them. Nevertheless, as should be clear from what we have already pointed out, enough is known to make a critical assessment possible.

In every field of knowledge apt to qualify as a scientific discipline three characteristics at least can be distinguished: the object, the method, and the program. In the case of alchemy, the object was clear, even though it was not quantitatively defined as it was when, with the work of Lavoisier and his contemporaries, the process of transition from alchemy to chemistry was concluded. That object consisted in the transformations of matter which, starting from certain chemical substances (materials that have the same properties down to the tiniest fraction), yield new chemical substances, possibly requiring the direct action of fire or of forces of nature such as those acting in volcanoes.

As to the method, it was already that of modern chemistry, for it consisted in the classical operations of purification and separation by means of distillation, sublimation, crystallization, fusion, calcination, and so on. It was doubtless an art, but an art in the same way that experimental chemistry is an art.

Finally, as to the program, alchemy aimed at attaining the know-how necessary for the transmutation of metals and at realizing the famous and mysterious *Opus Magnum*, the Great Work. There seems to be little agreement among historians as to what that expression meant. Much has been said about its identification with the "philosophical stone," the stone of wisdom. In a strange novel,[6] Charles Williams described it as a mysterious polyhedral jewel, supposedly belonging to the lost crown of King Solomon; it would allow the owner to voyage instantaneously in time and space, and to know the thoughts of men, but the man who would try to use it for money or power was bound to run into perdition. As is the case with the considerations of all genuine poets — and Williams was one[7] — that is a deep insight into the peculiar conception of the relation of man to the external reality that underlay alchemy; yet, some authors have suggested, not without good evidence, that the *Opus Magnum* was but the production of gold from less noble metals. Even granting this, one should not think that what was called since the beginning "genuine alchemy" had a utilitarian character in the degraded

6. C. Williams, *Many Dimensions* (1931; reprint, Grand Rapids, Michigan: W. B. Eerdmans, 1981).

7. Cf. H. Carpenter, *The Inklings: C. S. Lewis, J. R. R. Tolkien, C. Williams and Their Friends* (London: George Allen and Unwin, 1978).

sense of contemporary utilitarianism; if at all, it looked at usefulness in the sense given to it by Francis Bacon,[8] for it implied the elevation of the alchemist to the level of apprentice and cooperator of the Creator. To that end, it required a path of inner moral and religious perfection, that path which T. S. Eliot identified as

prayer, observance, discipline, thought and action,[9]

in order that the alchemist should become worthy of obtaining gold, the purest and noblest of all materials.

At least as regards the program, it might seem that alchemy did not pursue that aim of a rational and objective knowledge which characterized physics even before Galileo. Yet, a better look shows that it did have a rational and critical component as well as a cognitive motivation, the heritage of Greco-Roman thought. It seems probable that the great flourishing of alchemy in Europe, which started in the twelfth century, was related to the discovery of Aristotle's thought, transmitted by the Arabs — not least Avicenna, the Moslem philosopher and physician also known as Ibn Sina (980–1037), who wrote at least one treatise on alchemy — through translations into Latin. The scientific mind of Aristotle, which had introduced such very modern notions as information and complexity, provided theoretical principles on which a theory of alchemy independent of subjective factors could be built. The main principle, on which we shall pause again in a moment, was the notion that all material reality results from four invariant elements — fire, air, water, earth — which were thenceforth called "peripatetic," a historical name of Aristotle's followers: four centuries later that principle, revised through the operational definition of the elements and the acceptance of a larger number of them, became the foundation of modern chemistry. Thus, it seems reasonable to expect that, at least after the "Aristotelian revolution" of the late Middle Ages, alchemy possessed a scientific component in the modern sense. Let us see if we can draw it into light starting with the ideas of Albertus Magnus and Nicolas Flamel.

Albertus Magnus studied and practiced alchemy and mineralogy, and his writing earned him a lasting fame as an expert in these fields. His scientific mind is shown, among other things, by his belief that among the "arts," alchemy was that which best imitated nature,[10] and this proves that he was well aware that science must have an experimental foundation. His ideas in this matter stemmed from a careful, direct as well as

8. See e.g., P. Rossi, *Francesco Bacone* (Bari, Italy: Laterza, 1957).

9. T. S. Eliot, *Four Quartets*, "Dry Salvages," V, line 31.

10. J. A. Weisheipl, ed., *Albertus Magnus and the Sciences: Commemorative Essays 1980* (Toronto: Pontifical Institute of Mediaeval Studies, 1981). See in particular chapter seven by P. Kibre, chapter eight by J. M. Riddle and J. A. Mulholland, and chapter nine by N. F. George.

indirect observation of facts, and from what today the scientific world calls the "literature," that is to say the results and the theories transmitted by other men of science. Of course, Albertus was a man of his time, for he accepted the four-element theory and the doctrine of correspondences; and he had a measure of confidence in the influence of the stars, probably justified by the parallelism mentioned above; curiously enough, he also believed in the healing power of stones. Pearl Kibre[11] relates two significant considerations of his, one to the effect that art can produce by the heat of fire all that nature produces by means of the heat of the sun, provided that the fire be not stronger than the formative powers present in the metals; the other implying that the ablest alchemists work during the growing moon to produce purer metals and stones.

Flamel, who was no scholar, insisted on the patient quest for the conditions under which the *Opus Magnum* would be produced. His work is quite readable, although it relies on analogies presented in the form of pictures — a method of communication accessible even to illiterates, now adopted in popular computer programs. It presents in a concise form the fundamental principle on which we want to focus our attention. Flamel writes:

> [The metals] once formed are decomposed, in order that they may be made again [by combining opportunely sulfur and quicksilver (mercury)]. The latter are the sperms of the metals, cold as well as humid or hot; one of them is male, the other is female; this is their complexion. But there is no doubt that the two sperms in question are composed only by four elements.... The first sperm is male;...it is sulfur, and it is...Earth and Fire. This fixed sulfur is similar to fire, but invariable and metallic in nature — but I am not speaking of vulgar sulfur, for the latter has no metallic substance..., as I have personally proven.... The other, which is female, is that which...in occult philosophy is usually called quicksilver, and is but Water and Air.[12]

But for a few annotations, which we shall make presently, these few lines contain the theory on which alchemy was founded. It is perfectly rational. It starts by accepting the notion of element, defined as an ultimate component of matter, not susceptible of further decomposition. Then it adopts the assumption of the existence of just four elements — earth, fire, water, and air in certain ideal states — which give by combination under appropriate conditions all the existing substances, including those which form living beings. On the basis of the four-element hypothesis —

11. Weisheipl, *Albertus Magnus*, ch. 7.

12. N. Flamel, *Le livre des figures hiéroglyphiques* (1824) (Paris: Planète, 1971), with an introduction by René Alleau and a historical study by Eugène Canseliet.

which, until the time of Lavoisier, even rigorous scientists such as René Descartes utilized as a principle, much as we do with conservation of energy — gold, the philosophers' stone, living matter, in short the Great Work, are to be obtained by mixing materials, which contain precisely those elements in the opportune quantities and operational conditions. In that endeavor, the alchemists were forced by facts to admit that their four elements could not be isolated as such, a point which also holds for some of the most important elements of modern chemistry, e.g., oxygen. They tried, therefore, to preserve a certain theoretical simplicity by basing their experimental strategy on three substances, which actually could be isolated and manipulated — the three "alchemical principles": Sulfur, Mercury, and Salt.

In fact, a number of experimental observations already known in the time of Flamel showed, among other things, that:

- mercury has a great affinity for all metals, and in fact it dissolves many of them, particularly gold and silver, but is unique because of its liquid state at room temperature;

- sulfur forms metal sulfides with a marked metallic shine, e.g., galena, calchopyrite, and orpiment (arsenic trisulfide), all of which have been well-known since ancient times and have an aspect similar to gold;

- sulfur is highly polymorphic, and can change its color and its crystalline state if heated (there are yellow sulfur, red sulfur, plastic sulfur, liquid sulfur, gaseous sulfur, etc.); it catches fire easily and has been used for matches since antiquity; it attacks several metals, including mercury, forming sulfides.

These and other observations induced the alchemists to believe that purification and combination of mercury and sulfur, under appropriate circumstances, could yield not only orpiment, but real gold. In accordance with the four-element principle it was concluded that sulfur was made of Earth and Fire, and mercury was made of Water and Air, so that, if the right series of operations could be found, it would be possible to bring sulfur and mercury together so as to combine the four elements in the proportions present in any given metal. The confidence granted to this approach can be judged, for example, from the following statement of Albertus Magnus:

> Then undoubtedly it [sulphur] will impart to quicksilver a red colour;... from this copper is formed.[13]

13. Weisheipl, *Albertus Magnus*, ch. 8.

This way of thinking may explain why, having realized that orpiment (arsenic trisulfide) had some of the characteristics of gold, and contained sulfur, the alchemists (who thought that "mercury is the mother of all metals")[14] would make mercury sulfide, which is black, and then spend nights of patient work to find the conditions under which it would turn to something like orpiment and then to real gold, or to something even nobler; after all, they thought, the four elements were already present in mercury sulfide. It took centuries and the breakdown of the *ipse dixit* principle before the idea was accepted that — barring nuclear reactions — no technical operation will ever yield arsenic sulfide from mercury sulfide.

The rise of modern chemistry had begun, as that of science in general, a hundred years earlier. The transformation of alchemy was the work of those who started a revision of the four-element, three-principle theory in the Galilean spirit of rigor and fidelity to observed facts, particularly of Robert Boyle (1627–1691), fourteenth child of Richard Boyle, Earl of Cork. His masterpiece, the dialogue entitled "The Sceptical Chymist, or Chymico-physical Doubts and Paradoxes, touching the spagyrists'[15] principles commonly called hypostatical, as they are wont to be propos'd and defended by the generality of alchymists," is a demonstration of how superficial the alchemists were with respect to the traditional theoretical foundations of their field of inquiry. Paradoxically, however, it is also proof that not only the main operations of chemistry but its fundamental concepts — element, simple and compound body, atom and corpuscle, affinity — came from alchemy. The novelty was that certain points, such as the claim that there were only four elements, appeared to be untenable when an operational definition in the spirit of Galileo, as advocated by Boyle, was substituted for the merely intuitive notions handed down from antiquity.

Although Boyle, as other great scientists of the seventeenth century, was a deeply religious man, the separation between faith and science began in his time, partly because of the critical frame of mind introduced by him and the others. Indeed, the following century represented not only the introduction into alchemy of the operational definition of element and of quantitative laws, but a branch point, at which the impersonal component of alchemy developed into modern chemistry, and the personal commitment of the experimenter was no longer a matter of interest; the description and practical utilization in terms of objective laws grew and bore fruit while the relation to man of the phenomena studied and their significance in the context of the whole survived in a dormant state, if at all. With it, the belief in the unity of spiritual and

14. Cf., e.g., N. Flamel, *Le livre.*
15. The spagyrists were the followers of the school of Paracelsus (1493?–1561), who applied alchemical operations to the preparation of medicines.

material reality, one of the pillars of alchemy, was practically abandoned, and a dualistic frame of mind appeared, which was the premise to the current separation between humanism and science.[16]

The Spirit of Alchemy

The considerations presented so far can be summarized as follows: alchemy had a genuinely scientific interest in nature, which might partly explain its appeal for Albertus Magnus, Newton, and other men of the same caliber; however, that aspect was so strictly combined with a particular view of the relation between the scientist and his experimental operations that one may well wonder if those great scientists would have been so attracted by alchemy had it been simply a collection of "how-to" recipes and problems. In other words, alchemy was as much a science in the modern sense as was compatible with the state of culture before the eighteenth century; nevertheless, it was considered essential that the alchemist should participate in experimentation as the man he was, not as a pure, detached mind.

As far as the methods proper to science go, it is neither surprising nor particularly regrettable that a clear-cut distinction between what pertains to science (or technology) and what concerns the person doing it should have taken place in any field of inquiry. A long experience has shown that the aim of understanding nature's operations in view of emulating them is best reached by searching for cause-effect chains inherent in it (and formalized as logical statements). Still, it seems unlikely that progress — supposing there is something of that kind in intellectual matters — can justify the abandonment of what seemed theoretically valuable and inseparable from the scientific enterprise to the people of Hellenistic times and was still considered essential less than three centuries ago. History shows very clearly that there are fields in which the scholars of twenty-five centuries ago (or more, if you think of China) were far more advanced than we are. An American historian of philosophy emphasized this point very well in the 1930s:

> Greek philosophy leaped on to heights unreached again, while Greek science limped behind. Our modern danger is precisely the opposite: inductive data fall upon us on all sides like the lava of the Vesuvius, we suffocate with uncoordinated facts, our minds are overwhelmed with science breeding and multiplying into specialistic chaos for want of synthetic thought and a unifying philosophy. We are all mere fragments of what a man might be.[17]

No comment is probably necessary.

16. Torrance, "The Making of the Modern Mind," in *Transformation*, ch. 1.
17. Durant, *The Story of Philosophy*, 91.

A Path to Wisdom

We call "sapiential" — pertaining to wisdom — the personal, human component of alchemy, because in virtue of that component it became possible to look at scientific and technical knowledge as a contribution to wisdom. In fact, wisdom is that wide, diverse, humble learning and experience, which make a person capable of deciding on the right actions and points of view, in both a moral and a logical sense, and put that person in touch with the highest spiritual realities. Aspiration to wisdom, paradoxically preserved, albeit in a somewhat strange form, by a few modern alchemists, was not free from temptations, for the initiates of different sorts would often consider humility as the virtue of the weak, and make power their main goal. Nevertheless, the main spiritual philosophy of alchemy, that which saw the alchemist as an apprentice of God, placed the search for the secrets of nature in the context of a path toward elevation beyond ambitions and lust for power.

That approach, as we have already pointed out, is as old as alchemy itself. A hint in favor of the idea that it proceeds from the archetypal beliefs of man is that it appeared independently, as far as we can tell, in such diverse intellectual and religious environments as the Celestial Empire and the legendary Land of Ham. As already mentioned, there are traces of very ancient treatises of alchemy from China, while the treatise of the mythical Wei-po Yang, the "father of Chinese alchemy" goes back to the second century A.D., the golden period of Hellenistic "secret wisdom," although most probably it is not related to it. There seem to be no doubts that the Tao provided the metaphysical foundations for the *Opus Magnum* of the alchemists of the Far East. The *Tao-teh-Ching*, the "Book of the Principle and of Its Action," can be interpreted as a text on the principles governing alchemy.[18] It proposes a global view of reality, seen as the One, which is permanent and yet subject to unceasing change, realized by secret procedures. Because of this double nature, which reconciles in the way of poetry those views which were proposed to the West by the ancient Greek philosophers Parmenides and Heraclitus, the Tao is the principle which should inspire every action, particularly every operation of man. A perfect man is the person who in thought as well as in deed realizes complete harmony and equilibrium with the rest of the "cosmos," the universe seen as an ordered whole.

It is not surprising, therefore, that the Tao should be considered not only as the guide to all wisdom and justice, but as the key to any operation aimed at discovering the secret recipes by which nature produces the

18. Lao-Tzu, *Tao-teh-Ching*, Evola.

transformation of a substance into another. Thus, albeit perhaps without reaching the profound insight into the nature of man contained in the myth of Prometheus, Chinese thought had reached conclusions similar to those of Western thought: alchemy did not involve only *homo faber*, man as an animal which, by its very nature, transforms its environment, but also *homo religiosus*, man as an animal capable of elevating itself, in good and in evil, to become an aid or a competitor of the Creator. As is well known, the West deposited its alchemical tradition, in the first centuries of the Christian era, in the *Corpus Hermeticum*,[19] a collection of treatises generically attributed to the mythical figure of Hermes Trismegistos, Mercurius Thrice Great, to be identified with the Egyptian god Thoth, the scribe of the gods and god of wisdom. Hermes was neither a philosopher like Lao-Tzu nor a physician like Aesculapius: he was a master who transmitted to the initiate, the apprentice accepted after severe tests and examinations, the secrets of the Art which the Heavenly Artisan had applied to realize the marvelous variety of the physical world. It is not worth the while to pause on the use of those books by the powerful gnostic societies born with the Enlightenment, whose initiates claimed that they possessed the key for deciphering the secret knowledge concealed in their mysterious language, not surprisingly called "Hermetic": suffice it to mention that one of those initiates, active around 1860 as a professional freelance soldier, carried as his main title "Grand World-Hierophant of the Egyptian-Masonic Cult of Misraim-Memphis."[20] More interesting is the affinity between the *Tao-teh-Ching* and the *Corpus Hermeticum*, which share not only the enigmatic, sometimes paradoxical way of proposing concepts and methods, but the basic idea of the unity of spirit and matter. Compare these sentences:

> The whole Universe depends on a single Principle, and this principle itself proceeds from the One and Only *(Corpus, X.14)* — Preserve the One in order that spirit and body should come together never more to be divided (*Tao, 10*);

> [The World], keeping in its bosom all the seeds received from God, effectively produces in itself all beings, . . . and then, after they are dissolved, renews them all (*Corpus, IX, 6*) — The Tao is not Substance, but inexhaustible activity (*Tao, 4*).

Certainly, there is a great difference between the Father who is the source of the principles (Hermes) and the Lord of Heaven, who obeys the Principle (Lao-Tzu); but the affinity is evident: Lao-Tzu and Hermes

Trismegistos belong to the same strange mixture of mysticism, spiritual-ity, and esotericism, which has haunted since their origins the cultures of the East and the West, animated by the common underlying belief that spirit and matter are both present in the same, unitary reality.

As we have seen, the unity of nature, over and beyond the range of direct action of things on one another, appears to be the central point of a *Weltanschauung* based on the most recent advances of science; our re-flection on alchemy now suggests that perhaps we should go even beyond the unity of nature and consider the unity of reality, obviously admitting that the two are not the same because a spiritual dimension exists.

This is what alchemy did. In fact, the two main characteristics of the spirit of alchemy are

- the doctrine of analogies and correspondences;

- the mystical approach to alchemical operations.

We already briefly considered the first point in connection with magic, but it will be useful to review it again with special reference to its ap-plication to views on the nature of reality. As mentioned, it was in the late Hellenistic culture that analogies and correspondences were first put in comparatively systematic written form, but that heritage was received and transmitted largely by the Arabs soon after their expansion in North Africa and Spain during the seventh through ninth centuries. The under-lying world-view is usually qualified as Platonic, for it treats ideas as existing per se. The work of Ibn 'Arabî, a contemporary of Avicenna, the Arab scholar mentioned above, summarizes as it were the Hellenis-tic thought as it reached the Middle Ages, and gives a precise list of the points involved:

> In existence. all things, except Allah — exalted be He — can appear in one of four modes . . . :
>
>   i. the existence of the thing in its concrete reality;
>
>   ii. the existence of the thing in the knowing mind;
>
>   iii. the existence of the thing in words;
>
>   iv. the existence of the thing in writing,[21]

the last two modes being different inasmuch as the Uttered Word is at-tributed an intrinsic power, while the Written Sign passively waits for a mind to decipher it. If the four modes of existence are equivalent aspects of one and the same reality, then if the representation of an object in the

---

21. Ibn 'Arabî, *La Production des Cercles*, French trans. by P. Fenton and M. Gloton (Paris: Éd. de l'Éclat, 1996), 6.

mind is changed then its concrete reality too is modified; this, as we saw in the preceding chapter, is a principle of magic.

Actually, it is legitimate to accept the above list as referring to the fact that, although they are not necessarily equivalent, the four modes are all proper to any knowable thing. If a thing can be known, it can be given a name; if it does not exist, it cannot be known; and so on. But what is most important for the main theme of this book is that the four modes imply the belief that the observer and the observed reality are inextricably connected; the observer is involved not only as a pure mind, but, because of the psychological load every name carries, as the person he or she is. This is the foundation of the kind of coherence alchemy presupposed; we may expect that it is also the kind of coherence implied by the Great Dance image.

Analogies, Allegories, Correspondences

Let us now go back to the noncausal relations that the mind detects between the entities of which reality consists.

Analogies as such were extensively used in Hellenistic times — *viz.* in the culture of the Greek-speaking world after Alexander the Great. Perhaps the most significant example is provided by Philo of Alexandria (ca. 20 B.C.–40 A.D.), who, in his monumental effort to combine the Greek philosophical and the Hebrew religious traditions, set up a detailed allegorical interpretation of the Old Testament. On that interpretation the Scriptures described and prescribed the soul's progress toward a perfect spiritual life in God.[22] Although, according to the specialists,[23] Philo did not take a clear stand on the literal meaning of the Scriptures, later developments, especially those derived from the Hermetic books, practically accepted the view that in the relation between spirit and matter two or more faces of a single underlying reality are involved. It is not just a matter of interpretation; certain sentences are assumed to possess double or even multiple meanings,[24] for the words in them are taken to have multiple referents in different orders of reality. In other words, the same expression applies to two or more orders of reality, one corresponding to the immediate meaning, if any exists, the others corresponding to meanings beyond the reach of the senses, and therefore only describable by analogies or vague terms. For example, the sentence

---

22. F. H. Colson and G. H. Whitaker, *Philo in Ten Volumes* (London-Cambridge, Mass., 1929–1962).

23. E. Zeller and R. Mondolfo, *La filosofia dei Greci nel suo sviluppo storico* (Florence: La Nuova Italia, 1979), part 3, vol. 4 (ed. Raffaello Del Re), 486 and passim.

24. We are using here the term "meaning" where many philosophers of language would prefer the word "sense," since they reserve the former for the role of a word in a context. Here there seems to be no need for such a distinction.

"God made the living beings which swim in water,"[25] can be given a double meaning: the explicit one, and the "philosophical" one,[26] which, after a detailed analysis and checks for consistency all along the text of the Scriptures, might turn out to be something like: "By His grace, God made it possible for certain persons to be open to the world of spirit."

The belief that analogies describe multiple orders of reality may be seen as the root of the concept of correspondence, a concept which is officially absent from today's intellectual world, but, as already mentioned, is being rediscovered at the less educated level in the form of astrology, cosmic-energy theories, and so on. The step from analogies to correspondences was easy, at least before Galileo introduced a new way of thinking. The argument can be summarized as follows: if there is a correlation there must be an analogy and vice versa; if there is an analogy there must be some common reality underlying the relations and the modes of change of the terms of the analogy. Such was the argument by which one could establish correspondences between the celestial bodies, the seasons, the personalities of human beings born in different seasons or months, and so on. Particularly important for alchemy was the idea that objects playing a receptive role are feminine, while those playing an active role are masculine. According to this view, for example, the sun plays the role of the king, the moon that of the queen. This is not just an analogy, but a *correspondence*, if it is taken to imply, for example, that the presence or absence of the sun in the sky may be important for the success or failure of a chemical operation. In Platonic terms, one could say that the idea of masculinity is, so to speak, an entity in itself belonging to the "real reality" underlying everything; therefore, there must be basic patterns of behavior common to all masculine objects; those patterns may be more evident in certain objects, say celestial bodies, and then they can be detected by observing those objects; the knowledge thus gained serves to understand and predict the behavior of other masculine objects — say, sulfur — in which the same patterns are not evident for a variety of reasons.

Alchemy made extensive use of correspondences, both within the material level and between the material and the spiritual level. There seems to be some confusion in the literature, and specialists could perhaps clarify certain apparent disagreements or contradictions. For our illustrative purposes, the following corresponding pairs will suffice:[27]

25. Gen. 1:21.
26. Cf. Augustine, *Confessions*, ch. 13.
27. Cf. T. Burckhardt, *Alchemie*, ch. 11 and passim. As already mentioned, by the time of Paracelsus the pairs listed had been transformed into triads, particularly sulphur-mercury-salt, flesh-spirit-person, etc.

- matter and form in Aristotelian ontology;

- the moon and the sun in the sky;

- the queen and the king in human society;

- flesh and spirit (or body and soul) in human beings;

- mercury and sulfur in matter.

Roughly speaking, the alchemists of old expected that, *if the right procedure and conditions could be found,* then sulfur would fix mercury to yield gold, precisely as form unites with matter to yield a real object or as the king unites with the queen to engender the heir to the throne. The possible objections to this sort of theory are innumerable, and most of them are decisive. The objection of most interest to us is that the analogies are very crude. For example, what was called flesh in the gospel was (probably) a part or aspect of man that includes all instinctual psychic functions (e.g., fear of pain), and what was called spirit was related to the mind and the will.[28] The relation of these two concepts with Aristotelian matter and form seems therefore to be quite superficial, the main point in common being "noncommutativity": form gives actuality to matter, the spirit, within limits, consciously controls the flesh; in either case, the converse is false.

The same considerations apply to the analogy between the formation of mercury sulfide and the wedding of the queen and the king: one could easily admit that a new substance is formed by the union of mercury and sulfur, but the analogy stops there. What a difference with respect to the analogy between an electrostatic field and the velocity field of a flowing fluid, which provided the beautiful mathematical theory of fields and resulted in James Clerk Maxwell's discovery of electromagnetic waves! On the other hand, as Poincaré pointed out,[29] the equations of mathematical physics describe general relation patterns in material reality (what Einstein later saw as the space-time-matter continuum), of which the various classes of phenomena are realizations, to be described by models which are not necessarily unique.[30] Thus, the problem with alchemy was not analogies as such, but, as we have seen, the lack of a systematic attempt to determine reproducible facts and, not less important, of rigor in definitions. For example, the difficulty with the alchemical analogy between biological generation and chemical combination is not that analogies as such are outside science, but that all depends on what the

---

28. Cf. "The spirit is willing, but the flesh is weak," in Matt. 26:41.

29. Poincaré, *La science,* cf. following note.

30. This is why Poincaré was classified as a conventionalist, probably by philosophers who were not familiar with mathematical physics. In fact, a detailed analysis of his statements proves that he did believe that science describes reality; we have tried to make this point in a paper, "Poincaré et le mécanisme."

actual facts are. Suppose that mercury sulfide was formed of molecules capable of self-reproduction and resulting from the combination of one atom of mercury with one atom of sulfur. Then one might perhaps say that sulfur and mercury generate mercury sulfide. In fact, that famous alchemical view should have already aroused suspicions before the birth of modern chemistry, for actually mercury sulfide is a material that replaces the mercury and the sulfur which have yielded it, and no ordinary offspring grows by replacing its parents. Thus, the analogy in question is actually the recognition of a vague resemblance, and cannot be taken as more than a source of possibly poetical images.

The spirit-flesh analogy is different, for it connects different planes of what ordinary people treat as reality. As an introduction to its significance and implications, let us turn once again to hard science and consider the class of analogies that are the object of the general theory of systems: those centered on open self-regulated control systems. We saw in the preceding chapters the example of a planetary ecosystem, a living being, a human group, and we shall see in chapter twelve the case of human consciousness. If you read a book on the theory of control systems, you will find that the standard examples are actually devices such as electronic amplifiers or airplane autopilots; in fact, one normally thinks of those devices as genuine self-regulated control systems for the simple reason that they can be treated theoretically in a rigorous mathematical form.[31] Consequently, it is legitimate to claim that, when one treats as a system an entity such as a human group one is actually using an analogy. That the latter is fruitful and scientifically valid should be evident from the whole texture of this book, and is also supported by Poincaré's remarks on the nature of mechanism (chapter nine). The essential point is that the general features and possibly the mathematical description of the terms of the analogy are the same in the entity at hand as in a standard system. The entities under consideration are characterized by input and output channels, information processing units, feedback circuits, steady states, homeostasis, transition probabilities. Even the generation of new living beings could be described as a very special sort of output from a more or less undifferentiated input plus fertilization, resulting from a built-in development program and (in the case of sexual reproduction) an input signal coming from another system of the same type.

Now, the spirit-flesh analogy belongs more or less to the class of "system analogies." The reader can find in a paper by an influential American psychologist[32] a study showing why and in what sense the psyche is a

31. Cf., e.g., M. S. Lifschitz, *Operatory, Kolebanya, Vol'ny: Otkrytye Systemy* (Operators, oscillations, waves: open systems) (Moscow: Izdatel'stvo Nauka, 1966).

32. C. T. Tart, "The Basic Nature of Altered States of Consciousness: A Systems Approach," *Journal of Transpersonal Psychology* 8 (1976): 45–64; *States of Consciousness* (New York: Dutton, 1975).

closed-loop control system. Let us add that in the spirit-flesh diad the psyche is essentially seen as the seat of reason and will, the flesh as the seat of emotions, instincts, and sensations. They can be seen as sending and receiving subsystems, the former connected to (and largely conditioned by) the "flesh" and possibly to a nonmaterial reality, the latter connected and partly submitted to the "spirit" and to the outer material world. A person is fully realized when the whole system that he or she is has become perfectly balanced within itself and on both receiving channels; under conditions of stress a perfect man should be able to yield control of everything to the "spirit" moiety — a deed which, as Christ himself said, is extremely difficult precisely because it requires that the spirit-system ignore the compelling input from the flesh-system.

Once again, we see that the alchemical analogy has no strict scientific validity; it holds just in the sense that, as in man flesh and spirit combine to make the whole, so in matter sulfur and mercury might combine to yield gold. Still, it has a deep significance, for it says that the coherence and perfection of the world on the material plane is reflected in the coherence and perfect balance of man; indeed, alchemy claimed that as a condition for making matter proceed toward its ultimate perfection the operator should tread the same path on his own plane. Here the idea of the underlying unity of reality transforms the analogy into a strange yet profound way of looking at science: the operations leading to a nobler material are necessarily an enrichment in coherence of the whole, and therefore it is necessary that whatever or whoever in any way causes those operations to take place should be animated by the same motion toward a more perfect state; if it is a merely natural cause, that goes without saying; if it is a free being, then that being cannot succeed without striving toward its own moral and intellectual improvement. What if alchemy was right? What if war machines, poison gases, atomic bombs, and ecological disasters have been not only the proof of the abiding dark side of humanity, but the result of the separation between the scientists' activity as scientists and their human nature? There is a terrible sentence in an otherwise interesting and well-written book of popular science:

> But finally man got closer to nature's secret and discovered that by loosing a swarm of gaseous molecules he could throw his projectile seventy-five miles and then by the same force burst it into flying fragments.[33]

This passage refers to the discovery of explosives, and is included in the enthusiastic opening of a chapter on the scientific story of poison gases in the First World War. Readers can look up for themselves descriptions of

33. E. E. Slosson, *Creative Chemistry* (New York: Century, 1921), 219.

the horrors of poison gases; but even without doing so they might reflect on the use of the expression "nature's secret" in such a context.

In conclusion, a reflection on alchemy offers us a more emotional and personal side of the same considerations as were inspired in us by ecology in chapter eight. But what should a person do to satisfy the condition of perfect personal tuning in to the evolution of the universe toward order and beauty? Advice and suggestions in this direction are outside the scope of a book on the philosophy of nature; but the concrete answer of the alchemists is worth considering.

Alchemy, Mysticism, and Ethics

The alchemists believed in the existence of the soul. In our times, since the soul is often identified with an immortal principle present in man, it would seem that most opinion makers tend to discourage the very use of that word, for one thing by speaking disparagingly of "soulism." We shall return in chapter twelve to the scientific status of the soul; as far as a discussion of alchemy is concerned, there is no difficulty in giving up that unfashionable word, because it can be replaced by "psyche" to mean whatever imparts or summarizes the typical sensibility and inner activity of living beings. We shall reserve the word "spirit" to signify whatever is specific of man as a free rational animal. With this convention, it would seem that the "soulism" of alchemy had two facets:

- the attribution of some sort of psyche to inorganic matter ("pan-psychism");

- the belief that the success of transformations of matter induced by man would closely match the latter's spiritual progress.

The panpsychistic facet, to which we have already devoted some space (chapter nine), expressed in a rather fanciful way the existence of similarities deeper than one would normally think between nonliving objects and living beings. An example will be found in the analysis of the concept of meaning presented in the next chapter in the context of communication. A point pertaining to the natural sciences is that not only have chemistry and physical chemistry confirmed the existence of the "affinities" postulated by alchemy, but they have shown theoretically[34] and experimentally[35] that under appropriate conditions even nonliving matter tends to form structures of a greater and greater degree of order, possibly of organization. Taken in this sense and within the proper limits, the presence

34. I. Prigogine and I. Stengers, *La nouvelle alliance*.
35. Cf. V. Balzani and F. Scandola, *Supramolecular Photochemistry* (New York and London: Ellis-Horwood, 1991).

of a measure of lifelike activity of nonliving matter is thus confirmed by experimental work.

As to the second facet of alchemical "soulism," the discourse is more complex. At the most general level, one could invoke the subjective-objective problem of quantum mechanics to show that the participation of the subject in the manipulation of nature is a fact. Actually, such a consideration would be misleading because in quantum mechanics the observer is not conceived of as a complete human being, but merely as an outside operator. As we already mentioned, the point of alchemy was the involvement of the operator at the "spiritual" level, that is to say a psychological involvement calling into play the whole personality of the human operator. This is not so surprising because, as Blondel pointed out long ago,[36] conscious, deliberate action is a commitment of the whole person, and its success may depend on the frame of mind within which it is carried out.

The example of Thomas Alva Edison will clarify this point. Edison, as is well known, not only invented the electric lamp, but invested $40,000 (of his time) to realize the dream of making electric lamps cheap enough for everybody to afford them. It would seem (and I for one actually believe) that his dream really had little to do with money; Edison was certainly well aware of the fact that he would get the same profit with a lower investment had he accepted the idea that lamps should be available at a higher price only for the market of well-to-do families. If that is how things went, then Edison gave a good example of how unselfishness and genuine interest in the product rather than in sheer profit may be conditions for great technological realizations.

As we have seen, in the alchemical frame of mind the idea that all parallel processes are faces of a single process in the true underlying reality was applied to the experimenter, with the only novelty that the latter, as a human being, would be free not to change in the proper way, at which point his operations would follow a path different from the desired one. In the writings of Nicolas Flamel (and in general in the "white" alchemical tradition) this view always appears with reference to God: the alchemist is trying to emulate the operations by which the Supreme Technologist causes transformations to take place in matter; therefore, the alchemist should be a worthy apprentice. One can imagine Flamel and his wife Pernelle at the ceremony they performed in the antechamber of their laboratory before beginning their alchemical work. Upon their return from the chapel with great historiated glass windows where they had received Holy Communion, they would kneel in deep meditation for a quarter of an hour. Then they would put on immaculate white gowns like those of deacons, and then, in silent procession, they would move to

36. Blondel, *L'action.*

the laboratory, where crucibles were already glowing red on fires lit by their assistants, and the Athanor, the reaction vessel in which the Great Work would take place, towered on a brick furnace. Standing before their equipment, they would then intone together a prayer in the solemn language of the Church:

> *Omnipotens, aeterne Deus Pater coelestis luminis, a quo etiam omnia bona et perfecta dono proveniunt, rogamus infinitam tuam misericordiam, ut nos aeternam tuam sapientiam ... per quam omnia creata factaque sunt atque etiamnum reguntur et conservantur, recte agnoscere patiaris. ...*
>
> *Fac [ut illa] moderate nos comitetur in omnibus nostris operibus, ut per illius spiritum [inveniamus] verum intellectum, infallibilemque processum nobilissimae huius Artis, hoc est, sapientium miraculosam lapidem, quem mundo occultasti, et saltim electis tuis revelare soles. ...*
>
> *Primum recte et bene inchoemus, in eo ... labore(m) constanter progrediamur, et tandem [eum] etiam beate absolvamus, illoque aeterno cum gaudio fruamur, per coelestem illum et ab aeterno fundatum angularem miraculosumque lapidem.*[37]

Only after this prayer, written by Flamel himself in a somewhat approximate but humble and profound Latin, would they begin their work, in a silence interrupted by few words in a hushed voice.

Flamel's prayer is epistemologically interesting even for those who do not share his belief in the God of the Christians. The mystical path toward personal elevation is clearly implied by the request that God should grant a right and good beginning, ending with "eternal joy." It is a path at least partially open independently of adherence to a specific religion, for the term "God" may be taken to represent values, which man ought to respect and cultivate if he is to pursue the three Platonic ideals of truth, justice, and beauty. Let us say it again: the history of alchemy suggests that the practical operations of science and technology require a total personal involvement of the operator, indeed are parallel to the progress of the operator in the renunciation of his or her ego in favor of

37. N. Flamel, *Le livre.* "Almighty, eternal God the Father of celestial light, from whom also come as a gift all things good and perfect, we pray to your infinite mercy that you suffer that we recognize correctly your eternal wisdom, by which all things were created and made and in this very moment are ruled and held in being. Let it accompany us step by step in all our operations, so that by means of its spirit we can find the true knowledge and the infallible outcome of this very noble Art, that is, the miraculous stone of the wise, which you concealed from the world, and sometimes reveal to your elected. Grant to us in the first place a right and good beginning, [then] constancy in the progress of our work, that we should at last complete it in a blessed way, and that we may enjoy it with eternal joy, by that celestial and miraculous cornerstone laid before the beginning of time."

noble ideals. There is indeed a measure of literal truth in this. Consider specifically the operations of chemistry. It would be too much to claim that the end products of a reaction depend on the virtues of the chemist performing them. However, there may be a psychological component at least in the yield, which is often sensitive to small changes in the reaction conditions: a patient person, deeply interested not in personal success but in what he or she is doing, will obtain better results and maybe find unexpected byproducts, if for no other reason, because of the loving care applied to the least detail.

In general, all practical operations have this dependence on the experimenter's psychological attitude. If we consider technology developed in view of applications, then the role of the virtues of the operator is even more evident. Those who have a certain age and have worked with personal computers since the time of the glorious Apple II can testify to the enormous difference in quality and features between computer programs circulating before 1990 and the present expensive commercial programs. The essential difference is easily summarized: formerly, programs were made by people interested in programming as a means of providing tools for intellectual work; later, the aim of programs apparently became that of making the owners feel important by yielding plenty of colorful pictures and requiring faster microprocessors and more megabytes of random-access and hard-disk memory. It would seem that priority given to profit has affected the evolution of technology so as to encourage activities of very little value for improving the users' ability to enjoy beauty and knowledge. This development is probably a minor detail in the generally disquieting picture offered by our consumer society, and might even turn out, in the long run, to have a bright side; from the point of view of a philosopher of technology, however, though quantitatively far less dangerous, it may well be considered similar to the production and sale of chemical hallucinogens.

About Spiritual Standards

In short, those who develop technology without even a trace of the spirit of alchemy, i.e., without a parallel upgrading of their spiritual standards, particularly their sense of responsibility, may be contributing to the devastating ills of our society — ignorance and neuroses — which no vaccine can prevent. Truly enough, the spirit of alchemy was centered on worship and confidence in the God of Abraham; but even those who believe that religion should be replaced by merely human ideals should have grounds for lamenting its loss, since ideals seem to have vanished altogether. Edison invested his money in the dream that even low-income families could afford the joy of electric light; contemporary technological geniuses, if there are any, may be expected to use their minds to make money or gain fame by experimenting on the cloning of human beings.

The "white" alchemists believed that high spiritual standards were necessary because the Divine Master would not allow the unworthy to learn his secrets, or, if they did, such learning would result in ills without end. This belief sounds noble, but the implication that knowledge of a certain kind should be reserved to a limited number of people does not. History teaches that modern science thrived because the results obtained by each scientist were available to everybody. In point of fact, those who were capable of making use of those results were always very few: the novelty was merely that no special "worthiness" was expected. In our affluent society the situation is similar, but perhaps more serious, because science and technology have a greater potential for bad as well as evil use, and yet they are in the hands of a comparatively smaller number of "experts"; nor does education any longer provide the high-level cultural background that would allow "ordinary people" to control the experts. In light of this consideration, a remark by Girolamo Fracastoro — the famous doctor and humanist from Verona who already in 1538 fought against the doctrine that the course of illnesses was controlled by the stars — acquires a fresh sense and validity:

> It seems that what is deeply concealed in Nature [and] belongs to the realm of things divine and celestial should be the object of reticence and silence, or at least communicated not only modestly but as it were with a measure of decency; for it seems that it would not be without a measure of offense that one would repeat in public what Nature herself has wished to be profoundly hidden.[38]

This formulation of the spirit of alchemy does not mean that scientific and technological knowledge should be reserved to a few initiates; it means that, since in practice it is not possible to avoid the situation wherein only few people possess that knowledge, then these experts should have that view of man, that respect for nature, that sense of responsibility which would prevent them from giving priority to their own whims, power, and glory. Now, today's scientists belong to three different categories: those who consider research just a job, those who think of career and success, and those who are sincerely interested in science and its applications. According to Fracastoro's criterion only the third category should have access to the scientific and technological enterprise; in other words, if scientists cannot be but a small elite, then admission to that elite should

---

38. G. Fracastoro, *Scritti inediti*, ed. F. Pellegrini (Verona: Valdonega, 1955), 207, quoted in P. Rossi, *Francesco Bacone*, 97. "*Quae abditissima in natura sunt ad divina praesertim et caelestia pertinentia aut reticenda quidem et silentio continenda videntur, aut propalanda certe non modo modeste sed quodammodo verecunde; nam quae et natura ipsa occultissima esse voluit non sine quadam iniuria videntur palam proferri.*"

be based on high moral standards. This combination of human qualities with intellectual capacity, which amounts to a revival of the spirit of alchemy, has been advocated by many great minds of the recent past. It is condensed in a maxim by Albert Einstein:

> The true value of a man is first of all determined by the extent and the sense in which he has succeeded in freeing himself of his ego.[39]

This deliverance from one's ego is the essential point, because, like alchemy, the scientific and technological enterprise of today has a *Magnum Opus*, a "Great Work" that it should realize: making it possible for all human beings to realize their capacity for knowledge, love, and creation in full harmony with nature. A necessary condition for progress toward this goal is essentially the same as in the white alchemists' thought, namely that efforts in that direction should proceed parallel to an ever more loyal membership of scientists and technologists in what Einstein called late in his life[40] "the invisible community of those who strive for truth, beauty and justice."

39. A. Einstein, *Mein Weltbild* (The World as I See It) (1934; reprint, Frankfurt: Ullstein Materialien, 1979), 10. *"Der wahre Wert eines Menschen ist in erster Linie dardurch bestimmt, in welchem Grad und in welchem Sinn er zur Befreiung vom Ich gelangen ist."*

40. Cf. D. Brian, *Einstein: A Life* (New York: John Wiley, 1996), 234, reported by T. F. Torrance in a lecture on Einstein and God (Naples, Italy: IPE 1998).

Chapter 11

Universal Communication, Meaning, and Symbols

All things and beings appear to be directly or indirectly in touch with each other; in a sense, they "know" one another. In fact, an elementary form of meaning seems to be a feature of sensible reality falling within the scope of natural science. At the same time, communication and meaning reveal very special connotations when it comes to man, particularly in connection with symbols. Is this where the rigor of science and the intuitions of poetry meet?

Science and Communication – A Dialogue on Being and Communication – A Relation between Things and Processes – Gnosiomaton, the Knowing Machine – Meaning and Man – An Ocean of Symbols – Symbols in Science – The Divided Triangle, Symbol of Man – The Blessing of Fire – A Zoology of Symbols – A Window on Fairyland – Toward Other Seas

The study of communication is a convergence, or attempted convergence, of people who were trained, initially, in very different fields in history and philosophy, in literary and cultural studies, in sociology, technology and psychology. — RAYMOND WILLIAMS[1]

Science and Communication

For one thing, our journey along the abandoned paths of science has suggested that the Great Dance image may imply a commitment to a dimension of reality beyond the direct access of the five senses of man; for another, it has left us with the feeling that, after all, there may be something valid in such ideas as correspondences, influences, sympathies either in their past forms or under the new names of mental energy, auras, and what have you. Now, today's science does include a field of inquiry that seems to cover precisely whatever truth those vague and probably fanciful notions may conceal; indeed, it accounts for the existence of relations between things in the universe that cannot be reduced to the direct action of one body on another. The key concept involved is communication. Influences, sympathies, and the like could be but notions derived from the recognition of the basic fact that everything communicates with everything else. But, then, how can nonthinking objects participate in a communication network? Is communication not associated with meaning? These are but two of the questions we want to discuss in this chapter.

In ordinary language we tend to use the words "information" and "communication" without caring much about the difference. Science begins by giving a precise name to each concept, and by explaining what that name means. From operations of this sort often an entirely new chapter of science originates. In our case, there are in principle a science of communication and a science of information. We have already discussed the latter: and we have seen that information is the content of a message. Communication, on the other hand, is the process and the means by which information is transmitted. If you say: "I have received a communication from headquarters" you are using the word "communication" in a sense — that of "message" — admitted by your dictionary, but not by science, because you are implicitly giving two different meanings to that word. Even worse, a dictionary (i.e., current English usage)

---

1. Quoted by H. Hardt in *Communication, History and Theory in America* (London and New York: Routledge, 1992), 30.

allows the use of that same word to mean "information," i.e., to denote the content of the message. That happens because in ordinary language the meaning is made clear by the circumstances and by the context. In the example we are considering, the word "received" excludes the primary meaning of the word "communication" (act of communicating), while the meaning of "information" is superposed to that of "message" if it appears from the rest of what you say (the "context") that you are interested in the content of the message rather than in the message itself.

This is one of the main points which Claude Shannon, with whom we became acquainted in chapter two, had to consider when he made communication the key concept of a whole discipline. We have already examined its theoretical foundations in connection with information. Let us now try to understand, on the example just given, what communication really is. If you had had to be more precise, instead of the sentence "I have received a communication from headquarters" you should have used the following three sentences:

- The communication line between headquarters and us has been used by headquarters people;

- a message has been transmitted to us;

- I have been able to read and interpret the information contained in it.

Paradoxically, here you never mention communication as such, but only the communication line, for the simple reason that you do not care how messages are transmitted. The situation would be different if you said something like: "In order to make communication between us and headquarters possible I have had to use a protocol converter" — that device, you know, which allows a computer to receive on its serial port and process an input signal intended for a parallel port, or vice versa.

This analysis allowed Shannon to tackle in a scientific way the fundamental problem of finding a mathematical expression and an experimental procedure to measure how faithfully a given communication system would perform under given conditions.[2] We saw the solution in chapter two: it consists in assigning to a communication device a positive number lower than 1 telling the fraction of the information contained in an average message that will be preserved after transmission. If that number were, for example, 0.9, it would mean that upon arrival the message still contained with certainty 90 percent of the information it contained when fed to the communication system.

The definition thus obtained might seem to limit the scientific analysis of communication to devices such as telephones, computers, etc. In

2. Cf., e.g., R. G. Gallager, *Information Theory and Reliable Communication* (New York: John Wiley, 1968), 13–37.

fact, it also applies to another field of inquiry, communication such as is provided by the mass media, i.e., when the transmission line involves rewriting by a free agent having particular ideas and preconceptions. There are two reasons for this extension. First, the analysis we have made above is incomplete: the person who materially received the message from headquarters might be required to rewrite it for the others in his or her group, or, worse, might have to *report* on its content. Thus, the final result will depend on that person's ability to read and write well enough, and especially on that person's ability to forego all personal bias. We all know how important this is in journalism. Therefore, the theory of communication, seen as a branch of sociology, has after all the same problem as the engineering theory of communication.[3] The second reason is seen in Shannon's mathematical expression reported and discussed in chapter two. He takes as *data* of the transmission device the probabilities that different parts of a message will be forwarded correctly up to the end station. As long as no intermediate "recoding" (translation, explanation, etc.) by human beings is involved, those probabilities will only depend on the technology employed; but they will depend on who the interpreter is when there is a step — say, rewriting and commenting on a piece of news — whose reliability is a function of the interpreter's training and preconceptions. Here we have a limit to quantitative science because, as is well known, in the sciences of man — psychology, sociology, economics — fully reliable statistics cannot be obtained.

In conclusion, a sense of the word "communication" that is not a combination of distinct concepts, is probably "transfer of information." This transfer of information is the process by which a system A (a person, but, as will be seen, also a cell or a particle of nonliving matter) causes a system B to undergo *a specific change of state*. For example, if I wish to share with you certain ideas of mine, I have to write them down in a language that you understand, and then send you a letter with the resulting text. Because of dependence on the communication line, the information actually transferred may fail to be exactly the same, in quantity and quality, as that fed by the source to the transmission line; but I shall try to write in such a way that anyway your "state" changes as intended after reading. The change may be just in the content of your memory, but there can be no question about the fact that your state is no longer what it was before reading my letter.

We now know more or less what communication is. But does it not require a receiver capable of understanding a language, having a memory and possibly a consciousness? What do I mean when I say that everything

---

3. Cf. H. Hardt's book cited at the beginning of this chapter effectively illustrates the maze of vague notions, ideological preconceptions, and fragmentary data through which sociological communication theory is trying to make its way.

communicates with everything else? Do electrons write letters to cells? Do stars chatter with one another? Of course not; but I believe that, if we follow the lead given by the discussion just carried out, we shall be led to admit that it is legitimate to speak of communication in the sense just explained, albeit of a very rudimentary kind, between such low-complexity systems.

A Dialogue on Being and Communication

Perhaps I can make my point if I report here a reverie going back to a mild autumn evening of many years ago.

On a low hill from which one can contemplate the blue expanse of the southern Mediterranean sea, not far from the place where Aeneas, the mythical ancestor of the Romans, lost his pilot and friend Palinurus, there are the ruins of a town called Velia. It is the site of a still older Greek town of a time — several centuries before the Christian era — when the coastal regions of southern Italy were part of the Greek nation: Elea, the birthplace of the famous philosopher and legislator Parmenides. In my reverie, I found myself leisurely walking outside the walls of that town, along the main street, on that stretch which led, through groves of silver-leafed olive trees, to the blue expanse of the sea. After a while, I saw an elderly man, clad in a white tunic, apparently coming back to the town after a solitary walk. As he came nearer, he addressed me politely, as people of small places are wont to do. Here is the conversation we had.

P: Stranger, welcome to our land. What brings you here?

J: Nothing in particular. I am just taking a walk to relax and think about man and the world.

P: I am glad to meet you, for I am interested in the same sort of things. My name is Parmenides.

J: Mine is Joseph. But how curious that you should have the same name as the legislator of Elea. Did you know that? He was the thinker who, following the indications of the Daughters of the Sun, rode a chariot drawn by the Wise Mares and reached the doors of the Lady of Justice, Dike. She received him into the light of truth.

P: We must be meeting in a sort of no-time land, Stranger, for I am that Parmenides, and you are recalling the first lines of my poem on being and nonbeing.[4] You see, I was charged with writing down the laws of my town. Now, a lawmaker must base his laws on real facts and real possibilities, and therefore he must be able to distinguish what is real from what is not.

---

4. Parmenides, *Fragments*, ed. and trans. into German as *Über das Sein* by H. von Steuben (Stuttgart: Reclam, 1985).

J: If I remember correctly, the Lady Dike disclosed to you the basic truth: Being is permanent, and Change is but an appearance, like the waves of the sea. I find that a somewhat cryptic statement.

P: To me it seems clear. If something really exists, then that's it; it cannot be the product of nonbeing, nor can it cease to be. What really *is* cannot begin, evolve, and cease to be.

J: Yet, observation tells us that nothing remains for a long time what it seems to be at a certain moment. The science of my time has shown that not only do things change, but the processes by which they do so are irreversible.

P: Well, in my time there is already a nuisance who says so: his name is Heraclitus. Indeed, before visiting the Palace of Light, I had been asking myself if Heraclitus and his followers could possibly be right when they said that reality is a flowing river of perpetual change. If that were so, no just law would be possible because justice itself would be an ever changing reference, and what is right today could be wrong tomorrow.

J: But at this precise time of the world in which you live, have you already written those famous laws which your fellow citizens liked so much, that they would take every year an oath to respect them?

P: Yes, I have, and I have made up my mind: all change is actually a mysterious delusion of our minds, and what really exists is something that never changes: I call it "being."

J: I come from this same land twenty-five centuries ahead in your future. You know, your idea was regarded as a primitive view for a long time, but in my time it is creeping back through what we call science.

P: Tell me about it. In this no-time world, much of the new knowledge you people of the future have acquired emerges in my memory as mention is made of it. I expect I will understand what you refer to as if I were a man of your time.

J: Well, it is said that being is indeed what we get in touch with when we perceive the existence of something, but being has properties. As far as matter goes, what there is at the bottom of everything is space-time. Every object is like a bubble in space-time; it lasts a certain time; during that time it visits a certain region of space; and while it lasts it becomes.

P: Your space-time is akin to my unchanging sphere of being. So, what you are saying might be another way of saying that becoming is an illusion. But let me now ask you, Stranger: is that your major concern in your meditations?

J: Well, it isn't, although my problem is related to change and persistence just as yours.... Maybe on the material plane the overall persistence of all that exists is manifest in its unity, which is preserved by the interdependence of its parts or maybe just their intercommunication. Now, what I was thinking about when I met you is that, if it is granted that the universe is a network of relations, those relations should include communication between things.

P: I can see what communication between two human beings is; but I feel you will have to establish what you mean by that word, Stranger, if you want to apply it to every object in the universe.

J: A light ray arriving from a star is a message from that star.

P: Why is it not just energy arriving from it? Think of the sun.

J: Why not, indeed? But I guess that the only energy that does not carry information is heat... or maybe not: if there is a flow of heat, you know that there is something warmer in the direction from which it comes.

P: I see. And energy in the form of light carries much more information, for it also tells you the state of the matter that emits it, and in many cases the chemical composition of that matter. I seem to remember from my memory of the future that in the spectrum of the sun there are dark lines that tell which atoms are moving about in the corona of the sun.

J: Your foresight works quite well. Those dark lines are the Fraunhofer lines. So, you see, even the source of practically all energy on the earth sends us more than energy; it sends information.

P: And is that what you call "communication?"

J: It is. My view is that communication is but information transfer. Moreover, it seems to me that the earth sends information to the sun. For certainly there must be slight modifications in the shape of the sun's outer gaseous shell as the earth changes its relative position in space. Something like tiny tidewaves.

P: I grant you that. But communication, if I am not mistaken, implies a message and its decoding, i.e., the attribution of a meaning to the message, indeed to each part of the message. There does not seem to be anything similar in the relation between the earth and the sun.

J: Consider that the light of the sun has a variety of effects which do not depend just on the energy transported, but on the type of energy, and you will perhaps change your mind. If the same energy reached the earth in the form of gamma rays, all life would be destroyed in a short time. Moreover, light energy in the red-infrared region activates the photosynthetic process in plants. Thus, whatever exists on the earth receives more than just energy; it receives information and responds to it. Do you not think that responding is akin to understanding?

P: Perhaps. Nonetheless, all that is inseparable from energy as such.

J: I agree. But by the same token no communication takes place without some expense of energy. In the cases I have just mentioned the energy that carries the message — maybe just one signal — is also used to make important changes possible, whereas in other cases — say, a radio set — whatever energy is needed for special operations comes from other sources. But consider that at the beginning of radio communication there were radio sets that used the extremely small energy arriving with the radio waves to activate the earphones. Moreover, there are cases in which the sun's light is used simply as a message. I have already mentioned that the sun tells us something about its own chemical composition. But the main message of the sun is: "Look, here I am, a class-G star near you, and you would not be alive were I not here." We receive its radiation and read in it its presence and its nature; it is like reading a postcard from a friend.

P: What is the relation between the energy and the information received?

J: When you receive and interpret a message, your state changes in a way that depends on the content of the message. The same is true for every thing that reads a message. The energy required to switch on the necessary change of state may be very small, or it may be provided by other sources through amplification of the input signal. I think that the former case is the more frequent one, unless the system is sufficiently complex. The more so, the more complicated the message.

P: If you add that there are systems that search for the information contained in the energy arriving from other systems, and others that are merely passive receivers, though capable of some decoding, I can go along with you.

J: So, as you see, what a poet called "the great sea of being" is the real thing, as you said a long time ago, but at the same time it is a collection of objects, processes, and events somehow made one by communication between things.

P: Let me try to summarize. Nothing in the universe is completely isolated. There is some exchange of energy between all things, albeit extremely small. The important point is that, regardless of its quantity, that energy has characteristics such as direction, wavelength, and so on. Equal amounts of energy may be qualitatively much different. Therefore energy coming from a sender A and arriving at a receiver B functions as a message transporting information about A, and producing a response by B which depends on its quality. Unless it is so great that B is destroyed no matter what its qualitative characteristics are, it may or may not cause B to respond in a certain way depending on those characteristics.

J: A perfect summary.

P: I should like to discuss what that implies about the great sea of being, but the first stars have appeared in the sky. At any rate, many thanks. See you sometime, somewhere, Stranger from the future.

When I came back from my reverie, I was convinced more than ever that the claim that everything communicates with everything else is quite reasonable. But other questions remained. If the reality described by science is one where different layers of complexity can be distinguished, from elementary particles up to higher organisms and beyond, then a question arises: should we not think that communication only takes place horizontally, i.e., between systems belonging to the same complexity level, rather than vertically, i.e., between systems belonging to different complexity levels? For example: is it not illogical to expect that a molecule should communicate with a man? That is not an easy question, the more so as communication itself requires a carrier, which can be a system with its own degree of complexity.

To disentangle this side of the story, let us first of all make a list of examples.

a. communication at the same level

1. The anelastic collision of an atom A with another atom B: B is brought to an excited state, so that for a time, which is usually long on the atomic scale, it "remembers" that something happened to it. Here the message is energy above a certain threshold, and the interpretation is its use by B to get from the state before the collision to the one after the collision.

2. Production by a cell A of a molecule M, which influences another cell B, for example by stopping its replication. Here the message is the very structure of M, its "reading" is a chemical reaction binding M to the DNA of the receiving cell; its interpretation is the choice of the site at which the host molecule is bound, because it interrupts the production of the enzymes needed for the reproduction of B.

3. Control of an amplifier by feedback. The output device includes an electronic circuit A, of the same degree of complexity as the amplifier proper B, which sends to the input circuit of B a message in the form of a voltage or current change such that, if the output signal is too strong, the amplification factor is reduced, if it is too weak, the amplification factor is increased.

4. Letter exchange between two persons. This is the example we have already discussed.

b. communication between different levels

1. The anelastic collision of an electron A with an atom or molecule B. The electron is an elementary particle, and therefore (unless it undergoes the same fate as other elementary particles, now attributed a "structure") lies at the bottom of the complexity scale, and has no internal states. Nevertheless, it can communicate with another, more complex system, by exchanging kinetic energy. If a beam of electrons all with the same speed cross a region of space where molecules of a certain type are moving around, then some electrons will collide with molecules and yield energy to their internal degrees of freedom. After the passage through the swarm of molecules, therefore, there will be electrons slower than before and

moving in different directions: they have changed their state of motion because of a collision. By the same token, there will be molecules in a new state with a higher energy content. Since they will stay in that state for some time, it is permitted to say, albeit by analogy, that they have "learned" that electrons have collided with them. This might seem to be nothing more than an exchange of energy; but in fact, as has been said, the energy transfer only takes place with electrons having an energy beyond a certain threshold. Thus, something similar to the interpretation of a message has taken place.

2. The activation of certain enzymes by sodium or potassium ions. Enzymes, as is well known, are macromolecules presiding over chemical transformations in living systems. Those under consideration have the property that, when they trap, say, a potassium ion, they change their shape and acquire the ability to catalyze certain reactions. This phenomenon can be seen as the sending of a message from the potassium ion to the most remote parts of the macromolecule, which responds to it by changing its conformation.

3. The action of the psychological state of a human being or animal on the individual cells of its organism ("downward causation," cf. chapter twelve). For example, the nervous system of a person under stress may release certain molecules (chemical messengers), which affect the immunological efficiency of antibodies, thus increasing that person's risk of catching an infectious disease.

4. The change in body temperature when the external temperature changes. This is a well-known situation in which the body functions as a control system whose task is to keep its own temperature constant. The message here is the temperature of the environment, whose possible complexity, in this case, does not matter.

Note that case b1 is special, because (as far as the most recent information I have goes) the electron has no internal states, and therefore, although it can transport energy with respect to a specific energy frame, it cannot really memorize an event in such a way that a trace of it will persist for a while even if it stops. This remark is important in connection with a general consideration: all the examples given suggest that communication is possible because all the systems mentioned, except the electron, behave to a greater or lesser extent as systems in the proper sense, i.e., as open units capable of preserving their identities under a perturbation and at the same time capable of responding to external perturbations, even very weak, by suitable changes of state.

In accordance with the analysis carried out in the first section, in all the above examples communication consists of several steps:

- creation of a message, i.e., expression of the information to be transferred;

- transmission of the message;

- reading of the message at the receiving end;

- interpretation of the message.

Interpretation calls into play something that in human communication is called "language." This is a general aspect because normally the information transferred is not directly contained in the message. For example, in the case of temperature regulation in a warm-blooded organism, the signal received by the organism is not the change in average kinetic energy of the molecules of the environment, which, according to statistical physics, should be considered as the change in temperature proper, but some effect on the yield and rate of a chemical reaction. Unless the latter controls sweating directly, the organism must respond to that signal as if it knew that it meant that the temperature of the environment had changed. In general, a message has a "meaning" to be obtained by its translation into a language serving as a vehicle for its "content" (in the simple example of a letter to a friend). Here again, science demands that we should establish as rigorously as possible the scope of the word "language." Much has been written on this question.[5] For our purposes here — and in accordance with the realistic commitment of this book — language might be roughly defined as a conventional correspondence between sensible things acting as "signs" (say, the Chinese ideograms or simply written words) and facts, objects, or ideas. The acknowledgment of that correspondence for a particular sign is what we ordinarily call grasping its *meaning*.

As long as the receiver or the transmitter or both are inanimate objects, communication is simply a fact, an aspect of the coherence of the universe. But meaning and possibly signs come into play as soon as living beings are considered. Indeed, from the point of view of a science that has taken account of the systemic nature of living beings, meaning is a possible property of messages whenever the receiving system has a choice — to respond or not to respond, to act in one way or another. In other words, the rise of biology and of the science of communication has produced the discovery that meaning can (and should) be treated as something objective, as a fact of reality; indeed, as a feature of messages serving as criteria for choices.

---

5. As is well known, most of the philosophy of science of the twentieth century has been to a greater or lesser extent a philosophy of language; suffice it to recall names like Peirce, Russell, Wittgenstein, Cassirer, etc.

In the sense just discussed, meaning is associated with communication at the level characteristic of any living being, including the simplest bacteria. But a dramatically new extension of the general concept of meaning emerges, as it seems, at the level of human beings (and to some extent of higher animals). Then meaning is no longer limited to the simple type, "there is decaying fish in that direction," or "it is urgent to take cover," as with nocturnal ants smelling remnants of food or being hit by a light beam; more often than not it reveals information of the type, "the lights in the sky are stars," or "my good friend living a thousand miles from my home is well and remembers me," etc. Such complicated messages are transferred by conventional signs, e.g., those used to represent words. When the signs used are single objects or icons which put a person in touch with realities not directly accessible to the five senses, they are *symbols*. In the world of man, symbols are everywhere, from the equations of physics to the pillars of medieval cathedrals.

We are now going to examine both levels of communication at which the notion of meaning applies. Once again we shall see how the new science, more sober and humbler than the science of a few decades ago, takes us up and up the ladder of complexity and then leaves us, as Virgil left Dante on the top of the mountain of Purgatory, not pretending that the end of the line has been reached, but simply admitting that its task and scope are ended, and we should look for a different guide.

A Relation Between Things and Processes

I had my first contact with meaning when my friend Arturo Carsetti, a distinguished philosopher of science teaching in Rome, organized a meeting on the "emergence of meaning."[6] At first, I was somewhat surprised that meaning could emerge from anything: I had thought that either it is there or it is not. But then I had an illumination. As we have seen, in the current views about how the universe became what it appears to be, its development is seen as a process of complexification, i.e., evolution from lower to higher complexity levels.[7] After the Big Bang, there were elementary particles, such as quarks, hadrons, and what have you, then came molecules, cells, up to living beings: aggregation and complexification took place. At each level, as we have seen in chapter three, new features of reality appeared. The simplest example of those features is size: elementary particles have no size to speak of, atoms have different sizes but all extremely small, while molecules are larger and can have shapes. Emergence of meaning in the physical world would therefore mean that,

6. The proceedings have been published in *La Nuova Critica* (Rome) I–II (1992): 19–20.
7. Cf., e.g., Layzer, *Cosmogenesis*.

when the complexification of the universe reached that degree of complexity where it is possible to speak of entities behaving as wholes, there appeared a property which we may call, pending a justification of the term chosen, significance or *meaning*.

In the case of human beings, meaning[8] is usually associated with words, which represent things and actions and relations between them. When we say that "A means B," we imply that A "makes sense" to us and to the other members of our clan — those who speak the same language and live in the same environment — and makes it possible for us to make decisions, both as individuals and as a group. If you say, as a janitor in Naples said to me many years ago: "X is rich but he is not a gentleman," others will know how to behave with X and what to expect from him, provided they can associate meanings to the words "rich" and "gentleman." Thus, we certainly agree that meaningfulness is a distinctive feature of those statements that establish communication between human beings. If pursued along this familiar line, meaning is inextricably tied to the inner world of a self-conscious being. This is not a problem to such thinkers as Carnap,[9] for their interest appears to be centered on language and logic. Those thinkers are anyway very important; moreover, we too will presently consider the case of the reasoning animal, *animal rationale*, that is man; but for the time being we are interested in general in the members of the vast community of systems and beings that is the universe. Therefore, to begin at the most elementary level, let us record that a dictionary defines meaning as

1: that which you are intended to understand by something spoken or written or expressed in other ways, such as by signs; 2: importance or value; 3: an aim or intention.[10]

With the first and third definitions, the dictionary tends to stress the role of the sender of the message, and seems to ignore the fact that a meaning can be attributed to events or signs that were not intended as messages. Nonetheless, it hints at the meaning of a word or sign as "what it stands for." As to the second definition, it suggests that a coloring of importance and value (obviously in view of immediate or future action) is somehow present in the concept (or set of concepts) which the word "meaning" represents.

Further reflection along these lines suggests that three aspects of meaning should be considered at least as far as man is concerned: importance

8. We recall again that the specialists' distinction between "sense" and "meaning" is not relevant here.

9. R. Carnap, "Testability and Meaning," *Philosophy of Science* (1936): 420–471 and (1937): 2–40. For comments cf. A. J. Ayer, *Language, Truth and Logic* (London: Gollancz, 1946).

10. *Longman's Dictionary of Contemporary English* (London: Longman, 1987).

for choices, correspondence, and role in a context. Now imagine that we try to apply to meaning and meaningfulness the notion of emergence, and decide that meaning appeared in a certain epoch of the evolution of earth. Then, meaning no longer denotes a feature of a thinking person's relation with reality, ideas, and other human beings. It must be something similar, because otherwise one would not use that word, but it is not something characteristic of language and of man. It must be a relational property of reality, independent of a thinking subject, which has some basic aspects in common with meaning among human beings. We shall therefore try to associate meaning with the recognition of the existence of another reality, where "recognition" is not taken as an inner experience, but simply as a fact affecting the behavior of a living being.

We have already seen that organization, in the sense that applies to control systems and to living bodies, is a condition for individuality. It can be defined in strict relation to "homeostasis," i.e., the characteristic of certain complex systems, in particular of living being, which consists in their ability to perform a given task, to achieve certain goals, etc., in spite of changing environmental conditions. In this connection, a lead for the analysis of the emergence of meaning is provided by a consideration of Valerio Tonini, who wrote in 1980:

> A phylogenesis, an evolution or even just an ontogenesis not provided with disjunctive analyzers, that is selection mechanisms, would be impossible. *There is no informational process without disjunctive analyzers.* . . . Information, for a living being, is thus that which starts by *distinguishing* in the uncountable universe of events in which it is immersed two distinct sets: the class of *events that have a relevance* and the class of events that have no relevance for that system or being. . . . Life is the cybernetic organization of sequences of selective events.[11]

What Tonini calls "relevance" is having what we may call a "meaning." In other words, in the general sense valid for any living being, *meaningfulness* or significance is a relational property of reality by which a being feels, at its level of sensibility, that the message received provides information (direct or to be stored for future memory) important for its main aims — e.g., survival. Meaning is the specific information contained in the message in a form such that the being in question can make use of it.

Gnosiomaton, the Knowing Machine

According to the discussion just completed, meaning is discovered at the final stage of the processing of messages. In the case of human beings,

---

11. V. Tonini, *"Il corpo, la ragione, la psiche"* (Body, Reason, Psyche), *La Nuova Critica* 14 (Rome), no. 56 (1980): 49.

this implies that meaning increases knowledge. Therefore, if we extend the scope of meaning to all living beings, indeed to all homeostatic, self-regulated control systems, then we should also try to include knowledge among facts independent of thinking and self-consciousness. We shall see in the next chapter that this implies a strong limitation with respect to what knowledge appears to be if man's specific faculties are taken into account; but that is one more reason for making the attempt. To this end, the best strategy is to think of a model subject, which we shall call "Gnosiomaton" — the "knowing machine" — and show that its behavior and survival can only be explained in terms of a function having the properties of meaning. In order to "know," Gnosiomaton must be an "individual," capable of placing itself (however unconscious that action may be) in front of the rest of the world as an independent system. Such a system is nothing impossible for today's technology; just think of Sojourner, the little exploring machine that landed on Mars in July 1997. To be capable of "knowing" Gnosiomaton must have some sort of homeostasis, which, as discussed before, is a result of self-regulated organization and of an invariant informational core whose structure establishes a class of characteristic procedures for information processing. When Gnosiomaton is confronted with some perturbation from outside, it establishes its meaning at two levels. First, its disjunctive analyzers (e.g., if ... then devices coupled to its sensors) decide whether the message belongs to the class of messages important for the preservation of its working conditions or for the performance of its tasks; for example, it might ignore long-wave radio disturbances coming from space because they are mere radio noise as far as it is concerned. If the message is found to belong to the class of interesting messages, then Gnosiomaton will process it, i.e., it will translate the information received into its own machine code. This operation will make it possible to fit the message into the resident *organized* storage of instructions and data messages, and to take immediate action if any is required; it may be considered as the step at which the meaning of the message is detected. For example, Gnosiomaton's photocells might send an electric impulse, which is finally stored in its memory, to be activated when the location and intensity of light sources in the environment become important for charging the batteries. The process involved is detection of the meaning of the electric impulse received.

The correspondence aspect of meaning is included in the above analysis if knowledge is looked at as "grasping" (Latin: *intelligere = inter legere*), i.e., as a faithful internal description, written in the appropriate machine language, which Gnosiomaton makes of features of the outer world. There is more: to Gnosiomaton, as to a human baby, the final assessment of the *validity* ("truth-value") *of the meaning* could well be made by a test, by an action which verifies the theory — thus showing that the notion of meaning under consideration is scientific according to Popper's "falsifiability" criterion. Gnosiomaton, just as a small child, would reach out to seize an object and examine it by its various sensors. Thus, verification is somehow involved, but it is only possible if meaning in the structuralists' sense has already been established — i.e., if the input data have been stored and assigned a precise classification with respect to other stored data — and only correspondence with outer reality is in question. The latter has been called "validity" of the meaning, but it may be considered part of the very assignment of a meaning to a message inasmuch as it is indispensable for making the message a tool for decision and action.

Another point worth explicit mention is that meaning, as defined here, depends on the individual just as meaning in its familiar sense, unless identical machines in identical situations are considered; but this has nothing to do with subjectivity. The smell of a rose is a fact, indeed a chemical fact, but one has to have a nose to realize it is there, and the nose in question may well be different from all other noses, even if it belongs to a machine. There may be more features in the messages sent by a thing than meet the senses of a single individual, and those features that are detected by any given individual may be just a few of the total number. In short, the sentence, "Such and such an event has a meaning" possesses an objective (or, if you like, scientific) validity if it really stands for "such and such an event may cause some system in the universe to respond to it in a specific way, and we can tell what characteristics that system should have."

Since familiar expressions like "the meaning of life" seem to be general, one may wonder if the meaning of an event or set of events as defined above also holds without reference to a specific receiving system. Now, certain general questions of this kind, to some extent at least, can be answered by science, e.g., "What is the meaning of the death of a star?" Therefore, it would seem that they make sense; and that is because they essentially ask if the event to which they refer may force the selection of a particular evolution channel at a branch-point in the history of the universe. If so, however, they apply to events and processes treated *as messages of the parts to the whole;* that is to say, they concern the history of the world as such. Along this line, one could probably go so far as to claim that all events are meaningful, for every event is meaningful for at least one system in the universe.

I hope the reader will agree that at this point we have reached the core of the concept of meaning. The latter applies to all objects in the universe, except maybe those, like stars, which participate in the universal network of communication without actually needing information in order to stay tuned to the harmony of the whole. Even the exceptions, however, can at most be sources of meaning, in the sense that events involving them may have a meaning for other objects that are self-regulated systems out of equilibrium, and even for the whole universe.

As to the emergence of meaning, the underlying idea might now be clear. As complexity increases in the universe, more and more organized systems appear whose main characteristic is to participate in the Great Dance by performing a precise task against a background of unpredictable random fluctuations. Except possibly in the case of free agents, that task is automatically performed if the given system retains its identity. Conservation of identity involves analyzing "perceived" events as messages, and establishing if they require action, and, if so, which action. Since this kind of situation characterizes and perhaps even defines living systems (even possible living systems that are not chemically based), one could say that meaning is an essential characteristic of life; because the ability to assign meanings to messages from outside is a condition for preserving identity — a condition not only necessary but sufficient, as long as basic physical requirements are satisfied, such as the availability of energy in the appropriate form. Thus, the emergence of meaning in the history of the universe can be considered as an aspect of the emergence of life. Indeed, it is a very intriguing aspect, for it is what connects the individuality of a living being to its being an essential part of a larger context. In this sense, meaning probably emerged in the history of life by a slow process, because to primordial bacteria most events must have been inconsequential, and just a few responses sufficed for their *being themselves*, that is, for them to play their role in their environment. At the maximum complexity extreme we have human beings, whose nature is characterized by an unceasing search for meanings.

Meaning and Man

Certain thinkers claim that in human beings the search for meaning becomes almost pathological, for people cannot avoid what those thinkers consider to be pointless questions, such as the one about the meaning of life. However that may be, there seems to be in man an aspiration to the absolute which, as we have seen in chapter eight, can be understood by science as the fact that man can only maintain in perfect working condition its psychophysical individuality if it has a central set of rules that can guide the immense variety of decisions he has to make. Even those people who claim that their lives have meaning simply because they are always engaged in some useful activity, or because they are never despondent or in doubt, and so they need no recourse to a central reference idea,[12] probably mean that such a reference is a built-in feature of their subconscious,

---

12. Cf. K. Baier, "The Meaning of Life," in *Philosophy and Contemporary Issues*, ed. J. R. Bull and M. Goldinger (New York: Macmillan, 1976), 159ff.

possibly as part of their biological heritage, so that there are always good reasons for acting, and sufficient criteria for making what is felt to be the proper choice. We have already seen that, to the contrary, there are good grounds for believing that, as a matter of fact, the extreme adaptability of the human animal, the complexity of nature, and the permanent inner conflict between reason and subconscious drives make it necessary for the central set of guidelines to be independent of the individual — to be what we call absolute; so that the question about the meaning of exis-tence — which is essentially a question about general and absolute rules on which to base decisions — is not to be answered simply by a dive into the great stream of action. It would seem that *Homo sapiens* is the organ-ized system in which the emergence of meaning has reached its final stage by becoming the quest for the meaning of everything, independently of the immediate demands of a given situation.

It is in this connection that science can only provide partial informa-tion — the most significant piece being that it is not equipped to tread the paths leading into the forest bordering the shore she has reached. Let us at least state the problem and do as much as we can with the tools of science — stretching their scope as far as they can go.

An Ocean of Symbols

Two interrelated points seem particularly important in connection with man: communication with levels of reality not accessible to the senses, one of them being the spiritual one; and the objects and signs which allow human beings to stay in touch with those levels, namely symbols. We shall refer directly only to the latter, because they imply attention to the former. They form in themselves a most fascinating subject, and our exploration will of necessity be cursory and fragmentary, whereas the literature on them is incredibly rich. A few texts and dictionaries are cited below at the proper places. By way of introduction, we mention that modern research having symbolic expression as a central subject and taking into account both mathematics and anthropology, albeit within the philosophy of language, began with Ernst Cassirer (1874–1945).[13] However, the American philosopher Charles S. Peirce (1839–1914) is the thinker who best stated the rational and practical import of symbols. In the words of John Passmore,

> much of Peirce's philosophy is an attempt to work out a satisfac-tory theory of symbolism.... Peirce had been misunderstood, to his horror, as restricting science to the "practically useful" in its

13. An excellent introduction to Cassirer's well-known books is his *Wesen und Wirkung der Symbolbegriff* (Nature and action of the concept of symbol) (Darmstadt: Wissenschaft-liche Buchgesellschaft, 1956).

narrower sense. The meaning of a symbol, he now says, is the rational conduct which it stimulates. Thus we understand "lithium" if we know what steps to take in order to pick up our lithium from amongst other minerals. A sign is gibberish if, like many of the signs of traditional metaphysics, it does not lead us to some particular variety of rational conduct. This implies, of course, that we know how to decide what conduct is rational; Peirce happily accepts the consequence that "norms" of conduct are fundamental to inquiry.[14]

Peirce may have placed too great an emphasis on operational aspects, but he left a central role to reason. This should be kept in mind when considering famous studies on symbols by psychoanalysts, which stress their irrational side. Indeed, the term "symbol" is currently applied to many signs having a strong grip on subconscious associations of ideas and on imagination. Such symbols are extensively used in advertising and in general as "hidden persuaders." It is important to keep in mind that, to the contrary, our considerations will always be limited to symbols whose meanings, although they call into play the whole inner reality of a human being, can only be grasped as a result of a conscious and rational approach.

Distinctions are thus to be made. This is why we cannot follow those scholars who, in accordance with a fashionable but dangerous view, prefer to say that symbols are beyond definition. This is the case of the authors of an otherwise excellent dictionary of symbols.[15] Actually, if you consult that book, you will see that the authors really mean that the same word can be loosely applied to notions that have something in common, but are different. Now, as we have seen in the cases of communication and meaning, vague notions may constitute a good exploring ground, but a time must come when their scope must be restricted so as to make them susceptible of assessment. Therefore, let us briefly review attempts to understand what symbols are, following Marie-Madeleine Davy, a well-known student of symbolism in the Middle Ages.[16]

In ancient times, the word σύμβολον (pr. sewmbolon) stood for a tablet or other object broken in two pieces so that the two persons who possessed one half each could make sure of one another's identity even after several years by putting the two pieces together. For each of them the half ring or half tablet in his or her possession was a link with the invisible reality that was the absent friend — it was that friend's symbol. Symbols in the original Greek sense were used by towns and by the first Christians. Such a simple and practical identification document was probably that by which Paul of Tarsus proved that he was a Roman citizen when

14. Passmore, *A Hundred Years of Philosophy*, 110.
15. Chevalier and Gheerbrant, *Dictionnaire des Symboles* (Paris: Laffont, 1982).
16. M.-M. Davy, *Initiation à la symbolique romane* (Paris: Flammarion, 1977).

he arrived in Rome after appealing to the Emperor.[17] The transition from this technical meaning to the more general one is easily understood. The relation "Paul of Tarsus, half-tablet pair, Rome registry office" is a specific case of the general relation "first reality, symbol, second reality." The broken tablet plays a role similar — though, of course, not quite equivalent — to an interface allowing one-to-one communication between a person and the registry officer; a symbol, which borrows its name from the fragment pair, might be treated not just as a link at the intellectual and emotional level, but as a genuine interface capable of establishing communication between the psyche of a person and real things beyond the reach of that person's senses. No wonder that a symbol was considered in magic as a gate by which spirits jailed in a body of flesh could communicate with a world of free spirits, indeed command them.

The general quality of being a sign that establishes a relation was already mentioned by Jamblicus, a Neoplatonic philosopher who lived about the turn of the second century A.D. O. Clément, a well-known Christian-Orthodox theologian, pointed out that St. Ephraem Syrus (ca. A.D. 306–373) called the world an "ocean of symbols":

> In eastern mysticism, a symbol is a sign of identification between Heaven and Earth, between man and God through the Cosmos.... Symbolic knowledge reveals, almost vertically, the mystery present in things, God's glory that cannot be possessed but reveals itself when one is full of wonder.... It is knowledge of light and beauty, evident in an emotional involvement of the whole being, simple as a "sensation" but at the same time "sensation of God," as the Eastern Fathers had it.... In this light man enters communion with things, with the world.[18]

The Scotsman Johannes Scotus Erigena (810–877 A.D.), a doctor of the church, specified that a symbol is a sensible sign offering similarities to immaterial realities. The similarities may be pure or confused: they are pure if they are exact, they are confused if they are mixed with dissimilarities. Modern scholars have investigated the uses and applications of symbols. Davy mentions in her book that A. Schwaller de Lubitz stated that "symbols are signs one must learn to read, and symbolism is a language whose laws must be known; they have nothing to do with the grammatical structure of our languages." According to the Rumanian Mircea Eliade, an influential historian of religions,

> symbols, myths, images belong to the substance of spiritual life.... Symbolic thought ... precedes language and discursive reason. Sym-

---

17. Acts 25:12.

18. Cf. O. Clément, *"Cuore, simbolo, luce: realismo cristiano e armonia cosmica nei Padri della Chiesa"* (Heart, symbol, light: Christian realism and cosmic harmony in the Fathers of the Church), *La Nuova Europa* 2 (Milan), no. 6 (1995): 67–80.

bols unveil certain aspects of reality — the deepest ones — which lie beyond any means of knowledge.[19]

As mentioned, a scientific approach to symbols, albeit limited to psychology (and, in our opinion, somewhat biased by a professional tendency to treat pathological situations as the norm), was placed at the heart of analytic psychology by its founder, Carl Gustav Jung (1875–1961), the Swiss psychiatrist whose ideas greatly contributed to making the study of human psychology scientific, particularly by freeing psychology of Freud's questionable "pansexualism." Jung devoted a great part of his writings precisely to symbols. According to him,[20] symbols unify and activate the conscious as well as the subconscious, the future and the past of the observer, and thus guide the observer in his efforts to situate himself in relation to the whole of reality. In virtue of their complementary roles, the conscious and the unconscious shape as it were the internal connections of the observer's psyche so as to prepare its changes. A role is played in this not only by the present state and past history of the subject, but by the human group to which the observer belongs. Involved are both the built-in software (the "archetypes"), which is responsible for innate propensities and patterns of behavior common to all human beings, and the "collective unconscious," the acquired but unconscious response patterns that characterize human beings as social creatures or as belonging to a given social group.

Many authors like to emphasize that there is a profound difference between symbols on the one side, and allegories and signs on the other. Allegories proper are stories whose elements each stand for a clear-cut concept, and are akin to analogies, as mentioned in the preceding chapter in connection with Philo of Alexandria. For example, Dante's *Divine Comedy* begins with a description of the dark wood from which the poet emerges to find his guide Virgil; that wood stands for the emotional confusion of a man who, having decided to ignore values other than immediate personal satisfaction, realizes that he is unable to find the sense of freedom and fulfillment he expected. As to signs as such, we have already mentioned that they stand (or should stand) for precise concepts or objects; such is the case with words and icons. Indeed, any attempt to treat a symbolic expression as an analogy or as shorthand for a known thing will automatically transform the symbol into a mere sign.

The objects acting as symbols affect the minds participating in the Great Dance in a very special way. If they are inanimate they may well receive and send messages at a very rudimentary level; but since, as we

19. M. Éliade, *Images et symboles: Essais sur le symbolisme magico religieux* (Paris: Gallimard, 1952), 12.

20. Cf. C. G. Jung and M. L. von Franz, eds., *Man and His Symbols* (London: Aldus Books Ltd., 1964), and references therein.

shall see in more detail below, it is plausible that they are windows on a "spiritual reality," indeed, in a sense interfaces between embodied minds and other pure or embodied minds. I must say immediately that this possibility, as far as science is concerned, is precisely a possibility, nothing more; but we should take it seriously because, let us repeat it once more, we are reflecting on the kind of *Weltanschauung* or world-view that would be consistent with the recent advances and expansions of science, not just on what science can prove. With the reservations implicit in this reminder, we can doubtless include among the nonsensible entities with which symbols establish a connection the psyche of a person who is not in touch with us otherwise. Then certain objects, not in themselves intended as symbols — particularly artistic productions — turn out to play a similar role, for they put the person contemplating them in direct touch with the inner experience of another person. Now, the inner experience of man has been supposed to be relevant to science only in connection with the arrow of time;[21] even the famous paradoxes of quantum mechanics are far from calling it into play, for the kind of observer participation they invoke is only related to the fact that a system subjected to a measurement loses in part or entirely the memory of its previous history. Symbols open a far wider perspective. The inner experience of a sentient being can modify the whole of reality either directly, because an action induced by it can undergo spontaneous amplification, or indirectly, by modifying the inner experiences of other sentient beings, possibly through symbols and rituals, so as to induce those other sentient beings to self-amplifying actions. Expanding a strange suggestion by J. A. Wheeler,[22] we might say that the universe thus appears as an evolving communication network of processes involving in sentient and nonsentient systems having an independent existence.

Let us now examine symbols in more detail.

Symbols in Science

By acknowledging the existence and role of symbols, through those borderline disciplines that go under the general name of anthropology — sociology, psychology, semiotics, cognition theory, etc. — science has discovered a new world — the world of the primitive intuitional forms of understanding. But that is not the whole story. A short reflection shows that symbols have been present for a long time within physics, chemistry, and biology.

Think of the mathematical symbols of physics. You might say that they are names, like ψ, the Greek letter most used to represent quantum

21. Eddington, *The Nature of the Physical World*, 103.
22. Wheeler, "World as System," 4–15.

mechanical wave functions, but that is not enough. Upon seeing the letter ψ, an expert physicist will immediately think of particles and waves, the uncertainty principle, nonlocality, the Schrödinger equation, relativistic corrections, and so on. From the standpoint of pure logic, that single Greek letter is a conventional sign, and could stand for anything; in the context of the established tradition of quantum mechanics it is the gate to a whole world, which science has discovered not only by logic but also by imagination, a world full of mysteries, where a particle is a pointlike mass and a wave spread out in space, where the result of a measurement is often unpredictable. Thus, ψ is a genuine symbol; it speaks not only to the logical power of the mind, but to intuition and imagination, two faculties essentially involved in scientific discovery; and it thus establishes communication between the mind and the level of reality where matter can be looked at as a collection of interacting elementary particles.[23]

The symbols of physics also have something in common with what they represent: their mutual relations, which are logical at the formal level and causal at the sensible level. That is to say, they have in common with all symbols the property of connecting two different levels of reality, in their case the mathematical and the sensible; they have a distinctive character as they stand for specific physical quantities — energy, length, velocity, etc. — and are connected to one another by mathematical equations, which match the relations the symbolized quantities have in reality with one another. For example (ignoring a number of complicated considerations pertaining to philosophy of science), in Newton's equation $F = ma$ the letters F, m, a are symbols of force, mass, and acceleration because the values of those quantities, as measured in the real world, satisfy precisely that relation. However, that equation is not just a recipe for computing, say, the force from the mass and the acceleration; it tells you what happens to a body if you apply a force to it, namely that it changes its velocity.

Chemistry, the daughter of alchemy, has perhaps the most important universally accepted symbols of science, those of the elements. Consider the simple reaction by which iron reacts with diluted hydrochloric acid to yield hydrogen and a pale orange solution of ferric chloride. That reaction is represented as

$$2\,Fe + 6\,HCl = 2\,FeCl_3 + 3\,H_2.$$

In this equation Fe, HCl, $FeCl_3$ and H_2 are symbols, which stand for iron, hydrochloric acid, ferric chloride, hydrogen. Why do we not simply write the names? One reason is certainly that words would make the equations rather difficult to handle, but that is not the whole story. In alchemy, we would have written a circle with a little arrow sticking from

---

23. Of course, quantum mechanics is expected to hold at all levels of complexity, but, with a few exceptions, its use is superfluous in the case of macroscopic objects.

its upper right side, which also stood for the planet Mars: that would direct our minds to the one reality underlying iron, a particular celestial body, the god of war, and all that goes with it. In chemistry, as we saw in chapter ten, that wider scope has been lost; yet, Fe is more than an abbreviated word. It stands for a specific quantity (one gram atom) of the corresponding gray metal in any of its states (α-iron, γ-iron, liquid iron, gaseous iron, etc.), and for a single atom with twenty-six protons and electrons, thus connecting two different levels of reality, with all the notions and facts involved in the correlation. Peirce, as mentioned above, might have gone as far as saying that the very name of iron (a metal as lithium, mentioned in his example) is a symbol because it has many operational as well as rational implications.

The Divided Triangle, Symbol of Man

Let us now turn to those symbols outside science which are associated with the most mysterious aspect of human nature — our mythopoeic, mystical drives, which reveal the irrepressible feeling that a spiritual reality exists with which we share part of our existence. Madeleine Davy, in the book mentioned above, discusses many such symbols, most of them to be found in the medieval cathedrals of central Europe, for example, the cathedral of Reims. On one of those symbols, perhaps the simplest one, we are going to pause, because it represents in a way the epitome of what the Great Dance image makes of man. It is a triangle, not the perfect Pythagorean triangle representing divine wisdom, appropriated in the eighteenth century by secret gnostic societies,[24] but a half black, half white equilateral triangle; the symbol of man.[25] Here it is, in its unimposing simplicity.

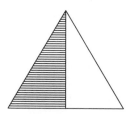

Being a true symbol, it covers a reality so much beyond all verbal expression that it is not possible to express its content in a few words.

24. H. Biedermann, *Dictionary of Symbolism: Cultural Icons and the Meanings behind Them,* trans. J. Hulbert (New York: Meridian 1994), under "triangle" and "Masonic symbols."

25. M.-M. Davy, *Initiation,* 198. Davy seems to refer to a rectangular triangle obtained by "generation" from the equilateral triangle which represents God. The bright moiety would then be invisible, but we prefer to treat it as visible.

But take a look at it. You are a human being; does that vertical division into black and white remind you of nothing at all? Perhaps, accustomed never to think about the quality of what you do, you might need a hint: what about that morbid curiosity with which people peruse the vilest tabloids, or what about that bitter impotent rage which burns in a person's heart when he or she sees injustice crushing people whose only fault is to be honest? Are these not manifestations of a dark and a bright side which cohabit within us? This is a first response; but on thinking a little longer you might find that the dark moiety also reminds you of our subconscious, where yet untamed primordial drives and archetypes concur both to give the right place to physiological needs and to generate bestial impulses.

Thus the dark moiety of the triangle need not represent the evil side of man; it may represent what we called "flesh" in the preceding chapter. By the same token, the white moiety may represent the "spirit," i.e., the self-conscious mind, including will. Then, the straight line separating the two parts hints at the fact that they should be perfectly adjusted to one another — the ideal condition of a human being, as we saw in chapter eight about the ecological niche of *Homo sapiens*. All right, you will say, but why a triangle? Why is the separation line vertical? Perhaps it is because the triangle is a closed figure with three corners; if the whole plane represents reality, then the triangle represents the portion of reality that is man. Then, the two lower vertices stand for the material reality of man, with flesh, corresponding to matter, on the left, and spirit, to the extent to which it is associated with matter, on the right. From the baseline joining the two lower vertices one can imagine a series of parallel lines, shortening as they approach the top: they remind us of the power human beings have to "sublimate" both their instincts and their reason, as when biological love for a person of the other sex becomes loyal affection going as far as renunciation of one's normal life. At the top sublimation coalesces into a point: that might be the dimensionless, immaterial gate at which a human being enters the world of pure spirits.

The above is a cursory attempt at expressing what the triangular symbol of man could convey; but it contains more. To circumscribe a little the interpretations one could add words, e.g.,

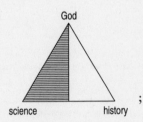

;

but then a discussion about word definitions and their possible correlations would be necessary. That was not the purpose of spending some time on the triangle; the purpose was to show how powerful and rich the suggestions of a symbol can be. Let us only add that, (a) once a lead is given (in our case, "this symbol stands for man"), those suggestions are largely accessible even to an illiterate person, although that person might not be able to express them in words; (b) the triangle we have discussed hints at another plane of reality only in a rather indirect way, for the whole figure is anyway centered on man.

There are symbols that clearly establish a connection between man's level of reality and other levels. The symbols of science are examples, but symbols having the immediacy and wealth of emotional overtones of the divided triangle are proposed by liturgy — the religious rituals of past and modern religions. Let us reflect on one such ritual, which also shows that signs and symbols need not be marks on paper or stone; many objects, especially objects familiar to everybody, can play that role.

The Blessing of Fire

One of the most fascinating rites of the Roman Catholic Church is the blessing of fire, on Easter Eve. Imagine that you happen to enter one of the great Gothic cathedrals of France, maybe in Chartres. The church is full of people in silent expectation. At a signal you do not even perceive, all stand up, and you note that everybody holds an unlit candle; your neighbor passes one to you. Suddenly, the lights are turned off. Then, a shimmer gradually builds up on the gothic pillars and on the walls, the dancing reflection of a light moving into the great medieval church through the historiated portal behind the congregation. The shimmer grows in intensity, and a glance tells you that the candles behind you are being lit one after the other. A procession, led by a priest holding the tall Paschal candle, slowly proceeds through the rows of pews. Now the procession is crossing your row, and the closest person lights his candle from the Paschal candle, his neighbor gets the light from his, and so on until your turn comes; and slowly a wave of light expands into the church until every candle is burning, and the nave, the aisles, and finally the apse are filled with a glory of lights, slightly swaying irregularly as if alive. Only later will you learn that another ceremony had preceded that in which you have participated: outside the church, a great fire had been lit, solemnly blessed, and the Paschal candle had been lit from it, to be taken into the church.

I do not know whether the Blessing of Fire was taken over from some pagan rite, as other feasts were in the early times of Christianity. But anyway the present meaning of the rite bears no trace of a possible pre-Christian origin, because the fire is intended as a symbol of the spiritual life given by the Word, transmitted by Jesus Christ to the people of God, who in turn light the flame of faith in their neighbors. Few people really know in detail the significance of the entire ceremony; but still fewer can escape a deep feeling of awe mixed with joy as their candles are lit. There will be people, of course, who will find some trivial psychological explanation for that feeling; but, aside from the fact that many of them are also those who see in every clock tower a phallic symbol, such a feeling can perhaps be explained, not explained away. The Roman Catholic Church itself would not encourage any supernatural interpretation, for, according to its doctrine, such an explanation is only reserved for the Eucharist, whose ritual is far less impressive. Nevertheless, there is something in every human being, believer or not, if he only knows the general idea and opens his heart, that makes him feel in that ceremony a "real presence," though he could not say of what. Let us leave the question open, only retaining that here the symbol is light transmitted without end from a main center to minor centers in wider and wider circles.

In many Christian churches candles also burn to prolong the presence of a worshipper before an image. There they are symbols which keep a person in touch with another person in Heaven. This example helps us appreciate the subtle emotional implications of a symbol. Just consider the difference between a real candle and one of those electric imitations which some modern parish priests place in their churches for the same purpose. I for one do not like that sort of innovation, probably because a candle is not a machine; it depends on its environment, and, most important, it slowly exhausts itself. When all the wax has been burned, it is no longer there; its silent burning is what my mortal life reduces to, whatever noise and incessant activity I try to produce — it is not just a sign that I paid a penny to light it. Shakespeare wrote the immortal lines which begin by "Out out, brief candle . . . " in a similar spirit; but his is just an analogy, however poetical: emphasis is placed on what life is like, whether a candle or a walking shadow. In contrast, in the case of a person lighting a candle before the image of a saint, the candle is a symbol in the original sense, like the ring or tablet broken to help friends to recognize one another; it stands for what I really am; in the context of prayer, it really is my life, and I feel that the blessed before whose image my life is burning will see me in it such as I am, a poor ephemeral creature of shadow longing for eternal light, and intercede for me.

A Zoology of Symbols

As to other symbols, specialized works[26] list an incredible number and variety of them; it must be kept in mind, however, that, since associations

---

26. Cf. the dictionaries by Chevalier and Gheerbrant (1982) and by Biedermann (1989).

are possible with almost every object familiar to a group of people, a rigorous selection should be made, and one may well expect that genuine symbols like the divided triangle are rare. However that may be, it is certain that not everything can be a symbol of everything; for example, a circle can hardly be a symbol of man. Tools, in general, can only be symbols representing human beings and their power; indeed, they can be found in friezes going back to the second half of the nineteenth century,[27] when worship of human reason was at its climax.

At least two types of symbols can play roles similar to that of a candle: the "gate" and the "center."

A gate is a symbol if it makes a person feel that through it one can get in touch with a part of reality not belonging to the sensible world, but communicating with him at the mental and emotional level. We have here a striking illustration of the limits of science. Is that communication real or not? Scientists might claim that a possible feeling of a real contact with other entities is only a psychological illusion; but that would be the same sort of claim as that of a deaf person, who, upon seeing people sitting with closed eyes and resting their heads on their hands during a performance of a chorale of Bach, insists that the orchestra is hypnotizing them by the strange motions of their hands on special instruments. Actually, at variance with altered states of consciousness induced by hallucinogens, mystical ecstasy has not been given any precise scientific explanation. This is in agreement with the notion that, if a reality exists with which only psychic (or mental) contact is possible, then it lies by its very nature beyond the reach of science. All science can do is to record the physical signs of a psychological change, as observed, say, in certain cases of religious conversion: a particular object, say the door of a church, perceived as a symbol of a supernatural reality can induce a change in attitude toward oneself and the world.[28] One might expect at first sight that no significant signs of such an experience would appear externally; but is that correct, even from a physiologist's point of view? In point of fact, if the change has been profound, it is even possible that people will doubt that they are observing the same person as before. Indeed, due to the well-established influence of the psyche on the chemistry of the human body, the psychological change might even have affected some biochemical processes. Science, as I said, can record all this; but such phenomena are not even reproducible at will, and no conclusion can be drawn. We can only say that, if an immaterial reality exists with which our minds

27. For example, those of the buildings of the municipality of Rome on the Capitoline Hill.

28. A beautiful description of such a conversion has been told by the famous French decadentist writer J.-K. Huysmans, *En route* (Paris: Tresse et Stock, 1895), ch. 2. The interested reader should also read Huysmans's masterpiece, *À rebours* (Paris: Charpentier, 1899).

and our psyches can establish contact by symbols or otherwise, then we must have grounds other than mere experimental science for accepting it, and other means to know something specific about it.

As to centers, shrines are certainly one example; mountains, of which human beings made places of worship long before the Iron Age, are another, as the history of mountaineering proves beyond any doubt. It is difficult to say precisely why that should be so; but, for that matter, how does science explain the pleasure one-year-old children take in being lifted from the ground and carried like that for a while? Is it a leftover of our supposed simian origin, or is it a sign that man carries within him the dream of freeing himself from the boundaries of earthly life? Be that as it may, a center exerts on human beings an attraction reminiscent of the attraction of an electric charge on charged particles in a gas. To see this, just think of pilgrimages in the Middle Ages, those centuries of great spirituality. Pilgrims would cross on foot several countries of Europe to pray in the most important shrines, the Holy Sepulchre in Jerusalem, St. Peter's Church in Rome, and the Cathedral of Santiago de Compostela on the Atlantic coast of Spain. Now imagine the pilgrims arriving at the shrine of Santiago de Compostela by night, each pilgrim carrying a candle or a torch. Imagine, too, that a man from the future is observing this strange phenomenon from a balloon: he will see swarms of tiny lights all slowly converging toward a mysterious black shadow. The lights do not collide with one another, as if a mysterious force kept them apart, just as electrostatic repulsion — the famous Coulomb hole — prevents the electrons of an atom from occupying the same place even if they have different spins. Thus, the attraction of a symbol acting as a center is almost a psychological equivalent of the attraction of, say, a large electric charge for charges of the opposite sign. A center is also felt as the site from which, like the light of a star, some mysterious incorporeal power is irradiated into the sensible world. According to Chevalier and Gheerbrant,

> the center, as a symbol, should not be conceived simply as a static position. It is the focus which is the origin of the movement of the one towards the many, from the inside to the outside, from the concealed to the manifest, from the eternal to the temporal, the origin of all emanation and divergence processes, and the focus where all processes of convergence are united, as in their principle, in their quest for unity.[29]

Coming back to symbols in general, let us pause briefly on symbols whose significance is not as serene and reassuring as in the cases we have examined. Jung's analytic psychology tends to emphasize not only the

---

29. Chevalier and Gheerbrant, *Dictionnaire*, s.v. "centre."

irrational components of symbols, but their negative, dark side, which is perhaps why psychoanalysis has failed to be a serious therapeutic tool. In the book cited above, Jung's followers mostly insist on this dark aspect, but a moment's reflection shows that they call "symbol" anything they consider irrational, particularly strange, primitive, or horrible signs, masks, or pictures used by various human groups. For example, a lion mask worn by a Cameroon wizard is presented as a symbol, with the comment that the wizard believes that by wearing it he has acquired the psyche of a lion. Those who know how easy it is for a two-year-old to pretend that he is repairing a car by a trick of the same kind will easily see how uncertain the whole idea is. There is an illuminating story in this connection about a Christian missionary in the Pacific Islands who was told everything about the complicated polytheistic religion of the natives. One day he started to explain that there was only one God, who was good, almighty, omniscient, and so on. As he spoke, the natives showed a growing uneasiness; at last, they stopped him, saying: "You are speaking of the Great Being, whom no one should openly mention." It turned out that they had a real religion, which was monotheistic and about which no one would speak openly because it was a serious thing. They had told the missionary myths and tales about gods as real to them as the adventures of Mr. Pickwick or Sir Lancelot are to us. In justice to Jung, it should be added that in general he was personally much more cautious than his followers. For example, the following consideration of his, which those who see in the response to symbols a strong rational component can certainly share, appears as an epigraph to the collection of essays on symbolism cited above:

> If a man understands and feels that already in this life he is connected to the unbounded, his desires and his mental attitude change. In the last analysis, man's value lies in the essential, and one who misses that has wasted his life.

A Window on Fairyland

There is a novel by George MacDonald (1824–1905)[30] in which, after many adventures in Fairyland, the hero ends up in his own familiar room and thinks his voyage has come to an end; but, on opening the window, instead of the usual fields and woods, he sees again the dense, endless forest of Fairyland. We are here in a similar situation. By reducing sympathies and correspondences to communication, by establishing that meaning can be treated as an objective feature of relations between living beings, quite independently of the inner experience of man, we could

---

30. MacDonald, *Phantastes*.

hope that we had reached two goals: (a) to show that the coherence that is the Great Dance is something science can acknowledge without going out of its limits; (b) to prove that, by the same token, whatever was valid in the strange world of elementals, demons, djinns, and cosmic energies in which magic believes could find a permanent place in the ivory tower of science. The idea that man is a special animal, that there is something special in his way of knowing and feeling could thus be dispelled, and the tower of science would appear again in its majesty as containing the whole of reality. Unfortunately, in the world of man's sensible experience, certain signs and objects, both natural and manmade, influence the activity of the animal *Homo sapiens* in a very curious way: they are symbols. Within limits, they can be the object of scientific studies, but they cannot be explained without calling into play the whole combination of instincts, archetypes, automatic responses, reason, and will that is man; and even thus there remains the possibility that, in some mysterious way, they establish communication between man and a plane of existence that does not belong to sensible reality. Thus, symbols open a window in the room science has assigned to communication as an ordinary, albeit new, object of study; and that window, as the window on Fairyland, shows an unfamiliar panorama. Of course, those who believe in nothing but science could never admit that it is real; yet, there seems to be no doubt that the sense of a presence given by certain symbols is not simply a reminder, but a deep feeling, which can move a person to act in one way rather than another, and is manifest in undeniable forms such as mysticism. Symbols certainly turn on complicated psychological processes, which in some regards are similar to the effects of hallucinations; but, as we have seen in the examples of the triangle and of the candle, they only work if a man uses his reason and will — that is to say, if he is in a normal state of consciousness. It thus seems that, like it or not, certain objects cause our senses to send to our brain *in its normal state* input that is construed as the feeling that something not sensed is present. This realization raises a question: why in the world should our senses play such a trick on a sane person, if there were nothing in our psychological structure that expects a plane of reality only capable of manifesting itself to our senses by means of symbols?

Science seems to be faced here with one more question that it cannot answer, and still make sense. It makes sense even granting that there are people who seem completely impervious to the meaning of symbols. I remember the uncomfortable feeling which pervaded me and the people standing near me in a church in Montreal, when, during the Easter Eve Blessing of the Fire, a man took out his cigarette lighter and lighted our candles; he was so convinced that he was being practical that no one had the courage to refuse his help. Of course, he had missed the meaning of the whole ceremony. This episode illustrates that genuine symbols, at variance with words and ideograms (in computer language, "icons"), can only be read by somebody who has a minimum of familiarity with the formalized, logical structure to which they belong (in this case the Christian doctrine and tradition); they are not just signs representing specific concepts or sounds, nor are they just tricks to switch on unknown unconscious or subconscious responses.

Another curious memory of mine goes back to 1964 in Budapest. The lady who provided bed and breakfast for me was a middle-aged widow. In her apartment, furnished in the old Austro-Hungarian style, there were little busts of Lenin everywhere: paradoxically, the image of the man who had ordered that churches in Russia should be destroyed even if that required firing on unarmed peasants[31] was being used as a sign of his presence after death. History provides plenty of experimental support, especially in connection with the history of religion, that nature has given human beings the strange and seemingly useless tendency to respond to symbols as if they placed them in touch with another plane of reality. Even today, it can be observed that in those countries where the traditional belief in a reality beyond the reach of the senses has practically vanished, cults and practices appear which propose that same reality, often with highly perplexing aspects.

If symbols are like windows showing a possible plane of reality lying beyond the reach of our senses, then the science of communication, which is necessarily a branch of psychology as well as a branch of engineering, suggests that in some way what ordinary people call spirit should be taken into account in the search for a *Weltanschauung* or a world-view founded on science but not blindly scientistic. It seems unquestionable that only human beings, inasmuch as they are capable of conscious, associative as well as logical thought, can find a symbolic meaning in a sign or other object. This limitation is a key to the role of intelligent beings in the Great Dance; it is they who can communicate with a possible reality beyond the objects their five senses can reach.

I am speaking of a *possible* reality for the simple reason that we have no criterion as compelling as those of science to prove that it is really there. In this connection, science is like a color-blind man who is being told that there must be some visible difference between a maple leaf in summer and the same leaf at the beginning of autumn. That person could even deny that the word "visible" makes sense, for to him there is no visible difference of the kind mentioned; he could only admit that other people behave as *if* there were such a difference. Similarly, being ultimately grounded on repeatable sensible experience, science cannot

---

31. This detail was confirmed, according to a press release of the time, by a letter of Lenin's photocopied and posted in the Red Square of Moscow in the wake of the collapse of the Communist regime.

apply its methods to statements about a reality only accessible by mental contact. It can, however, find indirect evidence or at least clues to the existence of that reality; as we have tried to show, symbols provide one such clue, to be added to the ethical and existential arguments given in the preceding chapters. It is a common observation that a man who accepts the existence of the spiritual level of reality which symbols such as the triangle and the candle point to normally achieves a relation with himself and with his environment that many others are looking for in vain. This is important because it confirms that the feeling of contact with a spiritual world realized by means of symbols is by no means an artificially induced state. As medical experience shows, psychoactive drugs and related techniques can at best favor recovery of a normal nervous state if other conditions are fulfilled; continued use of such drugs may be the lesser evil in certain cases, but then such usage requires continuous medical supervision and a rather frequent change of the dosage and chemical composition of the drugs.

Toward Other Seas

It would seem that here we have reached the limits of science. Still, there is one great problem left, which scientists are trying to tackle and which is related to spirit: the question of the soul. Throughout the centuries, there has been much confusion in discussions on the soul because there are two different meanings given to that word: the principle which distinguishes a living being from nonliving things, and some immortal part of a human being. This confusion, and the hegemony of mechanism, is the reason why an old scientific analysis was until recently largely ignored. A strictly related topic is the famous and somewhat dismal mind-body problem, solved today by decreeing that "mind" means "how the brain works" — a change in word meaning which, of course, amounts to moving to a different problem. We are going to explore this whole field in the next chapter, albeit only within the scope of this book.

Chapter 12

Mind, Soul, Psyche

The complexity viewpoint allows science to understand the peculiarity of being alive. Aristotle showed that the principle of life is not a vital fluid or field, but the coordinated dynamical activity that allows a living being to retain its identity and its unitary behavior. According to Aristotle, this is what his contemporaries called the "soul" (Greek ψυχή). The ψυχή of a plant is different from that of an animal; what is specific to the soul of a human being? This question leads, among other things, to the problem of self-consciousness, a major stumbling block for most eminent brain scientists of our time.

Two Modern Myths – On Being Alive – The ψυχή as a Whole; Complexity and Unity – Downward Causation – Faculties of Plant and Animal Souls – The Soul of Man – Affections – The Mind as Intellect – Mind as Free Will – Mind as Self-Consciousness – The Mind-Body Problem – What Do We Mean by Spirit? – About Immortality

*I found my philosopher forsaking mind or any other principle of order...
[and explaining my present condition by pointing out that,] as the bones
are lifted at their joints by the contraction or relaxation of the muscles, I
am able to bend my limbs, and this is why I am sitting here in a curved
posture — that is what he would say; and he would have a similar explanation of my talking to you, which he would attribute to sound, and air,
and hearing, and he would assign ten thousand other causes of the same
sort, forgetting to mention the true cause, which is, that the Athenians have
thought it fit to condemn me, and accordingly I have thought it better and
more right to remain here and undergo my sentence; for I am inclined to
think that these muscles and bones of mine would have gone off long ago
to Megara or Boeotia — by the dog, they would, if they had been moved
only by their own idea of what was best, and if I had not chosen the better
and nobler part, instead of playing truant and running away, of enduring
any punishment which the state inflicts. There is surely a strange confusion
of causes and conditions in all this. It may be said, indeed, that without
bones and muscles and the other parts of the body I cannot execute my
purposes. But to say that I do as I do because of them, and this is the way
in which mind acts, and not from the choice of the best, is a very careless
and idle mode of speaking. I wonder that they cannot distinguish the cause
from the condition, which the many, feeling about in the dark, are always
mistaking and misnaming.*   — SOCRATES[1]

Two Modern Myths

The conclusion reached by Socrates at the end of the passage above goes
back to twenty-five centuries ago; yet it applies even more to our time,
which grants a privileged status to "how" explanations. This is why, in
this chapter, more than elsewhere in this book, we are going to challenge,
in the name and for the sake of scientific honesty, what some people
call the "myths" of the modern mind: the myth that material progress
implies moral improvement and the myth that what really exists must
be spatially separable and susceptible of study in the laboratory. Both
myths continue to receive lip service by a vast majority in Europe and
America, as they did in ancient Greece in the time of Plato, although
they are contradicted by facts. Concerning progress, suffice it to recall
that it was already discussed by Kant in 1792.[2] As my friend Matteo

---

1. Plato, *Phaedo* 98c–99b. Cf. *The Portable Plato,* trans. B. Jowett and ed. S. Buchanan
(New York: Penguin Books, 1982), 252f.

2. I. Kant, *Der Streit der Fakultaten,* Part II. In *Gesammelte Schiften* (Berlin: Preußische
Akademie der Wissenschaften, 1902–1954).

Perrini pointed out, "Kant excluded a negative view on the grounds that otherwise mankind would tend to self-destruction; two names, Auschwitz and Hiroshima, suffice to prove that he was mistaken."[3] Realizations such as computers and antibiotics are certainly a great progress in the technical means available for improving the material side of the human condition, but there are good grounds for doubting that the material improvements have had a positive effect on the intellectual and moral quality of our life.

As to the existence of things not directly accessible to our senses or experimental devices, there is a story about Sir Ernest Rutherford, the great scientist who determined the structure of the atom, telling Samuel Alexander, a distinguished philosopher who believed in a spiritual reality, that his philosophy was just hot air, because the only scientifically measurable effect of his ideas was the rise in temperature of the room where he was speaking. Among philosophers who have no direct experience of how scientists work and even among scientists for whom science is essentially laboratory work, many really think in the way attributed to Rutherford in this story. They feel they are being modern, but the words of Socrates reported in the above epigraph tell a different story; such a "modern" viewpoint already existed in ancient Greece, confirming the biblical maxim *nihil sub sole novi*, nothing is new under the sun. One could perhaps compare these individuals to people who do not notice something only because it is too familiar, for it sounds incredible that they should deny, among other things, that organization, although it cannot be isolated and submitted to scientific experiments, exists as such: if as we saw in chapters two and three, the difference between a chaotic collection of parts and an organized system of the same parts is so real that it would be impossible to understand complex systems without accepting it as a fact.

Now, today's science, it seems, has even admitted that the "soul," seen as an essential aspect of living beings, does exist, although it can neither be weighed nor observed as such by any experimental device; it is called psyche, information, personality, and what have you, but it is accepted. To show why this is so, we shall go back to the reasoning of our old acquaintance Aristotle the Stagirite, and we shall apply to the soul and the mind those ideas of his which we have already met in connection with information. We shall see how, in its long travail toward the conquest of the secrets of matter, first inanimate, and then living, science has ended up by rediscovering something that had been found and lost so radically that we do not even possess a word for it — although the translators still

3. In a note to H. Bergson, *Le due fonti della morale e della religione* (The two sources of morals and religion), annotated translation into Italian by M. Perrini (Brescia, Italy: La Scuola, 1996) of H. Bergson, *Les deux sources de la morale et de la religion* (1932) (Paris: Presses Universitaires de France, 1959).

use for it the word "soul," which in the current usage only applies, if at all, in the case of man. The reason for this avatar is to be found in the fact that the rise of mechanistic reductionism from the time of Galileo (cf. chapter nine) caused not only the marvelous progress of physics up to our time, but also, until recent advances in theoretical biology, a regress in the understanding of life. We have already seen the fundamental aspects of this rediscovery in connection with complexity, but the time has come when we must tackle directly the question of the soul.

On Being Alive

Twenty-two centuries ago, ideas on the soul were as diverse as they are today.[4] Following his special calling, Aristotle decided that he would try to settle the matter once and for all. I for one believe that he succeeded; unfortunately, as I have said already, partly because of the drift of words toward new meanings, partly because his work was classed as "metaphysics" — whereas, in all respect for metaphysics, it was a rigorous study on the foundations of biology — about nineteen centuries later the rise of mechanistic reductionism (cf. chapter nine) made thinkers of all schools happy again by stirring up a debate on the very existence of the soul. Actually, Aristotle had examined the opinions current in his time, and had concluded that what people called the "soul" could be identified as that which characterizes the "being alive" of something. He was well convinced that life is an inherent potentiality of matter, not a sort of life fluid or force keeping the "flesh" alive, as was still believed by "vitalist" scientists a few decades ago; therefore, he solved his problem by introducing notions that were rediscovered by the mathematician Norbert Wiener about 1942 and made into a general theory by Bertalanffy and others (cf. chapter two).

In substance, Aristotle said to himself:

> Suppose one could keep the organs of a body in operation without allowing them to cooperate with one another; then one would have a body perfectly capable of living but not alive: a potentiality without an actuality. What would be missing? Not, perhaps, something more fundamental but not essentially different from what distinguishes an animal in full activity from an animal in irreversible coma?[5]

That is it, he said: what is missing is the characteristic organized and finalized activity of a living being — roughly speaking, the functioning of

4. Cf., e.g., Plato's *Phaedo*, *The Portable Plato*.
5. This is a paraphrase of a much more concise formulation quoted in a subsequent section.

the biological machinery as a unit oriented toward certain ends (survival, reproduction, etc.). If the heart does not pump the blood to the other organs, if the lungs do not inhale and exhale to change venous into arterial blood, if the kidneys do not purify the blood, if the nervous system does not transmit external stimuli to the brain, if the brain does not analyze external stimuli and make the body respond to them, and so on, and if all this does not take place in perfect coherence and so as to realize certain primary ends, then there is no life.

We shall review all this in more detail in the following sections. Here, let us point out that, despite the bad reputation his late followers of the sixteenth and seventeenth century gave him — and despite his limited interest in mechanics — Aristotle had discovered what is nowadays seen as the way out of the dilemma between mechanism and vitalism, i.e., between the view that life is nothing but the chemistry in the body and the view that there is a special undetectable substance that keeps the organs together and makes them collaborate, so that the body behaves as a whole performing specific functions and pursuing certain aims. The name given to the new view is "organismic" or, more appropriately, "integrationistic" biology. We already know, particularly from chapters two, three, and six, that the theoretical foundations of this view are to be found in the complexity-level description of sensible reality.

In one respect Aristotle's definition may sound strange, namely in the use of the Greek word ψυχή (pr. psewkhay; Latin *anima*) to denote what distinguishes being alive from not being alive. The reason is that, although words such as "animate" and "inanimate" correspond even today to that sense of the term "soul," in the popular usage of our times that same term refers to a specific aspect of man. Unless you are an animalist, you will find it curious if somebody spoke of the soul of a horse or of a spider, while Aristotle would have done so without hesitation; he concluded from a detailed analysis of the matter that the soul of the living being that is man should be viewed as a highly sophisticated version of something basically present also in a plant or a beast. The distinction between a "rational" soul like ours and a purely "sentient soul," like that of a frog, or a pure "vegetative soul," like that of a beech, is based on the "faculties" or natural powers of the being in question. If one ignores the limitations in this connection, as some North American Indians would do, then one may well believe, for example, that trees have a human-like soul, and, to overcome the inevitable inconsistencies, one may go as far as claiming that there are spirits in them, which can think and love. That is true in Fairyland, but the same feeling comes naturally to anybody in certain environments. I, for one, realized this on a small farm near Orvieto, the Italian town where Luca Signorelli painted his wonderful angels playing citterns, lutes, and violas in Heaven. On that farm, a great walnut tree stands isolated twenty feet above the sparse olive trees growing on the same land. It disdains care or attention; it always looks the same, indifferent to summer and winter, to stormy and clear skies; but in October it is full of walnuts. You might well think that it is not just a tree, but an alien being, living its own mysterious life for its own purposes, not communicating with you because it has nothing to share with you. No wonder that people could be tempted to make a minor god of such a tree. But, although it has a soul in Aristotle's sense, for all science can tell it is we who attribute to it faculties like our own or higher.

To keep track of the fact that we are speaking of all that goes with being alive, and not in particular the soul of man, let us agree that we shall use directly the Greek word ψυχή or "soul" between double quotation marks so that no confusion is possible. Even the English term "psyche" may cause confusion because, in the current acceptation (cf. chapter nine), one would not attribute a psyche, but at best a "psychism," to a bacterium or to an ant, whereas such creatures certainly have a ψυχή.

As we have seen, the ψυχή is a characteristic of a living being which results or, as one says today, "emerges" from its body. How then can we speak of it and even envisage a special study of it, without breaking it apart into a set of physiological processes, *viz.* those bodily processes which result in its operations? Why can we say that knowledge of all the possible neurophysiological processes is not equivalent to knowledge of the ψυχή? We already know Aristotle's answer. He wrote textually:

> The ψυχή is the first level of operation of a natural body having life potentially in it. The body so described is a body formed by organs.... If we have to give a general formula applicable to all kinds of ψυχή, we must describe it as the first level of operation of a natural organized body.[6]

Even modernized, this is a difficult text. For one thing, the philosophers who follow Aristotle and Aquinas might object to the word "operation" as used here because, when they speak of things like "the operations of the soul," they mean something different. But one should keep in mind

6. Aristotle *De Anima*, II, 412a. The classical English translation by J. A. Smith is given in Aristotle, *The Complete Works*, ed. J. Barnes (Princeton N. J.: Princeton/Bollingen, 1984). In it, Smith interpreted this passage as: "the soul is the first grade of actuality of a natural body having life potentially in it. The body so described is a body which is organized.... If we have to give a general formula applicable to all kinds of soul, we must describe it as the first grade of actuality of a natural organized body." The main difference with our rendering comes from the Greek word *entelecheia*, translated as "actualization" by J. A. Smith. It appears to mean here "the condition of a being or self-regulated control system actually operating as such," or, in general, the realization of one or all potentialities of a being or system. The word "activity" used by other translators is better in certain contexts. A specialist's discussion can be found in F. A. Trendelenburg, *Aristotelis de anima libri tres* (Graz: Akad. Druck- u. Verlagsanstalt, 1957), 242–244.

that, (a) the two senses of the word are easily distinguished if their context is taken into account, and (b) words slowly change their meanings with time, and no one can stop time. At any rate, as already pointed out, it seems clear that Aristotle had realized something that has been rediscovered only recently with the advent of integrationistic biology: a living being is a functioning open, self-regulated control system, and there must be something in it that distinguishes it from the same system when it is just a collection of parts having the same order and connections, but incapable of affecting one another. Let us try to see what this means by means of a familiar analogy.

Consider a TV set. When it is not connected to a source of electricity, its parts are exactly the same as when it is plugged in, but they do not and *cannot* perform any function; the set is as dead. No action except connecting it to a power source will result in a significant response. When it is plugged in, it can have two states: the stand-by state and the fully working state. In the stand-by state, the set is not producing images, but is sensitive to outside signals (e.g., those of the remote control), which as it were arouse it from its slumber. This analogy, with the obvious limitations of all analogies, can be used to get a better insight into the nature of the ψυχή provided an essential point regarding electronic circuits, especially solid-state ones, is kept in mind. The point in question is that connection to a power source is required not only to "feed" energy to the TV set, but to bring each component to a state in which it can operate and cooperate with the others in the correct way; it is this feature, not the energy consumption (which is the analog of metabolism in a living being), that interests us here. With this essential point in mind we can say that

1. when it is not connected to a power source, what we call a TV set is really nothing but a collection of connected electronic parts, for TV signals mean nothing to it: this is an analogy for what Aristotle calls a body with operational organs and hence capable of life, but not having life in it;

2. when it is connected to a power source, it becomes capable of receiving TV signals and performing other functions. However, it can have two states:

   a. one in which activity remains at a minimum level, waiting for the internal clock or an external command to set up the fully working state: this is an analogy for a living being in reversible coma or just at sleep;

   b. one in which it is working normally: this is an analogy for a living being awake and in full activity.

The example of the TV set (which could be made more effective by referring to more sophisticated devices, such as certain space probes) shows that there is something that can make a compound of parts of that kind (and *a fortiori* a "body complete with its organs, but capable of life and not alive") into a system capable of a coordinated activity, essentially consisting of receiving, processing, and sending signals of various kinds — e.g., images in the case of a TV set, words in the case of a human being.

The something in question, as we saw in chapter two, is "organization." Since this term is used in a somewhat ambiguous way (it often stands for "ordered structure"), it may be useful to remind the reader that in this book it is used only with the following meaning: Organization is an "organized and finalized dynamical activity resulting in unitary behavior," i.e., an active coordination of parts in view of the performance of some function or the obtention of some result.

The relation between the parts of a TV set that is established when it is connected to the power source, i.e., when it really becomes a TV receiver, is precisely of this nature. In this connection, it is important that a TV set is a different sort of machine from an automobile engine. Truly enough, there is some similarity: when not in operation, the engine is but a dead collection of pieces, albeit connected in a definite order, without which the engine would not work; whereas, if it is connected to the gasoline tank, an initial impulse is sufficient to initiate a regular activity, which only an external intervention can modify. That kind of activity is what laymen think of when they hear comparisons of living beings with machines. Actually, the TV set — not to mention more sophisticated artifacts — is essentially different from an engine in at least two respects: firstly, the parts of a disconnected TV set do not have the properties they have when the set is in operation, for they become active only when electric currents flow through them, and the behavior of each of them depends on the behavior of the others; secondly, the whole system is so designed that, out of the enormous number of signals arriving to the antenna, it detects those which it is designed to process; it changes "spontaneously" its performance depending on their fluctuations in frequency, intensity, and noise; it adjusts "spontaneously" to the external temperature and other conditions affecting the behavior of its parts by compensatory mechanisms, having the same function as, say, sweating in human beings.

Contrary to what people unfamiliar with modern technology might fear (or hope), the analogy just presented does not prove in any sense that living beings are equivalent to complicated electronic devices; suffice it to think of the enormous difficulties encountered after more than two decades of attempts to model cognition and consciousness by computer programs and/or ad hoc electronic devices. Indeed, this chapter, despite its reference to Aristotle, contains ideas that are only now attracting the attention of researchers in the field often called "mind science."[7]

The ψυχή as a Whole; Complexity and Unity

In this section we have to face again mechanistic reductionism. We have already recalled that, because of the great advances in knowledge resulting from the combination of Democritus's atomistic view and the replacement of the question "why?" by the question "how?", that approach to understanding reality reigned almost unchallenged from the seventeenth century to the second half of the twentieth century. If you read again Mersenne's passage quoted in chapter nine, you will realize that mechanism did away with the unifying principle that is the ψυχή, and that was only possible because in Mersenne's time the very notion of a self-regulated control system was unthinkable. More generally, as we have seen, particularly in chapter nine, mechanistic "nothingbuttery" — the claim that complex systems are nothing but their parts — is untenable, for it ignores all the advances of science that have given rise to the problem of complexity; but we have also seen that it would be superficial to reject the mechanistic explanation of phenomena just because it is radicalized by the reductionists. Today's scientists still tend to explain observed phenomena according to the mechanistic paradigm, which is the correct approach in most scientific disciplines, but they are gradually realizing that one way or the other the unity of a complex whole should also be accounted for. That is to say, two equally correct approaches to reality, the holistic and the mechanistic, should be reconciled. That can be done in general through the notion of complexity level.

Now, as we have already mentioned, the word "organization" conveys the image of coordinated and interacting parts all working coherently toward a specific end — say, self-preservation, propagation of the species, etc. In living beings (and to some extent in such machines as TV sets and computers), the attainment of that end is the result of elementary processes at a variety of levels, forming a sort of hierarchic scale. In living beings, there are a number of levels, for example:

1. the level that takes atoms as the ultimate building blocks of matter and at which the transmission of biological signals of all kinds appears as an extremely intricate set of interdependent physicochemical processes:[8]

7. Cf. the articles by F. M. Wuketits, H. Atlan, G. Longo, A. Carsetti, and myself in *La Nuova Critica* (Rome) 29 and 30 (1997); Stuart Sutherland's book review "Mind Traps," *Nature* 384 (1996): 228, and reviews of other books on the mind in the same journal.

8. The term "signal" is used here in the broad sense discussed in chapter eleven, and applies not only to nervous signals, but to processes such as the transport of glucose to the cells.

2. the level at which the "reference objects" are the enzymes and other biomacromolecules;

3. the level where the simplest units introduced to explain facts are the cells;

4. the level at which tissues and organs are the ultimate parts to be considered;

5. the level at which the organized system of the organs is studied independently of its material substrate.

The various descriptions are not alternative, but they refer to different aspects of the reality of the same object: in each level the properties associated with lower levels are implicit, those associated with higher levels are latent or indeterminate. Rather complicated objects of study may even be given different names depending on the complexity level at which they are examined — as when a doctor calls someone a patient and not a person — but in principle knowledge of all the levels is indispensable for complete knowledge of that object.

In the complexity-level approach, a fundamental characteristic of a living being is that, at the topmost level, it appears as an entity endowed with properties and capable of an activity that cannot be attributed to individual "components" or organs, nor to specific physiological processes. We can thus think of the ψυχή or "soul" in a genuinely holistic way as *the given being as characterized by the properties that emerge from the level at which neurophysiology works*. It is a new object of study, because its properties cannot be reduced to processes in the nervous system. It can be divided into parts (which of course are not material) and it is a system capable of many states, more precisely *states of consciousness*.[9] It is because of these features that psychology and psychiatry are genuine scientific disciplines.

Of course, the living being which we look at as a "psyche" also possesses a material substrate, and therefore the ordinary properties of a physical object: its weight, for example, is a physical property that can affect its behavior because of emotional reactions, say, to a fall, but can be treated as an external cause of the responses it causes. Therefore, it would seem legitimate to consider a living being as a composite reality, the ψυχή, which is what that being appears to be at the topmost level of complexity, and a material part, which we may call the body. This is an attractive way of looking at the body as distinct from the ψυχή, but the frontier between the two remains to be established. For example: are the basic instincts common to human beings and beasts to be attributed to the "body" or to the ψυχή? Taking into account modern

9. Cf., e.g., C. T. Tart, *States of Consciousness* (New York: Dutton, 1975).

views about information and steady-state systems out of equilibrium (cf. chapter two), we should expect that the answer will be found in the following equivalent definitions:

ψυχή = organized and finalized activity, which makes an ordered collection of parts into a living being;

ψυχή = finalized and organized information processing, which controls the continuous exchange of matter, energy, and information by which the steady-state system that is a living being maintains its identity in a changing environment.

With these definitions all that is typical of a living being as such — i.e., as a whole capable of activity and communication with its environment — belongs to the ψυχή: the body is just the collection of anonymous parts which support the show, as do the individual solid-state elements of a computer. According to this view, the most elementary instincts, since they vanish if life disappears, are properties of any "soul," just as ability to appreciate beauty and truth is a property of the human soul.

The conclusions reached so far can be summarized as follows: The ψυχή or soul is the dynamical organization of a living organism inasmuch as it is responsible for its being alive and for its behaving as a whole. In terms of the ladder of complexity levels it is what the being itself appears to be at the complexity level at which it behaves as a unitary whole. With reference to that complexity level, the ψυχή can be treated as an entity independently of its material support or "hardware," as is done in psychological studies. That may be sufficient for many purposes, but it should not be forgotten that an exhaustive comprehension of the ψυχή of a living being cannot dispense with properties associated with lower complexity levels, that is to say, the full reality of the whole living being to which it belongs.

It is important to recall that an entity can be treated as a separate object without implying that it is physically "separable." The ψυχή as defined here would have the same mode of existence as the personality of a human being. The difficulty we have in accepting its form of existence is due to the fact that scientism has accustomed us to believe that "existence" is the same as "observability by scientific methods as a separate object." We have already seen that this is not in agreement with current scientific as well as philosophical usage. The "physical separability" criterion would lead to the conclusion that neither the electric charge nor the structure of a molecule exist, and thus entire chapters of science would be devoted to things which do not exist. The fact is that there are different manners of existence; the manner of existence of the ψυχή (or the psyche, for that matter) is that of an object that exists on its own but cannot be isolated because it needs a support. A familiar example is a computer program; an even more obvious example is the shape of an object, which is independent of the nature of the material, but cannot be separated from it. This applies to the ψυχή such as has been defined above. Aristotle himself was explicit on this, and also pointed out its implications:

> From this it indubitably follows that the soul is inseparable from its body, or at any rate certain parts of it are (if it has parts), for the *actuality* of some of them is nothing but the actualities of their bodily parts. Yet, some may be separable because they are not the actuality of any body at all.[10]

In conclusion, we are justified in speaking of the "soul" as if it were separate from its neurophysiological substrate, as psychologists usually do for the psyche, without any contradiction with the claim that it results (or emerges) from processes taking place in the body as long as they form an organized whole. That, says Aristotle, is only contradictory for the parts of the ψυχή that perform operations which cannot possibly be viewed as the result of combined neurophysiological processes. The brain scientists and the artificial intelligence specialists of our time have had to face a difficulty of this kind in connection with self-consciousness.

Downward Causation

The organized activity that is the ψυχή has active and passive properties of its own. They are the result of combined processes at lower complexity levels, but they cannot be assigned to any single process or group of processes. We shall now examine them, and thus climb the ladder that will take us from the simple "soul" of a bacterium *E. coli* to the soul of a human being. As a premise we must consider a new type of process, which takes place between complexity levels: *downward causation*.

This expression can be found in a very interesting article by a distinguished Hungarian neurophysiologist.[11] It refers to a curious question, which, though particularly important in the case of *Homo sapiens*, applies to all living beings. Consider that disagreeable aspect of country walks, when you are suddenly roused from your daydreams full of peace and tranquility by the furious barking of an Alsatian dog, which, after waiting in silence until you were very close, now bursts into its noisiest performance. If you were an ideal scientist, you would not feel disturbed or afraid, but you would ask yourself the question: by what mechanism — i.e., by what cause-effect chain — has my passing by produced such an

---

10. *Op. cit.*, ch. 2, 12. J. A. Smith's translation.
11. J. Szentágothai, "Downward Causation?" *Annual Review of Neuroscience* 7 (1984): 1–11.

angry reaction in this dog, which appears to believe that a good bite in my leg is its most urgent duty? Your immediate tentative answer would certainly be: it is barking because it is defending its territory. But then you would decide that you have to examine the details, and you might be tempted to apply Mersenne's reasoning (chapter nine); the nose of the dog was exposed to an unfamiliar smell and its eyes perceived that the source of the smell was approaching; then the dog automatically started barking because that is what dogs do in such circumstances. But neither smell nor sight as such can activate the vocal cords of any animal. To make a long story short, you would have to admit that a central processor interpreted the signals coming from the senses, decided that, taken together, they belonged to the category of messages meaning "attempt to enter my territory under way," and caused the larynx to produce a sound. Let us assume that this analysis is correct. Then, there is not one, but *two* causal chains: one from the outer world to the brain, the other from the brain to the vocal cords. There is no direct connection between the two steps because the brain could have found that the smell was known, and then it would not have activated the barking mechanism. There has been a "decision," albeit instinctive; and the cause of the barking is precisely that decision. This is what may be called "downward causation." In humans, this kind of process is even more evident because the decision may be the result of an idea or a memory, and therefore the downward process will not be related in any way to stimuli immediately preceding it. It is from this consideration that the possibility of hypnosis or of a pure spirit acting on our psyche should be investigated.

Faculties of Plant and Animal Souls

We cannot say that there is life if there is no nutrition, no sensibility. Therefore, inasmuch as the entire life activity of a living being resides in its ψυχή, it is to the latter that the behavior schemes, both potential and actual, associated with feeding, reproduction, sensibility, etc. should be attributed. We may call "faculties" these and other natural powers of the ψυχή. Aristotle assigns to the ψυχή of all living beings a nutritive power or faculty, which includes growth and reproduction; then he lists the appetitive, the sensory, the locomotive, and the thinking powers. The difference between a plant, an animal, and a human being should be looked for in the number and quality of the faculties of their respective types of ψυχή. One could attribute to microorganisms and to plants a life that is essentially limited to nutrition, growth, and reproduction, with a low sensibility not associated with specific sense organs; the corresponding ψυχή might be called a "vegetative soul." The "souls" of macroscopic animals appear to have, in addition to the nutritive faculty, the ability to detect and process signals from the environment in the form of messages arriving through the sense organs; theirs might therefore be called "sentient souls,' meaning by that a ψυχή endowed with the power to *perceive*. Finally, the ψυχή of human beings has all the faculties of other animals, plus the ability to think; it is a "rational soul." It is in this case that it is a *soul* in the current sense.

The above is Aristotle's scheme. His discussion is extremely instructive. To be sure, a number of essential details should be updated; yet his knowledge of certain aspects of animal biology is surprisingly advanced, for example concerning the question of imagination in beasts, and, if one takes into account the use of words which nowadays have a more limited meaning (e.g., "touch"), then one sees that his ignorance of the microscopic world and of chemistry was less of a hindrance than could be expected. What makes his whole approach difficult for us, educated in a world where technology pervades all aspects of life, is that our way of formulating problems is entirely different from his. As previously mentioned, the faculties of the "soul" are proposed by Aristotle as the sources of the different patterns of behavior of living beings. We modern people can hardly understand why one should waste time on that problem, and we feel that the answer would have taught us nothing significant; what seems significant to us is rather the answer to the question: how does nature ensure that such a behavior pattern be realized?

This strange contrast can only be explained by looking at history. We briefly reviewed in chapter nine the history of mechanism, and pointed out that it degenerated into mechanistic reductionism, and as such should be disposed of, whereas genuine mechanism remains a fundamental tool of science. We also pointed out that the general approach to science current in Mersenne's time always chose first the "what-it-is?" approach to things. This priority was taken for granted, and the refusal of certain misuses and abuses it led to, even Mersenne's refusal of the existence of a ψυχή in animals, was always intended as a correction to it. Later, the success of mechanism and, still later, the abolition of philosophy as part of basic education led to the disappearance of the habit of beginning a study by giving definitions; indeed, certain popular philosophers of science — perhaps rather as a concession to their readers than because of a deep conviction — declared that one should never ask "what-is-it?" of anything. Thus, the general culture became one where only "how" explanations were considered satisfactory.

Yet, people have not really changed. The other day, in a TV movie for children, I heard a boy saying to a classmate, "You can write a report on that because of your superior intelligence." That boy was thinking in the what-is-it mode, and was presenting a faculty of his friend as the "cause" of something. Another typical expression is "my body"; its very use shows that, despite the discussions of scientists and philosophers, the same human beings who were brought up so that they would only accept "how" explanations are convinced that they are not just their bodies or, indeed, a collection of their bodily processes.

The way out of this *aporia* is one we already know: the complexity approach to reality, presented mainly in chapters two and three and above. The gist of the story is that the "what" explanation of the properties of a living being applies to the complexity level at which that being manifests all the properties it has as a result of being a unitary whole; whereas a "how" explanation applies at the complexity level of organs or even of enzymes, because at that level we have to deal with material components of the being under consideration and a mechanistic scheme applies. A "how" explanation usually corresponds to what one expects as an answer to the question "why?" in ordinary life; which is why it is accepted as satisfactory even when it is but a vague conjecture, as when you are told (hopefully as a joke) that the intelligence of a person is due to having eaten a lot of fish as a child. Consider how many times we answer the "why" questions of our children by telling them "how" a mysterious fact follows from an obvious one by a cause-effect chain. That does not mean that we do not think at higher complexity levels: not only do we use, as recalled above, expressions like "my body," but we currently say things like "I am tired," "you are walking," "she is writing"; and "do not disturb him because he is trying to think." In such expressions you might replace the personal pronoun by "body" or "mind"; but the meaning would be subtly changed: if you say "my body is tired" something else is expected in opposition to body; if you say "her hand is writing," you are clearly thinking of "writing" as a mere mechanical action, whereas in "she is writing" you also refer to the thinking which goes with it.

To sum up, we can say that it is correct to treat the ψυχή as the entity that possesses all the natural powers of the whole, and therefore determines the identity of a living being. Since the ψυχή results from physicochemical processes taking place in the body, one can say that it "emerges" from them; but, with an apparent paradox, one can also say that those processes are the "tools" or "computer hardware" by which the ψυχή operates. That paradox is resolved by consideration of "downward causation": once the ψυχή has emerged, it takes the lead and controls both the input and the output flow of information, matter, and energy that is the given being's life. At first sight, this might seem in contradiction with the "emergence" idea because the latter implies that the processes in question spontaneously form a coordinated network. But the facts are not so simple: even admitting, as we have done in chapter six, that there is a measure of spontaneous organization, then (according to current theories of the spontaneous origin of life) that embryonic organization would itself control further increases in organization, so that in fact it would use as tools certain physicochemical processes.

Thus, the "soul" in the Stagirite's sense is at the same time the product and the controller of bodily processes. There remains one source of perplexity: if there were operations of the ψυχή which did not depend on physicochemical processes, then how could they emerge from them or control them? This difficulty might be real in human beings, and then once again there might appear an intimation that man's reality partakes of something that is not matter as known by science.

The Soul of Man

When we come to man we need no more the precautions which have suggested use of the Greek word ψυχή. The term "soul" can be used without too great a risk of confusion, although we still give it a much more general import and significance than either "psyche" or "spirit." The soul of man takes special names depending on the perspective under which it is considered. The most important one is, of course, "consciousness." Under that name, as we have said, modern psychologists attribute to it "states" that are similar to those of control systems endowed with homeostasis. We shall examine the faculties of the human soul with reference to the question: "What can the soul do that the isolated organs, including the brain, cannot do?" In the language of complexity levels, this question becomes: "What properties of man belong to the complexity level at which the reference objects are the parts of the soul — memory, intellect, imagination, the subconscious, and so on?" We shall confine our attention to four fundamental faculties, possibly present to a greater or lesser extent in animals, but certainly particularly developed in human beings:

- affections;
- intelligence;
- will;
- self-consciousness.

Affections

Man's affections have their counterparts in the "souls" of beasts. No one would deny that maternal, paternal, and even conjugal love are basically instincts causing patterns of behavior that serve biological purposes in animals of the species *Homo sapiens*. In chapter eight we showed that science has much to say in this connection, provided it avoids temptations of monopoly. However, already in this connection there appears a characteristic of the human soul totally foreign to science, which we had occasion to mention in chapter eleven in connection with the symbol of the divided triangle: it is the ability to accept that certain affections become ideals. While I am writing this chapter, the last echoes of the solemn state funeral held in India for Mother Teresa of Calcutta are slowly fading away. That a great nation where Christianity is next to unknown and where, for a variety of reasons, little importance is attached to the sufferings of human beings, should have treated as a national hero a foreign Catholic nun who had done nothing to raise its reputation or its power or its gross national product, who in fact had confined her work and that of her companions to helping rejected and useless human beings, is ample experimental proof that the simple "new" commandment "love one another as I loved you"[12] is something which speaks to the soul of every man and woman, even though science has no explanation for its extension to pariahs dying on the side of a street.

The mind comes into play here, because the exercise of sublimated love, probably at variance with instinctual love, is not the result of a subconscious drive, but the deliberate identification of a stranger with a member of one's family; therefore, *ceteris paribus*, it demands intelligence, and intelligence of a special kind. Yet, it cannot be reduced to that. As far as the intention goes, it may partake of the will rather than of the intellect; moreover, its perfect consonance with the nature of man is rooted in our basic social instincts.[13]

Similar considerations apply to those extensions of love which are the wonder and curiosity the universe arouses in us and the spontaneous tendency of most people toward adoration for a supreme Author. They have been the driving forces behind some of the greatest realizations of man, and yet they could be traced back to tracts which we share with apes, for instance; in particular to a merely instinctive curiosity that is probably related to our belonging to a species highly versatile in finding solutions to survival problems. Thus, the "animality" of man is present in our souls as the very source of our spirituality, and that stands in favor of the inseparability of spirit and flesh in man.

The Mind as Intellect

Intelligence, will, and self-consciousness are usually assigned to that part of the soul which is called "mind." A number of thinkers identify it with the intellect, the Greek νοῦς (nous). Within that view, we can give it the following tentative definition: The word "mind" designates an immaterial object, which behaves as a system performing the functions which constitute the capacity, such as is found in human beings,

12. John 13:34.
13. A great novelist's perception of this is the leitmotif of H. Hesse's *Glasperlenspiel* (1943), Eng. trans., *The Glass Bead Game* (London: Cape, 1970).

i. to process information and organize it at a variety of levels of complexity;

ii. to integrate the result of (i) in the information previously received and already processed, with account of the actual state of the mind itself;

iii. to use (or "read") it in order to

- define actions to be carried out in the outer world with specific aims;

- detect implications and correlations, and consequently establish necessary revisions of the information already stored in the memory;

iv. reorganize already stored information accordingly.

This definition is in many ways more restrictive than others,[14] also often used, but we shall stick to it because it helps to pinpoint what we are going to consider in this section, the "intellect." Aristotle recognized two different parts of the mind as intellect:[15]

Since in every class of things, as in nature as a whole, we find two factors involved, (i), a matter which is potentially all the particulars included in the class, (ii), a cause which is productive in the sense that it makes them all (the latter standing to the former as, say, a technological process to the materials used), these distinct elements must likewise be found within the soul.

And in fact mind as we have described it is what it is by virtue of becoming all things, while there is another which is what it is by virtue of making all things; this is a sort of positive state like light; for in a sense light makes potential colors into actual colors.

Mind in this sense is separable, impassible, unmixed, since it is in its essential nature activity [ἐνέργεια] (for always the active is superior to the passive factor, the originating force to the matter which it forms).[16]

The gist of Aristotle's argument seems to be as follows. The mind automatically processes information from the outside world and arrives at constructs isomorphic with outside objects, i.e., "faithful" images of the

14. It was elaborated by a small study committee of scientists and philosophers who met in Naples, Italy, in 1990, in a study published as *Il rapporto di Napoli sul problema mente-corpo* (The Naples report on the mind-body problem) (Naples: IPE, 1991).

15. The parts in question, just like Freud's conscious and subconscious, are not necessarily separated or separable in space-time.

16. Aristotle, *De Anima* II (Γ, 5, tr. J. A. Smith). We have replaced the term "art" by the more familiar "technology."

sources of the information received; then it classifies them, and, what is
more, creates new concepts and derives suitable classification and correlation rules. Yet, this would not be knowledge if there were not in the
mind the ability to *realize* that it is in possession of information about
something. The active intellect is what does the realizing, and thus is
essentially consciousness. That it should be a part of the soul and have
a nature different from that of other parts — i.e., not emerging from
the body as an aspect of its dynamical organization — is suggested by
the analogy with light, but it is not clear whether or not it is logically
consistent with the rest of Aristotle's whole picture.

We shall have to come back to this question after dwelling on the two
other aspects of the mind, free will and self-consciousness. For the time
being, let us retain at least the consideration that the final stage of the
process by which the mind knows is, so to speak, the conscious identification and storage in the memory of a thing such as it becomes in a person's
inner world: a realization which is also a judgment. In today's language it
might be called the attribution of meaning. Here too, however, we must
distinguish: as seen in chapter eleven, meaning can be given a purely
operational definition, as the value (e.g., food-value) on which even a
unicellular animal bases its behavior, or it can be placed in relation to
the inner world of man. In either case it retains its role of making choices
possible in the presence of multiple possibilities; but, at variance with
behavior, the inner experience of man is only conditionally observable —
i.e., observable inasmuch as the reports of individuals about themselves
are accepted as objective — and that opens up a particular field of inquiry
within psychology.

Mind as Free Will

Will as a general notion could be assigned to some "appetitive" part
of the ψυχή of man, shared with all other living beings, but free will —
which, as we saw in chapter eight, is related to the special role the human
species appears to play in the universe — has a very special nature because
the "decision center" of each man cannot operate without the control
of the intellect; indeed, a really free decision is something that must be
preceded by a deliberation.

Donald M. MacKay, the already cited neurophysiologist, beautifully
analyzed the free-will problem in 1965:

> As human beings, our first datum is that we have a range of expe-
> rience which shades from "undergoing" or "suffering" to "doing."
> Some things happen *to* us; others, we bring about. In the domain of
> thought, the same gradation holds. Sometimes an idea "just strikes
> us"; but often we face an option and must decide it soberly by de-

liberate mental effort.... [A responsible act] can be distinguished from what may be termed "following through" — as for example in walking, where each leg movement may be almost unconscious, though the decision to walk was voluntary, and we call walking voluntary activity.[17]

Having stated this factual starting point, MacKay goes on to pinpoint the place of disagreement:

Our question, as Prof. Eccles has put it, is not, can we believe in our freedom on the basis of what we know in physiology, but quite the other way round: Do these facts of our experience create an embarrassment for theoretical physiology? Take first "having-an-idea" or "getting-an-inspiration." Here the element of control is minimal. Inspiration is something that "happens" to me. No embarrassment here for physiology, because we have no evidence in this experience to contradict the suggestion that what happened to us had a physical cause. For all we know the cause might sometimes be the kind of indeterminate chain of events to which Prof. Eccles alluded in his Waynflete lectures, with a Heisenberg indeterminate happening as their origin....

Facing an option, on the other hand, we have to *do* something. We may try to decide by mentally or physically tossing a coin. In that case I suggest that our experience partakes as much of "undergoing" as of doing, but it is just on the borderline. Here again, we have no grounds in our human experience to worry us as physiologists, because nothing in our experience of a mental toss-up says anything either way as to whether or not the outcome had a physical cause. It is merely something that happened to us, whose form we did not determine in any deliberate fashion.

Finally, MacKay goes over to the domain of free and responsible choice.

Here there might be an objection to our mechanistic physiology that we are neglecting; because when we take a deliberate step, one of our data is that *we face an option:* more than one possibility is open to us. We must therefore make sure that our physiological way of thinking does not deny the reality of this fact.

This lucid presentation shows that, even if computer science and cognitive science could one day demonstrate that a purely physical mechanism exists for self-consciousness, the problem of free will might turn out to

17. D. M. MacKay, *Semaine d'Étude sur Cerveau et Expérience consciente* (Study week on the brain and conscious experience) (Vatican City: Pontifical Academy of Sciences, 1965), 858–59. As to Prof. Eccles, mentioned by MacKay, *v. infra.*

be a much more difficult one. We may well believe, following Aristotle's main line of thought, that *also self-consciousness and free will are faces of the unitary reality of the "organized body,"* and therefore, in accordance with the approach of modern science, we may try to find the mechanisms by which they are realized; but the fact of our inner experience escapes by its very nature a scientific treatment. By the same token, I am afraid, it also escapes a strictly rational philosophical analysis, and remains a collection of facts on which an existential discourse, rather than a strictly philosophical one, should be built.

The problem of downward causation arises again in this connection. If the mind is an independent immaterial entity, how can it act on material processes? And, if it is a part of the soul, and the soul is an entity resulting from coordinated physicochemical processes, how can it act at the material level of enzymes and electrochemical potentials? The answer is not easy, because so far the biologists, the physicists, and the chemists have not paid much attention to the problems raised by the neurophysiologists. We have mentioned above one unquestionable fact: organization presupposes the possibility of control of the parts by the whole, which is but a compact way of saying that each part is controlled by all the others such as they are when they are engaged in organized activity. In a computer, this result could be realized because a central processor combines the input data, searches the memory for stored information connected with the input, evaluates the whole, and sends messages to the peripherals. As to humans, we know very little about the brain, which might be the central processor at the direct-access level, but we could accept the analogy with a computer as long as "evaluation" is treated as something automatic. But if there is free will, the preliminary processing of input and stored data is decoupled from the output, because the order "act in this way" must come from an evaluation center (e.g., the conscience), which might be open to inspirations, ideals, moral rules. One might push the computer analogy even that far, assuming that inspirations, ideals, moral rules can be taken into account by the central processor; but the often dramatic difference between what is done and what ought to be done is enough to show that a core of mystery would remain anyway.

Mind as Self-Consciousness

The analogy between knowing by the mind and light illuminating colored objects applies particularly to self-consciousness — the mind knowing itself — and to the related notion of conscience, which can be likened to knowing one's own image in a mirror.[18] The much criticized *cogito ergo*

18. Karol Wojtyla, "The Acting Person," in *Analecta Husserliana X* (Dordrecht: Reidel, 1979), 35–47.

sum of Descartes actually took self-consciousness as the basic certainty on which a world-view can be built: I know that I exist because I know that I think.

Unfortunately, the analogy between the active intellect and light leads to the question: "where does that light come from?" An attempt to answer it is both illuminating and a source of great uncertainty. In the course of history different answers have been proposed, from Averroës to Aquinas and to Leibniz. Aristotle makes the strange remark that the active intellect must be in nature different from the passive ("potential") one, for it cannot *become*, nor does it involve any operation of the brain. Therefore, he argues, it cannot be subject to decay, nor can it be thought to emerge as a property of a material whole.

The question of the nature of the self sounds like one of those problems debated by intellectuals in smoking rooms after dinner. That is a mistaken impression: just rephrase it as "what is man?" and you will see that it is the fundamental existential problem of all human beings, from people dying amidst general indifference (as travelers report) on the streets of certain cities in Asia to the young people spending their time at endless computer games in homes across America and Europe. Therefore, the patience which may be required to examine the question of the self is likely to be rewarded by a better understanding of what man is, even though, let me say it immediately, we are likely to end up with the conclusion that, as far as science goes, we are facing here another mystery — the mystery debated under the name of "mind-body" (or "mind-brain") problem.

The Mind-Body Problem

That the human being can be conceived as composed of two separate entities, one physical and one spiritual, was a thesis advocated around 400 B.C. by Plato in Europe and by the Hindu religion in Asia. Aristotle, a disciple of Plato, did not accept his master's dualism but had problems with the active intellect anyway. In the seventeenth century Descartes (and his friend Father Mersenne) proposed again that the mind is entirely distinct from the body, the latter being but a mechanical device (cf. chapter nine). One might say that in Mersenne's time people had lost sight of how complicated the organization of a living being is; but that same idea still appeals to the scientists of our time, particularly brain scientists, who are well aware of the existence of organization. A case in point is the eminent brain scientist John C. Eccles (1902–1997), a Nobel laureate for medicine, who adopted, under the name of "interactionism," precisely the belief that in man there is a separate entity, to be identified with the mind or, better, the self, i.e., whatever in a human being makes it possible for him or her to utter the word "I."[19]

This difficulty is paradoxically echoed by R. Hofstadter, an author whose analysis of thought processes in the brain, though restricted to logic and informatics, is well worth reading. He writes:

> You might think to yourself, "These speculations about brain and mind are all well and good, but what about the feelings involved in consciousness? These symbols [representations of concepts stored in the brain] may trigger each other all they want, but unless someone *perceives* the whole thing, there is no consciousness." This makes sense to our intuition on some level, but it does not make much sense logically. For we would then be compelled to look for an explanation of the mechanism which does the perceiving of all the active symbols, if it is not covered by what we have described so far.[20]

Hofstadter then goes on to introduce a "subsystem" in the collection of potential and actual symbols to whose interaction he reduces thought, and goes on to "prove" that such a subsystem can have all those functions we assign to the self. His analysis should be taken very seriously, but his belonging to a school of thought that reduces all knowledge to "how" explanations plays him a trick: he does not seem to realize that, in the course of his honorable endeavor to find a mechanism by which concepts form into thought up to the "I" concept, he assumes the existence of something which plays exactly the role of the separate mind postulated by Eccles. He associates it with "symbols" in the brain and proposes a mechanism to explain how it works, considering "logical" that one can take for granted two points: (i) that an entity capable of apprehension (he says "perception") of the "whole thing" cannot exist; (ii) that the apprehension in question cannot be a single event, but must be a process with a specific mechanism. Both assumptions are respectable parts of a scientistic creed; what is perhaps mistaken is to treat them as logical necessities.

Given the situation, we have to continue our exploration of the body-mind problem. A number of views, summarized by the famous metaphor "the smoke above the factory," simply deny the need to speak of a mind or of a psyche, except for convenience. Those views are related to the mechanistic reductionism still held by influential scientists, but, with the

---

19. Cf. J. C. Eccles, "Brain Research and the Brain-Mind Problem," in *Brain Research and the Mind-Body Problem: Epistemological and Metaphysical Issues*, ed. G. Del Re (Vatican City: Pontifical Academy of Sciences, 1992).

20. R. Hofstadter, *Escher, Gödel, Bach: An Eternal Golden Braid* (London: Basic Books, 1979), 385.

rise of integrationistic biology, they seem to be drifting into oblivion — until the next avatar.

Other views, summarized by the metaphor "the ghost in the machine," make a clear distinction between body and soul. They are "dualistic" views, as that advocated by several neurophysiologists in the more elaborate form called "interactionism," particularly, as mentioned, by John C. Eccles. Advocates of this point of view have been considered naïve even by some Christian philosophers; but it should suffice to recall that St. Augustine, one of the most profound minds in the history of Christianity, was a dualist to show that it is not fair to dismiss dualism by sarcasm or captious arguments. Here is a list of a few of the captious arguments and their flaws:

- appeal is made to irrelevant blunders of the dualists, such as Descartes's suggestion that the soul is situated in the pineal gland;

- it is considered evident that living organisms are not machines, but the argument is circular, since a machine is implicitly or explicitly defined as an artifact capable of a limited measure of autonomy but not having the properties of living organisms;

- the analogy between an organism and a machine is rejected by reference to the properties of the material of which a machine is made, in particular the fact that living tissues and organs decay very rapidly after death; according to what we know today, that difference is in principle of the same nature as the difference between a steel vase and a porcelain vase, or between a magnetic tape and a compact disc, which can carry exactly the same information;

- the modern concept of a machine as a control system of a very general nature is ignored, whereas a living body can be looked at precisely as a highly sophisticated instance of such a system, endowed with a very large degree of autonomy but open to input from some special kind of information source;

- it is considered self-evident that a nonmaterial entity cannot act on a material body, whereas

  i. forces, which are nonmaterial entities, have been used in physics for a long time, albeit with some hesitation as to their actual significance (cf. chapter six);

  ii. the belief in the ability of certain nonmaterial beings to control living beings has never been rejected by Christianity;

  iii. the distinction between material and nonmaterial entities has never been studied with due account of recent progress in theories about space and time;

- the pilot-boat metaphor is pushed beyond its intended limits — actually it only suggests the ontological independence of two entities which are attributed a relation similar to that between a pregnant woman and the child in her womb.

In short, many objections to interactionism are weak or captious. Nevertheless, there are real difficulties with it. The most significant one is probably found in determining which properties of man should be assigned to the separate entity that should be the mind or the soul proper. We have mentioned, for example, that instincts may take in man sublimated forms; we could have added the same sort of remarks about imagination and the sense of beauty. Now, it would seem that a dualistic view cannot easily account for such aspects of a person's soul. Aquinas offers perhaps the best formulation of this objection when he holds that logical consistency requires that Aristotle's "active intellect" should be looked at as a personal characteristic of man as are all other faculties of the soul.[21]

A third view, called "holistic," is precisely that of Aquinas. It might be rephrased in modern terms by saying that the "apprehension of the whole thing" mentioned in Hofstadter's passage quoted above is an operation of the mind consisting in a *single event* of a nature unknown to science, inasmuch as it does not involve any change in the material support of the soul. Such a view is in agreement with today's complexity approach to the physical world and is certainly consistent with what is known about man; even so, however, it does not seem that it removes the mystery of self-consciousness. In other words, in the perspective of a science that has accepted complexity, the existence of the soul in Aristotle's sense appears to be a fact not only compatible with science, that susceptible of scientific study; but, a core escaping scientific assessment remains.

Of course, one can always circumvent the mystery by changing the meaning of words. In well-known journals such as *Nature*,[22] the word "mind" is used as a term confusedly equivalent to "cognitive activity of the brain." People therefore speak of things like "a theory of the mind" when they only propose a mechanism by which the brain first collects and analyzes the information it receives from outside sources, then compares it to information already stored in its data banks, and finally puts it together again in an order of its own, to be eventually tested for its congruency to the intrinsic order of the external world. Proposals of this sort do not contribute to understanding the mind as intellect, but

---

21. T. Aquinas, *Summa contra gentiles*, part II, especially chs. 56–60. Eng. trans., with introduction and notes by J. F. Anderson, *Summa contra gentiles*, 2. *Creation* (Notre Dame, Ind.: University of Notre Dame Press, 1975).

22. Cf., e.g., the book reviews by E. S. Reed, "A Surfeit of Models," *Nature* 348 (1990): 23; and by L. H. Shaffer, "Modelling the Mind," *Nature* 351 (1991): 281.

they may be relevant to a theory of knowledge; for example, appeal to congruency implies a fundamental philosophical choice, strong realism, which purports that the outside world exists independently of us and can be known as *it is,* at least to come extent (cf. chapter three).

Current attempts to deal with the mind-body problem are especially valuable for the emphasis they place on the difficulties of both the holistic and dualistic solutions. Let us recall that the two subproblems under discussion are (a) whether or not a separable immaterial entity corresponding to the self exists, and (b) how it can act on matter without violating the laws of physics. In 1982, Henry P. Stapp published a physicist's account and proposal for their reconciliation.[23] Stapp's article is quite interesting and exhaustive, although, since it stays at the level of largely unknown neuronal processes, the central problem of explaining the unity of the mind with all the other psychological aspects of human beings is not discussed. An idea of the kind of considerations involved (and of their limitations) was given by the eminent American psychobiologist Roger W. Sperry (1913–1994):

> The individual nerve impulses and associated elemental excitatory events are obliged to operate larger circuit-system configurations of which they as individuals are only a part. These large functional entities have their own dynamics in cerebral activity with their own qualities and properties. They interact causally with one another *at their own level as entities.* It is the emergent dynamic properties of certain of these higher specialized cerebral processes that we interpret as the substance of consciousness.[24]

The largely conjectural images of circuits of neurons as the material seats of thought make this passage more readable than one by Aristotle; yet, the gist of the proposed interpretation of consciousness is essentially the same, that is, a complexity scheme in terms of parts that take on an organized state in which downward causation becomes possible.

What Do We Mean by Spirit?

At this stage we have probably said as much as is necessary within the scope of this book on views and counterviews on the mind-body problem. They certainly define a field of inquiry, indeed one pertaining partly to the sciences of matter, partly to the sciences of life, and partly to the human sciences. Its object is not just the intellect, the "thinking mind," since what Eccles calls the mind is rather the *self* of a human being; if

---

23. Cf. H. P. Stapp, "Mind, Matter and Quantum Mechanics," *Foundations of Physics* 12 (1982): 363–399.

24. R. W. Sperry, "Mind-Brain Interaction," *Psych. Rev.* 76 (1969): 532–536; cf. Stapp, "Mind, Matter." Italics are mine.

the self is seen as the center of thought and of free, deliberate action, and if we separate that aspect of man from everything else, we get the mind-body or mind-brain problem. Precisely because of that separation, the mind-body problem is probably relevant for the construction of a world-view or a *Weltanschauung* only in a particular connection: the existence in man of a spiritual principle. Precisely in that connection the separate self is logically a very nice solution, but it is deeply deceiving; for, in our attempt to make sense of our inner and outer experience, we should much prefer to think of a given individual's self as his or her *personality*, meaning by this word all that makes him or her — as Socrates in the example of chapter six — that particular person and none other; that is to say, thought, emotions, even instincts, the spirit and the flesh are all subsumed in what is usually called the self. Anyone who wants to make sense of the human condition and man's place in the universe is bound to take into account the material reality of man, just as he cannot avoid the spiritual issue, if only to reject it.

There is a problem here, which goes back to the Bible. Many languages, including ancient Greek, Latin, and English, have two words for the immaterial part (or aspect) of man, soul and spirit. The specialized dictionaries, including Lalande's and Audi's already cited dictionaries of philosophy, attribute to the two words essentially the same meaning. J. L. McKenzie[25] states explicitly that in the Bible the word spirit, when referred to human beings, does not usually stand for the soul, but — to summarize a beautiful and detailed analysis — for what is not associated with rationality in humans. In fact, the Gospel of Luke reports that the Mother of Christ said to Elizabeth:

> *Magnificat anima mea Dominum*
> *et exultavit spiritus meus in Deo Salvatore meo.*[26]

Here, a distinction is clearly made: *spiritus* appears to coincide *grosso modo* with what Jaspers called the "thymopsyche" (from Gk. θυμός, desire)[27] for it is capable of emotions like rejoicing; *anima* has the characteristics of Jasper's "noopsyche" (from Gk. νοῦς, intellect), since it realizes that the Lord is great and expresses that realization in words.

In a technical study, it would not be admissible to ignore *sic et simpliciter* the biblical acceptation, the more so as, despite the decline of religiousness in formerly Christian countries, the Bible is still an important source of inspiration and beliefs. However, since we are interested

---

25. J. L. McKenzie, *Dictionary of the Bible* (New York: Bruce, 1971).

26. My soul praises the Lord, and my spirit rejoices in God my Savior, Luke 1:46–47. The Greek text has ψυχή for "anima" and πνεῦμα (pneuma) for "spirit," so that the Latin terms are perfectly appropriate.

27. K. Jaspers, *Allgemeine Psychopathologie* (*General Psychopathology*) (Berlin: Julius Springer, 1923). Jaspers's subdivision of the psyche was pointed out to me by D. Gherardi, professor of psychiatry at the University of Rome "La Sapienza."

in the existential exigencies of modern men, we should perhaps prefer the notion of spirit implicit in the spirit-flesh correlation, which is also of biblical origin, and accept the identification of the spirit of man with what current usage calls the soul, *viz.* all that in man transcends the strict exigencies of material life. This amounts to excluding from the ψυχή, the soul in Aristotle's sense, those faculties (or aspects of faculties) that human beings have in common with other animals, and retaining only that which in our being "soars above the bodily ties."

We may seem to be wasting our time on a mere matter of words, but just consider the procedures by which the hidden persuaders of the mass media make people accept their ideas, and you will realize that words have a great power, and the only defense against the persuaders is to know exactly what words mean. Now, in our exploration aimed at finding out what sort of *Weltanschauung* or world-view is emerging from the most recent advances of science, we reached several times a boundary beyond which gleamed a reality not accessible to our senses or devices. We have called that reality spiritual, relying on some intuitive meaning of that word; here, since we have seen what it means to say that there is in man something spiritual, we should try to see what the whole thing boils down to. The first question, of course, is: "Is there really anything spiritual in man?" The positivists, of course, give a completely negative answer. For example, John Dewey, an evolutionary instrumentalist who inspired after the second world war a reform of American education whose results are evident today, believed that "the brain is an organ of a certain kind of behaviour, not of knowing the world";[28] that thought is but an instrument of readaptation of the human animal, etc. That, as it seems, is intended to explain away the mind as an incorporeal entity. The well-known French philosopher Henri Bergson (1859–1941), whose insistence on basing knowledge on experienced facts is in full agreement with the spirit of modern science, said a similar thing about the brain, but pointed to the opposite direction as to thought:

> The body is, for us, a means for acting, but also an obstacle to perception.... It is a filter or a screen which, by keeping in a virtual state all that, by becoming actual, could interfere with action, helps us to see in front of us what is in the interest of what we have to do.... In short, our brain does not create or preserve our representations, only sets for them boundaries rendering them active. It is the *organ of attention to life.*[29]

Thirteen years earlier he had summarized his view by an effective analogy:

28. Cited from J. Dewey, *Creative Intelligence* (1917) by Will Durant, *The Story of Philosophy*, 523.
29. Bergson, *Les deux sources.*

Brain activity is to mental activity what the movements of the conductor's baton are to a symphony. The symphony exceeds in all respects the movements which scan it; in the same way, the life of the spirit exceeds the life of the brain.[30]

We have seen at the end of chapter eight and elsewhere that exactly the same class of arguments about the human species, in light of the advances of science since Dewey's time, lead to the conclusion that the human species cannot do without a reference to the absolute. And "absolute," let us admit it, means "God." The persistence of religion throughout the whole known history of mankind, even in distorted and sometimes horrifying forms, proves that point beyond any possible doubt. But God means a spiritual reality: how can man refer to it if man does not possess a spark of that reality? The whole discussion of symbols in chapter eleven points in the same direction. But it is Aristotle's analysis of the nature of living beings, which is scientific, not metaphysical, that provides perhaps the strongest suggestion of something in human nature that is not of a material nature: the fact that man is able to say "I know." The mind-body problem, as we have seen, is ample evidence that here we are facing a mystery. The answer to the question about a spiritual component of man can therefore be formulated as follows: The existence of such a component appears to be consistent with the scientific evidence we have; but it is in the nature of the case that we should look elsewhere for decisive arguments. Science has done all she could by showing that she cannot pronounce upon this matter.

If we decide that "how" explanations are not complete explanations, and that the study of man gives strong hints that a dimension of reality exists that is "spiritual," i.e., inaccessible to our five senses or to experimental devices, then another problem remains. As we saw in our discussion of magic, alchemy, and communication, there are grounds for believing that the spirit of man can also communicate in some mysterious way with something which is neither spatially localized nor sensible, and therefore is merely spiritual, but has will and intellect, and can intervene in the material world. In other words, there are grounds for believing that certain faculties of the human soul also belong to beings that do not need a material support ("a body") for their activity. Of course, there are no "proofs" of that in the mathematical or the experimental sense; indeed, as is well known, even the famous "five proofs" of the existence of God given by Thomas Aquinas are "ways" showing that belief in the existence of God is highly reasonable; they are not demonstrations of the same kind as proofs of Newton's law or of Pythagoras's theorem. By definition, neither God nor lesser spirits, in general, have a predictable

---

30. H. Bergson, *L'énergie spirituelle* (1919; reprint, Paris: Presses Universitaires de France, 1959), 850.

behavior; and that would rule out science, even if their very spiritual nature did not already do so. Moreover, as we have seen, if there are such beings, the only way we have to contact them is through our spiritual component, that is to say, through our inner experience, and the only objective data we have in this connection are those of history. What history teaches is known to everybody; suffice it to recall the picture of the Greek culture of many centuries B.C. that emerges from Homer's poems. That culture included a deeply rooted belief that there exists an unseen world of beings who rule or guide the lives of human beings, or at least can influence them. It is so clear that neither is the poet describing a primitive society nor is he paying lip service to some official religion that the reader is almost tempted to believe with him that Athena and Zeus really exist, and are something akin to what an angel and Yahweh are in the biblical tradition.[31]

Apart from historical considerations, we are touching here a topic which, as has been pointed out in chapter nine, might well deserve further consideration by science, at least in view of clearly fixing a borderline. We have seen that organization as such cannot be denied existence per se on the grounds that it presupposes a material support, something that plays the role computer "hardware" plays with respect to programs. We are speaking now of something like information without any support that our senses can perceive and science can study. Can science provide clues for or against the existence of such a "free" form of information? Considering the nature of what physics calls a "field," one may be tempted to think that it can. When Faraday and Clerk Maxwell introduced the electromagnetic field, the scientific world of their time was scandalized, precisely because they had introduced an entity without any material support.[32] Of course, there are reasons why fields are anyway sensible objects, but further reflection will most probably show that those reasons essentially amount to the fact that they can be produced and tested at will under reproducible conditions chosen by the observer — and that might well be the main difference between them and possible "pure" spirits. Thus, we have here another mystery, whose scientific aspects have not yet been cleared up; and today's science is expected to be much more cautious on this matter than the science of one hundred fifty years ago.

It could be claimed that spiritual beings, since they do not depend on matter for their existence, are not subject to decay and extinction; and that was in fact the view taken by Aristotle and Aquinas. But can we say that information is not subject to decay? A field might be perma-

---

31. In fact, there was a tendency in the Middle Ages to consider Zeus as essentially a name for the Christian God, and the lesser pagan gods as mythical personages corresponding to actual angels or demons. That is shown, for example, by certain passages of Dante's *Divine Comedy*.

32. Cf. our chapter seven and Torrance, *Transformation*, ch. 6.

nent in ideal conditions, but if it participates in physical transformations, it is bound sooner or later to lose energy, and therefore decay. In contrast, it would seem that Aristotle was right in claiming that, since true knowledge is the indivisible act of becoming conscious of processed information, it is not a material process. Therefore — to make a long, still largely unwritten story short — whatever the reality of spiritual creatures is who are intermediate between human beings and God, the question of the possible immortality of the human soul should be looked at as a separate problem. In fact, having accepted that, in the context of reflections on the nature of man, the term "spirit" designates a part of the ψυχή, of the soul in Aristotle's sense, we should also admit, in accordance with the conclusions reached in the preceding section, that it cannot be conceived of as an entity entirely independent of a material support, just as organization cannot be thought of as subsisting by itself. This means that, if the question of the "immortality of the soul" makes any sense at all in the case of man, it should probably concern the human soul as defined by Aristotle in the modified form proposed by Aquinas (a personal active intellect), and not merely the spiritual principle present in it. What attitude should one take in this connection, with due account of all that science has learned about man and nature? Why should man be singled out among living beings by this mysterious fact of immortality?

About Immortality

Well, even if it sounds like arrogance vis-à-vis other animals, it would seem that nobody, perhaps not even the animalists, can or will deny what, in ordinary speech, we all accept: that the soul is what makes a man what he is, a creature of shadow with a longing for light, a mammal which, in spite of intellectual fashions, has a freedom of choice and action that no other known animal has, and the power to grasp in himself the whole universe. This intuitive view of man is what makes it impossible to forget the words with which the mad Prince Hamlet describes the human condition:

> O God, I could be bounded in a nut-shell and count myself the king of infinite space, were it not that I have bad dreams.[33]

Science has nothing to say about this, although it can accept and handle the notion of soul, understood as the organization that makes a being a unit, i.e., a being attaining a level of complexity at which it is a fully integrated whole of complex parts; a being capable of interacting and communicating with everything else in the universe while remaining distinct from everything else. When it comes to humans (and possibly to

33. *Hamlet*, 2.2.52–54 in *Complete Works of William Shakespeare* (New York: Doubleday, 1936).

other living beings with which we cannot communicate fully enough to grasp their complexity), the soul has that faculty or set of faculties that some call the "self," and all that goes with it is a mystery. Science, having progressed enough to acknowledge its own limitations, today recognizes that the problem associated with that mystery makes sense, even if it cannot solve it by its methods. On the question of the soul, as on other topics we took up in the preceding chapters, science opens perspectives on lands which it cannot explore.

In this case the land discovered and yet inaccessible is the realm of a recurrent dream of mankind, not a bad dream, but a beautiful one: uninterrupted enjoyment of being, mere being, as when, in a serene evening on a lonely seashore, you sit down, and just listen to the wash of the groundswell, occasionally broken by distant bird cries; or when you let your mind wander, and unexpectedly discover that you have the answer to questions you had always asked yourself in vain. This dream of eternal bliss, in the face of the evidence of death, has suggested the idea of the immortality of that which people everywhere understand as the "soul" — not exactly the ψυχή of man, but something closely resembling it, an immaterial entity identical with the human being to whom it belongs except for the material base to which it imparts all the properties that make it into a human being.

I am speaking of a dream that becomes an idea, but in all times the vast majority of people have actually *believed* in a life after death. The reason is that they have always believed that they are in touch with another dimension of reality. We saw that in connection with symbols in chapter eleven and in connection with the "optimum state" of a human group at the end of chapter eight. There we found a clue to the explanation of our instinctive belief in spirit, but it lay at the borderline between science (in its broadest sense) and intuition or mysticism. F. J. Tipler, in a provocative book, has tried to fit even immortality and God into physics.[34] It is not surprising that, being a physicist, he should believe that atheism arises from the inability of science to tackle theological problems. Other thinkers believe that atheism is the result of the fragmentation of culture, which brings about the inability of many scientists to see the point of any question except those formulated in the language of their own discipline. Now, Tipler's book presents an attempt to set up a consistent "theory" of God and the immortality of the soul in the language that is familiar to theoretical physicists — more precisely to theoretical cosmologists. Some points in Tipler's book are very well taken, as when he claims, in full agreement with Aristotle and Aquinas, that life is "information processing": that is a very abstract way of expressing the meaning of that term ἐντελέχεια (entelechy), which we met in discussing Aristotle's ideas. But

---

34. Tipler, *Physics of Immortality.*

there are at least two general reasons for regarding Tipler's book as only a chapter, albeit extremely stimulating and original, of what should be a far longer study. One reason is that he seems to leave little room for an analysis of the sort of information processing that the soul is; the other is that his whole argumentation is based on a number of principles, assumptions, and simplifications of the kind made in cosmological theories of the universe, e.g., the "Postulate of Eternal Life." It would seem that a detailed assessment of those assumptions could lead to plausibility judgments, but would still leave the final decision to our belief. At any rate, Tipler's work illustrates a main point we are trying to make in this book: science, particularly physics, has at last realized that denying sense to issues with which it is not able to cope is a poor solution to the existential problems of man.

As to immortality, Aristotle opened the way to a different sort of solution, as we saw above, by suggesting that the active intellect cannot belong to the same order of reality as the body. Aquinas, in turn, realized that there is some inconsistency in a possible limitation to a "light-like" intellect of that part of man which survives death. Truly enough, as a Thomist whose memory is very dear to me wrote,

> The immortality of the soul which we admit [apart from religious belief] is immortality of the intellect, since only in the intellect, in thought, does the soul free itself from its ties, however intimate, to the body and soars as it were beyond the present life and temporality.[35]

However — let us say it again — Aquinas's idea is that the active intellect is part of the human soul, although it partakes of the properties of entities that are not corruptible and ephemeral as the body; it thus imparts to the whole human soul the ability to communicate, by symbols or otherwise, with that world of permanence, which we call "spiritual." In other words, the mystery which the scientific analysis of Aristotle was forced to recognize, and which the brain science of John Eccles faced again twenty-three centuries later, appears to imply that the human soul, although rooted in matter as a tree is rooted in earth, is spiritual, and rests on the Platonic — and Christian — interconvertibility of Truth, Beauty, and Justice. In this sense, the primacy of the "intellect" stands for much more than the ability to know: by having something of the nature we attribute to the godhead, our whole soul has a double citizenship, that of sensible reality and that of spiritual reality. If our relatives and friends now dead have actually migrated to the unknown land of Heaven, and

---

35. R. Del Re, "L'immortalità dell'anima," *La Scuola e L'Uomo (The School and Man)* (Rome), no. 10 (1978): 292–296.

if the Father of us all is there, then truly, as a preacher in a small church on the outskirts of Waterloo, Ontario, once said,

with our last breath we shall return home.

Nevertheless, it is not obvious that immortality, in such a perspective, should mean a continuity of existence of the soul, even separated from the body. Significantly, after a discussion on self-organization in the nervous system, the neurophysiologist J. Szentágothai, whom we mentioned in connection with downward causation, reminded the audience that:

> According to the Apostolic Creed we believe in the resurrection of the flesh and not [necessarily] in the continuity of some immaterial soul.... There is no material or immaterial continuity needed for God to fulfill His promise.[36]

That is theology, even in the context of a neurophysiologist's reflections; as to science, it must accept in its better (and probably intended) sense the often quoted last point of Ludwig Wittgenstein's *Tractatus logico-philosophicus:*

Whereof one cannot speak, thereof one must be silent.[37]

If we compare Tipler's noble attempt to fit immortality into a cosmological theory with the symbol that is a candle lit before the image of the Lady of Mercy we will realize that, regardless of whether or not Tipler has done more than call attention to a number of questions, science cannot aspire to replace God's direct revelation. Immortality remains a mystery, and science is obliged to stop on the brink of the great cliff separating the realm of what it can ascertain and verify from the rest of the great chain of being. At variance with the past, also in this matter today's science admits its limits, and, by so doing, leaves to each of us the task of choosing — in the words of the declared atheist Jacques Monod — between the Kingdom and the Darkness.

---

36. G. Del Re, ed., *Brain Research and the Mind-Body Problem* (Vatican City: Pontifical Academy of Sciences, 1992), 64.

37. For an interpretation cf. P. Engelmann, ed., *Letters of Ludwig Wittgenstein* (It. tr. *Lettere de Ludwig Wittgenstein* [Florence: La Nuova Italia, 1970]), 69ff.

Chapter 13

About a Scientific World-View

Wonder at the immensity and complexity of the universe is perhaps the main reason why we want to found on science our Weltanschauung. Now, the latter is essentially a simplified, largely intuitive "theory of the world" on which a man's practical decisions are based. Can such a theory be built in accordance with the building rules that have made science so convincing? If not, what are the difficulties?

Science and Mystery – Nightmares – The Story of Rama – A Sense of Wonder – Applying the Methods of Science – Science and Facts – Human Knowledge as Knowledge of Reality – On the Reality of Certain Entities – What Is Science? – Principles as Keys to Answers – A Scientific Principle: Energy Conservation – Metascientific Principles and Beliefs – From Science to a Standpoint on Reality – A "Scientific" *Weltanschauung*

We shall not cease from exploration
And the end of all our exploring
Will be to arrive where we started
And know the place for the first time.
Through the unknown, remembered gate
When the last of earth left to discover
Is that which was the beginning;
At the source of the longest river
The voice of the hidden waterfall
And the children in the apple-tree
Not known, because not looked for
But heard, half-heard, in the stillness
Between two waves of the sea.

— T. S. ELIOT[1]

Science and Mystery

We are at the end of our exploration. It could continue, since the quest for understanding has no end, but hopefully what was essential is already clear: the science of the latter decades of the second millennium has revealed a far more complex picture of reality than the science of fifty years ago would have dreamed, confirming the words of caution which such geniuses as Pascal, Poincaré, Einstein had pronounced or written on so many occasions so long ago. It does not "present to us for our belief" the relentless march of the blind power of nature — as the Bertrand Russells of all ages have thought since the beginning of history — but a world where every object or being participates in a general harmony of the universe with its own individuality and a varying measure of independence, at its own level of size and complexity; a world where each object or being contributes with its own value and qualities to the Great Dance of all things, which combines decay and emergence of order, return to a shapeless chaos and blossoming into unimagined wonders of order; a world open on the mystery of yet undiscovered relations and properties, open on a dimension of reality inaccessible to scientific observation but as it were discreetly signaling its presence in a variety of ways.

The wiser and humbler spirit of the new science still has a long way to go before the many scientists who have become influential as a result

1. T. S. Eliot, *Four Quartets*, "Little Gidding," V, lines 26–38.

of excellence in specialized research accept with an equal mind that competence in any particular field is not sufficient for a *vue d'ensemble*. But this anomaly will disappear in due course, unless the decline in education continues.[2] A good sign is that the new science has discovered that it can ignore neither man nor history; indeed, as we have seen in chapter eight, it shows that even on merely biological grounds every human being is expected to use his or her freedom and intelligence to tune-in, as finely as these gifts make it possible, to the harmony and coherence of the universe, to cooperate in the creation of more order and beauty. We are surrounded by examples of this. Anyone who has ever gazed at the clear aerial outline of the Chesapeake Bay Bridge, spanning in one jump the great pale-blue estuary of the Susquehanna River, or seen a big airplane clumsily taxiing toward its take-off strip, and then, with a roar, taking up speed to become a silver creature of the air, will certainly agree that manmade wonders are not monuments to the power of human reason and know-how but the proof that science and technology, using what nature has placed at man's disposal, are meant for harmony and beauty, provided, of course, that they conform to the unwritten alliance between man and nature.

Yet, on thinking of the direction in which this book had led us, it is difficult not to feel a bit of wistfulness. We started with a general reflection on the unity and order of the world, we went on to becoming, we moved to finalism. There, mainly because of the notion of "explanation," the problem of man crept in. Man's presence was significant already in the chapter on regularity and variety, but then we had to devote a full chapter to his place in the universe (chapter eight). Subsequent chapters treated man's relation to science, to the physical universe, and to a possible spiritual reality in many ways; those explorations were (as far as that is possible for a writer) a dispassionate examination of facts, but of facts which of necessity involved or regarded man. Finally, a chapter was devoted to what, as far as we know, characterizes us as distinct from all other living beings — the ability to think and freely decide a course of action. This greater and greater presence of man is the reason why a wistful feeling comes to a scientist's heart. After all, was Laplace — whose belief in mechanistic determinism has become a classic — to be blamed if he longed for a world in which there was no room for the free intervention of man, where there was no room for good or evil? If such a world were possible, then a scientist could dream of the self as a pure mind, discovering one after the other the secrets of nature, and living in a pure atmosphere, far from the weakness and meanness and stupidity which human beings, scientists included, put in their everyday actions.

Unfortunately, not only was deterministic science an illusion, but there

2. F. Seitz, "Decline of the Generalist," *Nature* 403 (2000): 483–84.

were people who used it — arguably with good intentions — to deny any significance to personal aspirations to beauty, justice, and truth. Marx and Freud, with their versions of reductionism, according to which every single man was a mere wave in the sea of an economy-driven mass, or a machine driven by instincts lurking in the darkness of the psyche, are the emblematic figures of that tragic anti-human trend, which eventually found its application in the social structures of the twentieth century. Therefore, after all, it is good that, led by its very advances toward more humility and openness, science should be looking again at mankind, its place in the universe, its history, its soul. To be sure, in this crazy planetary society, which the media display before us in all its worst and most morbid details, we may find it difficult to believe that human beings deserve special consideration. But this feeling is as biased as the opposite one. Let us rather remember what somebody wrote long ago, that wisdom is first of all courage to face facts, all facts, those we like and those we dislike, those we find encouraging and those we find depressing. In the case of man, as Pascal remarked,[3] it would not do that we should comprehend how close we are to the beasts, if we did not realize at the same time that there is in us a potential for great and noble deeds; it would also be dangerous if we should realize how wonderful our reason and creativity are, and ignored our potential for baseness and perversion; and it would be even more dangerous if we ignored either; indeed we should proceed through life in full awareness of both sides of our nature.

In short, it seems that, rather than yield to regret for the impossible dream of rising, by the pursuit of science, above our human condition, we should accept science and ourselves as we are, and listen to the new message that seems to emerge from the newer lines of research: every individual, indeed every object in the universe belongs to a secret network of causal and noncausal relations, whose unceasing change, whether toward complexification or decay, appears to be like a Great Dance, harmoniously evolving in ever newer figures, following a mysterious suite of which our reason cannot grasp but a few themes. If only because we know that a particular tiny light in the starry winter sky is the red giant star Betelgeuse, and we can somehow imagine and feel its majestic solitude in the depths of space, we are in relation with it, and we are subtly different from what we should be if we did not know about its existence; and through each of us, others may be subtly changed by that seemingly useless piece of information.

And here we come to a consideration implicit in all that we have explored so far. Man, as any other living being, is an open self-regulated system receiving and emitting signals, a steady-state two-way information processor which, though slowly aging, retains from conception to

---

3. B. Pascal, *Pensées*, Lafuma, 121–418.

death a permanent core of properties constituting its identity. This means that man's relation to the rest of the universe is active, as well as passive, on two accounts: not only does he and his devices emit signals of all sorts, but reception of a signal often stimulates a person to act, either automatically or deliberately, in a certain way. This fact prompts a question: apart from immediate biological ends, are there general ends that characterize man's conscious, deliberate activity? We have seen in chapter eight that human beings need some set of absolute rules as criteria for choices. Most rules may be expected to be interdictions, as in the case of respect for life or for nature in general; but it is in the nature of man that he should realize himself in action, so one wonders if there are rules which do not interdict, but command a certain type of action. Clearly, if the universe evolves toward a greater and greater coherence, those rules should guide man to act always so as to contribute to the harmony of the universe. What that might imply in a *Weltanschauung* satisfying our existential needs will be our concern in the latter part of this chapter; here let us just emphasize that, if such a participation in the Dance is possible, then, despite our shortcomings, we may begin to think that life is worth living.

Thus, even though ours is perhaps a time of regress, in which people who have reached living standards inaccessible in the past do not seem to be taking any advantage of their unprecedented opportunities, grounds for hope are offered by genuine science — behind which popular and alas! textbook science is usually lagging, with a delay of several decades: grounds for hope to wake up at last not from ordinary human folly and pathological behavior, for history teaches us that that is the lot of the children of Eve, but from the existential nightmares built up in the latter three or four centuries, the centuries devoted in the West to the worship of "human reason" as the supreme legislator.

Nightmares

It is a dismal task to pause on those nightmares. But we have spent so much time to get an idea of the sort of *Weltanschauung* or world-view inspired by the new science and summarized by the Great Dance image that it would be a pity if we did not briefly reflect on the problems for which a new way of looking at the world is needed.[4]

Much has been written on the birth and rise of the ideologies treating ordinary people as nothing but anonymous members of a mass, only

---

4. We remind the reader that, in this book, the German word *Weltanschauung* is used to denote a concept similar, but not identical to "world-view"; at variance with the latter, which is expected to have been consciously constructed, it refers to that essentially intuitive and partly subconscious pattern of personal views on life and the world on which even the least educated man bases his choices.

requiring material welfare and free material pleasures to be good and happy. In a novel written in 1932, Aldous Huxley described a future society whose details — from sex as mere entertainment to genetically selected test-tube babies — have been or are being realized one after the other in the Western society.[5] The result is what C. S. Lewis called "the abolition of man"[6] and there seems to be no reaction. Now, as the Roman historian P. C. Tacitus (55–117 A.D.) wrote at the beginning of the Christian era,

> *Ut corpora nostra lente augescunt, cito extinguuntur, sic ingenia studiaque represseris facilius quam revocaveris; subit quippe etiam ipsius inertiae dulcedo et invisa primo desidia postremo amatur.*

> As our bodies slowly grow, but are quickly extinguished, so it is easier to repress talents and will to acquire knowledge and abilities than to restore them; for sweetness is found even in inertia itself, and the inactivity at first hated is eventually loved.[7]

If what Tacitus wrote is true, then, what with the collapse of the family institution and the decline of education, it would seem that at least for Western society there is little hope of changing the trend. People are not complaining and even less planning revolutions. Therefore, as it seems, Einstein's "invisible community" of those who fight for the three Platonic values should accept their defeat: human society has no need for values or heroes.

The process toward a society free from ideals and heroes gained momentum in the more advanced parts of the world after the second world war.[8] The Western "organization man" and the Communist "party member" were for a while the reference models. Even the rise of biology and the great scientific synthesis proposed by the general theory of systems and by Ilya Prigogine's work, which opened the way to the collapse of reductionism, went largely unheeded among men of science and of letters. Yet, there were warnings coming from reputed scientists, like Ludwig von Bertalanffy, founder of the general systems theory. In a paper of 1970, after showing that the recovery of the notion of organism was necessary, he moved to consider the possibility that this recovery could help to correct the course society was taking. He even made a precise suggestion, recalling Huxley's prophecy:

> At this point a humanistic psychology and education shall have to be introduced — humanistic entirely in the sense of natural sciences,

---

5. A. Huxley, *Brave New World* (1932; reprint, New York: Harper-Collins, 1989).
6. Lewis, *Abolition of Man.*
7. Tacitus, *Agricola* 3.1.
8. Cf. Schlesinger, "The Decline of Heroes."

meaning what is specific of man. We do not know if such a reassessment of values, in the sense of a reintroduction of specifically human values, is still possible in our society. But we know that the progressive bestialization of man, its scientific and technical conditioning by means of psychological techniques, coupled with the subhuman drives to aggression, bloodthirst and pleasure in destruction — that such a development leaves only few end results: in the best case a *Brave New World* in the sense of Aldous Huxley, human machines conditioned from the fertilized egg to their disposal as used machine parts; or, in the less favorable case, the atomic self-destruction of a humanity which has given up the heritage received from God for the lentil soup of a factitious civilization.[9]

It seems that Bertalanffy, an eminent scientist pleading for humanism, was right. We have avoided atomic self-destruction probably because no winner would have been left, and we seem to be heading for Huxley's *Brave New World*. Yet, there is, I insist, hope for the future because there are men and women who still work against the stream, and the young are not as passive as they might seem. University professors of all disciplines will tell you that the young still would like to fight for ideals inspired by the great Platonic values. Attempts to give back to them what Bertalanffy called "specifically human values" are being made.[10] Therefore, let us move to more serene considerations, from nightmares to dreams.

The Story of Rama

A dream about the relationship between man's understanding and the course of things in the universe was told by a British writer in a book which, despite interludes which are clearly concessions to the supposed tastes of today's readers, reveals a genuine poetical inspiration.[11] One day in the near future, the astronomers of the solar system detect Rama, a mysterious asteroid from outer space approaching the sun at a speed just below that of light. Initially only the astronomers are interested in Rama; but then things change.

On a billion television screens, there appeared a tiny featureless cylinder, growing rapidly second by second. By the time it had doubled its size, no one could pretend any longer that Rama was a natural object. Its body was a cylinder so geometrically perfect that

9. M. Lohmann, *Wohin führt die Biologie? Ein interdisziplinäres Kolloquium (1970)* (Munich: Deutscher Taschenbuch Verlag, 1977), 13–31.

10. E.g., in an educational program based on J. M. Templeton's book *Worldwide Laws of Life: 200 Eternal Spiritual Principles* (Philadelphia-London: Templeton Foundation Press, 1997).

11. A. C. Clarke, *Rendezvous with Rama* (New York: Ballantine, 1974).

it might have been turned on a lathe — one with centres fifty kilo-metres apart. The two ends were quite flat, apart from some small structures at the centre of one face, and were twenty kilometres across.

An exploration team finds that it is an inside-out cylindrical world, now dead as dead can be, with a cylindrical deep-frozen sea like a belt at its middle, and all details — including islands, which look like cities — repeated thrice. Then, one day, three gigantic fluorescent tubes suddenly light up, the cylindrical sea starts to melt, and a process similar to that which is thought to have initiated life on earth is completed in a few days. Half-biological, half-mechanical beings emerge from the sea, and begin to go about simple maintenance tasks, without heeding the intrud-ers, even when the latter use force to enter one of the strange buildings on one of the islands. Mankind is more and more nervous, but the politi-cians waste their time in endless palaver. Therefore, certain that Rama is a menace to the solar system, the Hermians, the inhabitants of Mercury, place an atomic bomb near it; Lieutenant Rodrigo, a member of the in-spection team who belongs to the "Fifth Church of Christ, Cosmonaut," deactivates it at the risk of his own life, with the tacit encouragement of his captain.

But Rama continues its voyage toward the sun. One day, the three "linear suns" begin to flash, a long emergency sound is heard, and Rama quickly returns to its sleep. The sun is close and the explorers have to leave.

> Rama was now two hundred thousand kilometres away, and dif-ficult to see against the glare of the Sun. But they could obtain accurate radar measurements of its orbit. And the more they ob-served, the more puzzled they became. . . . It looked as if the fears of the Hermians, the heroism of Rodrigo, and the rhetoric of the General Assembly had been utterly in vain. . . . Everyone had been so certain that Rama would lose speed, so that it could be captured by the Sun's gravity, and thus become a new planet of the solar system. It was doing just the opposite. It was gaining speed in the worst possible direction. Rama was falling ever more swiftly into the Sun.

It appears that Rama is tapping energy and matter from the sun. Then, after a few revolutions inside the sun, it takes a last ninety-degree swing and leaves:

> It was dropping out of the ecliptic, down into the southern sky, far below the plane in which all the planets move. Though that, surely, could not be its ultimate goal, it was aimed squarely at the Greater Magellanic Cloud, and the lonely gulfs beyond the Milky Way.

A Sense of Wonder

Clarke's *Encounter with Rama* is an efficacious parable of the sensation that remains in an open mind after considering what we know about the universe, living and nonliving alike. We know today far more than the preceding generations, but we understand as little as they did, and it is not to be expected that further data will reduce significantly the mystery behind most of the information we already possess. It is often pointed out that the more answers we get to our questions about the universe, the more new questions arise. If we learned that there are intelligent beings on the planets of Sirius, we would immediately wish to learn something about their aspect and habits; and then we would try to meet them; and then we would wonder about the possible inhabitants of other stars; and so on without end. But the mass media of our paradoxical society have found a way to quench our scientific curiosity: they transform the vaguest guesses into certainties, and explain to us, for example, the habits of the dinosaurs with details which no serious scientist would ever acknowledge as more than just possible. So they keep the fable alive that science knows everything, and at the same time banalize everything, adroitly passing over whatever might cause perplexity and doubt. That is a very effective way of fighting against the sense of wonder and mystery genuine science gives to those scientists who, as Carlyle's metaphor says, have eyes behind their spectacles: we are left with the sensation that there are people like us who have understood what we have not, we watch pictures which fill our imagination, and there we are, satisfied with intellectual garbage. But in our hearts we know that there is something fishy in the whole story; moreover, we realize that the real point is not to know, for example, that certain dinosaurs actually lived on the eggs of other dinosaurs, but to know what sense it makes that there should have been dinosaurs, which thrived for millions of years and then utterly vanished. As to questions about other intelligent beings living on remote worlds, the motives for our curiosity are even clearer: we hope that the answers would make better guesses possible concerning the sense of everything. What motivates us could be expressed as follows: "Before the mystery of the universe, two emotions fill my heart: a sense of profound awe, and a deep desire to know more about it. Perhaps, if I had more information, it would be possible for me to find what I should do in order that my existence may fully belong to this beautiful and great reality." Now, precisely on expressing our feelings explicitly we realize that what we miss is not so much additional scientific information as something lying beyond the limits of science. And then we see something we had perhaps overlooked in Clarke's parable, the implications of the fact that it leaves a central question unanswered: what was the purpose of Rama? We do not even know if that question makes sense, for the hypothetical beings who had built it might well be so different from human beings that purpose, instinct, thought, emotions would be completely foreign to their nature; and the only way to find out would be to ask them, if only they could hear us and if they were prepared to come down to our level, so as to answer in terms we could understand. Do you not feel in this, as I do, a faint echo of other Parables and Teachings, which many of us heard about in childhood and then forgot, and others never had an opportunity to know?

It would seem that our desperate longing for a place in the universe is of the same category as the strange archetypes, briefly discussed in chapter eleven, which make a person light a candle before the image of a saint. Science cannot help us in this connection, but, as we have seen throughout these reflections, it tells us that the species *Homo sapiens* has, as all other living beings, peculiar characteristics, and — if it is not a monstrous error of nature, contradicting whatever may be valid in any theory of evolution — those characteristics suggest for it the ecological niche of a highly pioneering species, whose habitat is the whole universe. Thus the archetype, the built-in psychological structure, which makes us feel that our real place is the very universe that fills us with awe, seems to be of biological origin; but, as we have also seen, some of the issues it raises refer us to something that lies beyond science, a reality far above ours, which knows what the optimum state and the possible role of mankind is. That reality, with which we are in touch in mysterious ways, of which we partake with that part of our soul which is not common to all animals, is what man has always called the world of spirit.

It is not within the scope of this book to dwell more than we have already done on the difference between spirit and matter. Maybe the difference, though decisive for us who depend on our five senses, is a minor one from the point of view of a superior being. What matters is that the mystery surrounding us from all sides, the unknown land which our exploration descried at the end of each voyage, be it the voyage through the land of chance or through the theories of the cosmos, is the mystery of spirit, the mystery of God. We can very well shut our eyes tightly, and declare that it is all illusions, epiphenomena, blind chance, but there are a number of objections to that sort of attitude. We have already seen them, but allow me to briefly recount how I came across a little apologue which summarizes them all in a nutshell.

Once upon a time, I was doing research in Germany, and from time to time visited my parish church, whose priest was a nice elderly man from Nuremberg. He was a good priest, who put his faith in all he did, even when he played the choir director by making the faithful in different rows of seats sing the same melody starting one after the other, as the parts in a canon. He had placed in the bookstand of his church certain nice

booklets entitled "for every new day."[12] In a way, I think those booklets
are typical of the special kind of religiosity of Germany, whose great
spiritual wealth has been largely forgotten in the wake of the terrible
events of World War II — despite admonishments like that of Father Bro,
who, in a Lent sermon at the Cathedral in Paris, said: "If you believe
that you and your countrymen would not be capable of doing the same,
then you have understood nothing of human nature."

Well, those booklets are collections of short poems and reflections on
ordinary life which, without rhetoric or high-brow doctrinal statements,
offer guidelines and suggestions for the day-to-day moral and existential problems of man. The first one I bought was divided into several
minichapters. In it, at page seven, I found "The Legend of the 'Modern'
Man," which goes as follows.

A "modern" man lost his way in the desert.
The relentless rays of the Sun were drying him out.
Then he saw at a distance an oasis.
"Aha, a mirage," thought he,
"a reflection in the air which is deluding me,
for in fact there is nothing at all."
He came closer to the oasis, but it would not disappear.
He could see clearer and clearer the date palms,
the grass and above all the source.
"Of course a hunger phantasy of my half crazy brain," thought he;
"such delusions are known of people in my state.
Now I even hear the water bubbling.
A hearing hallucination. How cruel is Nature."
A short time later two Beduins found him dead.
"Can you make sense of such a thing?" said one of them to the
        other.
"The dates almost grew in his mouth.
And close to the source he lies,
dead from hunger and thirst. How is that possible?"
The other answered: "He was a modern man."

So much for blind chance, epiphenomena, and what have you. A science refusing a *Weltanschauung* open on the spiritual dimension of reality
is not science, it is a delusion liable to make a man die from thirst on
the bank of a water stream.

This does not mean — shall I say it again? — that all we have seen
so far tells us what that spiritual reality is, whether or not God exists,
whether or not it is possible for man to find moral guidance in rules

12. H. Dickel, W. Disselnkötter, D. Gläsche, W. Meing, *An jedem neuen Tag* (Stuttgart:
Arbeitsgemeinschaft Missionarische Dienste, 1980).

rooted in the absolute. On the other hand, since science has guided us so far, as Virgil guided Dante to the threshold of Paradise, let us see what we can still learn from it, before concluding our exploration. We wish to see if a *Weltanschauung*, indeed a world-view, can be built and assessed following the same scheme as if it were a scientific theory, so that it will be logically justified just as much as any scientific theory can be, pending, of course, criteria of verification that cannot be those of science.

Applying the Methods of Science

In the preceding chapters, we paused very little on that "dismal science" (as Will Durant called it), which is called sometimes epistemology, sometimes philosophy of science: the study of knowledge, particularly of scientific knowledge. It is dismal because it puts all in question, including whatever makes a fact a fact, so that, when reading the speculations of its students, you feel like a man trying to stand on a surfboard in the middle of a stormy sea. Yet, epistemology has real problems to tackle; the trouble is that one who discusses them should be at the same time a philosopher and a scientist with experience in the carrying out and interpretation of experiments. This was by no means the case with most philosophers of science; a remarkable exception was the Hungarian physical chemist Michael Polanyi (1891–1976),[13] who contributed to major advances in the study of proteins, and later moved to philosophy of science. Being a strong realist, he was ignored by the most influential philosophers of science of his time — Popper, Kuhn, Lakatos, Feyerabend, and many others. One way or the other, these philosophers were all connected with logical positivism, which, as we already had occasion to mention, considers science merely as a logically consistent language putting order to sensations arriving from a chaotic, unknowable "outer world." As we shall see, logical positivism had a constructive side, but the objection remains that genuine scientists do not see how reason and logic can make an engine work, unless the laws they discover and use are objective laws of nature.

Given the unquestionable success of science as a way to knowledge, and the unending disagreements in other fields of inquiry — from psychology to theology — we must admit that not even the growing evidence that scientific knowledge borders on a land of mystery and wonder inaccessible to it can remove the sensation that only science is reliable. This is also due to the fact that the information a man can get on the processes taking place in nature, however important it may be, will not involve him as a person; whereas a conclusion reached about existential problems will always demand something of the self, like requiring a change

13. M. Polanyi, *Personal Knowledge: Towards a Post-Critical Philosophy* (Chicago: University of Chicago Press, 1958; New York: Harper, 1964). Cf. Torrance, *Transformation*, ch. 5.

of attitude toward other people, or maybe the acknowledgment that we should obey rules that admit of no lawyer's trick, or at least accept some kind of renunciation. In that land beyond science the inner life of a man is all that matters, and its pattern

> is new in every moment
> And every moment is a new and shocking
> Valuation of all we have been. We are only undeceived
> Of that which, deceiving, could no longer harm.
> In the middle, not only in the middle of the way
> But all the way, in a dark wood, in a bramble,
> On the edge of a grimpen, where is no secure foothold,
> And menaced by monsters, fancy lights,
> Risking enchantment.[14]

If we try to make sense of the land unknown to science, we must be prepared to risk deception, enchantment, doubts; but there is a hope that, if we adopt the same scheme by which science constructs an interpretation of experimental data, we may find a personal path toward answers that will make our lives more serene and productive. That is to say, we are liable to find answers to those questions that most of us simply suppress in our subconscious, much as the officers of the court during the trial described in *Alice in Wonderland* suppressed the cheers of a guinea-pig:

> As that ["suppressed"] was rather a hard word, I will explain to you how it was done. They had a large canvas bag, which tied up at the mouth with strings; into this they slipped the guinea-pig, head first, and then sat upon it.[15]

The canvas bag is a good image for our subconscious, if we make it capacious enough. But we may decide that, after all, tackling those suppressed questions is worth the candle; then it would probably be advisable to proceed in accordance with the well-established pattern by which scientific theories are constructed and verified — though with different verification protocols. But what is the established pattern in question? Let us begin from the beginning, the nature of the evidence on which a reliable theory should be based.

Science and Facts

An ordinary person might well wonder why in the world he or she should waste time on the evident truth that science deals with facts. Indeed, everybody grants that this is so, but are what you and I call facts the

---

14. T. S. Eliot, *Four Quartets*, "East Coker," II, lines 35–43.
15. L. Carroll: *Alice's Adventures in Wonderland*, in *The Annotated Alice*, with an introduction and notes by M. Gardner (Cleveland: World Publishing Co. 1963), 149.

same thing that science studies? Before Kant, there was an almost general consensus that the answer should be an emphatic "yes." After him things changed. This was probably because, with his attempt to construct a solid theory of cognition, he provided a scheme which was eventually interpreted as follows:

- whatever surrounds me, if it exists at all, is merely an unknowable transmitter, which sends input to my nervous system, and I cannot know anything about it as it really is;

- however, I can put order in my sensations, and thus declare that I know something;

- therefore, what I call a fact is but a construction I have made out of my sensations;

- moreover, even assuming that it is caused by something "out there," that cause cannot be but the production of signals, some "event" or "process," certainly not some *thing*.

The philosophers directly or indirectly adhering to logical positivism, whom we had occasion to mention, particularly in chapter nine, declared that what science calls a fact is just something on which a logically consistent discourse is possible, and its actual reality is not a condition for truth. They would add the condition that the statements taken as axioms can only refer to our sensible experience (although we do not know whether there really are objects causing it). Paul K. Feyerabend (1924–1996) realized that this additional "dogma" does not ensure the *uniqueness* of a theory putting order in our sensations, and coined the famous slogan "anything goes," meaning — as it seems — that any theory is equally acceptable, provided it is logically consistent.[16]

If this view of science provided a complete account of what science is, then not only all existential problems and a possible spiritual dimension of reality, but the very notion of objective truth would be ruled out. If, on the other hand, it is taken as only part of the whole story, then it is extremely significant, for it emphasizes two very important points:

- every scientific theory, and science itself as a whole, must be coherent, i.e., its statements must be at least logically compatible;

- precisely because it is a logical construction, any scientific theory, and science in general, cannot do without a number of *postulates*, i.e., statements which a scientist is asked to accept, albeit on grounds of plausibility and experimental evidence, without that strong evidence required, say, to sentence a person to jail;

16. P. K. Feyerabend, *Against Method: Outline of an Anarchistic Theory of Knowledge* (London: NLB; Atlantic Highlands, N.J.: Humanities Press, 1975).

- science rests on a small number of most general postulates or axioms, called *principles;* the more important ones, particularly the first and second principle of thermodynamics, have been so successful in explanations and predictions that they are now accepted as fundamental truths.

That much is certainly an important contribution of recent epistemology to the understanding of science.

Human Knowledge as Knowledge of Reality

As to the existence of facts and things that are not constructs of our minds, but are fully independent of us, it is at least an existential necessity. This is why one is bound to accept "strong realism" (chapter three) at least as far as the direct-access level of reality — whatever is directly accessible to our five senses — is concerned.[17] But such an acceptance is void of implications unless one also disposes of appropriate "criteria of existence," that is, the rules to be applied to make sure that "ontological" judgments (e.g., "in that stable there is a horse") are valid. Otherwise, how could we be sure that individual facts or objects are not mere personal or collective illusions? If no such criterion exists, as Kant feared, then it is useless to claim that a physical or spiritual reality independent of us exists.

To clarify this matter, we must briefly consider the process by which knowledge is attained by human beings. We shall divide it into two stages, which we shall call here *apprehension* and *comprehension.*

The apprehension stage is *grosso modo* the preconscious identification of an object among the pictures presented by the nervous system to the recognition machinery of the brain. All that arrives at the conscious level is that a certain thing exists and is distinct from everything else, as when we recognize somebody from his or her face and are not capable of telling *what* has enabled us to identify that person. The comprehension stage is the *critical processing* of the apprehended information, which involves analysis and synthesis within the context of data and experiences previously processed and memorized. The new information is thus brought to a level susceptible of expression in a language, which can range from a strictly logical one (mathematics) to a merely associative one (painting, music). It is at this stage that certain irrational, subconscious schemes and structures of the mind come into play — particularly ultimate beliefs and archetypes, together with consciously chosen principles.

17. If one tries instead to extend to the direct-access level the results of science concerning elementary particles, one is still forced to accept realism in order to avoid treating everything as a mere illusion, but one can speak of a "veiled" reality. That was the thesis of D'Espagnat, *À la recherche*, already cited in chapter three.

The apprehension stage includes a tentative judgment of reality, which must be subjected to a critical evaluation during subsequent processing. For example, I may want to know if the wine is really sweet or bitter, as Socrates in the *Theaethetus* of Plato, or I may want to understand what is happening when, thinking I am alone in my room, I suddenly see a stranger looking at me, only to realize that it is my own face reflected by a mirror. Let us pause on this example. The question to be posed could be either: "Is there *really* another person here?" or: "Can I *truly* say that another person is here?" This equivalence between reality and truth at the level of knowledge could perhaps explain much of the success of views that reduce reality to a superfluous notion only needed for emotional equilibrium. But along this line, one can arrive at the absurd, as in that story where certain things ceased to exist when the little ape Lucy closed its eyes. What we should keep in mind is that there are two sorts of truth: logical correctness (as in the case of "if...then" statements) and faithfulness to reality (where no "if" is allowed).

In the latter case, as we have said, man needs a criterion of existence because he has to make operative decisions — *man must act*. Now, such a criterion may concern chains of events in space-time, and entities either belonging to space-time or sharing with entities in space-time certain characteristics — particularly individuality and will. Science may be seen as a refined tool for establishing what is real and what is not (at least in space-time) because it is capable of setting up a network of relations whose ultimate function is to prove that if entity E or fact F is real, then entity E' and fact F' are also real (or cannot be real). In the process of dealing with reality questions, i.e., of trying to understand the world, laws are discovered that can be used for technological applications; however, as we have just seen, the usefulness of science does not lie primarily in those applications, the more so as technology provides means, and means are useless without ends.

The central point in this analysis of the scientific enterprise is the reality chain whose rings are, in the formalism used above, $E \to E'$ (or $F \to F'$ or $E \to F'$ or $F \to E'$). Such a chain must end with a primary fact or thing P_0 which is self-evident. René Descartes (1596–1650) pointed this out long ago, when he said that a fact whose reality cannot be questioned must be the starting point of any serious body of knowledge. He took for P_0 his famous *cogito, ergo sum*,[18] but perhaps thought is much too complicated as a reference fact. The same role might be played by a fact whose reality is especially undeniable as it is unwelcome: death. If a scientific theory allows the construction of a device capable of killing — for example the atom bomb — it is legitimate to think that at least some of the facts on which that theory has been built are as real as the result of its application.

---

18. "I think, therefore I exist," in *Discours de la Méthode* (Discourse on method), part IV.

The nature of the individual facts science tries to correlate can be incredibly varied. They range from the results of reproducible experiments at the direct-access level (e.g., the fall of a body) to the existence of invisible and intangible material entities (e.g., elementary particles, space-time) established by theoretical consistency arguments, and to facts established by analogy and plausibility arguments (e.g., that a certain bone-shaped stone was the bone of a dinosaur, which lived millions of years ago). They all refer to primary facts by some complicated theoretical chain of the type mentioned above; and what is especially interesting for us is that in certain cases no direct communication with the senses is involved, in others there is no rigorous theoretical connection. Since no experiment can reproduce a fossil bone a million years old, nor is there a mathematical theory showing that the "laws of nature" require that such an object can only be the present state of what was a genuine bone, we can only say that it is extremely implausible that by chance chemical processes should have formed a structure so similar to a bone, found in several specimens, together with fossils that could be attributed to related animals, or interpreted as eggs, etc. It is thus *morally* certain that it was a bone; but the reader will no doubt see what this implies: the existence of dinosaurs is a fact deduced in two quite indirect ways: the logical way, similar to that which leads to belief in the existence of the electron, and the plausibility way, based on analogy and coherence with other facts.

Considering a world-view based on what man knows today, it seems unquestionable that facts that do not belong to the reality studied by science should be taken into account because otherwise the existential problems of man would not find a place in it; but that means neither that those additional facts should be accepted without a rigorous critical assessment, nor that they are facts in a sense different from those of science. Their assessment will have to be carried out largely by means of analogies and coherence arguments — much as in the case of the existence of dinosaurs — on the basis of history, anthropology, and natural sciences; but we should not be deterred by the necessity to supplement merely logical deductions by other kinds of arguments; in fact physics, the standard model for methods ensuring reliable conclusions, provides ample justification for doing so.

On the Reality of Certain Entities

We mentioned the existence of the electron in connection with the existence of dinosaurs. It seems opportune to pause a little on this in connection with the more general question of the existence of entities postulated by scientific theories but not accessible to direct observation, considering its relationship with the possible existence of a spiritual reality.

No one can see or touch the electron. Yet, no physicist would speak of it as merely a useful hypothesis, except when paying lip service to the tenets of certain philosophers of science. The fact is that, when it comes to questions like the existence of the electron, physical science behaves as a judge trying to decide on indirect evidence whether or not the facts reported are a crime and, if so, who is the criminal. The only difference is that, whereas a judge need only assign the qualification of "author of this crime" to a person whose existence is known from other sources, in the case of the electron a physicist is faced with having to derive from the given facts the very existence of an entity not otherwise known. The additional assumption is that material entities *may exist*, which cannot be detected by our five senses except in huge numbers and combined with other entities of the same sort. The way out of this difficulty can be found by considering that a particle is seen intuitively as the limit of a sequence of subdivisions of directly observed matter into smaller and smaller parts. More generally, as discussed in the preceding section, if we can construct a chain from familiar facts of man's direct-access level to the existence of the electron, then the existence of the latter is a fact.

Let us now turn to those invisible and intangible entities which by their very nature cannot be expected to respond to prearranged experimental conditions, either because they are endowed with free will or because their manifestations in the sensible world obey a project unknowable to man. The problems which arise in connection with them concern not only the existence of a Supreme Being, but that of demons, such as are claimed to exist by magic and witchcraft, of angels, and in general of "nonmaterial beings" (cf. chapter nine). Obviously, science can help very little; for science, in the case of a free being not otherwise observable, could at best detect those interventions of that being on sensible reality that are repeated in similar circumstances with the same clear-cut pattern; and even then such interventions could be attributed to a free nonmaterial agent only if at least a hint about their possible aim were available.

This consideration rules out every possibility of knowing something about the plans and aims of lesser spirits; it could apply to the God of Christianity, as Giambattista Vico suggested (cf. chapter seven), inasmuch as history might reveal the existence of sequences of events explicable in terms of a (revealed) salvation plan. But that is all, and we know very well that free will itself cannot be proved by logical or operational arguments. Human life is a thin thread supported by several basic beliefs; one of them is belief in moral responsibility, which implies free will; but, as we shall see presently, basic beliefs cannot be deduced logically. Either they are innate, or, like the principles of physics, they are generalization from limited evidence.

In sum, direct or indirect evidence for the existence of pure spirits should be obtained in some ad hoc way. We shall return to this issue presently. For the time being, as is our wont when questions important for our human condition arise, let us prepare the ground by calling upon a poet to speak. The Belgian poet Maurice Maeterlinck, in the passage cited in chapter two, wrote:

> Here is the great question which has priority on all others: is the existence of pure spirits possible?

> We have never seen any. That proves nothing. We have never seen our thought, and yet we know that it exists, that it moves matter. Yes, it will be said, but at least in our world it always has a material support, it is always issued from it, it feeds on it; and as the matter feeding it dies, it too ceases to live.

> Is that sure? Is it well established that our thought is indissolubly bound to our body and needs it absolutely in order that it may subsist? Need one admit that it is instantaneously asphyxiated or fulgurated as it goes out of the flesh? Why could it not immediately begin to absorb another matter, the matter dispersed under other forms in space, and thus find in it what it needs in order to maintain its existence and evolve in it?

> Would it not be possible for it to reach regions where spirit and matter coexist, are mingled and no longer separated, as is normally the case on Earth?

What Is Science?

We are now in a position to examine science, such as it is after the end of physicalism, with the aim to see more explicitly how a reliable theory, including a world-view, should be built according to its praxis.[19] Keeping in mind that there are at most a few facts which can be considered evident, science appears to have the three tasks already hinted at by Plato two and a half thousand years ago:

- establishing what is real and what is not (in the sensible world);

- discovering the rules of change — if any — of the sensible reality;

- detecting entities and facts not accessible to the senses without ad hoc instruments;

19. It may be useful to remind the reader that, in accordance with the spirit of this book, we are not forwarding a final view on the nature of science; we are only presenting what seems to be a sensible opinion based on realism and accepting most current views as far as is possible without contradictions.

- providing the basic framework for a coherent *Weltanschauung*, while keeping the utmost openness to extensions of knowledge inside and outside science itself.[20]

The method of science can be experimental in the strict sense of verifying its statements by ad hoc tests, but it can also utilize experiments made by nature and check them for their consistency with all other information. The essence of the scientific method is the search for coherence, using basically

- the efficient-cause scheme and the mechanical model;
- the final-cause scheme and the biological model;

and aiming at offering human beings, using those schemes, a "formalized" explanation of facts, i.e., explicit descriptions and correlations of them in terms of a language allowing for logical connections (not just consisting of icons and cartoons) of the aspect of reality each particular discipline studies. This way of looking at science is probably consistent in its main lines with the basic tenets of the majority of contemporary epistemologists, but precisely because of that it does not give the right place to the single disciplines, each of which works with a specific class of facts. Those classes are as diverse as the buying of a stock of oriental carpets by a merchant and the flash produced by the impact of an electron on a television screen. Remarks on the difference between fields of inquiry (the specific subjects of the various disciplines) were given in the preceding chapters as the opportunity presented itself. As to aspects in common, they are probably limited to those mentioned at the end of the preceding section.

Science should also have an aim. The modern tradition has adopted usefulness as that aim, following Francis Bacon:

Now the true and lawful goal of the sciences is none other than this: that human life be endowed with new discoveries and powers.[21]

From Bacon to contemporary pragmatists the choice of practical usefulness as the supreme value has proven disastrous, and it was certainly not the motive of Galileo, Clerk Maxwell, and Einstein, to name just three of the greatest scientists of history. Nevertheless, in the course of this book, we have often adopted the same view. The explanation is simple: as in the case of mechanism and of logical positivism, if the ideas of the pragmatists are freed of their ideological ballast — power worship, materialism, relativism, and what have you — then the standpoint that science is a tool for survival does provide a key to the appreciation of scientific results, as

20. Plato, *Theaethetus* (Oxford: Clarendon, 1900).
21. F. Bacon, *Novum Organon* (1620) (reprint Florence: Sansoni, 1942), I, 81.

we saw particularly in chapter eight; the difference lies in the allowance for the fact that the usefulness of science extends beyond welfare, for the right relation between man and nature should be included among the conditions for survival of the human species. Therefore, the usefulness of science should be looked at in the context of the existential conditions of the *human person*, which implies an individualistic and not necessarily materialistic anthropology; its significance is not limited to the evolution of the species, although that side of the story is not ruled out.

In other words, the idea that the value of something depends on its usefulness is acceptable as a general principle — provided usefulness is not limited to the realm of the material conditions of man — because then it corresponds to what we have had to acknowledge all along our exploration of the borders of science: that there is a continuity between the biological collocation of man and his ideals and aspirations toward a different sphere of being. A utilitarian point of view is not necessarily in contrast with the classical values of truth, beauty, and justice. The claim that these three values are the basic values can be rephrased by saying that they are built-in features of the world in which we live; a corollary is that any deviation from their pursuit is incompatible with perfect integration in the world (and hence survival) of any species whose members are endowed with reason and free will; another corollary is that, if there is a Creator, then those values are an aspect of the Creator's very nature.

Principles as Keys to Answers

A most important point, which lies at the origin of many conflicts of opinion, in the natural sciences as well as in nonscientific fields of inquiry, is that every explanation necessarily rests on "axioms" in the etymological sense of the word — i.e., assertions believed to deserve confidence, though not proven beyond doubt — which are first taken as working hypotheses, then accepted by an act of faith, and finally submitted to a great number of tests to prove their ability to support a coherent explanation of facts; whereafter they are accepted as "principles." Perhaps at variance with science, which only requires working assumptions as starting points, in the case of a world-view or *Weltanschauung*, certain questions cannot be answered without prior acceptance, by a sort of act of faith, in some general principle. The principle chosen is then tested, at least at the level of personal experience, for its ability to support a coherent explanation of all the data and facts on which those questions bear. The most important example of such a general principle is the existence of a Creator. St. Augustine, a few years before 400 A.D., summarized the faith-test process on it in a rightly famous, deeply poetical formulation:

Quaeram te, Domine, invocans te, et invocem te credens in te.

I shall look for you, Lord, invoking you, and I shall invoke you believing in you.[22]

He meant that one could not experience the import of belief in God without accepting the existence of God to the point of praying to Him; nevertheless, faith is only the beginning of a quest, for one who does not really understand (within the limits of the human mind, of course) who and what God is might pray to the wrong god.

Evidence in favor of the need to start, by an act of faith, from something like the "God principle" is that adherence without a scientific proof to a principle of the same kind is also characteristic of those who, like Jacques Monod, believe that the physical universe is the only reality, and "chance, blind chance" is to be invoked whenever science does not find a law according to which a particular fact or object is bound to be what it is (cf. chapter seven). A choice between the two principles must be made, let us say it once again, on the basis of their ability to offer a coherent explanation of our inner and outer experience. For example, the "blind chance" principle can settle all questions without further reflection, for it amounts to agreeing with the King of Hearts:

"If there is no meaning in it," said the King, "that saves a world of trouble, you know, as we needn't try to find any...."[23]

Unfortunately, coherence is not attained, because, as Monod himself pointed out, at least the problem of choosing between the Kingdom and the Darkness remains. Therefore, one might not accept as a satisfactory solution to all problems the denial of meaning to all that is not susceptible of a "scientific proof," preferring, instead, to work at the creation principle; but then one would have a long way to go, beginning with something we have played down in the preceding chapters in order to be as impartial as possible, namely evidence of purpose in the universe.[24] Before that, however, the decisive objection should be countered: "Granting that Monod's principle is just a matter of faith, the 'God principle' is worse, for Monod confines himself to the unshakable laws of science, whereas the 'God principle' will never be as evident as the principles of science, such as the principle of energy conservation." Clearly, if this objection is correct, the well known (and deleterious) splitting between science and faith in a Creator — at least for people who are not prepared to accept chance as the ultimate ruler — is beyond repair. But is the objection really serious? To find an answer, let us see how principles work in science on the example of energy conservation.

22. Augustine, *Confessions*, ch. I, sec. 1.
23. L. Carroll, *Alice's Adventures in Wonderland*, 159.
24. Cf. Templeton, *Evidence of Purpose*.

A Scientific Principle: Energy Conservation

We have already seen that in science facts alone do not suffice: science needs ordering principles. One might think that in science principles too are facts; but that is not really the case, if by "facts" you mean "experimental evidence."

Consider now the conservation of energy, well known as the most important principle of science. That principle is not a fact, but an extrapolation from facts, accepted as a basic truth because it has proved to be both fully general and capable of surviving the most difficult crises of science.[25] Scientists came close to a nervous breakdown when the "black-body problem" resulted in the "ultraviolet catastrophe" around 1880, and the energy conservation principle ran into apparently insurmountable difficulties.

A body that is capable of absorbing any electromagnetic radiation is called "black." Although it is an idealization, a small window in an oven closely approximates this definition. Now, the laws of physics predict that a black body must also emit electromagnetic radiation, with a "spectrum" — i.e., an intensity distribution versus wavelength (color) — that only depends on its temperature. Thus, the light emitted by a heated oven is in a one-to-one correspondence to its temperature, and in fact the temperature of an oven can be measured by observing the light it emits. The sun behaves as a black body, and that is why one can tell that its surface temperature is approximately 6000°C. Now, when the physicists tried to derive the spectrum of a black body from the principles of physics (energy conservation, laws of electromagnetism, Boltzmann's statistical distribution), they found that the black body was predicted to emit an *infinite energy*, concentrated at very short wavelengths (UV, x-rays, and beyond). This result was called "the ultraviolet catastrophe," and it was indeed a catastrophe, because it contradicted not only experiment, but the most fundamental among the very principles from which it had been derived, conservation of energy. Planck found a way out of the impasse by discovering the quantization of energy (which, by the way, was shown thirty years later to respect energy conservation only in the mean), but it was a narrow escape.

This story is an illustration of the last consideration Henri Poincaré makes in the discussion recalled above, written in the very years when Planck made his momentous discovery:

> I wish to retain only one impression of the whole of this discussion, and that is, that Mayer's law [the energy conservation principle] is a form flexible enough for us to be able to put into it almost anything

25. A masterful discussion of the epistemological status of the principle of conservation of energy was given by Poincaré, *La science*.

we like. I do not mean by that that it corresponds to no objective reality, or that it reduces to mere tautology; since, in each particular case, and provided we do not wish to extend it to the absolute, it has a perfectly clear meaning.

This flexibility is a reason for believing that it will last long; and, as, on the other hand, it will only disappear to be blended in a higher harmony, we may work with confidence and utilize it, certain beforehand that our work will not be lost.[26]

As you can see, despite its extraordinary and fascinating successes, science is a construction which rests on foundations which do not stem from a logical or factual necessity, but from intuitions and extrapolations;[27] and yet, because of their ability to serve as key laws ensuring the consistency of a particular theoretical analysis with the rest of science, those foundations are treated as incontrovertible facts by all scientists; for example, if one of my students asks me how to work out a physics problem, I will answer that one should first of all apply the principle of conservation of energy, or at least make sure that it is respected.

Meta-Scientific Principles and Beliefs

Mayer's principle is a quantitative law directly used in scientific research. But man, whether doing science or not, must rely on principles of other kinds. One such principle is the principle of unity of nature, which goes back to the beginning of history, and has been fully recovered by the new science reviewed in this book. It is meta-scientific — "meta" is Greek for "beyond" — because (i) it also applies to aspects of reality not covered by scientific theories, (ii) it is not a law establishing a relation between observable quantities, but a criterion for choosing procedures and approaches.

Simplicity of nature is another principle of the same kind. When a scientist finds a possible law governing some set of phenomena, he or she is the more sure that it is correct the simpler it is, on the grounds that "nature is simple." A case in point is again Mayer's principle of energy conservation. See what Poincaré wrote:

Half a century ago [ca. 1850] it was frankly confessed and proclaimed abroad that Nature loves simplicity; but Nature has proved the contrary since then on more than one occasion. We no longer

---

26. Poincaré, *Science and Hypothesis*, 134f. The translation of the French word "souple" has been corrected to "flexible."

27. This consideration corresponds to what was called the "nomological-deductive model" of science by C. G. Hempel, *Philosophy of Natural Sciences* (Englewood Cliffs, N.J.: Prentice Hall Inc., 1966).

confess this tendency, and we only keep of it what is indispensable, so that science may not become impossible....

In a law immediately deduced from experiments, such as [Boyle and] Mariotte's law, this simplicity would rather appear as a reason for distrust; but here this is no longer the case. We take elements that at the first glance are unconnected; these arrange themselves in an unexpected order, and form a harmonious whole. We cannot believe that this unexpected harmony is a mere result of chance. Our conquest appears to be valuable to us in proportion to the efforts it has cost, and we feel the more certain of having snatched its true secret from Nature in proportion as Nature has appeared more jealous of our attempts to discover it...the imposing simplicity of Mayer's principle contributes to strengthening our faith in it.[28]

Although Poincaré was extremely cautious in this statement, subsequent developments largely confirmed his inclination in favor of nature's simplicity. For example, the introduction of the notion of tensor and relativity theory allowed the physicists to write the fundamental laws of electromagnetism as a simple relation between two quantities, one representing together the magnetic and electric fields, the other representing the properties of the medium. Also quantum mechanics and the theory of nonlinear processes respect the principle that the equations representing the basic patterns of nature are simple. It is with the application of those theories to control nature and to predict its behavior that the story changes completely. We saw in chapter five deterministic chaos emerging from an innocuous second degree algebraic equation; imagine what might emerge from slightly less innocuous expressions. In short, Poincaré's remark that the simplicity of nature is a condition for science not to become impossible has been confirmed by later successes of physics; but — as he certainly knew from his work on the three-body problem — it has also been found that man's mind is forced to acknowledge its limitations precisely when it tries to cope with the details of relations which are extremely simple in themselves.

In the passage quoted above Poincaré used the words "faith" and "believe." This is not without significance: they imply what Polanyi stated half a century later, that — regardless of our grounds for our accepting them — the principles governing our understanding of the world are adopted by an act of faith, even if they are strictly scientific ones. This shows how thin is the barrier separating what we called the "God principle" from other principles by which we try to obtain in our mind a *faithful* representation of the reality which communicates with us

28. Poincaré, *Science and Hypothesis*, 130f.

through our senses or which we experience within ourselves. As to meta-scientific principles such as the unity and simplicity of nature, they are at the same time conditions for understanding (as Poincaré pointed out) and features of a *Weltanschauung* inseparable from many other intuitive principles and beliefs guiding our approach to life and nature. The implications of this remark in connection with science can be summarized by a consideration of T. F. Torrance's, who devoted many years of reflection to them:

> In natural science we are concerned ultimately, not with convenient arrangements of observational data which can be generalized into universal explanatory form, but with movements of thought, at once theoretical and empirical, which penetrate into the intrinsic structure of the universe in such a way that there becomes disclosed to us its basic design and we find ourselves at grips with reality.... We cannot pursue natural science scientifically without engaging at the same time in meta-scientific operations.[29]

Concerning the role of belief in principles we could follow Polanyi and go beyond meta-scientific ones, which have a measure of formalization, over to those beliefs which we adopt even when in words we contradict them, say, that truth and falsehood are real alternatives, that most decisions imply a choice between Good and Evil, that beauty is not just a matter of personal taste or social conventions, and so on. Those beliefs may be called "ultimate."[30] They are involved in the process of understanding, but they have a counterpart in the irrational component of the human psyche, if we accept C. G. Jung's idea that there are in our psyche structures (or structuring principles) common to all human beings, the "archetypes," which shape the activity of our imagination and our emotional responses.[31] Although the professional psychiatrist's tendency to reduce everything to psychological mechanisms of a somewhat morbid kind is present in Jung's applications of the archetype idea, what seems particularly worth retaining in a broader context is the implication that the creative cognitive processes by which man builds science as well as a world-view start from ultimate built-in principles, which are partly connected with processes involving aspects of our psyche other than the intellect.

The idea that our knowledge is based on beliefs seems to go back at least to David Hume. Hume, writes Torrance, held that there are

> natural beliefs which control the relation of the reason to matters of fact and existence.... That is to say, our rational arguments operate

---

29. Torrance, *Divine and Contingent Order*, 3.
30. Torrance, *Transformation*, ch. 5.
31. A fairly concise and clear definition is given by Jung himself in *Man and His Symbols*, chapter eleven, note 11.

with beliefs that are not themselves rational, or logically demonstrable. As Hume understood it, it was particularly important to establish the status of two forms of natural belief, belief in continuing and independent existence, and belief in causal dependence, for without it no physical science, let alone objective, rational behaviour, would be possible. Hume himself contrasted belief and knowledge, much as John Locke had done before him, but he did see that belief has an essential role to play in the establishment of knowledge in spite of its non-logical character.

In our own days, however, it has become more and more apparent as the foundations of knowledge have been exposed, not least in connection with active scientific discovery, that belief and knowledge cannot be contrasted in the way advocated by Locke and Hume, for belief plays an essential if informal part in the basic operations of knowing as well as in formal, symbolic operations through which the body of our knowledge is established in a consistent form. But today we have also come to realize more clearly that true beliefs of this kind are not open to logical proof or disproof.[32]

Not surprisingly, the skeptical logician Bertrand Russell wrote:

> The attempt to prescribe to the universe by means of *a priori* principles has broken down; logic, instead of being, as formerly, a bar to possibilities, has become the great liberator of the imagination, presenting innumerable alternatives which are closed to unreflective common sense, and leaving to experience the task of deciding, where decision is possible, between the many worlds which logic offers for our choice.[33]

Because of his professional training, he recognized, precisely as the logical positivists were doing in the same epoch, the need for drawing the starting points of science from outside it. Probably for the same reason he did not pay much attention to the scientist's commitment to faithfulness to factual reality: otherwise he might have added that imagination makes us free, but free to find the truth, not free from the obligation to look for the truth.

What are the ultimate beliefs? To a large extent, they are principles similar to that of simplicity of nature, but they lie deeper in our mental structure because they guide our choices even when we consciously reject them. As Torrance recalled, Einstein, Heisenberg, and many others identified as an ultimate belief the possibility to grasp reality with our theoretical constructions and the inner harmony of the world. Hume

---

32. Torrance, *Transformation*, ch. 5, 192f.
33. Russell, *An Outline of Philosophy*, 308.

mentioned, as we have seen, causality and the continuing, independent existence of things. Another belief we all have purports that real chance cannot exist. Whenever we speak of chance, we make of it a cause of events, as the Romans did with the goddess Fortuna; thus, however shameful it may sound to modern enlightened culture, we must admit that an ultimate belief of all men is that all events have a cause. Along the same line, one should admit as an ultimate belief that all events have a role or function in the "whole show," as the Great Dance image implies.

Can an ultimate belief be wrong? Can one do without ultimate beliefs? As to the first question, the answer is double-faced. There is in principle a way to prove that an ultimate belief is wrong: examining the consequences of its adoption. However, since in that very examination we will most probably use that belief, the procedure might produce "undecidable" statements. The question would be better posed if it were phrased as follows: can an ultimate belief be misapplied? That seems possible, but then the critical task of the conscious mind is precisely to remove the crowd of ill-justified intuitions and emotional overtones that accompany certain ultimate beliefs, e.g., the belief in supernatural beings, which could lead to the most horrifying consequences, as in the human sacrifices of the Aztecs of Mexico. As to the second question, it would seem that the answer is negative. A simple example is the paradoxical faith of that remarkable unlogical logician who, after denying the existence of any grounds for beliefs, spoke of *noble* ideals, thus asking his readers to accept a term that implies belief in the possibility of distinguishing, at least subjectively, between what is noble and what is ignoble.

Ultimate beliefs provide an answer to a remark by Einstein and at the same time they open another problem. Einstein said that what he found most difficult to understand was why nature should be understandable. In answer to Einstein, one might recall that man is part of nature: why should one be so surprised that nature should be intelligible, when we are built with the same materials and the same laws as everything else? After all, we know that logical operations can be realized by pieces of matter (the microprocessors of computers), and that may be seen as an experimental proof that physical processes match exactly our (logical) mental processes. It would have been different if we had found that nature is *intelligent*; but then — and here is the new question — should we not take the intelligibility of nature as an argument in favor of a "God principle" according to which God is a supreme intelligence? In other words, we might argue as follows: nature is intelligible, and obeys the laws of logic, but, as far as we can see, it is not capable of self-conscious knowing; it is similar to a sheet of paper that contains the solution of a difficult mathematical problem, but does not realize that important fact. Now, nature is not our creation; the principle that it has been created by a personal God, with whom we share a little of the same "active intellect" (cf. chapter twelve) makes the existence of something intelligible and not intelligent perfectly acceptable. One can assume that nature itself is God, as was done by the Jewish-Dutch philosopher Benedict Spinoza (1632–1677) but the history of philosophy suggests that the resulting world-view is not sufficient to warrant the acceptance of Spinoza's pantheistic version of the "God principle."

From Science to a Standpoint on Reality

We can now face our last task: examining what questions a world-view should answer, how it should be constructed, and how far it is possible to transfer to its construction the epistemological scheme, the structure, and the cognitive procedure of science. Let us start from the idea that what we want is a coherent picture based, precisely as science, on certain primary facts and on certain principles. The following scheme substantially matches the structure of science as described above, and indicates where the differences are.

a. The problems a world-view is supposed to tackle are more general and in part essentially different from those of science. What is demanded is an answer to existential and philosophical questions arising from science, the inner experience of man, history and sociology.

b. Among the questions to be answered the following, listed somewhat at random, are probably the most important ones:

- Is the universe a reality to be accepted as such?
- Is it reasonable to attribute design and purpose to the universe?
- Is there intelligence in the universe?
- What is the place of man in the universe?
- Is free will a fact?
- Are there ethical rules independent of social conventions?
- Is there a spiritual dimension of reality, meaning by "spiritual" beings or properties inaccessible to science, but accessible to our inner experience and to an examination of patterns in history?
- Has man a spiritual side to his nature?
- Is there a purpose to human life beyond the pursuit of material satisfactions?
- Is death the end of a person?
- Is there a supreme spiritual being?

c. The primary facts are largely the same as those of science, although science must ignore those facts which it cannot explain in terms of its principles and of (at least statistically) reproducible experimental results. They have already been briefly reviewed in the preceding chapters, and are reviewed in other books. However, there are facts resulting from history and from psychological experiences not reproducible at will (e.g., mysticism), which a world-view should address.

d. The logical rules are the same.

e. The requirement of self-consistency or internal coherence is the same. However, there is an additional requirement of the same kind: the scheme to be found should be in full accord with established results of the three fields of knowledge mentioned above.

f. The principles or axioms required will of necessity be different in nature from those of science because the questions to be answered are different. For example, if you want an answer to the question, "Does every human being have an assignment in this world deriving from his or her very nature?" the principles on which your arguments should rely cannot be the same as the answer to a question concerning the motion of the molecules in a gas. They, however, should fulfill the same conditions as those of science, namely they should result from

- generalization of facts or rules;
- significant analogies;
- ability to ensure an optimum coherence of the theory.

A detailed discussion of the questions listed under b, which a world-view should address, is out of the scope of this book, for it would amount to constructing a philosophical system or to proposing a theological theory of the world. What we should do next is rather what we began with, and use the ideas just reviewed to look at the world-view suggested by the considerations made in the preceding chapters and conveyed by the image of the Great Dance. As I have pointed out several times since the first chapter, what matters in real life is one's personal *Weltanschauung* — i.e. one's partly subconscious manner of making sense of inner and outer experience — rather than a systematic philosophical construction. Nevertheless, a discussion of the nature and scope of a world-view and the way in which it could be constructed is important, because a *Weltanschauung* is anyway a world-view as it were at draft level: as somebody said — in answer to the well known maxim "first live, then philosophize" — *vivere est philosophari*, to live *is* to philosophize, i.e., to try to make sense of the facts of life. In this spirit we should now conclude our attempt to find out, keeping in mind the points listed above, on what grounds a scientifically sound world-view should rest, why different solutions might be adopted in perfect good faith, and what sort of world-view would be consistent with the Great Dance image.

A "Scientific" *Weltanschauung*

We have seen that, in constructing a world-view as well as in adopting a *Weltanschauung*, we should have, as in the natural sciences, a specific kind of questions, evidence to work on, interpretive principles, and criteria for the assessment of both facts and principles. The evidence consists of facts which we accept as such as is done in science, not only because of tests in the laboratory but because of analogies and inferences, as science does for example with the existence of dinosaurs. The principles serve as general laws connecting the facts to one another; not necessarily in terms of a cause-effect relationship, but also as a means-end one, as is normally the case in biology. The final acceptance of the principles and their implications rests on the ability of the "theory" to accommodate all ascertained facts and to provide, in a noncontradictory way, indeed with a maximum of coherence, arguments in favor of a decision about facts that are still *sub judice*.

If this is how things stand, why are there so many antithetic answers to the fundamental existential questions of humanity? The answer is easy: it is partly because science works on observable phenomena for which there is a regularity everybody accepts, partly — perhaps mainly — because the acceptance of a conclusion concerning the meaning of our existence implies a definition of our responsibilities and duties, and many of us do not see why we should sacrifice our supposed freedom to do what we like to a *Weltanschauung* or a world-view which, in order to be coherent, requires that we ourselves should behave in accordance with it. It follows that we might choose certain principles not because they account best for the world and ourselves, but because they leave us as free as possible to act as we like. It is perhaps wise not to give examples, for there are too many of them around, and to recall them might be branded as moralism. But consider one thing: it may be very well that a man considers himself all right because he would never kill anybody, but what if he campaigns, for ideological motives, in favor of ideas — say, the "value" of transgression — which might lead many young people to become drug addicts?

If science demanded a personal commitment such as a coherent *Weltanschauung* demands, many people would be against science. Let me recall the curious example of this which I have already mentioned. The animal rights activists are against testing drugs on animals, and one may be sympathetic to their views. But some such activists, in a full page advertisement, began the exposition of their reasons with the statement that "experimenting on animals cannot really be useful for man because they belong to other species." Considering that the first vaccine was the anti-rabies vaccine, tested (as all the others) on animals, one can see how what is felt to be a good cause can make people blind to the most evident facts.

Now imagine what happens when the issues at hand lie beyond the limits of science. A parable reported in the Gospel of Luke makes this point very clearly, quite apart from its religious significance. A rich man had been sent to Hell, particularly for his indifference to the sufferings of Lazarus, a poor man now in Paradise. He called to Abraham for help, but Abraham explained that it was impossible for him to do anything, because of the laws which rule those places.

> The rich man said, "Well, father, I beg you, send Lazarus to my father's house, where I have five brothers, so that they, at least, will not come to this place of pain." Abraham said: "Your brothers have Moses and the prophets to warn them; let your brothers listen to what they say." The rich man answered: "That is not enough, father Abraham! But if someone were to rise from death and go to them, then they would turn from their sins." But Abraham said, "If they will not listen to Moses and the prophets, they will not be convinced even if someone were to rise from the dead."[34]

This example applies to the questions that many eminent scientists today recognize as most fundamental, even when they are only interested in their own specialty: the place of man in the universe and the values which should guide him. If we are not prepared to do our best to put our egos aside, and if we only listen to what pleases us, then we have made our choice, and our ideas are likely to be biased beyond remedy.

---

34. Luke 16:19–31. The translation is that of the American Bible Society, reprinted by Days Inns.

Chapter 14

Envoy

What questions would take shape in the mind of a man contemplating the world around him while it passes from night into daylight? Might he not end up by sharing Pascal's and Einstein's feeling that the study of sensible reality establishes communication with something or someone beyond matter?

The Image of the Dance – Meditation – The Rules of the Dance – Science and a Spiritual Outlook

Yes or no, has human life a meaning, and has man a destiny? I act, but without even knowing exactly who I am nor indeed if I am....

I will clear this off my heart. If there is something to see, I want to see it. Perhaps shall I learn if, yes or no, that ghost I am to myself, with this universe which I carry in my eyes, with science and its magic, with the strange dream of consciousness, has any solidity....

The problem is inevitable; man solves it inevitably; and the solution, right or wrong, but voluntary and at the same time necessary, is carried by each person in his actions. — MAURICE BLONDEL[1]

The Image of the Dance

The reader might expect that we now gather up the threads and suggest a *Weltanschauung*. But, as we have seen in the preceding chapter, a manner of interpreting the world to guide a person's actions demands a personal commitment, and a personal path of justification: it is a spiritual enterprise. We have seen that science often arrives at results which would make sense if a spiritual dimension of reality existed; we have also seen that it suggests how a satisfactory *Weltanschauung* could be chosen; yet the actual choice is a matter of wisdom, not just of knowledge. That is why we must leave our exploration as it stands. But one thing we can perhaps say: if the Great Dance image is correct, if all beings and objects in the universe have a role to play in the harmony of the whole, if man is a responsible animal, then the choice is already restricted. For example, at least at first sight, neither the belief in the primacy of human reason nor the belief in abstention from action as a way to reach perfect tuning to the Dance seem consistent with the picture of the universe offered by today's science. The Great Dance seems to require that a being such as man should play an active personal role guided by loving attention and respect for all other beings. That is as much as one can perhaps say without abandoning science altogether. As to what it implies, before saying farewell to the reader, let me propose what Einstein called a *Gedanken-*

---

1. *Oui ou non, la vie humaine a-t-elle un sens, et l'homme a-t-il une destinée? J'agis, mais sans connaître au juste qui je suis ni même si je suis....*

J'en aurai le coeur net. S'il y a quelque chose à voir, j'ai besoin de le voir. J'apprendrai peut-être si, oui ou non, ce fantôme que je suis à moi-même, avec cet univers que je porte dans mon regard, avec la science et sa magie, avec l'étrange rêve de la conscience, a quelque solidité....

Le problème est inévitable; l'homme le résout inévitablement; et cette solution, juste ou fausse, mais volontaire en même temps que nécessaire, chacun la porte dans ses actions. Blondel, *L'action*, viif.

experiment, a thought-experiment, on the relation of man to himself, life, and the universe.

Meditation

Think of a clear, mild night in the countryside, say, somewhere in the Great Plains of North America. For some unaccountable reason, you wake up in the uncertain hour before the morning. Finding that sleep is not coming back, you put on something heavy and go out to wait for sunrise in the large wooden armchair which somebody placed on the patio, facing the east, ages ago. Before you, the plain recedes to the end of the world, still covered by the deep shadows of the night. There is no wind. The world is enwrapped in silence. Only the lonely call of a night bird, coming from far away, breaks it at long intervals.

You gaze for a while at the remote horizon, then you raise your eyes to the sky. It is full of stars. Among a crowd of tiny dots of light just at the limit of vision, luminous gems shine, and here and there the deep blue background is replaced by a diffuse nebulosity — a dust of stars or a luminous fog. You think of what science has discovered. The tiny lights may be small stars, but some of them are actually great beacons shining in space, millions of times more remote and brilliant than those stars which shine most brightly in the sky. Some may well be like our sun, supplying their planets with energy and life; others are probably lonely jewels, sending their light into empty space for some mysterious purpose, or for no purpose at all. The tools man shaped — telescopes, radiotelescopes, spectrometers, space probes — have also revealed other objects in the depths of space, visible and invisible, double stars, quasars, black holes, pulsars, dark dust clouds, and so on. You think of the dreams written down in certain books, about dark clouds many times the solar system in size, magnetic winds producing terrible storms, asteroid belts circling as reefs of space beyond the orbit of Pluto, swarms of comets traveling from one galaxy to another.

Those may be dreams, but one thing is certain: in the lights in the sky great wonders are hidden; science is slowly discovering some of them — but the greater mysteries remain unriddled. You pause on the strangest of them: why do those lights fill man, an animal living on a tiny dot in the immensity of the universe, with awe and longing for something indefinite, but great? The mystery is made yet deeper by the fact that whatever man knows or will know about those lights in the sky is an inexplicable gift without apparent motives: for it is they that send us messages allowing us to guess something about what they are, where they are, how long they will live. "Is it possible," you wonder, "that they give us no hints as to why they exist?"

*   *   *

You listen to the stillness, but your mind refuses to relax. "Is it possible," you think, "that such wonders are just the product of chance? Why should chance have produced such beauty and variety? Maybe beauty is merely a human feeling; but, then, why do I feel that they are so beautiful? Why were my remote ancestors so impressed by the mystery of the stars, even in times when they did not know what the stars could be? In those times, they thought they could see in the sky figures of people and animals. They realized that the yearly change of those constellations marked the seasons, as if they were mysterious powers ruling the world. What if, after all, they were right? What if, up there, among the stars, or beyond them in some invisible and intangible portion of reality, there are intelligences or one intelligence which made everything for some unimaginable purpose?"

*   *   *

Your eyes pause on a star, low on the eastern horizon, which you had not noticed before: it is so bright that the stars near it appear paler. It must be the Bringer of Light, the Morning Star — not a remote sun, probably, but the planet Venus. And another question comes to your mind. Science has made it possible to send space probes to Venus. Fifty years ago, it was thought to be similar to the earth in its youth, maybe with herds of dinosaurs and forests of giant ferns. It now seems that it is hostile to life as we know it. What a deception, what a new source of wonder. Maybe traces of a past life can be found on Mars, but what would the use be of that discovery? And again: why are we so eager to know?

"All right," you think, "let us grant that it is a mystery man will never unveil. But one thing is sure: we want to belong in the wonder science is disclosing day by day, we want to find in the universe not only life, but intelligent life. We want to be there, in communion with the universe, with the intelligences which surely inhabit it. That is our home, and we shall be unquiet until we are sure that the planet where we happen to be is part of our home." The poetical dream of Olaf Stapledon, when he dreamed that he could leave his body and wander among the stars and the galaxies, meeting manlike beings everywhere at all stages of evolution, had something in it. Perhaps Stapledon missed many things, perhaps he accepted too easily the extension of evolutionism and rationalism to the future of mankind, but his was a meditation on intelligence in the universe, and on something science is only now discovering: the subtle network of communication, the underlying communion — which science calls coherence — of all things. Maybe that communion is already full, though changing and evolving all the time, and it is men who, because of lack of humility and discipline, are not capable of tuning all their actions to it; maybe the Dance is steadily developing toward some unimaginable finale — but anyway it would seem that what man wants in order to be at peace is full participation in it — perfect tuning to the Dance.

*   *   *

Lulled by the silence and the solitary regular cry of the night bird far in the plain, you pause on the implications. And then, like one suddenly recalled from a dreaming state to full wakefulness by the recollection of a past moment of terror, you realize that most of what you are imagining beyond the appearances of the firmament is but what human science says. Is it all really true? Science makes sense, facts seem to support it as far as can be reasonably expected, but why should man be so efficient in getting knowledge of the world and interfering with it? Here is another mystery: if science is true, should we not feel about it as the ancients did when they made up the myth of Prometheus, to remind men that fire had been stolen from the gods? Were the alchemists not right, when they kneeled down humbly to thank the Source of all wisdom for the knowledge they had been granted, and prayed that he, Master and Father, would grant them still more of that knowledge which is also wisdom?

"Here," you think, "lies a mystery in the mystery. Some say that man appeared by chance in the universe. But is it possible that a tiny creature like man should be able to understand anything in the universe if he is just a chance product of the blind, relentless march of an unconscious power? Or is the self-consciousness of man a spark of the unimaginable perfection of a Being that is more one and more permanent than any being could be, even at the highest complexity level of organized matter?"

*   *   *

Dawn points. A gleam is emerging from below the horizon. Soon the world around you will wake up, activity will begin. You wait. And you hear birds beginning their songs of welcome to the new day, a cow mooing far away, even what sounds like a human call. The change is slow, but unmistakable: the mystery of the night is passing into the mystery of the day. And the new mystery becomes all the more impressive when the red disk of the sun appears at the horizon.

With sunrise, everything is changed. The stillness of the night is only a memory. No longer is the bird singing which nature had chosen as a sentinel of the night, in exchange, perhaps, for a few prey: no longer are a multitude of creatures asleep under the bushes and in holes in the ground. Activity has begun again. From the trees behind the house you can hear the birds: you had not realized till today how noisy those small graceful creatures can be: like small children at school when the teacher is not there.

That thought reminds you of the people in the city, getting ready for work. In a short time they too will all be in full activity, driving big machines, collecting documents, watching their monitors, attending school,

preparing burglaries. A movie of many years ago comes to your mind —
Koyaniskatsi, "crazy life." You remember a remark of a French friend:
"Qu'est-ce qui les fait courir?" — what is driving them?

You think of the standard answer: money, power, and sex. But you are
not convinced. "Perhaps," you think, "that is not enough, supposing it is
correct. Money, power, sex are only efficacious ways to forget a void in
one's soul. For that matter, even absorbing activities like painting a landscape or writing a computer program are ways to forget one's existence
and responsibilities. That seems to be what certain social psychologists
had in mind, when they begged the question by claiming that 'there is
only one meaning to life: the act of living itself.' But there are people
who feel grateful to their gods if, at the end of a day's toil, they can bring
to their families enough for the next day's needs; there are people for
whom even personal success is worth nothing if it is not a way to make
oneself useful to others; there are people who think that life has such a
deep meaning that they devote their lives to assist human beings dying
alone on sidewalks among the indifference of the passersby; and there are
people who believe that prayer is the highest occupation. What should
one make of them? Explain their choices as the results of complicated
Freudian mechanisms?" Here you pause. For you have the feeling that
if the ideas of those social psychologists were in accordance with the
genuine nature and condition of man, everybody would be happy and
wise in the affluent permissive societies of our time. As happened with
other recipes for a social paradise, a test is under way; and the results
are frightening.

You realize you have allowed your emotions to take control of your
mind. You let your eyes wander toward the remote horizon and slowly
calm down. "Be that as it may," you think, "I feel that there should be a
more general driving force for the apparently senseless activity of nature
and, particularly, of human beings. The evidence science provides could
help a lot in this connection."

That is an intriguing thought. A comparison of what is known about
the various animal species suggests that *Homo sapiens* is a pioneering
species, which can only play its role by combining social instincts with
reliance on the free initiatives of individuals. Maybe that is the key to the
incessant activity of people, over and beyond their primary needs: the
social instinct of the human individual, who wants to find a place among
other people, is somehow actualized as desire for power and money;
the instinct which drives a human being to find a complement to his or
her personality in a family is actualized in the search for mere physical
pleasure. Those actualizations seem incomplete; perhaps they result when
the individuals do not apply their freedom and their reason, as nature
expects, to control their drives in accordance with suitable standards.
"All right," you think, "but why should they?"

And then an answer comes to your mind. It is a common experience that an ordinary man is bound to lose touch with all that is beautiful and true, to lose peace with himself and with the world, to begin a personal descent into hell if he gives up the quest for a meaning of life. He will always find that whatever power or money or pleasures he has are not enough, and, far from finding peace, he will slowly become a slave of his own lust. Lost will be the wonders of the stars, the beauty of poetry, the everyday miracle of sunrise. "There must be rules," your inner voice says, "which a man should follow in order to avoid such a dismal fate. But how can one find them? Can the study of how the things change that are immersed in space-time provide an answer?" You go back in your mind to the results discussed in the chapters of this book, and the answer seems clear. It cannot. First, the scientists now know too much to believe that science can offer a complete and coherent picture of the universe in all its interrelated patterns of change. Second, rules guiding us to adjust as finely as possible to the evolving, unpredictable Harmony of the Great Dance could only be known by the composer who has it all in his mind. "No wonder," you continue, "that some people say that either there are no rules, or they are spontaneously applied whenever we act. I for one am ready to believe that they are inscribed in our nature; but they are subconscious, and take control only when the species is in danger, otherwise atrocities and perversions would not exist. As an individual, I am expected to find them and accept them freely. But where can I find them, if nothing and no one gives me a hint? Only if there is a spiritual dimension of reality, as the billions of men and women believe who pray every day, only if one chooses, as Augustine did, to believe in a Creator who has sent us a message, then perhaps can one really learn how to tune in to the Harmony of the Whole."

*   *   *

The sun is already several degrees above the horizon. The images and sounds of every day surround you. Perhaps it is time for you too to start your day's activities. But something retains you. From far away, accompanied by long moos, a noise arrives which at first sounds unfamiliar: a freight train passing somewhere in the distance. After a while, you hear a rumble, rapidly growing in volume and pitch to the unmistakable noise of a jet engine. It fills the air, and an arrow-like silhouette passes over you, vanishing with its noise behind the house. A military plane on a training flight?

Great advances indeed have taken place since the time of the Wright brothers. For a moment, you think that after all there are grounds for a just pride. But then you pause. Pride of what? Of the fact that man has a mind capable of entering communion with Nature, of learning her laws and applying them? Or pride of all the good which man, with discipline and renunciation, has been able to do with high technology? Something rings false, here. A few of the missiles that airplane could fire would do enough harm to balance all the good the technology behind it has made possible. Or, for that matter, can all the useful information one can find by means of worldwide computer networks compensate for just one horrible episode of slavery and abuse of children which those networks made possible?

"Nevertheless," you consider, "the fault is not with Science and Technology: it is with ourselves. We flee from responsibility, we define freedom as 'nonsubmission to any *higher* power,' we kill the voice of our conscience by using whatever talents and power we have to campaign against those who preach love and wisdom. We keep saying 'there is no spiritual dimension of reality, hence there is no supreme Lawmaker,' while a tide is rising against the very future of our species, against children. Is that not scientific evidence that the human animal cannot survive if it refuses to the spiritual dimension of reality?"

*   *   *

Somebody is calling for breakfast. "Perhaps, my need for a good breakfast points to the solution," you think; "let me forget everything, and let me live everyday life as it comes. Was that not a piece of advice by a great teacher of the past?" But you know that that is only part of the story. Breakfast is necessary; as our ancestors used to say, *mens sana in corpore sano*, the mind can only be healthy in a healthy body. But the problem is precisely what one should do with life, when the mind and the body are correctly working. Play a computer game? Go jogging? Read advertisements to find a new exciting restaurant? Meet colleagues to organize actions for more free time? Get a new, more exciting horoscope from the reputed Madame Sesostris?

*   *   *

It is time to attend to ordinary occupations. In going out, you have a last look at the sky. The stars and the silence of the night are no longer real. Were they ever there? Is the world of spirit like the stars in a land where night never comes, where no sensory experience will ever tell the inhabitants that there are stars?

The Rules of the Dance

That was the end of our thought experiment.[2] Try it yourself, and see if you do not come up with the same kind of questions. Here is what

2. The book by O. Stapledon to which the "meditator" referred is *Starmaker* (1937; reprint, New York: Berkley, 1961). Madame Sesostris is a character in T. S. Eliot's *Wasteland*.

they will boil down to. From man's viewpoint, the Dance is like a great, complicated, evolving puzzle. Under the guidance of the great principles and the rigorous methods of science, the pieces discovered by the various disciplines find their place one after the other. But great gaps remain. Some can be filled by facts about man and his psyche, others by the study of history. But the complete picture is not to be reconstructed except if some great ordering principle is found outside science. We have already recalled the concise statement of this fact by Jacques Monod, the eminent biologist famous for his faith in "blind chance": if science tells us all there is to know about the world and ourselves, then

> man is alone in the indifferent immensity of the Universe. Neither his destiny nor his duty are written anywhere. It is up to him to choose between the Kingdom and the Darkness.[3]

Monod was right, but he was too pessimistic; for, as we have seen, science gives us hints in the form of missing pieces of the puzzle that is the Dance of all things, the most important piece being the very universality of coherence and harmony. Apart from that, the great ordering principle is outside its scope.

Monod's great ordering principle was that whatever science cannot assess in the laboratory is chance or illusion. We have tried to suggest that such a view is not really consistent with the story science appears to tell; for if a man accepts it, then he may have to give up truth, beauty and justice at the same time, lest he be accused of incoherence. It would seem that the only alternative is to face a truth which is neither pleasant nor comfortable for most of the people of affluent societies: that the path to living a full life is opened neither by a lot of free time nor by the cult of transgression. Was it Francis Bacon who, for all his emphasis on the power of man over nature, said that if a Creator did not exist, we should invent one?

As we said already, it is not within the scope of this book to discuss religious issues. As far as this book is concerned, it is up to the reader to choose between the Kingdom and the Darkness. Our emphasis on the former is justified by the fact that "darkness" is far more popular and well known — meaning by it the decision to ignore spiritual issues altogether. At any rate, should the reader be tempted to adopt the spiritual solution, or, having already adopted it, to examine in more detail what it implies, then a few comments will be useful.

Science and a Spiritual Outlook

Those great men in history, like St. Augustine and Blaise Pascal, who represent the conjunction of a high scientific spirit with a genuine reli-

---

3. J. Monod, *Le hasard*, 195.

gious faith, even went as far as explaining how one could proceed in choosing a theistic ordering principle. Of Augustine, we have already said something; as to Pascal, let us recall his famous *pari*, the bet on the Christian God.[4] By saying that the religious choice is a bet, he meant that it is not possible to give a logical proof of the existence of God, which is a principle, and cannot be derived logically from any other premise;[5] moreover, at least in the case of God as Christianity conceives Him, it demands a lot in terms of discipline, renunciation and hard work with no sensible reward. Therefore, Pascal says, if you decide to be a (loyal) Christian, you take a risk and should consider the price you have to pay. But, he adds, there is also a gain, in terms of coherence, of love given and received, of freedom from the obsession of success, of a life beyond the threshold of death.

The analogy with a bet makes it easier to understand why it is not enough to accept a vague notion of Supreme Being. As the title of a strange science fiction novel by Clifford Simak says,[6] one has "a choice of gods," at the philosophical as well as at the religious level. Indeed, our time offers at least four great religions. Now, having chosen to consent to the existence of a spiritual reality, one will have to consider which view of it is most likely to complete the picture whose pieces form the puzzle of the universe, so as to make, out of the incredibly varied and yet harmonious and coherent universe which science is discovering, a whole to which man is perfectly tuned, in which duty and destiny are inscribed. Some think that, since communication, active and passive, is a feature of the Great Dance, strictly connected with its always novel development in time, the best choice for man would be a personal God, who has set as the ideal optimum state of mankind that in which the will of each individual to help others to be in measure with the Dance is maximum; a personal God who has set love of other men and of nature as the basic reference value for each human person.

Far from providing an easy path toward passive acceptance of everything, the choice of a "loving Creator" as the basic principle of a *Weltanschauung* requires an active commitment as well as renunciation and discipline. Moreover, it cannot be expected to clarify many mysteries, if only because the human mind is limited; but it could supply pieces filling the gaps in the puzzle picture offered by science. Those pieces will probably do so only in outline, but clearly enough to make the puzzle into that coherent view a man wants if he is to understand how to play his part of the Dance.

4. B. Pascal, *Pensées*, Lafuma, 418.

5. We say "logically" thinking of the proof of a mathematical theorem. This does not mean that there are no rational arguments for the existence of God; the famous "five ways" of Thomas Aquinas are the best known such arguments.

6. C. D. Simak, *A Choice of Gods* (New York: G. P. Putnam's Sons, 1972).

Such a choice also requires courage. You have to believe in a God who is at the same time a person and the entity in which truth, beauty and justice are realities in themselves; and you have to decide that the mystery of evil will not diminish commitment to love. Paradoxically, it is to Lucien Goldmann, a man who studied religion as a thing of the past, who had granted full faith to Marxism-Leninism, that we owe a very interesting commentary on the Christian faith of Pascal:

> It is because the existence of God is no longer for the fallen man absolutely and simply certain that Pascal could, indeed had to elaborate a theory of the world and of earthly physical, biological, and social reality. It is because man, being man, cannot be satisfied in any way and to any degree by an insufficient and relative world that this theory could attain a realism free from all intramundane illusion, all caution and all compromise, and it could situate itself on the highest scientific and philosophical plane compatible with his time and historical situation.

> One can thus see the importance, for a coherent interpretation of the life and work of Pascal, along with the absolute insufficiency of any intramundane reality, along with the impossibility to find rest in this world, of the impossibility, not less radical, to have a certitude simple and not paradoxical of the existence of God, the impossibility to ignore the world and find refuge in loneliness and eternity.[7]

Being a Marxist, Goldmann limited the validity of Pascal's views to his time and historical situation. As the breakdown of recipes for a paradise on earth has shown, the "contradictions and paradoxes" which prompted Pascal's world-view are present also in today's planetary civilization. Indeed, with the discovery of randomness in natural processes, of the spontaneous emergence of order, of universal coherence and communication, science has given stronger support to the belief that the "intramundane" reality, the reality of nature and society, is not sufficient for the psychological needs of man.

Of course, it would be illusory to expect that even fully open-minded acceptance of a spiritual dimension of reality would eliminate all problems and unveil all mysteries; if that is what one is looking for, then it would be much easier (though not so easily justified) to dismiss all mysteries and problems as mere psychological constructs. If, on the other hand, one wants to know what one's role in the Dance is, belief in the existence of a Composer and Director of the Dance might be the answer. That was the foundation of the world-view of men like Pascal long before modern biology and cosmology made the Dance image actual.

7. L. Goldmann, *Le Dieu caché* (Paris: Gallimard, 1959), 316f.

Paradoxically, what those creative men believed in was full acceptance of the will of God. That was not a contradiction, because for them the will of the Cosmic Choreographer was that each human being should take a creative part in the harmoniously evolving figures of the Dance. Indeed, if a joyful acceptance of one's role in it is what was meant by the man who said that the meaning of life is the act of living, then, in the frame of Pascal's views, that man had stated a far more profound truth than he thought.[8] For, in that frame, it is the will of God that gives meaning to our life, and God's will is precisely that a person should fully live his or her life as a free, creative, passionate participant in the cosmic Dance. Pascal more than others realized how much there is that man cannot understand, not least the reason why a loving, almighty Being should allow pain and grief to mar the perfection of the Dance. But, being a genius, he knew more than others how little man knows, and he was content with having grasped the meaning of life. In that sense, also Einstein, who limited his religiosity to belief in a supreme intelligence revealing itself in the physical world, would probably have agreed with the spirit of Piccarda Donati, when she said to Dante:

> *E'n la sua volontade è nostra pace:*
> *ell' è quel mare al qual tutto si move,*
> *ciò ch'ella cria o che natura face.*

> And his will is our peace; this is the sea
> To which is moving onward whatsoever
> It doth create, and all that nature makes.[9]

It is a peace — shall I say it again? — which is not resignation, but serene confidence that, even in circumstances which seem unpropitious, the choice to fight for truth, beauty, and the dignity of every human person is the right one; that it is indeed the only choice consistent at the same time with the exigencies of our inner self and with the role we are expected to play in the world which today's science offers to us for our belief.

8. If the reader would like to reflect on action and science in this direction, he should perhaps read the lucid and profound studies offered by M. Blondel and by K. Wojtyla in the works cited above.

9. Dante Alighieri, *Divine Comedy*, 33.85–87, Longfellow tr.

Bibliography

The following list of books and articles is intended, (a), to provide a quick reference to repeated citations in the footnotes of this book and, (b), to give additional information about books and their translations. Of course, for complete details the reader should consult library sources, particularly the Library of Congress catalog, available on Internet.

Agazzi, E., ed. *Probability in the Sciences.* Dordrecht: Kluwer, 1988.

———. *Il bene e il male nella scienza* (Good and evil in science). Milan: Rusconi, 1992.

Alighieri, Dante. *Divina Commedia* (ca. 1310), in Dante Alighieri, *Opere di Dante, testo critico.* Ed. M. Barbi. Florence: Società Dantesca Italiana, 1921. Eng.-Am. trans. H. W. Longfellow, *Divine Comedy.* Internet: ELT web, Digital Dante Project, Columbia University.

Aquinas, Thomas. *Summa contra gentiles,* book 2, especially chs. 56–60. Eng. trans., with an intro. and notes, J. F. Anderson, *Summa contra gentiles, 2. Creation.* Notre Dame, Ind.: University of Notre Dame Press, 1975.

———. *In Aristotelis Libros Physicorum.* In *Selected Philosophical Writings.* Sel. and trans. T. McDermott. Oxford and New York: Oxford University Press, 1993.

Ibn'Arabî, M. *La Production des Cercles.* Trans. from Arab into French by P. Fenton and M. Gloton. Paris: Éd. de l'Éclat, 1996.

Aristotle. *De anima,* see F. A. Trendelenburg, J. D. Kaplan.

———. *Metaphysics.* Ed. and trans. J. Warrington London: Dent, 1956.

Audi, R. *The Cambridge Dictionary of Philosophy.* Cambridge: Cambridge University Press, 1995.

Augustine, Saint. *The Confessions.* Trans. M. Boulder. London: Hodder and Stoughton, 1997.

Ayer, A. J. *Language, Truth and Logic.* London: Gollancz, 1946.

Bacon, F. *Novum Organon.* 1620: reprint, Florence: Sansoni, 1942.

Barrow, J. D., and F. J. Tipler. *The Anthropic Cosmological Principle.* Oxford: Oxford University Press, 1986.

Baudrillard, J. *L'illusion de la fin:* ou *La grève des événements.* Paris: Galilée, 1992. Eng. trans. Charles Dudas, York University, Canada, as *Pataphysics of the Year 2000.* Internet text at www.CTheory.com.

Bergson, H. *L'énergie spirituelle.* 1919; reprint, Paris: Presses Universitaires de France, 1959.

———. *Les deux sources de la morale et de la religion.* 1932; reprint, Paris: Presses Universitaires de France, 1959. Eng. trans. R. Ashley-Avdra and C. Bereton, *The Two Sources of Morality and Religion.* Notre Dame, Ind.: University of Notre Dame Press 1977.

Bertalanffy, L. v. "General System Theory — A Critical Review," *General Systems* (1962): 1–20.

Biedermann, H. *Dictionary of Symbolism — Cultural Icons and the Meanings behind Them.* Trans. J. Hulbert. New York: Meridian 1994.

Blondel, M. *L'action.* 1893; reprint, Paris: Quadrige/Presses Universitaires de France, 1993. Eng. trans. O. Blanchette, *Action.* Notre Dame, Ind.: University of Notre Dame Press, 1986.

Blumenfeld, H. *Paradigmen zu einer Metaphorologie* (Paradigms for a science of metaphors). Vol. 6 of the series Archive für Begriffgeschichte. Bonn: H. Bouvier and Co., 1960.

Bocheński, J. M. *Wege zum philosophischen Denken.* Freiburg i. B., Germany: Herder, 1959.

Bodart, R. *Maurice Maeterlinck.* Paris: Seghers, 1962.

Brandmüller, W. *Galilei e la Chiesa, ossia il diritto ad errare* (Galileo and the church, the right to make mistakes). Vatican City: Libreria Editrice Vaticana, 1992.

Brian, D. *Einstein: A Life.* New York: John Wiley, 1996.

Brooke, J. H. *Science and Religion: Some Historical Perspectives.* Cambridge: Cambridge University Press, 1991.

Buchanan, S., ed. *The Portable Plato.* New York: Penguin Books, 1982.

Bull, J. R., and M. Goldinger. *Philosophy and Contemporary Issues.* New York: Macmillan, 1976.

Bullock, A., O. Stallybrass, and S. Trombley, eds. *The Fontana Dictionary of Modern Thought.* London: Fontana Paperbacks, 1988.

Burckhardt, T. *Alchemie: Sinn und Weltbild.* Olten, Switzerland: Walter, 1960. Eng. trans. W. Stoddard, *Alchemy: Science of the Cosmos, Science of the Soul.* Shaftesbury: Element, 1986.

Capra, F. *The Tao of Physics.* New York: Wildwood House, 1975.

Carlyle, T. *Sartor Resartus.* 1838; London: Dent, Everyman's Library, 1973.

Carnap, R., and Y. BarHillel. *An Outline of a Theory of Semantic Information.* Boston: MIT Res. Lab. of Electronics, Technical rep. 247, 1952.

Carpenter, H. *The Inklings: C. S. Lewis, J. R. R. Tolkien, C. Williams and Their Friends.* London: George Allen & Unwin, 1978.

Carroll, L. *Alice's Adventures in Wonderland.* In *The Annotated Alice,* with intro. and notes by Martin Gardner. Cleveland: World Publishing Co., 1963.

———. *The Hunting of the Snark.* 1876; London: Chatto and Windus, 1941.

Cassirer, E. *Wesen und Wirkung der Symbolbegriff* (Nature and action of the concept of symbol). Darmstadt: Wissenschaftliche Buchgesellschaft, 1956.

Chalmers, D. *The Conscious Mind: In Search of a Fundamental Theory.* Oxford: Oxford University Press, 1996.

Chesterton, G. K. *The Ball and the Cross.* London: Wells Gardner, Darton & Co., 1910.

Chevalier, J., and A. Gheerbrant. *Dictionnaire des Symboles.* Paris: Robert Laffont/Jupiter, 1982. Eng. trans. J. Buchanan-Brown, *A Dictionary of Symbols.* Oxford and Cambridge, Mass.: Blackwell, 1994.

Clarke, A. C. *Rendezvous with Rama.* New York: Ballantine, 1974.

——. *The City and the Stars.* New York: Harcourt, Brace and World, 1953.

Colson, F. H., and G. H. Whitaker. *Philo in Ten Volumes.* London: Heinemann, and Cambridge, Mass.: Harvard University Press, 1929–1962.

Coyne, G. V., M. Heller, and J. Žičinski, eds. *The Galileo Affair: A Meeting of Truth and Science.* Città del Vaticano: Specola Vaticana, 1985.

D'Espagnat, B. *A la recherche du réel.* Paris: Gauthiers-Villars, 1979.

Darlton, C., and Perry Rhodan. *Das Mutanten Korps.* Ed. W. Voltz. Rastatt, Germany: Moewig, 1979.

Davies, P. *About Time: Einstein's Unfinished Revolution.* New York: Simon & Schuster, 1995.

Davy, M. M. *Initiation à la symbolique romane.* Paris: Flammarion, 1977.

Defoe, D. *Robinson Crusoe,* 1719.

Del Re, G., ed. *Brain Research and the Mind-body Problem: Epistemological and Metaphysical Issues.* Vatican City: Pontifical Academy of Sciences, 1992.

——. "Poincaré et le mécanisme." *Philosophia Scientiae* (Nancy), special issue 1, 1 (1996): 55–69.

Descartes, R. *Discours de la méthode.* (1637) Paris: Flammarion, 2000. Eng. trans., *Discourse on the Method and Meditations on First Philosophy.* Ed. D. Weissman. New Haven and London: Yale University Press, 1996.

Dewey, J. *Creative Intelligence.* New York: H. Holt & Co, 1917.

Donne, J. *Liriche sacre e profane: Sacred and Profane Poems.* Critical English Edition. Ed. G. Melchiori. Milan: Mondadori, 1983.

Eddington, A. S. *The Nature of the Physical World.* 1935; London: Dent, Everyman's Library, 1947.

Eigen, M., and P. Schuster. *The Hypercycle: A Principle of Natural Self Organization.* New York, Springer, 1979.

Einstein, A. *Mein Weltbild* (*The World as I See It*). 1934; reprint, Frankfurt: Ullstein Materialien, 1979.

Éliade, M. *Images et symboles: Essais sur le symbolisme magico-religieux.* Paris: Gallimard, 1952. Eng. trans. P. Mairet, *Images and Symbols.* London: Harvill Press 1961.

Eliot, T. S. *Four Quartets.* In *The Complete Poems and Plays 1909–1950.* New York: Harcourt Brace Jovanovich, 1971.

Engelmann, P. *Letters of Ludwig Wittgenstein.* Italian trans. Florence: La Nuova Italia, 1970.

Flamel, N. *Le livre des figures hiéroglyphiques.* 1624; Paris: Planète, 1971. Eng. trans. Eirenaeus Orandus, *Nicholas Flammel, His Exposition of the Hi-erographicall Figures Which He Caused to Be Painted upon an Arch in*

St. Innocent Church-Yard in Paris. London: T. S. for T. Walkley, 1624; ed. Laurinda Dixon. New York: Garland, 1994.

Fracastoro, G. Scritti inediti. Ed. F. Pellegrini. Verona: Valdonega, 1955.

Galilei, G. Dialogo sopra i due massimi sistemi del mondo. Florence: Landini, 1632. Eng. trans. S. Drake, Dialogue about the Two Chief Systems of the World. Berkeley: University of California Press, 1953.

Gallager, R. G. Information Theory and Reliable Communication. New York: John Wiley, 1968.

Galtier, G. Maçonnerie Égyptienne, Rose-Croix et Néochevalerie [Les fils de Cagliostro]. Alençon, France: Éditions du Rocher, 1989.

García Bazán, Francisco. Plotino y la gnosis. Buenos Aires: Fundación para la Educación, la Ciencia y la Cultura, 1981.

Gibbon, E. The Decline and Fall of the Roman Empire. 1776–1794; reprint, London: Dent, Everyman Library, 1966.

Gilchrist, C. Alchemy. Longmead, England: Element Books, 1991.

Gleick, J. Chaos. New York: Penguin, 1987.

Goldmann, L. Le Dieu caché. Paris: Gallimard, 1959.

Hardt, H. Communication, History and Theory in America. London and New York: Routledge, 1992.

Hartmann, N. Neue Wege der Ontologie. 1942; Stuttgart: Kohlhammer, 1949. Eng. trans. R. C. Kuhn, New Ways of Ontology. Westport, Conn.: Greenwood Press, 1975.

Heidegger, M. Holzwege. 5th ed. Frankfurt a.M.: Klostermann, 1972.

Heine, H. Buch der Lieder. 1827; Munich: Kindler, 1964.

Heisenberg, W. The Physical Principles of the Quantum Theory. Chicago: University of Chicago, 1930.

Hempel, C. G. Philosophy of Natural Sciences. Englewood Cliffs, N.J.: Prentice Hall, 1966.

Heschel, A. Who Is Man? Stanford, Calif.: Stanford University Press, 1965.

Hesse, H. Glasperlenspiel. 1943; reprint, Frankfurt a. M.: Suhrkamp, 1979. Eng. trans. R. and C. Winston, The Glass Bead Game (Magister Ludi). London: Cape, 1970.

Hippel, A. R. v., ed. Molecular Science and Molecular Engineering. New York: John Wiley and the Technology Press of M.I.T., 1959.

Hofstadter, R. Escher, Gödel, Bach: An Eternal Golden Braid. London: Basic Books, 1979.

Hurd, D. L., and J. J. Kipling, eds. The Origins and Growth of Physical Science. Harmondsworth, Eng.: Penguin Books, 1964.

Huxley, A. Brave New World. 1932; New York: Harper-Collins, 1989.

Huysmans, J.-K. A rebours. Paris: Charpentier, 1884. Eng. trans. with an intro. H. Ellis, Against the Grain. New York: Dover Publications, 1969.

———. En route. Paris: Tress & Stock 1895. Eng. trans. C. K. Paul. New York: H. Fertig, 1976.

Jacob, R. La logique du vivant: Une histoire de l'hérédité. Paris: Gallimard, 1971.

Jaspers, K. Allgemeine Psychopathologie. 1913. Eng. trans. J. Hoenig and M. W. Hamilton, General Psychopathology. Baltimore: Johns Hopkins University Press, 1997.

Jeans, J. H. *The Dynamical Theory of Gases.* New York: Dover, 1954, reprint of 4th ed. of 1926.

Journet, C. *Le mal: Essai théologique.* Paris: Desclée De Brouwer, 1961.

Jung, C. G., and M. L. von Franz, eds. *Man and His Symbols.* London: Aldus Books Ltd., 1964.

Jung, C. G. *The Role of the Unconscious.* 1918. In *Collected Works.* Vol. 9. Princeton, N.J.: Princeton/Bollingen, 1959.

Kant, I. *Der Streit der Facultäten.* In *Gesammelte Schriften.* Berlin: Preußische Akademie der Wissenschaften, 1902–1954. Eng. trans. M. J. Gregor, *The Conflict of the Faculties.* Lincoln: University of Nebraska Press, 1992.

Kaplan, J. D., and W. D. Ross, eds. *The Pocket Aristotle.* New York: Pocket Books, 1958.

Kemble, E. C. *The Fundamental Principles of Quantum Mechanics.* New York: Dover, 1937.

Kircher, A. *Musurgia Universalis.* Rome: Haer. Franc. Corbelletti, 1650.

Lamont, C. *Freedom of Choice Affirmed.* New York: Horizon, 1967.

Landau, L. L., E. M. Lifshits, and L. P. Pitaevski. *Statistical Physics.* Moscow: MIR, 1976.

Lao-Tzu. *Tao-teh-Ching.* Italian trans. and comments by J. Evola. Milan: Ceschina, 1959. The author cannot recommend the English translations he has been able to peruse.

Layzer, D. *Cosmogenesis.* New York: Oxford University Press, 1990.

Leoni, S. *Le armonie del mondo.* Genoa: ECIG, 1988.

Lewis, C. S. *Miracles.* London: Pan Books, 1947.

———. *The Abolition of Man.* London: Collins, 1944.

Lifschitz, M. S. *Operatory, Kolebanya, Vol'ny — Otkrytye Systemy* (Operators, oscillations, waves — open systems). Moscow: Izdatel'stvo Nauka, 1966.

Lohmann, M., ed. *Wohin führt die Biologie? Ein interdisziplinäres Kolloquium* (Where is biology leading us?) 1970; Munich: Deutscher Taschenbuch Verlag, 1977.

Lovelock, J. E. "Hands Up for the Gaia hypothesis." *Nature* 344 (1990): 100–102. Cf. *Nature* 207 (1965): 568–70.

MacDonald, G. *Phantastes.* 1858; Grand Rapids, Mich.: Eerdmans, 1981.

MacKay, D. *The Clockwork Image.* London: Inter-Varsity Press, 1974.

Manzoni, A. *I promessi sposi.* Milan: Ferrario, 1840. Eng. trans. A. Colquhoun, *The Betrothed.* London: Dent, Everyman's Library, 1950.

Maxwell, J. C. *A Dynamical Theory of the Electromagnetic Field (1864), with an Appreciation by A. Einstein.* Ed. and intro. T. F. Torrance. Edinburgh: Scottish Academic Press, 1982.

McKenzie, J. L. *Dictionary of the Bible.* New York: Bruce, 1971.

Mersenne, M. *Harmonie universelle.* Paris, 1636–37; reprint, Centre National de la Recherche Scientifique, 1963.

———. *Quaestiones in Genesim.* Paris: Sumptibus Sebastiani Cramoisy, 1623.

Monod, J. *Le hasard et la necessité.* Paris: Seuil, 1970. Eng. trans. Austryn Wainhouse, *Chance and Necessity.* New York: Knopf, 1972.

Morin, E. *Introduction à la pensée complexe.* Paris: ESF, 1990.

Nock, A. D., ed. *Corpus Hermeticum.* French trans. A.-J. Festugière. Paris: Belles Lettres, 1960.

Olby, R. *The Path to the Double Helix.* 1974; reprint, Mineola, N.Y.: Dover, 1994.

Parmenides. *On Being.* Ed. and trans. into German as *Über das Sein* by Hans v. Steuben. Stuttgart: Reclam, 1985.

Pascal, B. *Pensées.* Ca. 1660. Ed. Louis Lafuma. Paris: Éd. du Seuil, 1963. Eng. trans. *The Thoughts of Blaise Pascal.* Westport, Conn.: Greenwood Press, 1978.

Passmore, J. *A Hundred Years of Philosophy.* London: Penguin, 1968.

Pauwels, L., and J. Bergier. *Le matin des magiciens.* Paris: Gallimard, 1960. Eng. trans. R. Myers, *The Morning of the Magicians.* Chelsea, Mich.: Scarborough House, 1991.

Pedersen, O. *The Book of Nature.* Vatican City: Vatican Observatory Foundation, 1992.

Peitgen, H. O., and P. H. Richter. *The Beauty of Fractals: Images of Complex Dynamical Systems.* Heidelberg and New York: Springer, 1986.

Plato. *Phaedo.* Eng. trans. Benjamin Jowett, in Buchanan, *The Portable Plato,* q.v.

———. *Theaethetus.* Oxford: Clarendon, 1900.

Poincaré, H. *La science et l'hypothèse.* 1902; Paris: Champs-Flammarion, 1968. Eng. trans. *Science and Hypothesis.* New York: Dover, 1952.

Polanyi, M. *Personal Knowledge: Towards a Post-Critical Philosophy.* Chicago: University of Chicago Press, 1958; New York: Harper, 1964.

Popper, K. R., and J. C. Eccles. *The Self and Its Brain.* Berlin: Springer International, 1978.

Portmann, A. *Aufbruch der Lebensforschung.* Frankfurt a.M.: Suhrkamp, 1965.

Prigogine, I., and I. Stengers. *Entre le temps et l'éternité.* Paris: Flammarion, 1992.

———. *La nouvelle alliance.* Paris: Gallimard, 1979.

Pullman, B., ed. *The Emergence of Complexity.* Vatican City: Pontifical Academy of Sciences, 1996.

Purves, W. K., and G. H. Orians. *Life: The Science of Biology.* Sunderland, Mass.: Sinauer Associates, 1987.

Quine, W. O. *From a Logical Point of View.* Cambridge, Mass.: Harvard University Press, 1953, 1961.

Redfield, J. *The Celestine Prophecy.* New York: Warner Books, 1993.

Rensch, B. *Das universale Weltbild.* Frankfurt a.M.: Fischer, 1977.

Rossi, P. A. *Francesco Bacone.* Bari, Italy: Laterza, 1957.

Rubin, V. C., and G. V. Coyne, eds. *Large Scale Motions in the Universe.* Vatican City: Pontifical Academy of Sciences, 1988.

Ruskin, J. *Unto This Last and Other Writings.* Ed. Clive Wilmer. New York: Viking Penguin, 1985.

Russell, B. *An Outline of Philosophy.* 1927; New York: World, Meridian Books, 1960.

Salviucci, P., ed. *Semaine d'Étude sur Cerveau et expérience consciente.* Vatican City: Pontifical Academy of Sciences, 1965.

Schlesinger, A. M., Jr. "The Decline of Heroes." In Thruelsen and Kobler, *Adventures of the Mind,* q.v.

Schummer, J. *Realismus und Chemie.* Würzburg: Königshausen u. Neumann, 1996.

Shannon, C. E., and W. Weaver. *The Mathematical Theory of Complexity.* Chicago: University of Illinois Press, 1949.

Simak, C. D. *A Choice of Gods.* New York: G. P. Putnam's and Sons, 1972.

Slosson, E. E. *Creative Chemistry.* New York: Century, 1921.

Stapledon, O. *Starmaker,* 1937; reprint, New York: Berkley, 1961.

Stebbing, L. S. *Philosophy and the Physicists.* Harmondsworth, Eng.: Penguin, 1944.

Tacitus, P. C. *Agricola.* 98 A.D.. Eng. trans., with an intro. H. Mattingly and revision by S. A. Handford, *The Agricola and The Germania.* Harmondsworth, Eng.: Penguin, 1971.

Tart, C. T. *States of Consciousness.* New York: Dutton, 1975.

Teilhard de Chardin, P. *Le Phénomène humain.* Paris: Seuil, 1955. Eng. trans. B. Wall, *The Phenomenon of Man.* New York: Harper, 1959.

Templeton, J. M. *The Humble Approach.* New York: Continuum, 1995.

———. *Worldwide Laws of Life: 200 Eternal Spiritual Principles.* Philadelphia and London: Templeton Foundation Press, 1997.

Templeton, J. M., ed. *Evidence of Purpose.* New York: Continuum, 1994.

Templeton, J. M., and R. L. Herrmann. *Is God the Only Reality?* New York: Continuum, 1994.

Thom, R. *Prédire n'est pas expliquer.* Paris: Eshel, 199', Champs-Flammarion, 1993.

Thorpe, T. E. *Essays in Historical Chemistry.* 1894. Italian trans. R. Pitoni, *Storia della Chimica.* Turin: STEN, 1911.

Thruelsen, R., and J. Kobler, eds. *Adventures of the Mind.* First series. New York: Vintage Books, 1959.

Tipler, F. J. *The Physics of Immortality.* New York: Doubleday, 1994.

Tolkien, J. R. R. *The Lord of the Rings.* 1965; New York: Ballantine, 1973.

Torrance, T. F. *Divine and Contingent Order.* Oxford: Oxford University Press, 1981.

———. *Transformation and Convergence in the Frame of Knowledge.* Belfast: Christian Journals Ltd., 1984.

Toulmin, S., ed. *Quanta and Reality: A Symposium.* London: Hutchinson, 1962.

Trendelenburg, F. A. *Aristotelis de anima libri tres.* Graz: Akad. Druck- u. Verlagsanstalt, 1957. Cf. Kaplan et al.

Verne, J. *L'Ile mystérieuse.* Paris: Hetzel, 1874; photographic reprint, Paris: Hachette, 1977). Eng. trans., *The Mysterious Island.* New York: Permabooks/Pocket Books, 1961.

Vico, G. B. *Principi di una scienza nuova d'intorno alla comune natura delle nazioni.* 1732. Eng. trans. *The New Science of Giambattista Vico.* Ithaca, N.Y.: Cornell University Press, 1984.

Wahl, F. *Qu'est-ce que le structuralisme? 5. Philosophie.* Paris: Seuil, 1973.

Wassermann, C., R. Kirby, and B. Rordorff, eds. *The Science and Theology of Information.* Geneva: Labor et Fides, 1992.

Webster, A. G. *The Dynamics of Particles*. 1912; reprint, New York: Dover, 1959.

Weisheipl, J. A., ed. *Albertus Magnus and the Sciences — Commemorative Essays*. Toronto: Pontifical Institute of Mediaeval Studies, 1981.

Wheeler, J. A. "World as System Self-Synthetized by Quantum Networking." *IBM Journal of Research and Development* 32 (1988): 4–15.

Whitehead, A. N. *Process and Reality: An Essay in Cosmology.* New York: Free Press, 1978.

Whitrow, G. J. *The Natural Philosophy of Time*. Oxford: Clarendon Press, 1980.

Williams, C. W. *Many Dimensions*. 1931; reprint, Grand Rapids, Mich.: W. B. Eerdmans, 1981.

———. *The Greater Trumps*. 1932; reprint, Grand Rapids, Mich.: W. B. Eerdmans, 1976.

Wirth, O. *Les tarots des imagiers du Moyen Age*. Paris: Claude Tchou, 1966. Eng. trans. *The Tarot of the Magicians*. York Beach, Me.: S. Weiser, 1985.

Wojtyla, K. (Pope John Paul II). *The Acting Person*. Analecta Husserliana X, Dordrecht: Reidel, 1979.

Zeller, E., and R. Mondolfo. *La filosofia dei Greci nel suo sviluppo storico* (Greek Philosophy in its historical development). Ed. R. Del Re. Florence: La Nuova Italia, 1979. Part 3, vol. 4.

Index of Names

Index of Subjects

absorption of light. *See also* light
action, person's, 22, 26–27, 52, 78, 100, 158, 170, 189–92, 195–96, 301–4, 209, 211–13, 218, 224, 238, 255, 260, 269, 292, 297, 327, 336–37, 340, 348, 350, 381, 383, 391. *See also* activity, specific, of human being
activity
    of system or being and its parts, 18, 39–41, 48, 50, 136, 144, 168, 199, 222, 241, 251, 262, 268–69, 292, 309, 313, 315–17, 319–22, 327, 329–30, 334, 338, 394–95
    specific, of human being, 23, 37, 39, 72–73, 78, 155, 203, 212, 250–51, 267, 271, 302, 306, 350, 371, 385
actuality and actualization, 43–44, 68–69, 102, 153, 250, 265, 313, 315, 321
adaptability, 201, 293
affections, 325–26
affinities, 232, 238, 268
aggregates, as distinct from structured wholes, 76
alchemy and alchemical principles, 41, 196, 215, 218, 226, 245, 249–55, 258–61, 263–65, 267–72, 298, 338
allegories, 247, 263, 296
alphabet, 138, 230
amino acids, 137
ammonia, 128
amoeba, 18, 75–76, 190
amplification, amplifier, 17–18, 22, 78, 118, 120, 135, 169, 172, 181, 224, 236–37, 242, 244, 266, 283–84, 297
analogy, 5, 19, 40, 50, 78, 88, 104, 135, 146, 155, 157, 177, 180, 219, 224, 241, 264–67, 285
analytic psychology. *See* psychoanalysis
angels and demons, 215, 233, 238, 240, 241, 245, 253, 306, 314, 339, 363

anthropic principle, 20–21, 41, 83, 104, 159, 173–74, 176, 183, 235
apprehension, 332, 334, 360, 361
archetypes, 40, 95, 296, 300, 306, 355, 361, 371
arrow of time. *See* time
astrology, 6, 7, 11, 13, 215, 218, 229–30, 232, 235–36, 238, 245, 249, 251, 264
astronomy and astrophysics, 11, 13, 25, 41, 70, 80–82, 92, 109, 249–51
atmosphere, Earth's, 22, 129, 242
atom, 14, 16–17, 23, 34, 38–39, 41, 43–46, 51, 65, 67–70, 82–83, 96, 102–3, 128, 130, 138, 158, 227–28, 252, 258, 266, 282, 284, 287, 299, 304, 312, 318, 361
autopoiesis, 121, 127, 133, 135–36
axiom, 359, 360, 366, 375

bacterium, 115, 287, 292
becoming, 10, 24, 34, 84, 91–98, 102, 156–57, 177, 190, 213, 224, 227, 238, 281, 293, 327, 337, 341, 348. *See also* change
behavior, 10, 14–17, 20, 33, 40, 48, 50, 52, 71, 96, 205–7, 210, 221, 242, 244, 264, 289, 290. *See also* activity
being
    living. *See* living being
    fact of, 42, 62–63, 89–91
    immaterial. *See* reality, spiritual
Bhagavad Gita, 208
Big Bang, 89, 174, 287
biocenose, 200
biochemistry and biochemical processes, 100, 200, 251, 303
biodiversity, 201, 203, 210
bioethics and biological manipulations, 195, 197

405